The DevOps 2.4 Toolkit: Continuous Deployment To Kubernetes

Continuously deploying applications with Jenkins to a Kubernetes cluster

Viktor Farcic

The DevOps 2.4 Toolkit: Continuous Deployment To Kubernetes

Continuously deploying applications with Jenkins to a Kubernetes cluster

Viktor Farcic

This is a Leanpub book. Leanpub empowers authors and publishers with the Lean Publishing process. Lean Publishing is the act of publishing an in-progress ebook using lightweight tools and many iterations to get reader feedback, pivot until you have the right book and build traction once you do.

Also By Viktor Farcic

The DevOps 2.0 Toolkit

The DevOps 2.1 Toolkit: Docker Swarm

The DevOps 2.2 Toolkit: Self-Sufficient Docker Clusters

The DevOps 2.3 Toolkit: Kubernetes

Contents

Preface

Soon after I started working on The DevOps 2.3 Toolkit: Kubernetes[1], I realized that a single book could only scratch the surface. Kubernetes is vast, and no single book can envelop even all the core components. If we add community projects, the scope becomes even more extensive. Then we need to include hosting vendors and different ways to set up and manage Kubernetes. That would inevitably lead us to third-party solutions like OpenShift, Rancher, and DockerEE, to name a few. It doesn't end there. We'd need to explore other types of community and third-party additions like those related to networking and storage. And don't forget the processes like, for example, continuous delivery and deployment. All those things could not be explored in a single book so *The DevOps 2.3 Toolkit: Kubernetes* ended up being an introduction to Kubernetes. It can serve as the base for exploring everything else.

The moment I published the last chapter of The DevOps 2.3 Toolkit: Kubernetes[2], I started working on the next material. A lot of ideas and tryouts came out of it. It took me a while until the subject and the form of the forthcoming book materialized. After a lot of consultation with the readers of the previous book, the decision was made to explore continuous delivery and deployment processes in a Kubernetes cluster. The high-level scope of the book you are reading right now was born.

---

[1]https://amzn.to/2GvzDjy
[2]https://amzn.to/2GvzDjy

Overview

Just like the other books I wrote, this one does not have a fixed scope. I did not start with an index. I didn't write a summary of each chapter in an attempt to define the scope. I do not do such things. There is only a high-level goal to explore **continuous delivery and deployment inside Kubernetes clusters**. What I did do, though, was to set a few guidelines.

The first guideline is that *all the examples will be tested on all major Kubernetes platforms*. Well, that might be a bit far-fetched. I'm aware that any sentence that mentions "all" together with "Kubernetes" is bound to be incorrect. New platforms are popping out like mushrooms after rain. Still, what I can certainly do is to choose a few of the most commonly used ones.

Minikube and **Docker for Mac or Windows** should undoubtedly be there for those who prefer to "play" with Docker locally.

AWS is the biggest hosting provider so **Kubernetes Operations (kops)** must be included as well.

Since it would be silly to cover only un-managed cloud, I had to include managed Kubernetes clusters as well. **Google Kubernetes Engine (GKE)** is the obvious choice. It is the most stable and features rich managed Kubernetes solution. Adding GKE to the mix means that Azure Container Service (AKS) and **Amazon's Elastic Container Service (EKS)** should be included as well so that we can have the "big trio" of the hosting vendors that offer managed Kubernetes. Unfortunately, even though AKS is available, it is, at this moment (June 2018), still too unstable and it's missing a lot of features. So, I'm forced to scale down from the trio to the GKE and EKS duo as representatives of managed Kubernetes we'll explore.

Finally, a possible on-prem solution should be included as well. Since **OpenShift** shines in that area, the choice was relatively easy.

All in all, I decided to test everything in minikube and Docker for Mac locally, AWS with kops as the representative of a cluster in the cloud, GKE for managed Kubernetes clusters, and OpenShift (with minishift) as a potential on-prem solution. That, in itself, already constitutes a real challenge that might prove to be more than I can chew. Still, making sure that all the examples work with all those platforms and solutions should provide some useful insights.

Some of you already chose the Kubernetes flavor you'll use. Others might still wonder whether to adopt one or the other. Even though the comparison of different Kubernetes platforms is not the primary scope of the book, I'll do my best to explain the differences as they come.

To summarize the guidelines, the book has to **explores continuous delivery and deployment in Kubernetes using Jenkins**. All the examples have to be tested in **minikube, Docker for Mac (or Windows), AWS with kops, GKE, OpenShift with minishift, and EKS**.

The moment I finished writing the previous paragraph I realized that I am repeating the same mistakes from the past. I start with something that looks like a reasonable scope, and I end up with something much bigger and longer. Will I be able to follow all of those guidelines? I honestly don't know. I'll do my best.

I was supposed to follow the "best practice" by writing the overview at the end. I'm not doing that. Instead, you are reading about the plans for the book, not the end result. This is not an overview. You can consider this as the first page of the diary. The end of the story is still unknown.

Eventually, you might get stuck and will be in need of help. Or you might want to write a review or comment on the book's content. Please join the DevOps20[3] Slack channel and post your thoughts, ask questions, or participate in a discussion. If you prefer a more one-on-one communication, you can use Slack to send me a private message or send an email to viktor@farcic.com. All the books I wrote are very dear to me, and I want you to have a good experience reading them. Part of that experience is the option to reach out to me. Don't be shy.

Please note that this one, just as the previous books, is self-published. I believe that having no intermediaries between the writer and the reader is the best way to go. It allows me to write faster, update the book more frequently, and have more direct communication with you. Your feedback is part of the process. No matter whether you purchased the book while only a few or all chapters were written, the idea is that it will never be truly finished. As time passes, it will require updates so that it is aligned with the change in technology or processes. When possible, I will try to keep it up to date and release updates whenever that makes sense. Eventually, things might change so much that updates are not a good option anymore, and that will be a sign that a whole new book is required. **I will keep writing as long as I continue getting your support.**

---

[3]http://slack.devops20toolkit.com/

Audience

This book explores continuous deployment to a Kubernetes cluster. It uses a wide range of Kubernetes platforms and provides instructions how to develop a pipeline on few of the most commonly used CI/CD tools.

This book is not your first contact with Kubernetes. I am assuming that you are already proficient with Deployments, ReplicaSets, Pods, Ingress, Services, PersistentVolumes, PersistentVolumeClaims, Namespaces and a few other things. This book assumes that we do not need to go through the basic stuff. At least, not through all of it. The book assumes a certain level of Kubernetes knowledge and hands-on experience. If that's not the case, what follows might be too confusing and advanced. Please read The DevOps 2.3 Toolkit: Kubernetes[4] first, or consult the Kubernetes documentation. Come back once you're done and once you think you can claim that you understand at least basic Kubernetes concepts and resource types.

---

[4]https://amzn.to/2GvzDjy

About the Author

Viktor Farcic is a Principal Consultant at CloudBees[5], a member of the Docker Captains[6] group, and author.

He coded using a plethora of languages starting with Pascal (yes, he is old), Basic (before it got Visual prefix), ASP (before it got .Net suffix), C, C++, Perl, Python, ASP.Net, Visual Basic, C#, JavaScript, Java, Scala, etc. He never worked with Fortran. His current favorite is Go.

His big passions are containers, distributed systems, microservices, continuous delivery and deployment (CD) and test-driven development (TDD).

He often speaks at community gatherings and conferences.

He wrote The DevOps Toolkit Series[7], and Test-Driven Java Development[8].

His random thoughts and tutorials can be found in his blog TechnologyConversations.com[9].

---

[5]https://www.cloudbees.com/
[6]https://www.docker.com/community/docker-captains
[7]http://www.devopstoolkitseries.com/
[8]https://www.packtpub.com/application-development/test-driven-java-development
[9]https://technologyconversations.com/

Dedication

To Sara, the only person that truly matters in this world.

Prerequisites

Each chapter will assume that you have a working Kubernetes cluster. It doesn't matter whether that's a single-node cluster running locally or a fully operational production-like cluster. What matters is that you have (at least) one.

We won't go into details how to create a Kubernetes cluster. I'm sure that you already know how to do that and that you have kubectl installed on your laptop. If that's not the case, you might want to read Appendix A: Installing kubectl and Creating A Cluster With minikube. While minikube is great for running a local single-node Kubernetes cluster, you'll probably want to try some of the ideas in a more production-like cluster. I hope that you already have a "real" Kubernetes cluster running in AWS, GKE, DigitalOcean, on-prem, or somewhere else. If you don't, and you don't know how to create one, please read *Appendix B: Using Kubernetes Operations (kops)*. It'll give you just enough information you need to prepare, create, and destroy a cluster.

Even though *Appendix A* and Appendix B explain how to create a Kubernetes cluster locally and in AWS, you do not need to limit yourself to minikube locally and kops in AWS. I did my best to provide instructions on some of the most commonly used flavors of Kubernetes clusters.

 All the examples in the book are tested against Kubernetes clusters created with **minikube and Docker For Mac (or Windows) locally, kops in AWS, OpenShift with minishift, Google Container Engine (GKE), and Amazon Kubernetes Service (EKS)**.

In most cases, the same examples and commands will work in all of the tested combinations. When that is not the case, you'll see a note explaining what should be done to accomplish the same result in your favorite Kubernetes and hosting flavor. Even if you use something else, you should have no problems adapting the commands and specifications to comply with your platform.

Each chapter will contain a short list of requirements that your Kubernetes cluster will need to meet. If you are unsure about some of the requirements, I prepared a few Gists with the commands I used to create them. Since each chapter might need different cluster components and sizes, the Gists used for setting up a cluster might differ from one chapter to another. Please use them as guidelines, not necessarily as the exact commands you should execute. After all, the book assumes that you already have some Kubernetes knowledge. It would be tough to claim that you are not a Kubernetes newbie and yet you never created a Kubernetes cluster.

Long story short, the prerequisites are hands-on experience with Kubernetes and at least one Kubernetes cluster.

 I will assume that this is not your first contact with Kubernetes. If my assumption is wrong, please consider going through The DevOps 2.3 Toolkit: Kubernetes: Deploying and managing highly-available and fault-tolerant applications at scale[10] first.

---

[10]https://amzn.to/2GvzDjy

Rumblings Of An Old Man

 Continuous Deployment is about making a decision to do things right. It is a clear goal and a proof that the changes across all levels were successful. The primary obstacle is thinking that we can get there without drastic changes in the application's architecture, processes, and culture. Tools are the least of our problems.

I spend a significant chunk of my time helping companies improve their systems. The most challenging part of my job is going back home after an engagement knowing that the next time I visit the same company, I will discover that there was no significant improvement. I cannot say that is not partly my fault. It certainly is. I might not be very good at what I do. Or maybe I am not good at conveying the right message. Maybe my advice was wrong. There can be many reasons for those failures, and I do admit that they are probably mostly my fault. Still, I cannot shake the feeling that my failures are caused by something else. I think that the root cause is in false expectations.

People want to improve. That is in our nature. Or, at least, most of us do. We became engineers because we are curious. We like to play with new toys. We love to explore new possibilities. And yet, the more we work in a company, the more we become complacent. We learn something, and then we stop learning. We shift our focus towards climbing company ladders. The more time passes, the more emphasis we put on defending our positions which often mean the status quo.

We become experts in something, and that expertise brings us to glory and, hopefully, it lands a promotion, or two. From there on, we ride on that glory. *Look at me, I'm a DB2 expert. That's me, I set up VMWare virtualization. I brought the benefits of Spring to our Java development.* Once that happens, we often try to make sure that those benefits stay intact forever. We won't switch to NoSQL because that would mean that my DB2 expertise is not as valuable anymore. We won't move to Cloud, because I am the guru behind VMWare. We will not adopt Go, because I know how to code in Java.

Those voices are critical because they are being voiced by senior people. Everyone needs to listen to them, even though the real motivations behind those voices are selfish. They are not based on actual knowledge, but often on repeated experience. Having twenty years of experience with DB2 is not truly twenty years of improvement, but rather the same experience repeated twenty times. Yet, twenty years has weight. People listen to you, but not because they trust you, but because you are senior and management believes in your capabilities to make decisions.

Combine voices from the old with management's fear of unknown and their quest for short-term benefits. The result is often status quo. *That worked for years, why would we change it to something else. Why would I trust a junior developer telling me what to do?* Even if a claim for change is backed by the experience from giants like Google, Amazon, and Netflix (just to name a few), you are likely to get a response along the following lines. *"We are different". "That does not apply here." "I'd like to do that but regulations, which I do not truly understand, prevent me from changing anything."*

Still, sooner or later, a directive to change comes along. Your CTO might have gone to the Gartner meeting where he was told to switch to microservices. Too many people spoke about Agile for upper management to ignore it. DevOps is a huge thing, so we need to employ it as well. Kubernetes is everywhere, so we'll start working on a PoC soon.

When those things do happen, when a change is approved, you might be ecstatic. This is your moment. This is when you'll start doing something delicious. That is often the moment when I receive a call. *"We want to do this and that. Can you help us?"* I usually (not always) say yes. That's what I do. And yet, I know that my engagement will not produce a tangible improvement. I guess that hope dies last.

Why am I so pessimistic? Why do I think that improvements do not produce tangible benefits? The answer lies in the scope of required changes.

Almost every tool is a result of specific processes. A process, on the other hand, is a product of a particular culture. Adopting a process without making cultural changes is a waste of time. Adopting tools without accepting the processes behind them is a futile effort that will result only in wasted time and potentially substantial license costs. In infrequent occasions, companies do choose to accept the need to change all three (culture, processes, and tools). They make a decision, and sometimes they even start moving in the right direction. Those are precious cases that should be cherished. But they are likely to fail as well. After a while, usually a few months later, we realize the scope of those changes. Only the brave will survive, and only those committed will see it through.

Those who do choose to proceed and indeed change their culture, and their processes, and their tools, will realize that they are incompatible with the applications they've been developing over the years. Containers work with everything, but benefits are genuinely tremendous when developing microservices, not monoliths. Test-driven development increases confidence, quality, and speed, but only if applications are designed to be testable. Zero-downtime deployments are not a myth. They work, but only if our applications are cloud-native, if they follow at least some of twelve factors[11], and so on.

It's not only about tools, processes, and culture, but also about getting rid of the technical debt you've been accumulating over the years. By debt, I don't necessarily mean that you did something wrong when you started, but rather that time converted something awesome into a horrible monster. Do you spend fifty percent of your time refactoring? If you're not, you're accumulating technical debt. It's unavoidable.

When faced with all those challenges, giving up is the expected outcome. It's human to throw down the towel when there's no light at the end of the tunnel. I don't judge you. I feel your pain. You're not moving forward because the obstacles are too big. Still, you have to get up because there is no alternative. You will continue. You will improve. It'll hurt a lot, but there is no alternative, except slow death while your competition is looking over your soon-to-be corpse.

---

[11]https://12factor.net/

You got this far, and I can assume only two possible explanations. You are one of those who read technical books as a way to escape from reality, or you are applying at least some of the things we discussed thus far. I hope it's the latter. If that's the case, you do not fall into "yet another failure of mine." I thank you for that. It makes me feel better.

If you do employ the lessons from this book, without faking, you are indeed doing something great. There is no way of pretending continuous delivery (CD). Every commit you make is ready for production if all the stages are green. The decision whether to deploy it to production is based on business or marketing needs, and it is not technical in any sense. You can even take a step forward and practice continuous deployment (CDP). It removes the only action performed by a human and deploys every green commit to production. Neither of the two can be faked. You cannot do CD or CDP partly. You cannot be almost there. If you are, you're doing continuous integration, it-will-be-deployed-eventually process, or something else.

All in all, you are, hopefully, ready to do this. You will take a step towards continuous deployment inside a Kubernetes cluster. By the end of this book, the only thing left for you is to spend an unknown amount of time "modernizing" architecture of your applications or throwing them to thrash and starting over. You'll be changing your tools, processes, and culture. This book will not help you with all of those. We're focused on tools and processes. You'll have to figure out what to do with your culture and architecture. The same holds true for the way you write your tests. I won't teach you testing, and I won't preach TDD. I'll assume that you already know all that and that we can focus on continuous deployment pipeline only.

At this moment, you might feel desperate. You might not be ready. You might think that you don't have a buyout from your management, that the people in your company will not accept this direction, or that you don't have enough time and funds. Do not get depressed. Knowing the path is the most crucial part. Even if you cannot get there any time soon, you should still know what the destination is, so that your steps are at least moving you in the right direction.

What Is Continuous Deployment?

 Practicing continuous deployment means that every commit to the master branch is deployed to production without human intervention.

That's it. That's the shortest, and probably the most accurate definition of continuous deployment you'll ever find. Is that too much for you? If you don't think you can (or should) ever get there, we can fall back to continuous delivery.

 Practicing continuous delivery means that every commit to the master branch is deployable to production unless it failed a fully automated pipeline.

The only substantial difference between continuous deployment (CDP) and continuous delivery (CD) is that one deploys to production while the other requires that we choose which commit is deployed to production. That's much easier, isn't it? Actually, it isn't. It's almost the same since in both cases we are so confident in the process that every commit is or can be deployed to production. In the case of continuous delivery, we (humans) do need to make a decision on what to deploy. However, that is the cause of significant confusion. What follows is the vital part so please read it carefully.

 The decision which commit to deploy to production is based on business or marketing needs, and it has nothing to do with engineers.

If every commit (that did not fail the pipeline) is deployable to production, there is no need for an engineer to decide what will be deployed. **Every commit is deployable**, we just might not want to have a feature available to users straight away. It's a business decision. Period.

As a learning experience, you should take the least technical person in a company and put him (or her) in front of a screen with the builds and let him (or her) choose which release to deploy. Someone from cleaning services is an excellent candidate to be that person. Now, before that person clicks the button to deploy a random release, you need to remove yourself from that room.

Here comes the critical question. How would you feel in that situation? If you'd go to the closest bar to have a coffee confident that nothing wrong will happen, you are in the right place. If you would have a nervous breakdown, you're still far from being there. If that's the case, do not despair. Most of us would have a nervous breakdown from letting a random person deploy a random release. That's not what matters. What is important is whether you want to get there. If you do, read on. If you don't, I hope you're reading a free sample of the book, and you can make an educated decision not to waste money. Get something else to read.

"Hold on," you might say. "I am already doing continuous integration," could be the thought in your head right now. "Is continuous delivery or deployment truly that different?" Well, the answer is that it's not, but that you probably misunderstood what continuous integration is. I won't even try to define it for you. Over fifteen years passed since CI became a thing. I will, however, ask you a few questions. If you answer with "no" to at least one of them, you're not doing CI. Here it goes.

- Are you building and, at least partially, testing your application on every commit without exceptions and no matter to which branch that commit is pushed to?
- Is everyone committing at least once a day?
- Do you merge your branches to the *master* after a couple of days, if not more frequently?
- Do you stop doing whatever you're doing to fix a failed build? Is that the highest priority (after fire emergency, earthquakes, and other life-threatening events)?

That's it. Those are the only questions you need to answer. Be honest with yourself. Did you really respond with "yes" to all four of those questions? If you did, you're my hero. If you didn't, there is only one more question left to answer.

Do you really want to do continuous integration (CI), delivery (CD), or deployment (CDP)?

Deploying Stateful Applications At Scale

 Stateless and stateful application are quite different in their architecture. Those differences need to be reflected in Kubernetes as well. The fact that we can use Deployments with PersistentVolumes does not necessarily mean that is the best way to run stateful applications.

Most of the applications are deployed to Kubernetes using Deployments. It is, without a doubt, the most commonly used controller. Deployments provide (almost) everything we might need. We can specify the number of replicas when our applications need to be scaled. We can mount volumes through PersistentVolumeClaims. We can communicate with the Pods controlled by Deployments through Services. We can execute rolling updates that will deploy new releases without downtime. There are quite a few other features enabled by Deployments. Does that mean that Deployments are the preferable way to run all types of applications? Is there a feature we might need that is not already available through Deployments and other resources we can associate with them?

When running stateful applications in Kubernetes, we soon realize that Deployments do not offer everything we need. It's not that we require additional features, but that some of those available in Deployments do not behave just as we might want them to. In many cases, Deployments are an excellent fit for stateless applications. However, we might need to look for a different controller that will allow us to run stateful applications safely and efficiently. That controller is StatefulSet.

 If we are to implement continuous delivery or deployment processes across the whole organization, we cannot ignore the fact that not all the applications are stateless. Having a state is unavoidable, and we need to be sure that we know how to handle stateful applications.

Let's experience some of the problems behind stateful applications, and the benefits *StatefulSets* bring to the table. To do that, we need a cluster.

 This chapter asssumes that you are already familiar with Namespaces, Ingress, Services, and Deployments. If you're not, please refer to The DevOps 2.3 Toolkit: Kubernetes[12] for more info.

We'll skip the theory (for now), and dive straight into examples. To do that, we need a cluster.

---

[12]https://amzn.to/2GvzDjy

Creating A Cluster

We'll start the hands-on walk-through by cloning the `vfarcic/k8s-specs` repository that contains all the example definitions we'll use throughout the book.

 A note to Windows users

Please run all the examples from *GitBash* (installed through *Git*). That way the commands you'll see throughout the book will be same as those executed on *MacOS* or any *Linux* distribution. If you're using Hyper-V instead of VirtualBox, you may need to run the *GitBash* window as an Administrator.

 All the commands from this chapter are available in the 01-sts.sh[13] Gist.

```
1  git clone \
2      https://github.com/vfarcic/k8s-specs.git
3
4  cd k8s-specs
```

Now that you have a repository with the examples we'll use throughout the book, we should create a cluster unless you already have one.

For this chapter, I'll assume that you are running a cluster with **Kubernetes version 1.9** or higher. Further on, I'll assume that you already have an **nginx Ingress Controller** deployed, that **RBAC** is set up, and that your cluster has a **default StorageClass**. If you are unsure about some of the requirements, I prepared a few Gists with the commands I used to create different clusters. Feel free to choose whichever suits you the best, or be brave and roll with your own. Ideally, you'll run the commands from every chapter on each of the Kubernetes flavors. That way, you'll not only learn the main subject but also gain experience in running Kubernetes in different combinations and, hopefully, make a more informed decision which flavor to use for your local development as well as for production.

The Gists with the commands I used to create different variations of Kubernetes clusters are as follows.

- docker4mac.sh[14]: **Docker for Mac** with 2 CPUs, 2GB RAM, and with **nginx Ingress** controller.
- minikube.sh[15]: **minikube** with 2 CPUs, 2GB RAM, and with `ingress`, `storage-provisioner`, and `default-storageclass` addons enabled.

---

[13]https://gist.github.com/505aedf2cb268837983132d4e4385fab
[14]https://gist.github.com/06e313db2957e92b1df09fe39c249a14
[15]https://gist.github.com/536e6329e750b795a882900c09feb13b

- kops.sh[16]: **kops in AWS** with 3 t2.small masters and 2 t2.medium nodes spread in three availability zones, and with **nginx Ingress** controller (assumes that the prerequisites are set through Appendix B).
- minishift.sh[17]: **minishift** with 2 CPUs, 2GB RAM, and version 1.16+.
- gke.sh[18]: **Google Kubernetes Engine (GKE)** with 3 n1-standard-1 (1 CPU, 3.75GB RAM) nodes (one in each zone), and with **nginx Ingress** controller running on top of the "standard" one that comes with GKE. We'll use nginx Ingress for compatibility with other platforms. Feel free to modify the YAML files if you prefer NOT to install nginx Ingress.
- eks.sh[19]: **Elastic Kubernetes Service (EKS)** with 2 t2.medium nodes, with **nginx Ingress** controller, and with a **default StorageClass**.

 The purpose of those Gists is to serve as guidance, not necessarily as a set of steps you should execute blindly. I assume that you already know how to create a cluster with the specified requirements.

Using StatefulSets To Run Stateful Applications

Let's see a StatefulSet in action and see whether it beings any benefits. We'll use Jenkins as the first application we'll deploy. It is a simple application to start with since it does not require a complicated setup and it cannot be scaled. On the other hand, Jenkins is a stateful application. It stores all its state into a single directory. There are no "special" requirements besides the need for a PersistentVolume.

A sample Jenkins definition that uses StatefulSets can be found in `sts/jenkins.yml`.

```
1  cat sts/jenkins.yml
```

The definition is relatively straightforward. It defines a Namespace for easier organization, a Service for routing traffic, and an Ingress that makes it accessible from outside the cluster. The interesting part is the `StatefulSet` definition.

The only significant difference, when compared to Deployments, is that the `StatefulSet` can use `volumeClaimTemplates`. While Deployments require that we specify PersistentVolumeClaim separately, now we can define a claim template as part of the `StatefulSet` definition. Even though that might be a more convenient way to define claims, surely there are other reasons for this difference. Or maybe there isn't. Let's check it out by creating the resources defined in `sts/jenkins.yml`.

---

[16]https://gist.github.com/2a3e4ee9cb86d4a5a65cd3e4397f48fd
[17]https://gist.github.com/c9968f23ecb1f7b2ec40c6bcc0e03e4f
[18]https://gist.github.com/5c52c165bf9c5002fedb61f8a5d6a6d1
[19]https://gist.github.com/5496f79a3886be794cc317c6f8dd7083

A note to minishift users

OpenShift does not allow setting `fsGroup` in the security context, it uses Routes instead of Ingress, and Services accessible through Routes need to be the `LoadBalancer` type. Due to those changes, I had to prepare a different YAML specification for minishift. Please execute `oc apply -f sts/jenkins-oc.yml --record` instead of the command that follows.

```
1  kubectl apply \
2      -f sts/jenkins.yml \
3      --record
```

We can see from the output that a Namespace, an Ingress, a Service, and a StatefulSet were created. In case you're using minishift and deployed the YAML defined in `sts/jenkins-oc.yml`, you got a Route instead Ingress.

 # A note to GKE users

GKE uses external load balancer as Ingress. To work properly, the `type` of the service related to Ingress needs to be `NodePort`. We'll have to patch the service to change its type. Please execute the command that follows.

```
kubectl -n jenkins patch svc jenkins -p '{"spec":{"type": "NodePort"}}'
```

Let's confirm that the StatefulSet was rolled out correctly.

```
1  kubectl -n jenkins \
2      rollout status sts jenkins
```

Now that `jenkins` StatefulSet is up and running, we should check whether it created a PersistentVolumeClaim.

```
1  kubectl -n jenkins get pvc
```

The output is as follows.

```
1  NAME                    STATUS VOLUME   CAPACITY ACCESS MODES STORAGECLASS AGE
2  jenkins-home-jenkins-0 Bound  pvc-...  2Gi      RWO          gp2          2m
```

It comes as no surprise that a claim was created. After all, we did specify `volumeClaimTemplates` as part of the StatefulSet definition. However, if we compare it with claims we make as separate resources (e.g., with Deployments), the format of the claim we just created is a bit different. It is a combination of the claim name (`jenkins-home`), the Namespace (`jenkins`), and the indexed suffix (`0`). The index is an indication that StatefulSets might create more than one claim. Still, we can see only one, so we'll need to stash that thought for a while.

Similarly, we might want to confirm that the claim created a PersistentVolume.

```
1  kubectl -n jenkins get pv
```

A note to minishift users

You'll see a hundred volumes instead of one. Minishift does not (yet) uses default storage classes. Instead, we have a hundred volumes without a storage class so that enough volumes are available for testing purposes. Only one of them will be with the status Bound.

Finally, as the last verification, we'll open Jenkins in a browser and confirm that it looks like it's working correctly. But, before we do that, we should retrieve the hostname or the IP assigned to us by the Ingress controller.

A note to GKE users

Please change hostname to ip in the command that follows. The jsonpath should be {.status.loadBalancer.ingress[0].ip}. Please note that GKE Ingress spins up an external load balancer and it might take a while until the IP is generated. Therefore, you might need to repeat the command that follows until you get the IP.

A note to minikube users

Please change the following command to CLUSTER_DNS=$(minikube ip).

A note to minishift users

Please change the following command to CLUSTER_DNS=jenkins-jenkins.$(minishift ip).nip.io.

```
1  CLUSTER_DNS=$(kubectl -n jenkins \
2      get ing jenkins \
3      -o jsonpath="{.status.loadBalancer.ingress[0].hostname}")
4
5  echo $CLUSTER_DNS
```

We retrieved the hostname (or IP) from the Ingress resource, and now we are ready to open Jenkins in a browser.

```
1  open "http://$CLUSTER_DNS/jenkins"
```

A note to Windows users

Git Bash might not be able to use the open command. If that's the case, replace the open command with echo. As a result, you'll get the full address that should be opened directly in your browser of choice.

 In some cases (e.g., GKE), it might take a few minutes until the external load balancer is created. If you see 40x or 50x error message, please wait for a while and try to open Jenkins in the browser again.

You might see browser's message that the connection is not private. That's normal since we did not specify an SSL certificate. If that's the case, please choose to proceed. In Chrome, you should click the *ADVANCED* link, followed by *Proceed to...* For the rest of the browsers... Well, I'm sure that you already know how to ignore SSL warnings in your favorite browser.

You should see a wizard. We won't use it to finalize Jenkins setup. All we wanted, for now, is to explore StatefulSets using Jenkins as an example. There are a few things we're missing for Jenkins to be fully operational and we'll explore them in later chapters. For now, we'll remove the whole jenkins Namespace.

```
1  kubectl delete ns jenkins
```

From what we experienced so far, StatefulSets are a lot like Deployments. The only difference was in the volumeClaimTemplates section that allowed us to specify PersistentVolumeClaim as part of the StatefulSet definition, instead of a separate resource. Such a minor change does not seem to be a reason to move away from Deployments. If we limit our conclusions to what we observed so far, there are no good arguments to use StatefulSets instead of Deployments. The syntax is almost the same, and the result as well. Why would we learn to use a new controller if it provides no benefits?

Maybe we could not notice a difference between a StatefulSet and a Deployment because our example was too simple. Let's try a slightly more complicated scenario.

Using Deployments To Run Stateful Applications At Scale

We'll use go-demo-3 application throughout this book. It consists of a backend API written in Go that uses MongoDB to store its state. With time, we'll improve the definition of the application. Once we're happy with the way the application is running inside the cluster, we'll work on continuous deployment processes that will fully automate everything from a commit to the vfarcic/go-demo-3 GitHub repository, all the way until it's running in production.

We need to start somewhere, and our first iteration of the go-demo-3 application is in the sts/go-demo-3-deploy.yml directory.

```
1  cat sts/go-demo-3-deploy.yml
```

Assuming that you are already familiar with Namespaces, Ingress, PersistentVolumeClaims, Deployments, and Services, the definition is fairly straightforward. We defined a Namespace go-demo-3 in which all the other resources will reside. Ingress will forward external requests with the base path /demo to the Service api. The PersistentVolumeClaim does not have a storageClassName, so it will claim a PersistentVolume defined through the default StorageClass.

There are two Deployments, one for the API and the other for the database. Both have a Service associated, and both will create three replicas (Pods).

Now that we have a very high-level overview of the go-demo-3 definition, we can proceed and create the resources.

```
1  kubectl apply \
2      -f sts/go-demo-3-deploy.yml \
3      --record
4
5  kubectl -n go-demo-3 \
6      rollout status deployment api
```

We created the resources defined in sts/go-demo-3-deploy.yml and retrieved the rollout status of the api Deployment. The API is designed to fail if it cannot access its databases, so the fact that it rolled out correctly seems to give us a reasonable guarantee that everything is working as expected. Still, since I am skeptical by nature, we'll double-check that all the Pods are running. We should see six of them (three for each Deployment) in the go-demo-3 Namespace.

```
1  kubectl -n go-demo-3 get pods
```

The output is as follows.

```
1  NAME      READY STATUS            RESTARTS AGE
2  api-...   1/1   Running           2        55s
3  api-...   1/1   Running           2        55s
4  api-...   1/1   Running           2        55s
5  db-...    1/1   Running           0        55s
6  db-...    0/1   CrashLoopBackOff  2        55s
7  db-...    0/1   CrashLoopBackOff  1        55s
```

A disaster befell us. Only one of the three db Pods is running. We did expect a few restarts of the api Pods. They tried to connect to MongoDB and were failing until at least one db Pod started running. The failure of the two db Pods is a bit harder to explain. They do not depend on other Pods and Services so they should run without restarts.

Let's take a look at the `db` logs. They might give us a clue what went wrong.

 Â A note to GKE users

GKE will not be able to mount a volume to more than one Pod. Two of the `db-` Pods with have `ContainerCreating` status. If you `describe` one of those Pods, you'll see `Multi-Attach error for volume "pvc-..."` `Volume is already exclusively attached to one node and can't be attached to another`. That's a typical behavior since the default PersistentVolumeClass used in GKE creates volumes that can be attached only to one Pod at a time. We'll fix that soon. Until then, remember that you will not be able to see the logs of those Pods.

We need to know the names of the Pods we want to peek into, so we'll use a bit of "creative" formatting of the `kubectl get pods` output.

```
1  DB_1=$(kubectl -n go-demo-3 get pods \
2      -l app=db \
3      -o jsonpath="{.items[0].metadata.name}")
4
5  DB_2=$(kubectl -n go-demo-3 get pods \
6      -l app=db \
7      -o jsonpath="{.items[1].metadata.name}")
```

The only difference between the two commands is in `jsonpath`. The first result (index 0) is stored in `DB_1`, and the second (index 1) in `DB_2`. Since we know that only one of the three Pods is running, peeking into the logs of two will guarantee that we'll look into at least one of those with errors.

```
1  kubectl -n go-demo-3 logs $DB_1
```

The last lines of the output of the first `db` Pod are as follows.

```
1  ...
2  2018-03-29T20:51:53.390+0000 I NETWORK   [thread1] waiting for connections on port 27\
3  017
4  2018-03-29T20:51:53.681+0000 I NETWORK   [thread1] connection accepted from 100.96.2.\
5  7:46888 #1 (1 connection now open)
6  2018-03-29T20:51:55.984+0000 I NETWORK   [thread1] connection accepted from 100.96.2.\
7  8:49418 #2 (2 connections now open)
8  2018-03-29T20:51:59.182+0000 I NETWORK   [thread1] connection accepted from 100.96.3.\
9  6:43940 #3 (3 connections now open)
```

Everything seems OK. We can see that the database initialized and started `waiting for connections`. Soon after, the three replicas of the `api` Deployment connected to MongoDB running inside this Pod.

Now that we know that the first Pod is the one that is running, we should look at the logs of the second. That must be one of those with errors.

```
1  kubectl -n go-demo-3 logs $DB_2
```

The output, limited to the last few lines, is as follows.

```
1   ...
2   2018-03-29T20:54:57.362+0000 I STORAGE  [initandlisten] exception in initAndListen: \
3   98 Unable to lock file: /data/db/mongod.lock Resource temporarily unavailable. Is a \
4   mongod instance already running?, terminating
5   2018-03-29T20:54:57.362+0000 I NETWORK  [initandlisten] shutdown: going to close lis\
6   tening sockets...
7   2018-03-29T20:54:57.362+0000 I NETWORK  [initandlisten] shutdown: going to flush dia\
8   glog...
9   2018-03-29T20:54:57.362+0000 I CONTROL  [initandlisten] now exiting
10  2018-03-29T20:54:57.362+0000 I CONTROL  [initandlisten] shutting down with code:100
```

There's the symptom of the problem. MongoDB could not lock the /data/db/mongod.lock file, and it shut itself down.

Let's take a look at the PersistentVolumes.

```
1  kubectl get pv
```

The output is as follows.

```
1  NAME     CAPACITY ACCESS MODES RECLAIM POLICY STATUS CLAIM           STORAGECLASS REA\
2  SON AGE
3  pvc-... 2Gi       RWO          Delete          Bound  go-demo-3/mongo gp2             \
4      3m
```

There is only one bound PersistentVolume. That is to be expected. Even if we'd want to, we could not tell a Deployment to create a volume for each replica. The Deployment mounted a volume associated with the claim which, in turn, created a PersistentVolume. All the replicas tried to mount the same volume.

MongoDB is designed in a way that each instance requires exclusive access to a directory where it stores its state. We tried to mount the same volume to all the replicas, and only one of them got the lock. All the others failed.

If you're using kops with AWS, the default StorageClass is using the kubernetes.io/aws-ebs provisioner. Since EBS can be mounted only by a single entity, our claim has the access mode set to ReadWriteOnce. To make thing more complicated, EBS cannot span multiple availability-zones, and we are hoping to spread our MongoDB replicas so that they can survive even failure of a whole zone. The same is true for GKE which also uses block storage by default.

Having a `ReadWriteOnce` PersistentVolumeClaims and EBS not being able to span multiple availability zones is not a problem for our use-case. The real issue is that each MongoDB instance needs a separate volume or at least a different directory. Neither of the solutions can be (easily) solved with Deployments.

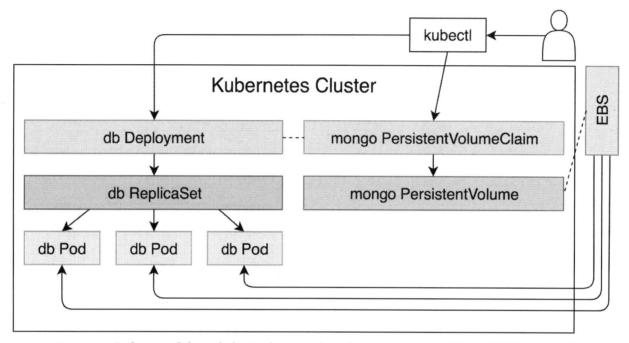

Figure 1-1: Pods created through the Deployment share the same PersistentVolume (AWS variation)

Now we have a good use-case that might show some of the benefits of StatefulSet controllers.

Before we move on, we'll delete the `go-demo-3` Namespace and all the resources running inside it.

```
1  kubectl delete ns go-demo-3
```

Using StatefulSets To Run Stateful Applications At Scale

Let's see whether we can solve the problem with PersistentVolumes through a StatefulSet. As a reminder, our goal (for now) is for each instance of a MongoDB to get a separate volume.

The updated definition is in the `sts/go-demo-3-sts.yml` file.

```
1  cat sts/go-demo-3-sts.yml
```

Most of the new definition is the same as the one we used before, so we'll comment only on the differences. The first in line is StatefulSet that replaces the `db` Deployment. It is as follows.

```yaml
 1  apiVersion: apps/v1beta2
 2  kind: StatefulSet
 3  metadata:
 4    name: db
 5    namespace: go-demo-3
 6  spec:
 7    serviceName: db
 8    replicas: 3
 9    selector:
10      matchLabels:
11        app: db
12    template:
13      metadata:
14        labels:
15          app: db
16      spec:
17        terminationGracePeriodSeconds: 10
18        containers:
19        - name: db
20          image: mongo:3.3
21          command:
22            - mongod
23            - "--replSet"
24            - rs0
25            - "--smallfiles"
26            - "--noprealloc"
27          ports:
28          - containerPort: 27017
29          resources:
30            limits:
31              memory: "100Mi"
32              cpu: 0.1
33            requests:
34              memory: "50Mi"
35              cpu: 0.01
36          volumeMounts:
37          - name: mongo-data
38            mountPath: /data/db
39    volumeClaimTemplates:
40    - metadata:
41        name: mongo-data
42      spec:
43        accessModes:
```

```
44        - ReadWriteOnce
45      resources:
46        requests:
47          storage: 2Gi
```

As you already saw with Jenkins, StatefulSet definitions are almost the same as Deployments. The only important difference is that we are not defining PersistentVolumeClaim as a separate resource but letting the StatefulSet take care of it through the specification set inside the volumeClaimTemplates entry. We'll see it in action soon.

We also used this opportunity to tweak mongod process by specifying the db container command that creates a ReplicaSet rs0. Please note that this replica set is specific to MongoDB and it is in no way related to Kubernetes ReplicaSet controller. Creation of a MongoDB replica set is the base for some of the things we'll do later on.

Another difference is in the db Service. It is as follows.

```
1   apiVersion: v1
2   kind: Service
3   metadata:
4     name: db
5     namespace: go-demo-3
6   spec:
7     ports:
8     - port: 27017
9     clusterIP: None
10    selector:
11      app: db
```

This time we set clusterIP to None. That will create a Headless Service. Headless service is a service that doesnâ€™t need load-balancing and has a single service IP.

Everything else in this YAML file is the same as in the one that used Deployment controller to run MongoDB.

To summarize, we changed db Deployment into a StatefulSet, we added a command that creates MongoDB replica set named rs0, and we set the db Service to be Headless. We'll explore the reasons and the effects of those changes soon. For now, we'll create the resources defined in the sts/go-demo-3-sts.yml file.

```
1  kubectl apply \
2      -f sts/go-demo-3-sts.yml \
3      --record
4
5  kubectl -n go-demo-3 get pods
```

We created the resources and retrieved the Pods. The output of the latter command is as follows.

```
1  NAME      READY  STATUS            RESTARTS AGE
2  api-...  0/1    Running           0        4s
3  api-...  0/1    Running           0        4s
4  api-...  0/1    Running           0        4s
5  db-0     0/1    ContainerCreating 0        5s
```

We can see that all three replicas of the api Pods are running or, at least, that's how it seems so far. The situation with db Pods is different. Kubernetes is creating only one replica, even though we specified three.

Let's wait for a bit and retrieve the Pods again.

```
1  kubectl -n go-demo-3 get pods
```

Forty seconds later, the output is as follows.

```
1  NAME      READY  STATUS            RESTARTS AGE
2  api-...  0/1    CrashLoopBackOff  1        44s
3  api-...  0/1    CrashLoopBackOff  1        44s
4  api-...  0/1    Running           2        44s
5  db-0     1/1    Running           0        45s
6  db-1     0/1    ContainerCreating 0        9s
```

We can see that the first db Pod is running and that creation of the second started. At the same time, our api Pods are crashing. We'll ignore them for now, and concentrate on db Pods.

Let's wait a bit more and observe what happens next.

```
1  kubectl -n go-demo-3 get pods
```

A minute later, the output is as follows.

```
1  NAME        READY  STATUS           RESTARTS  AGE
2  api-...      0/1    CrashLoopBackOff  4        1m
3  api-...      0/1    Running          4         1m
4  api-...      0/1    CrashLoopBackOff  4        1m
5  db-0        1/1    Running          0         2m
6  db-1        1/1    Running          0         1m
7  db-2        0/1    ContainerCreating 0        34s
```

The second db Pod started running, and the system is creating the third one. It seems that our progress with the database is going in the right direction.

Let's wait a while longer before we retrieve the Pods one more time.

```
1  kubectl -n go-demo-3 get pods
```

```
1  NAME        READY  STATUS           RESTARTS  AGE
2  api-...      0/1    CrashLoopBackOff  4        3m
3  api-...      0/1    CrashLoopBackOff  4        3m
4  api-...      0/1    CrashLoopBackOff  4        3m
5  db-0        1/1    Running          0         3m
6  db-1        1/1    Running          0         2m
7  db-2        1/1    Running          0         1m
```

Another minute later, the third db Pod is also running but our api Pods are still failing. We'll deal with that problem soon.

What we just observed is an essential difference between Deployments and StatefulSets. Replicas of the latter are created sequentially. Only after the first replica was running, the StatefulSet started creating the second. Similarly, the creation of the third began solely after the second was running.

Moreover, we can see that the names of the Pods created through the StatefulSet are predictable. Unlike Deployments that create random suffixes for each Pod, StatefulSets create them with indexed suffixes based on integer ordinals. The name of the first Pod will always end suffixed with -0, the second will be suffixed with -1, and so on. That naming will be maintained forever. If we'd initiate rolling updates, Kubernetes would replace the Pods of the db StatefulSet, but the names would remain the same.

The nature of the sequential creation of Pods and formatting of their names provides predictability that is often paramount with stateful applications. We can think of StatefulSet replicas as being separate Pods with guaranteed ordering, uniqueness, and predictability.

How about PersistentVolumes? The fact that the db Pods did not fail means that MongoDB instances managed to get the locks. That means that they are not sharing the same PersistentVolume, or that they are using different directories within the same volume.

Let's take a look at the PersistentVolumes created in the cluster.

```
1   kubectl get pv
```

The output is as follows.

```
1   NAME      CAPACITY  ACCESS MODES  RECLAIM POLICY  STATUS  CLAIM                      STORAG\
2   ECLASS  REASON  AGE
3   pvc-...  2Gi       RWO           Delete          Bound   go-demo-3/mongo-data-db-0  gp2    \
4           9m
5   pvc-...  2Gi       RWO           Delete          Bound   go-demo-3/mongo-data-db-1  gp2    \
6           8m
7   pvc-...  2Gi       RWO           Delete          Bound   go-demo-3/mongo-data-db-2  gp2    \
8           7m
```

Now we can observe the reasoning behind using `volumeClaimTemplates` spec inside the definition of the StatefulSet. It used the template to create a claim for each replica. We specified that there should be three replicas, so it created three Pods, as well as three separate volume claims. The result is three PersistentVolumes.

Moreover, we can see that the claims also follow a specific naming convention. The format is a combination of the name of the claim (`mongo-data`), the name of the StatefulSet `db`, and index (`0`, `1`, and `2`).

Judging by the age of the claims, we can see that they followed the same pattern as the Pods. They are approximately a minute apart. The StatefulSet created the first Pod and used the claim template to create a PersistentVolume and attach it. Later on, it continued to the second Pod and the claim, and after that with the third. Pods are created sequentially, and each generated a new PersistentVolumeClaim.

If a Pod is (re)scheduled due to a failure or a rolling update, it'll continue using the same PersistentVolumeClaim and, as a result, it will keep using the same PersistentVolume, making Pods and volumes inseparable.

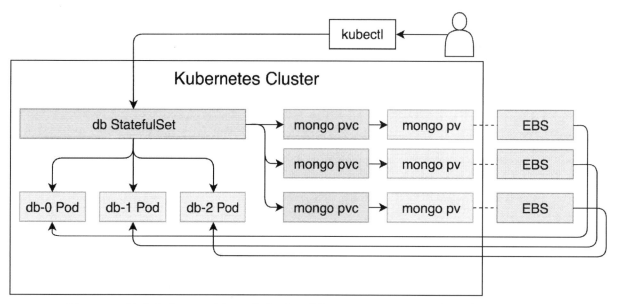

Figure 1-2: Each Pod created through the StatefulSet gets a PersistentVolume (AWS variation)

Given that each Pod in a StatefulSet has a unique and a predictable name, we can assume that the same applies to hostnames inside those Pods. Let's check it out.

```
1  kubectl -n go-demo-3 \
2      exec -it db-0 -- hostname
```

We executed hostname command inside one of the replicas of the StatefulSet. The output is as follows.

```
1  db-0
```

Just as names of the Pods created by the StatefulSet, hostnames are predictable as well. They are following the same pattern as Pod names. Each Pod in a StatefulSet derives its hostname from the name of the StatefulSet and the ordinal of the Pod. The pattern for the constructed hostname is [STATEFULSET_NAME]-[INDEX].

Let's move into the Service related to the StatefulSet. If we take another look at the db Service defined in sts/go-demo-3-sts.yml, we'll notice that it has clusterIP set to None. As a result, the Service is headless.

In most cases we want Services to handle load-balancing and forward requests to one of the replicas. Load balancing is often round-robin even though it can be changed to other algorithms. However, sometimes we don't need the Service to do load-balancing, nor we want it to provide a single IP for the Service. That is certainly true for MongoDB. If we are to convert its instances into a replica set, we need to have a separate and stable address for each. So, we disabled Service's load-balancing by setting spec.clusterIP to None. That converted it into a Headless Service and let StatefulSet take over its algorithm.

We'll explore the effect of combining StatefulSets with Headless Services by creating a new Pod from which we can execute nslookup commands.

 nslookup does not work in all Kubernetes clusters. If you experience errors, please ignore them and follow the logic from the books' output.

```
1   kubectl -n go-demo-3 \
2       run -it \
3       --image busybox dns-test \
4       --restart=Never \
5       --rm sh
```

We created a new Pod based on busybox inside the go-demo-3 Namespace. We specified sh as the command together with the -ti argument that allocated a TTY and standard input (stdin). As a result, we are inside the container created through the dns-test Pod, and we can execute our first nslookup query.

```
1   nslookup db
```

The output is as follows.

```
1   Server:     100.64.0.10
2   Address 1: 100.64.0.10 kube-dns.kube-system.svc.cluster.local
3
4   Name:       db
5   Address 1: 100.96.2.14 db-0.db.go-demo-3.svc.cluster.local
6   Address 2: 100.96.2.15 db-2.db.go-demo-3.svc.cluster.local
7   Address 3: 100.96.3.8 db-1.db.go-demo-3.svc.cluster.local
```

We can see that the request was picked by the kube-dns server and that it returned three addresses, one for each Pod in the StatefulSet.

The StatefulSet is using the Headless Service to control the domain of its Pods. The domain managed by this Service takes the form of [SERVICE_NAME].[NAMESPACE].svc.cluster.local, where cluster.local is the cluster domain. However, we used a short syntax in our nslookup query that requires only the name of the service (db). Since the service is in the same Namespace, we did not need to specify go-demo-3. The Namespace is required only if we'd like to establish communication from one Namespace to another.

When we executed nslookup, a request was sent to the CNAME of the Headless Service (db). It, in turn, returned SRV records associated with it. Those records point to A record entries that contain Pods IP addresses, one for each of the Pods managed by the StatefulSet.

Let's do nslookup of one of the Pods managed by the StatefulSet.

The Pods can be accessed with a combination of the Pod name (e.g., db-0) and the name of the Service. If the Pods are in a different Namespace, we need to add it as a suffix. Finally, if we want to use the full CNAME, we can add svc.cluster.local as well. We can see the full address from the previous output (e.g., db-0.db.go-demo-3.svc.cluster.local). All in all, we can access the Pod with the index 0 as db-0.db, db-0.db.go-demo-3, or db-0.db.go-demo-3.svc.cluster.local. Any of the three combinations should work since we are inside the Pod running in the same Namespace. So, we'll use the shortest version.

```
1  nslookup db-0.db
```

The output is as follows.

```
1  Server:      100.64.0.10
2  Address 1:   100.64.0.10 kube-dns.kube-system.svc.cluster.local
3
4  Name:        db-0.db
5  Address 1:   100.96.2.14 db-0.db.go-demo-3.svc.cluster.local
```

We can see that the output matches part of the output of the previous nslookup query. The only difference is that this time it is limited to the particular Pod.

What we got with the combination of a StatefulSet and a Headless Service is a stable network identity. Unless we change the number of replicas of this StatefulSet, CNAME records are permanent. Unlike Deployments, StatefulSets maintain sticky identities for each of their Pods. These pods are created from the same spec, but they are not interchangeable. Each has a persistent identifier that is maintained across any rescheduling.

Pods ordinals, hostnames, SRV records, and A records are never changed. However, the same cannot be said for IP addresses associated with them. They might change. That is why it is crucial not to configure applications to connect to Pods in a StatefulSet by IP address.

Now that we know that the Pods managed with a StatefulSet have a stable network identity, we can proceed and configure MongoDB replica set.

```
1  exit
2
3  kubectl -n go-demo-3 \
4      exec -it db-0 -- sh
```

We exited the dns-test Pod and entered into one of the MongoDB containers created by the StatefulSet.

```
1   mongo
2
3   rs.initiate( {
4      _id : "rs0",
5      members: [
6         {_id: 0, host: "db-0.db:27017"},
7         {_id: 1, host: "db-1.db:27017"},
8         {_id: 2, host: "db-2.db:27017"}
9      ]
10  })
```

We entered into mongo Shell and initiated a ReplicaSet (rs.initiate). The members of the ReplicaSet are the addresses of the three Pods combined with the default MongoDB port 27017.

The output is { "ok" : 1 }, thus confirming that we (probably) configured the ReplicaSet correctly.

Remember that our goal is not to go deep into MongoDB configuration, but only to explore some of the benefits behind StatefulSets.

If we used Deployments, we would not get stable network identity. Any update would create new Pods with new identities. With StatefulSet, on the other hand, we know that there will always be db-[INDEX].db, no matter how often we update it. Such a feature is mandatory when applications need to form an internal cluster (or a replica set) and were not designed to discover each other dynamically. That is indeed the case with MongoDB.

We'll confirm that the MongoDB replica set was created correctly by outputting its status.

```
1   rs.status()
```

The output, limited to the relevant parts, is as follows.

```
1   ...
2     "members" : [
3       {
4         "_id" : 0,
5         ...
6         "stateStr" : "PRIMARY",
7         ...
8       },
9       {
10        "_id" : 1,
11        ...
12        "stateStr" : "SECONDARY",
13        ...
14        "syncingTo" : "db-0.db:27017",
```

```
15        ...
16      },
17      {
18        "_id" : 2,
19        ...
20        "stateStr" : "SECONDARY",
21        ...
22        "syncingTo" : "db-0.db:27017",
23        ...
24      }
25    ],
26    "ok" : 1
27 }
```

We can see that all three MongoDB Pods are members of the replica set. One of them is primary. If it fails, Kubernetes will reschedule it and, since it's managed by the StatefulSet, it'll maintain the same stable network identity. The secondary members are all syncing with the primary one that is reachable through the db-0.db:27017 address.

Now that the database is finally operational, we should confirm that the api Pods are running.

```
1  exit
2
3  exit
4
5  kubectl -n go-demo-3 get pods
```

We exited MongoDB Shell and the container that hosts db-0, and we listed the Pods in the go-demo-3 Namespace.

The output of the latter command is as follows.

```
1  NAME      READY STATUS  RESTARTS AGE
2  api-...   1/1   Running 8        17m
3  api-...   1/1   Running 8        17m
4  api-...   1/1   Running 8        17m
5  db-0      1/1   Running 0        17m
6  db-1      1/1   Running 0        17m
7  db-2      1/1   Running 0        16m
```

If, in your case, api Pods are still not running, please wait for a few moments until Kubernetes restarts them.

Now that the MongoDB replica set is operational, api Pods could connect to it, and Kubernetes changed their statuses to Running. The whole application is operational.

There is one more StatefulSet-specific feature we should discuss.

Let's see what happens if, for example, we update the image of the db container.

The updated definition is in sts/go-demo-3-sts-upd.yml.

```
1  diff sts/go-demo-3-sts.yml \
2      sts/go-demo-3-sts-upd.yml
```

As you can see from the diff, the only change is in the image. We'll update mongo version from 3.3 to 3.4.

```
1  kubectl apply \
2      -f sts/go-demo-3-sts-upd.yml \
3      --record
4
5  kubectl -n go-demo-3 get pods
```

We applied the new definition and retrieved the list of Pods inside the Namespace.

The output is as follows.

```
1  NAME     READY  STATUS             RESTARTS  AGE
2  api-...  1/1    Running            6         14m
3  api-...  1/1    Running            6         14m
4  api-...  1/1    Running            6         14m
5  db-0     1/1    Running            0         6m
6  db-1     1/1    Running            0         6m
7  db-2     0/1    ContainerCreating  0         14s
```

We can see that the StatefulSet chose to update only one of its Pods. Moreover, it picked the one with the highest index.

Let's see the output of the same command half a minute later.

```
1  NAME     READY  STATUS             RESTARTS  AGE
2  api-...  1/1    Running            6         15m
3  api-...  1/1    Running            6         15m
4  api-...  1/1    Running            6         15m
5  db-0     1/1    Running            0         7m
6  db-1     0/1    ContainerCreating  0         5s
7  db-2     1/1    Running            0         32s
```

StatefulSet finished updating the db-2 Pod and moved to the one before it.

And so on, and so forth, all the way until all the Pods that form the StatefulSet were updated.

The Pods in the StatefulSet were updated in reverse ordinal order. The StatefulSet terminated one of the Pods, and it waited for its status to become Running before it moved to the next one.

All in all, when StatefulSet is created, it, in turn, generates Pods sequentially starting with the index 0, and moving upwards. Updates to StatefulSets are following the same logic, except that StatefulSet begins updates with the Pod with the highest index, and it flows downwards.

We did manage to make MongoDB replica set running, but the cost was too high. Creating Mongo replica set manually is not a good option. It should be no option at all.

We'll remove the go-demo-3 Namespace (and everything inside it) and try to improve our process for deploying MongoDB.

```
1  kubectl delete ns go-demo-3
```

Using Sidecar Containers To Initialize Applications

Even though we managed to deploy MongoDB replica set with three instances, the process was far from optimum. We had to execute manual steps. Since I don't believe that manual hocus-pocus type of intervention is the way to go, we'll try to improve the process by removing human interaction. We'll do that through sidecar containers that will do the work of creating MongoDB replica set (not to be confused with Kubernetes ReplicaSet).

Let's take a look at yet another iteration of the go-demo-3 application definition.

```
1  cat sts/go-demo-3.yml
```

The output, limited to relevant parts, is as follows.

```
1  ...
2  apiVersion: apps/v1beta2
3  kind: StatefulSet
4  metadata:
5    name: db
6    namespace: go-demo-3
7  spec:
8    ...
9    template:
10     ...
11     spec:
```

```
12          terminationGracePeriodSeconds: 10
13          containers:
14          ...
15          - name: db-sidecar
16            image: cvallance/mongo-k8s-sidecar
17            env:
18            - name: MONGO_SIDECAR_POD_LABELS
19              value: "app=db"
20            - name: KUBE_NAMESPACE
21              value: go-demo-3
22            - name: KUBERNETES_MONGO_SERVICE_NAME
23              value: db
24  ...
```

When compared with `sts/go-demo-3-sts.yml`, the only difference is the addition of the second container in the StatefulSet `db`. It is based on cvallance/mongo-k8s-sidecar[20] Docker image. I won't bore you with the details but only give you the gist of the project. It creates and maintains MongoDB replica sets.

The sidecar will monitor the Pods created through our StatefulSet, and it will reconfigure `db` containers so that MongoDB replica set is (almost) always up to date with the MongoDB instances.

Let's create the resources defined in `sts/go-demo-3.yml` and check whether everything works as expected.

```
1  kubectl apply \
2      -f sts/go-demo-3.yml \
3      --record
4
5  # Wait for a few moments
6
7  kubectl -n go-demo-3 \
8      logs db-0 \
9      -c db-sidecar
```

We created the resources and outputted the logs of the `db-sidecar` container inside the `db-0` Pod.

The output, limited to the last entry, is as follows.

---

[20]https://hub.docker.com/r/cvallance/mongo-k8s-sidecar

```
1   ...
2   Error in workloop { [Error: [object Object]]
3     message:
4     { kind: 'Status',
5       apiVersion: 'v1',
6       metadata: {},
7       status: 'Failure',
8       message: 'pods is forbidden: User "system:serviceaccount:go-demo-3:default" can\
9   not list pods in the namespace "go-demo-3"',
10      reason: 'Forbidden',
11      details: { kind: 'pods' },
12      code: 403 },
13    statusCode: 403 }
```

We can see that the db-sidecar container is not allowed to list the Pods in the go-demo-3 Namespace. If, in your case, that's not the output you're seeing, you might need to wait for a few moments and re-execute the logs command.

It is not surprising that the sidecar could not list the Pods. If it could, RBAC would be, more or less, useless. It would not matter that we restrict which resources users can create if any Pod could circumvent that. Just as we learned in *The DevOps 2.3 Toolkit: Kubernetes* how to set up users using RBAC, we need to do something similar with service accounts. We need to extend RBAC rules from human users to Pods. That will be the subject of the next chapter.

 ## A note to Docker For Mac/Windows users

On Docker for Mac (or Windows), the db-sidecar can list the Pods even with RBAC enabled. Even though Docker for Mac/Windows supports RBAC, it allows any internal process inside containers to communicate with Kube API. Be aware that even though the sidecar could list the Pods in Docker For Mac/Windows, it will not work in any other cluster with RBAC enabled.

To StatefulSet Or Not To StatefulSet

StatefulSets provide a few essential features often required when running stateful applications in a Kubernetes cluster. Still, the division between Deployments and StatefulSets is not always clear. After all, both controllers can attach a PersistentVolume, both can forward requests through Services, and both support rolling updates. When should you choose one over the other? Saying that one is for stateful applications and the other isn't would be an oversimplification that would not fit all the scenarios. As an example, we saw that we got no tangible benefit when we moved Jenkins from a Deployment into a StatefulSet. MongoDB, on the other hand, showcases essential benefits provided by StatefulSets.

We can simplify decision making with a few questions.

- Does your application need stable and unique network identifiers?
- Does your application need stable persistent storage?
- Does your application need ordered deployments, scaling, deletion, or rolling updates?

If the answer to any of those questions is *yes*, your application should probably be managed by a StatefulSet. Otherwise, you should probably use a Deployment. All that does not mean that there are no other controller types you can use. There are a few. However, if the choice is limited to Deployment and StatefulSet controllers, those three questions should be on your mind when choosing which one to use.

What Now?

We're finished with the exploration of StatefulSets. They will be essential since they will enable us to do a few things that will be critical for our Continuous Deployment processes. For now, we'll remove the resources we created and take a break before we jump into Service Accounts in an attempt to fix the problem with the MongoDB sidecar. Who knows? We might find the usage of Service Account beyond the sidecar.

```
1  kubectl delete ns go-demo-3
```

We deleted the go-demo-3 Namespace and, with it, all the resources we created. We'll start the next chapter with a clean slate. Feel free to delete the whole cluster if you're not planning to explore the next chapter right away. If it's dedicated to this book, there's no need to waste resources and money on running a cluster that is not doing anything.

Before you leave, please consult the following API references for more information about StatefulSets.

- StatefulSet v1beta2 apps[21]

---

[21]https://v1-9.docs.kubernetes.io/docs/api-reference/v1.9/#statefulset-v1-apps

Enabling Process Communication With Kube API Through Service Accounts

 Humans are not the only ones who rely on a cluster. Processes in containers often need to invoke Kube API as well. When using RBAC for authentication, we need to decide which users will have permissions to perform specific actions. The same holds true for the processes running inside containers.

When we (humans) try to access a Kubernetes cluster with RBAC enabled, we are authenticated as users. Our username provides an identity that API server uses to decide whether we are allowed to perform intended actions. Similarly processes running inside containers might also need to access the API. In such cases, they are authenticated as a specific ServiceAccount.

ServiceAccounts provide a mechanism to grant permissions to processes running inside containers. In many ways, ServiceAccounts are very similar to RBAC users or groups. With humans, we use RoleBindings and ClusterRoleBindings to relate users and groups to Roles and ClusterRoles. When working with processes, the main difference is in the name and the scope. Instead of users or groups, we create ServiceAccounts which we bind to roles.However unlike users that can be global, ServiceAccounts are tied to specific Namespaces.

 This chapter assumes that you are already familiar with Namespaces, Ingress, Deployments, Roles, ClusterRoles, RoleBindings, ClusterRoleBindings, Users, and Groups. If you're not, please refer to The DevOps 2.3 Toolkit: Kubernetes[22] for more info.

We won't go into any more theory. Instead, we'll try to learn different aspects of ServiceAccounts through hands-on examples.

Creating A Cluster

We'll start the hands-on walk-through by entering the directory where we cloned the vfarcic/k8s-specs repository.

---

[22]https://amzn.to/2GvzDjy

All the commands from this chapter are available in the 02-sa.sh[23] Gist.

```
1   cd k8s-specs
2
3   git pull
```

Next, we'll need a cluster which we can use to experiment with ServiceAccounts. The requirements are the same as those we used in the previous chapter. We'll need **Kubernetes version 1.9** or higher as well as **nginx Ingress Controller, RBAC**, and a **default StorageClass**. If you didn't destroy it, please continue using the cluster you created in the previous chapter. Otherwise, it should be reasonably fast to create a new one. For your convenience, the Gists and the specs we used before are available here as well.

- docker4mac.sh[24]: **Docker for Mac** with 2 CPUs, 2GB RAM, and with **nginx Ingress**.
- minikube.sh[25]: **minikube** with 2 CPUs, 2GB RAM, and with `ingress`, `storage-provisioner`, and `default-storageclass` addons enabled.
- kops.sh[26]: **kops in AWS** with 3 t2.small masters and 2 t2.medium nodes spread in three availability zones, and with **nginx Ingress** (assumes that the prerequisites are set through Appendix B).
- minishift.sh[27]: **minishift** with 2 CPUs, 2GB RAM, and version 1.16+.
- gke.sh[28]: **Google Kubernetes Engine (GKE)** with 3 n1-standard-1 (1 CPU, 3.75GB RAM) nodes (one in each zone), and with **nginx Ingress** controller running on top of the "standard" one that comes with GKE. We'll use nginx Ingress for compatibility with other platforms. Feel free to modify the YAML files if you prefer NOT to install nginx Ingress.
- eks.sh[29]: **Elastic Kubernetes Service (EKS)** with 2 t2.medium nodes, with **nginx Ingress** controller, and with a **default StorageClass**.

Now that we have a cluster, we can proceed with a few examples.

Configuring Jenkins Kubernetes Plugin

We'll start by creating the same Jenkins StatefulSet we used in the previous chapter. Once it's up-and-running, we'll try to use Jenkins Kubernetes plugin[30]. If we're successful, we'll have a tool which could be used to execute continuous delivery or deployment tasks inside a Kubernetes cluster.

[23]https://gist.github.com/5fdca8e7f7bb426003abf4ad55745807
[24]https://gist.github.com/06e313db2957e92b1df09fe39c249a14
[25]https://gist.github.com/536e6329e750b795a882900c09feb13b
[26]https://gist.github.com/2a3e4ee9cb86d4a5a65cd3e4397f48fd
[27]https://gist.github.com/c9968f23ecb1f7b2ec40c6bcc0e03e4f
[28]https://gist.github.com/5c52c165bf9c5002fedb61f8a5d6a6d1
[29]https://gist.github.com/5496f79a3886be794cc317c6f8dd7083
[30]https://github.com/jenkinsci/kubernetes-plugin

```
1   cat sa/jenkins-no-sa.yml
```

We won't go through the definition since it is the same as the one we used in the previous chapter. There's no mystery that has to be revealed, so we'll move on and create the resources defined in that YAML.

A note to minishift users

OpenShift does not allow setting fsGroup in the security context, it uses Routes instead of Ingress, and Services accessible through Routes need to be the LoadBalancer type. Due to those changes, I had to prepare a different YAML specification for minishift. Please execute oc apply -f sa/jenkins-no-sa-oc.yml --record instead of the command that follows.

```
1   kubectl apply \
2       -f sa/jenkins-no-sa.yml \
3       --record
```

Next, we'll wait until jenkins StatefulSet is rolled out.

```
1   kubectl -n jenkins \
2       rollout status sts jenkins
```

A note to GKE users

GKE uses external load balancer as Ingress. To work properly, the type of the service related to Ingress needs to be NodePort. We'll have to patch the service to change its type. Please execute the command that follows.

```
kubectl -n jenkins patch svc jenkins -p '{"spec":{"type": "NodePort"}}'
```

Next, we'll discover the DNS (or IP) of the load balancer.

A note to GKE users

Please change hostname to ip in the following command. The jsonpath should be {.status.loadBalancer.ingress[0].ip}. Please note that GKE Ingress spins up an external load balancer and it might take a while until the IP is generated. Therefore, you might need to repeat the command that follows until you get the IP.

A note to minikube users

Please change the following command to CLUSTER_DNS=$(minikube ip).

A note to minishift users

Please change the following command to `CLUSTER_DNS=jenkins-jenkins.$(minishift ip).nip.io`.

```
1  CLUSTER_DNS=$(kubectl -n jenkins \
2      get ing jenkins \
3      -o jsonpath="{.status.loadBalancer.ingress[0].hostname}")
4
5  echo $CLUSTER_DNS
```

Now that we know the address of the cluster, we can proceed and open Jenkins UI in a browser.

```
1  open "http://$CLUSTER_DNS/jenkins"
```

 In some cases (e.g., GKE), it might take a few minutes until the external load balancer is created. If you see 40x or 50x error message, please wait for a while and try to open Jenkins in the browser again.

Now we need to go through the setup wizard. It's a dull process, and I'm sure you're not thrilled with the prospect of going through it. However, we're still missing knowledge and tools that will allow us to automate the process. For now, we'll have to do the boring part manually.

The first step is to get the initial admin password.

 ## A note to Windows users

The command that follows might result in `no such file or directory` error. In that case, please replace / with // in the path. Continue applying the same fix throughout the book if you continue experiencing the same problem.

```
1  kubectl -n jenkins \
2      exec jenkins-0 -it -- \
3      cat /var/jenkins_home/secrets/initialAdminPassword
```

Please copy the output and paste it into the *Administrator password* field. Click the *Continue* button, followed with a click to *Install suggested plugins* button. Fill in the *Create First Admin User* fields and press the *Save and Finish* button.

Jenkins is ready, and only a click away. Please press the *Start using Jenkins* button.

If we are to use the Kubernetes plugin[31], we need to install it first. We'll do that through the *available plugins section* of the *plugin manager screen*.

---

[31]https://github.com/jenkinsci/kubernetes-plugin

```
1  open "http://$CLUSTER_DNS/jenkins/pluginManager/available"
```

Type *Kubernetes* in the *Filter* field and select the checkbox next to it.

Since we are already in the plugin manager screen, we might just as well install BlueOcean as well. It'll make Jenkins prettier.

Type *BlueOcean* in the *Filter* field and select the checkbox next to it.

Now that we selected the plugins we want, the next step is to install them. Please click the *Install without restart* button and wait until all the plugins (and their dependencies) are installed.

We are not yet finished. We still need to configure the newly installed Kubernetes plugin.

```
1  open "http://$CLUSTER_DNS/jenkins/configure"
```

The plugin adds Kubernetes as yet another *Cloud* provider. Please expand the *Add a new cloud* drop-down list inside the *Cloud* section, and select *Kubernetes*. The section you're looking for should be somewhere close to the bottom of the screen.

Now that we added Kubernetes as a Cloud provider, we should confirm that it works. Please click the *Test Connection* button.

Unless you forgot to unable RBAC in your cluster, the output should be similar to the one that follows.

```
1  Error testing connection : Failure executing: GET at: https://kubernetes.default.svc\
2  /api/v1/namespaces/jenkins/pods. Message: Forbidden!Configured service account doesn\
3  't have access. Service account may have been revoked. pods is forbidden: User "syst\
4  em:serviceaccount:jenkins:default" cannot list pods in the namespace "jenkins".
```

 A note to Docker For Mac/Windows users

Even though Docker for Mac/Windows supports RBAC, it allows any internal process inside containers to communicate with Kube API. That is quite the opposite from what you'll experience in other Kubernetes platforms. As a result, you'll see a few discrepancies between the outputs in this chapter and those you'll see in your cluster. You'll notice that you'll be able to perform actions that are forbidden in other Kubernetes platforms.

API server rejected our request to list the Pods in the `jenkins` Namespace. Such a reaction makes perfect sense. If any process in any container could request anything from the API, our security efforts would be useless. What would be the point of trying to restrict users (humans), if all it takes is to create a single Pod that sends a request to the API server? Kube API rightfully denied our request to list the Pods.

Just as a username provides a sort of identity to humans, a ServiceAccount is an identity for all the processes that run in containers. Since we did not specify any ServiceAccount for the Pod where Jenkins is running, Kubernetes assigned one for us. The Pod is authenticated as the default account which happens to be bound to roles that give almost no permissions. In other words, if we do not define a ServiceAccount for a Pod, it'll be associated with the ServiceAccount default, and the processes inside that Pod will not be able to requests almost anything from the API server.

The default ServiceAccount is created for every Namespace in the cluster. It is, in a way, similar to the default StorageClass. If a Pod does not have a ServiceAccount, it'll get the default. That ServiceAccount has insufficient privileges, and it cannot do almost anything. We can bind more permissive role to the default ServiceAccount, but that would be a very uncommon solution to the problem.

We need to associate Jenkins process with an entity that has more permissions. As a minimum, we should be able to list the Pods in the jenkins Namespace. To do that, we have to learn about ServiceAccounts first.

We'll delete jenkins Namespace and search for a simple way explore ServiceAccounts.

```
1   kubectl delete ns jenkins
```

Exploring the default ServiceAccount

Jenkins might not be the best starting point in our exploration of ServiceAccounts. Too many things are happening that are out of our control. There's too much "magic" hidden behind Jenkins code. Instead, we'll start with something simpler. We'll run kubectl as a Pod. If we manage to make that work, we should have no problem applying the newly acquired knowledge to Jenkins and other similar use-cases we might have.

Unfortunately, there is no kubectl official image (at least not in Docker Hub), so I built one. The definition is in the vfarcic/kubectl[32] GitHub repository. Let's take a quick look.

```
1   curl https://raw.githubusercontent.com/vfarcic/kubectl/master/Dockerfile
```

The Dockerfile is so uneventful and straightforward that there's probably no need going through it. It's a kubectl binary in an alpine based image. Not more, not less.

Let's run it.

---

[32]https://github.com/vfarcic/kubectl

```
1  kubectl run kubectl \
2      --image=vfarcic/kubectl \
3      --restart=Never \
4      sleep 10000
```

We should wait for a few moments until the image is pulled and the container that forms the Pod is running.

Let's start by checking out the serviceAccount entry in the Pod specification.

```
1  kubectl get pod kubectl \
2      -o jsonpath="{.spec.serviceAccount}"
```

The output is as follows.

```
1  default
```

Since we did not specify any ServiceAccount, Kubernetes automatically assigned the default. That account was created with the Namespace.

We might be able to dig a bit more information in the kubectl container.

```
1  kubectl exec -it kubectl -- sh
```

No matter which ServiceAccount is used, Kubernetes always mounts a secret with the information about that account. The secret is mounted inside the /var/run/secrets/kubernetes.io/serviceaccount directory.

```
1  cd /var/run/secrets/kubernetes.io/serviceaccount
2
3  ls -la
```

We entered into the secret's directory and listed all the files. The output is as follows.

```
1  total 4
2  ... .
3  ... ..
4  ... ..2018_05_07_00_35_25.899750157
5  ... ..data -> ..2018_05_07_00_35_25.899750157
6  ... ca.crt -> ..data/ca.crt
7  ... namespace -> ..data/namespace
8  ... token -> ..data/token
```

We can see that it created three soft-links (ca.crt, namespace, and token) which are pointing to a directory that contains the actual files. You should be able to guess what those files contain. The token and the certificate are used for authentication when communicating with the API server. The third file contains only the Namespace in which the Pod is running.

Let's try a very simple operation.

```
1  kubectl get pods
```

The output is as follows.

```
1  Error from server (Forbidden): pods is forbidden: User "system:serviceaccount:defaul\
2  t:default" cannot list pods in the namespace "default"
```

We got a similar error message as when we tried to use Jenkins' Kubernetes plugin without credentials. Once again we're faced with limited permissions bound to the default account. We'll change that soon. For now, we'll exit the container and remove the kubectl Pod.

```
1  exit
2
3  kubectl delete pod kubectl
```

We saw the limitations of the default account. We'll try to overcome them by creating our own ServiceAccounts.

Creating ServiceAccounts

Let's take a look at service accounts currently available in the default Namespace.

```
1  kubectl get sa
```

The output is as follows.

```
1  NAME     SECRETS AGE
2  default 1        24m
```

At the moment, there is only one ServiceAccount called default. We already saw the limitations of that account. It is stripped from (almost) all the privileges. If we check the other Namespaces, we'll notice that all of them have only the default ServiceAccount. Whenever we create a new Namespace, Kubernetes creates that account for us.

 ## A note to minishift users

OpenShift is an exception. Unlike most other Kubernetes flavors, it created a few ServiceAccounts in the default Namespace. Feel free to explore them later when you learn more about ServiceAccounts and their relations to Roles.

We already established that we'll need to create new ServiceAccounts if we are ever to allow processes in containers to communicate with Kube API. As the first exercise, we'll create an account that will enable us to view (almost) all the resources in the default Namespace. The definition is available in the sa/view.yml file.

```
1  cat sa/view.yml
```

The output is as follows.

```
1  apiVersion: v1
2  kind: ServiceAccount
3  metadata:
4    name: view
5
6  ---
7
8  apiVersion: rbac.authorization.k8s.io/v1beta1
9  kind: RoleBinding
10 metadata:
11   name: view
12 roleRef:
13   apiGroup: rbac.authorization.k8s.io
14   kind: ClusterRole
15   name: view
16 subjects:
17 - kind: ServiceAccount
18   name: view
```

The YAML defines two resources. The first one is the `ServiceAccount` named `view`. The ServiceAccount kind of resources is on pair with Namespace in its simplicity. Excluding a few flags which we won't explore just yet, the only thing we can do with it is to declare its existence. The real magic is defined in the RoleBinding.

Just as with RBAC users and groups, RoleBindings are tying Roles to ServiceAccounts. Since our objective to provide read-only permissions that can be fulfilled with the ClusterRole `view`, we did not need to create a new Role. Instead, we're binding the ClusterRole `view` with the ServiceAccount with the same name.

If you are already experienced with RBAC applied to users and groups, you probably noticed that ServiceAccounts follow the same pattern. The only substantial difference, from YAML perspective, is that the `kind` of the subject is now `ServiceAccount`, instead of being `User` or `Group`.

Let's create the YAML and observe the results.

```
1   kubectl apply -f sa/view.yml --record
```

The output should show that the ServiceAccount and the RoleBinding were created.

Next, we'll list the ServiceAccounts in the `default` Namespace and confirm that the new one was created.

```
1   kubectl get sa
```

The output is as follows.

```
1   NAME     SECRETS AGE
2   default 1        27m
3   view    1        6s
```

Let's take a closer look at the ServiceAccount `view` we just created.

```
1   kubectl describe sa view
```

The output is as follows.

```
1   Name:       view
2   Namespace:  default
3   Labels:     <none>
4   Annotations: kubectl.kubernetes.io/last-applied-configuration={"apiVersion":"v1","ki\
5   nd":"ServiceAccount","metadata":{"annotations":{},"name":"view","namespace":"default\
6   "}}
7                kubernetes.io/change-cause=kubectl apply --filename=sa/view.yml --recor\
8   d=true
9   Image pull secrets: <none>
10  Mountable secrets:  view-token-292vm
11  Tokens:             view-token-292vm
12  Events:             <none>
```

There's not much to look at since, as we already saw from the definition, ServiceAccounts are only placeholders for bindings.

We should be able to get more information from the binding.

```
1   kubectl describe rolebinding view
```

The output is as follows.

```
1   Name:       view
2   Labels:     <none>
3   Annotations: kubectl.kubernetes.io/last-applied-configuration={"apiVersion":"rbac.au\
4   thorization.k8s.io/v1beta1","kind":"RoleBinding","metadata":{"annotations":{},"name"\
5   :"view","namespace":"default"},"roleRef":{"ap...
6                kubernetes.io/change-cause=kubectl apply --filename=sa/view.yml --recor\
7   d=true
8   Role:
9     Kind: ClusterRole
10    Name: view
11  Subjects:
12    Kind            Name Namespace
13    ----            ---- ---------
14    ServiceAccount view
```

We can see that the ClusterRole named view has a single subject with the ServiceAccount.

Now that we have the ServiceAccount that has enough permissions to view (almost) all the resources, we'll create a Pod with kubectl which we can use to explore permissions.

The definition is in the sa/kubectl-view.yml file.

```
1  cat sa/kubectl-view.yml
```

The output is as follows.

```
1   apiVersion: v1
2   kind: Pod
3   metadata:
4     name: kubectl
5   spec:
6     serviceAccountName: view
7     containers:
8     - name: kubectl
9       image: vfarcic/kubectl
10      command: ["sleep"]
11      args: ["100000"]
```

The only new addition is the serviceAccountName: view entry. It associates the Pod with the account.
Let's create the Pod and describe it.

```
1  kubectl apply \
2      -f sa/kubectl-view.yml \
3      --record
4
5  kubectl describe pod kubectl
```

The relevant parts of the output of the latter command are as follows.

```
1   Name: kubectl
2   ...
3   Containers:
4     kubectl:
5       ...
6       Mounts:
7         /var/run/secrets/kubernetes.io/serviceaccount from view-token-292vm (ro)
8   ...
9   Volumes:
10    view-token-292vm:
11      Type:       Secret (a volume populated by a Secret)
12      SecretName: view-token-292vm
13  ...
```

Since we declared that we want to associate the Pod with the account `view`, Kubernetes mounted a token to the container. If we defined more containers in that Pod, all would have the same mount.

Further on, we can see that the mount is using a Secret. It contains the same file structure we observed earlier with the `default` account.

Let's see whether we can retrieve the Pods from the same Namespace.

```
1  kubectl exec -it kubectl -- sh
2
3  kubectl get pods
```

We entered into the Shell of the container and listed the Pods.

The output is as follows.

```
1  NAME     READY STATUS   RESTARTS AGE
2  kubectl 1/1    Running 0         55s
```

Now that the Pod is associated with the ServiceAccount that has `view` permissions, we can indeed list the Pods. At the moment, we can see the `kubectl` Pod since it is the only one running in the `default` Namespace.

 ## A note to minishift users

You should see three Pods instead of one. When we created the OpenShift cluster with minikube, it deployed Docker Registry and a Router to the `default` Namespace.

Even though you probably know the answer, we'll confirm that we can indeed only view the resources and that all other operations are forbidden. We'll try to create a new Pod.

```
1  kubectl run new-test \
2      --image=alpine \
3      --restart=Never \
4      sleep 10000
```

The output is a follows.

```
1  Error from server (Forbidden): pods is forbidden: User "system:serviceaccount:defaul\
2  t:view" cannot create pods in the namespace "default"
```

As expected, we cannot create Pods. Since we bound the ClusterRole `view` to the ServiceAccount, and that allows us only read-only access to resources.

We'll exit the container and delete the resources we created before we continue exploring ServiceAccounts.

```
1  exit
2
3  kubectl delete -f sa/kubectl-view.yml
```

Jenkins' Kubernetes plugin needs to have full permissions related to Pods. It should be able to create them, to retrieve logs from them, to execute processes, to delete them, and so on. The resources defined in sa/pods.yml should allow us just that.

```
1  cat sa/pods.yml
```

The output is as follows.

```
1  apiVersion: v1
2  kind: ServiceAccount
3  metadata:
4    name: pods-all
5    namespace: test1
6
7  ---
8
9  kind: Role
10 apiVersion: rbac.authorization.k8s.io/v1beta1
11 metadata:
12   name: pods-all
13   namespace: test1
14 rules:
15 - apiGroups: [""]
16   resources: ["pods", "pods/exec", "pods/log"]
17   verbs: ["*"]
18
19 ---
20
21 apiVersion: rbac.authorization.k8s.io/v1beta1
22 kind: RoleBinding
23 metadata:
24   name: pods-all
25   namespace: test1
26 roleRef:
27   apiGroup: rbac.authorization.k8s.io
28   kind: Role
29   name: pods-all
30 subjects:
```

```
31  - kind: ServiceAccount
32    name: pods-all
```

Just as before, we are creating a ServiceAccount. This time we're naming it pods-all. Since none of the existing roles provide the types of privileges we need, we're defining a new one that provides full permissions with Pods. Finally, the last resource is the binding that ties the two together. All three resources are, this time, defined in the Namespace test1.

Let's create the resources.

```
1  kubectl apply -f sa/pods.yml \
2      --record
```

So far, we did not explore the effect of ServiceAccounts to Namespaces other than those where we created them, so we'll create another one called test2.

```
1  kubectl create ns test2
```

Finally, we'll run kubectl as a Pod so that we can test the new account. Let's take a very quick look at the updated kubectl Pod definition.

```
1  cat sa/kubectl-test1.yml
```

The output is as follows.

```
1  apiVersion: v1
2  kind: Pod
3  metadata:
4    name: kubectl
5    namespace: test1
6  spec:
7    serviceAccountName: pods-all
8    containers:
9    - name: kubectl
10     image: vfarcic/kubectl
11     command: ["sleep"]
12     args: ["100000"]
```

The only differences from the previous kubectl definition are in the namespace and the serviceAccountName. I'll assume that there's no need for an explanation. Instead, we'll proceed and apply the definition.

```
1 kubectl apply \
2     -f sa/kubectl-test1.yml \
3     --record
```

Now we're ready to test the new account.

```
1 kubectl -n test1 exec -it kubectl -- sh
2
3 kubectl get pods
```

We entered the kubectl container and retrieved the Pods.

The output is as follows.

```
1 NAME      READY STATUS   RESTARTS AGE
2 kubectl 1/1    Running 0            5m
```

We already experienced the same result when we used the ServiceAccount with the view Role, so let's try something different and try to create a Pod.

```
1 kubectl run new-test \
2     --image=alpine \
3     --restart=Never \
4     sleep 10000
```

Unlike before, this time the pod "new-test" was created. We can confirm that by listing the Pods one more time.

```
1 kubectl get pods
```

The output is as follows.

```
1 NAME       READY STATUS   RESTARTS AGE
2 kubectl    1/1    Running 0            6m
3 new-test 1/1    Running 0            17s
```

How about creating a Deployment?

```
1 kubectl run new-test \
2     --image=alpine sleep 10000
```

As you hopefully already know, if we execute a run command without the --restart=Never argument, Kubernetes creates a Deployment, instead of a Pod.

The output is as follows.

```
1  Error from server (Forbidden): deployments.extensions is forbidden: User "system:ser\
2  viceaccount:test1:pods-all" cannot create deployments.extensions in the namespace "t\
3  est1"
```

It's obvious that our ServiceAccount does not have any permissions aside from those related to Pods, so we were forbidden from creating a Deployment.

Let's see what happens if, for example, we try to retrieve the Pods from the Namespace test2. As a reminder, we are still inside a container that forms the Pod in the test1 Namespace.

```
1  kubectl -n test2 get pods
```

The ServiceAccount was created in the test1 Namespace. Therefore only the Pods created in the same Namespace can be attached to the pods-all ServiceAccount. In this case, the principal thing to note is that the RoleBinding that gives us the permissions to, for example, retrieve the Pods, exists only in the test1 Namespace. The moment we tried to retrieve the Pods from a different Namespace, the API server responded with an error notifying us that we do not have permissions to list pods in the namespace "test2".

 While user accounts are global, ServiceAccounts are namespaced. After all, a human user is almost always invoking the API from outside the cluster while the processes inside containers are always inside the Pods which are inside the Namespaces.

We'll exit the container and delete the resources we created, before we explore other aspects of ServiceAccounts.

```
1  exit
2
3  kubectl delete -f sa/kubectl-test1.yml
```

We saw that, with the previous definition, we obtained permissions only within the same Namespace as the Pod attached to the ServiceAccount. In some cases that is not enough. Jenkins is a good use-case. We might decide to run Jenkins master in one Namespace but run the builds in another. Or, we might create a pipeline that deploys a beta version of our application and tests it in one Namespace and, later on, deploys it as production release in another. Surely there is a way to accommodate such needs.

Let's take a look at yet another YAML.

```
1  cat sa/pods-all.yml
```

The output is as follows.

```
1    apiVersion: v1
2    kind: ServiceAccount
3    metadata:
4      name: pods-all
5      namespace: test1
6
7    ---
8
9    kind: Role
10   apiVersion: rbac.authorization.k8s.io/v1beta1
11   metadata:
12     name: pods-all
13     namespace: test1
14   rules:
15   - apiGroups: [""]
16     resources: ["pods", "pods/exec", "pods/log"]
17     verbs: ["*"]
18
19   ---
20
21   kind: Role
22   apiVersion: rbac.authorization.k8s.io/v1beta1
23   metadata:
24     name: pods-all
25     namespace: test2
26   rules:
27   - apiGroups: [""]
28     resources: ["pods", "pods/exec", "pods/log"]
29     verbs: ["*"]
30
31   ---
32
33   apiVersion: rbac.authorization.k8s.io/v1beta1
34   kind: RoleBinding
35   metadata:
36     name: pods-all
37     namespace: test1
38   roleRef:
39     apiGroup: rbac.authorization.k8s.io
40     kind: Role
41     name: pods-all
42   subjects:
43   - kind: ServiceAccount
```

```
44    name: pods-all
45
46  ---
47
48  apiVersion: rbac.authorization.k8s.io/v1beta1
49  kind: RoleBinding
50  metadata:
51    name: pods-all
52    namespace: test2
53  roleRef:
54    apiGroup: rbac.authorization.k8s.io
55    kind: Role
56    name: pods-all
57  subjects:
58  - kind: ServiceAccount
59    name: pods-all
60    namespace: test1
```

We start by creating a ServiceAccount and a Role called pods-all in the test1 Namespace. Further on, we're creating the same role but in the test2 Namespace. Finally, we're creating RoleBindings in both Namespaces. The only difference between the two is in a single line. The RoleBinding in the test2 Namespace has the subjects entry namespace: test1. With it, we are linking a binding from one Namespace to a ServiceAccount in another. As a result, we should be able to create a Pod in the test1 Namespace that will have full permissions to operate Pods in both Namespaces.

The two Roles could have been with different permission. They are the same (for now) only for simplicity reasons. We could have simplified the definition by defining a single ClusterRole and save ourselves from having two Roles (one in each Namespace). However, once we get back to Jenkins, we'll probably want to have different permissions in different Namespaces, so we're defining two Roles as a practice.

Let's apply the new definition, create a kubectl Pod again, and enter inside its only container.

```
1  kubectl apply -f sa/pods-all.yml \
2      --record
3
4  kubectl apply \
5      -f sa/kubectl-test2.yml \
6      --record
7
8  kubectl -n test1 exec -it kubectl -- sh
```

There's probably no need to confirm again that we can retrieve the Pods from the same Namespace so we'll jump straight to testing whether we can now operate within the test2 Namespace.

```
1  kubectl -n test2 get pods
```

The output shows that no resources were found. If we did not have permissions to view the files, we'd get the already familiar forbidden message instead.

To be on the safe side, we'll try to create a Pod in the test2 Namespace.

```
1  kubectl -n test2 \
2      run new-test \
3      --image=alpine \
4      --restart=Never \
5      sleep 10000
6
7  kubectl -n test2 get pods
```

The output of the latter command is as follows.

```
1  NAME       READY STATUS   RESTARTS AGE
2  new-test 1/1   Running 0           18s
```

The Pod was created in the test2 Namespace. Mission was accomplished, and we can get out of the container and delete the Namespaces we created, before we try to apply the knowledge about ServiceAccounts to Jenkins.

```
1  exit
2
3  kubectl delete ns test1 test2
```

Configuring Jenkins Kubernetes Plugin With ServiceAccounts

Now that we got a grip on ServiceAccounts, it should be relatively straightforward to correct the problem we experienced with Jenkins. As a reminder, we could not configure the Kubernetes plugin. We experienced the same forbidden message as when we tried to use kubectl container with the default ServiceAccount. Now that we know that ServiceAccounts provide permissions to processes running inside containers, all we have to do is to define one for Jenkins.

We'll spice it up a bit with a slightly more complicated use-case. We'll try to run Jenkins master in one Namespace and perform builds in another. That way we can have a clear separation between Jenkins and "random" stuff our builds might be doing. Through such separation, we can guarantee that Jenkins will (probably) not be affected if we do something wrong in our builds.

Our example will not set up LimitRanges and ResourceQuotas. I'll assume that you're familiar with them and that you understand that a more serious setting must have them defined. If you're a newbie to those things, please consult the official documentation or explore related chapters in The DevOps 2.3 Toolkit: Kubernetes[33].

Let's take a look at yet another Jenkins definition.

```
1  cat sa/jenkins.yml
```

The relevant parts of the output are as follows.

```
1  ...
2  apiVersion: v1
3  kind: Namespace
4  metadata:
5    name: build
6
7  ---
8
9  apiVersion: v1
10 kind: ServiceAccount
11 metadata:
12   name: jenkins
13   namespace: jenkins
14
15 ---
16
17 kind: Role
18 apiVersion: rbac.authorization.k8s.io/v1beta1
19 metadata:
20   name: jenkins
21   namespace: build
22 rules:
23 - apiGroups: [""]
24   resources: ["pods", "pods/exec", "pods/log"]
25   verbs: ["*"]
26 - apiGroups: [""]
27   resources: ["secrets"]
28   verbs: ["get"]
29
30 ---
```

---

[33]https://amzn.to/2GvzDjy

```
31
32    apiVersion: rbac.authorization.k8s.io/v1beta1
33    kind: RoleBinding
34    metadata:
35      name: jenkins
36      namespace: build
37    roleRef:
38      apiGroup: rbac.authorization.k8s.io
39      kind: Role
40      name: jenkins
41    subjects:
42    - kind: ServiceAccount
43      name: jenkins
44      namespace: jenkins
45    ...
46    apiVersion: apps/v1beta2
47    kind: StatefulSet
48    metadata:
49      name: jenkins
50      namespace: jenkins
51    spec:
52      ...
53      template:
54        ...
55        spec:
56          serviceAccountName: jenkins
57            ...
```

This time we are creating a second Namespace called build and a ServiceAccount jenkins in the jenkins namespace. Further on, we created a Role and a RoleBinding that provides required permissions in the build Namespace. As such, we bound the Role with the ServiceAccount in the jenkins Namespace. As a result, Jenkins should be able to create Pods in build, but it won't be able to do anything in its own Namespace jenkins. That way we can be relatively safe that a problem in our builds will not affect Jenkins. If we specified ResourceQuotas and LimitRanges for both Namespaces, our solution would be even more bulletproof. But, since I assume that you know how to do that, I excluded them in an attempt to simplify the definition.

Let's apply the config and observe the result.

 A note to minishift users

Due to the changes required for OpenShift, we'll use a different YAML specification. Please execute oc apply -f sa/jenkins-oc.yml --record instead of the command that follows.

```
1  kubectl apply \
2      -f sa/jenkins.yml \
3      --record
```

 ## A note to GKE users

GKE uses external load balancer as Ingress. To work properly, the type of the service related to Ingress needs to be NodePort. We'll have to patch the service to change its type. Please execute the command that follows.

```
kubectl -n jenkins patch svc jenkins -p '{"spec":{"type": "NodePort"}}'
```

We can see from the output that the resources were created. All that's left is to wait until Jenkins rolls out.

```
1  kubectl -n jenkins \
2      rollout status sts jenkins
```

Now that Jenkins is up-and-running, we should open it in a browser and repeat the same setup steps we did before.

```
1  open "http://$CLUSTER_DNS/jenkins"
```

The first step is to get the initial admin password.

```
1  kubectl -n jenkins \
2      exec jenkins-0 -it -- \
3      cat /var/jenkins_home/secrets/initialAdminPassword
```

Please copy the output and paste it into the *Administrator password* field. Click *Continue*, followed by the *Install suggested plugins* button. The rest of the setup requires you to *Create First Admin User*, so please go ahead. You don't need my help on that one.

Just as before, we'll need to add *Kubernetes* and *BlueOcean* plugins.

```
1  open "http://$CLUSTER_DNS/jenkins/pluginManager/available"
```

You already know what to do. Once you're done installing the two plugins, we'll go to the configuration screen.

```
1   open "http://$CLUSTER_DNS/jenkins/configure"
```

Please expand the *Add a new cloud* drop-down list in the *Cloud* section and select *Kubernetes*.

Now that we have the ServiceAccount that grants us the required permissions, we can click the *Test Connection* button and confirm that it works.

The output is as follows.

```
1   Error testing connection : Failure executing: GET at: https://kubernetes.default.svc\
2   /api/v1/namespaces/jenkins/pods. Message: Forbidden!Configured service account doesn\
3   't have access. Service account may have been revoked. pods is forbidden: User "syst\
4   em:serviceaccount:jenkins:jenkins" cannot list pods in the namespace "jenkins".
```

Did we do something wrong? We didn't. That was the desired behavior. By not specifying a Namespace, Jenkins checked whether it has necessary permission in the Namespace where it runs. If we try to invoke Kube API from a container, it'll always use the same Namespace as the one where the container is. Jenkins is no exception. On the other hand, our YAML explicitly defined that we should have permissions to create Pods in the `build` Namespace. Let's fix that.

Please type *build* in the *Kubernetes Namespace* field and click the *Test Connection* button again.

This time the output shows that the `connection test` was `successful`. We managed to configure Jenkins' Kubernetes plugin to operate inside the `build` Namespace. Still, there is one more thing missing.

When we create a job that uses Kubernetes Pods, an additional container will be added. That container will use JNLP to establish communication with the Jenkins master. We need to specify a valid address JNLP can use to connect to the master. Since the Pods will be in the `build` Namespace and the master is in `jenkins`, we need to use the longer DNS name that specifies both the name of the service (`jenkins`) as well as the Namespace (also `jenkins`). On top of all that, our master is configured to respond to requests with the root path `/jenkins`. All the all, the full address Pods can use to communicate with Jenkins master is should be `http://[SERVICE_NAME].[NAMESPACE]/[PATH]`. Since all three of those elements are `jenkins`, the "real" address is `http://jenkins.jenkins/jenkins`. Please type it inside the *Jenkins URL* field and click the *Save* button.

Now we're ready to create a job that'll test that everything works as expected.

Please click the *New Item* link from the left-hand menu to open a screen for creating jobs. Type *my-k8s-job* in the *item name* field, select *Pipeline* as the type, and click the *OK* button. Once inside the job configuration screen, click the *Pipeline* tab and write the script that follows inside the *Pipeline Script* field.

```
1   podTemplate(
2       label: 'kubernetes',
3       containers: [
4           containerTemplate(name: 'maven', image: 'maven:alpine', ttyEnabled: true, co\
5   mmand: 'cat'),
6           containerTemplate(name: 'golang', image: 'golang:alpine', ttyEnabled: true, \
7   command: 'cat')
8       ]
9   ) {
10      node('kubernetes') {
11          container('maven') {
12              stage('build') {
13                  sh 'mvn --version'
14              }
15              stage('unit-test') {
16                  sh 'java -version'
17              }
18          }
19          container('golang') {
20              stage('deploy') {
21                  sh 'go version'
22              }
23          }
24      }
25  }
```

ⓘ   If you prefer to copy and paste, the job is available in the my-k8s-job.groovy Gist[34].

The job is relatively simple. It uses podTemplate to define a node that will contain two containers. One of those is golang, and the other is maven. In both cases the command is cat. Without a long-running command (process 1), the container would exit immediately, Kubernetes would detect that and start another container based on the same image. It would fail again, and the loop would continue. Without the main process running, we'd enter into a never-ending loop.

Further on, we are defining that we want to use the podTemplate as a node and we start executing sh commands in different containers. Those commands only output software versions. The goal of this job is not to demonstrate a full CD pipeline (we'll do that later), but only to prove that integration with Kubernetes works and that we can use different containers that contain the tools we need.

Don't forget to click the *Save* button.

---

[34]https://gist.github.com/2cf872c3a9acac51409fbd5a2789cb02

Now that we have a job, we should run it and validate that the integration with Kubernetes indeed works.

Please click the *Open Blue Ocean* link from the left-hand menu followed by the *Run* button.

We'll let Jenkins run the build and switch to Shell to observe what's happening.

```
1  kubectl -n build get pods
```

After a while, the output should be as follows.

```
1  NAME               READY STATUS          RESTARTS AGE
2  jenkins-slave-... 0/3   ContainerCreating 0       11s
```

We can see that Jenkins created a Pod with three containers. At this moment in time, those containers are still not fully functional. Kubernetes is probably pulling them to the assigned node.

You might be wondering why are there three containers even though we specified two. Jenkins added the third to the Pod definition. It contains JNLP that is in charge of communication between Pods acting as nodes and Jenkins masters. From user's perspective, JNLP is non-existent. It is a transparent process we do not need to worry about.

Let's take another look at the Pods in the `build` Namespace.

```
1  kubectl -n build get pods
```

The output is as follows.

```
1  NAME               READY STATUS  RESTARTS AGE
2  jenkins-slave-... 3/3   Running 0        5s
```

This time, if you are a fast reader, all the containers that form the Pod are running, and Jenkins is using them to execute the instructions we defined in the job.

Let's take another look at the Pods.

```
1  kubectl -n build get pods
```

The output is as follows.

```
1  NAME               READY STATUS      RESTARTS AGE
2  jenkins-slave-... 3/3   Terminating 0        32s
```

Once Jenkins finished executing the instructions from the job, it issued a command to Kube API to terminate the Pod.

Jenkins nodes created through `podTemplate` are called on-shot agents. Instead of having long-running nodes, they are created when needed and destroyed when not in use. Since they are Pods, Kubernetes is scheduling them on the nodes that have enough resources. By combining one-shot agents with Kubernetes, we are distributing load and, at the same time, using only the resources we need. After all, there's no need to waste CPU and memory on non-existing processes.

We're done with Jenkins, so let's remove the Namespaces we created before we move into the next use-case.

```
1  kubectl delete ns jenkins build
```

Using ServiceAccounts From Side-Car Containers

We still have one more pending issue that we can solve with ServiceAccounts. In the previous chapter we tried to use `cvallance/mongo-k8s-sidecar` container in hopes it'll dynamically create and manage a MongoDB replica set. We failed because, at that time, we did not know how to create sufficient permissions that would allow the side-car to do its job. Now we know better.

Let's take a look at an updated version of our *go-demo-3* application.

```
1  cat sa/go-demo-3.yml
```

The relevant parts of the output are as follows

```
1   ...
2   apiVersion: v1
3   kind: ServiceAccount
4   metadata:
5     name: db
6     namespace: go-demo-3
7
8   ---
9
10  kind: Role
11  apiVersion: rbac.authorization.k8s.io/v1beta1
12  metadata:
13    name: db
14    namespace: go-demo-3
15  rules:
```

```
16  - apiGroups: [""]
17    resources: ["pods"]
18    verbs: ["list"]
19
20  ---
21
22  apiVersion: rbac.authorization.k8s.io/v1beta1
23  kind: RoleBinding
24  metadata:
25    name: db
26    namespace: go-demo-3
27  roleRef:
28    apiGroup: rbac.authorization.k8s.io
29    kind: Role
30    name: db
31  subjects:
32  - kind: ServiceAccount
33    name: db
34
35  ---
36
37  apiVersion: apps/v1beta1
38  kind: StatefulSet
39  metadata:
40    name: db
41    namespace: go-demo-3
42  spec:
43    ...
44    template:
45      ...
46      spec:
47        serviceAccountName: db
48        ...
```

Just as with Jenkins, we have a ServiceAccount, a Role, and a RoleBinding. Since the side-car needs only to list the Pods, the Role is this time more restrictive than the one we created for Jenkins. Further down, in the StatefulSet, we added `serviceAccountName: db` entry that links the set with the account. By now, you should be familiar with all those resources. We're applying the same logic to the side-car as to Jenkins.

Since there's no need for a lengthy discussion, we'll move on and `apply` the definition.

```
1  kubectl apply \
2      -f sa/go-demo-3.yml \
3      --record
```

Next, we'll take a look at the Pods created in the go-demo-3 Namespace.

```
1  kubectl -n go-demo-3 \
2      get pods
```

After a while, the output should be as follows.

```
1  NAME     READY STATUS  RESTARTS AGE
2  api-... 1/1   Running 1        1m
3  api-... 1/1   Running 1        1m
4  api-... 1/1   Running 1        1m
5  db-0    2/2   Running 0        1m
6  db-1    2/2   Running 0        1m
7  db-2    2/2   Running 0        54s
```

All the Pods are running so it seems that, this time, the side-car did not have trouble communicating with the API.

To be on the safe side, we'll output the logs of one of the side-car containers.

```
1  kubectl -n go-demo-3 \
2      logs db-0 -c db-sidecar
```

The output, limited to the last entries, is as follows.

```
1   ...
2       { _id: 1,
3         host: 'db-1.db.go-demo-3.svc.cluster.local:27017',
4         arbiterOnly: false,
5         buildIndexes: true,
6         hidden: false,
7         priority: 1,
8         tags: {},
9         slaveDelay: 0,
10        votes: 1 },
11      { _id: 2, host: 'db-2.db.go-demo-3.svc.cluster.local:27017' } ],
12   settings:
13     { chainingAllowed: true,
```

```
14    heartbeatIntervalMillis: 2000,
15    heartbeatTimeoutSecs: 10,
16    electionTimeoutMillis: 10000,
17    catchUpTimeoutMillis: 2000,
18    getLastErrorModes: {},
19    getLastErrorDefaults: { w: 1, wtimeout: 0 },
20    replicaSetId: 5aef9e4c52b968b72a16ea5b } }
```

The details behind the output are not that important. What matters is that there are no errors. The side-car managed to retrieve the information it needs from Kube API, and all that's left for us is to delete the Namespace and conclude the chapter.

```
1    kubectl delete ns go-demo-3
```

What Now?

ServiceAccounts combined with Roles and RoleBindings are an essential component for continuous deployment or any other process that needs to communicate with Kubernetes. The alternative is to run an unsecured cluster which is not an option for any but smallest organizations. RBAC is required when more than one person is operating or using a cluster. If RBAC is enabled, ServiceAccounts are a must. We'll use them a lot in the chapters that follow.

Please consult the APIs that follow for any additional information about ServiceAccounts and related resources.

- ServiceAccount v1 core[35]]
- Role v1 rbac[36]
- ClusterRole v1 rbac[37]
- RoleBinding v1 rbac[38]
- ClusterRoleBinding v1 rbac[39]

One more thing before you leave. Please consult jenkins-kubernetes-plugin[40] for more information about the plugin.

---

[35]https://v1-9.docs.kubernetes.io/docs/reference/generated/kubernetes-api/v1.9/#serviceaccount-v1-core
[36]https://v1-9.docs.kubernetes.io/docs/reference/generated/kubernetes-api/v1.9/#role-v1-rbac
[37]https://v1-9.docs.kubernetes.io/docs/reference/generated/kubernetes-api/v1.9/#clusterrole-v1-rbac
[38]https://v1-9.docs.kubernetes.io/docs/reference/generated/kubernetes-api/v1.9/#rolebinding-v1-rbac
[39]https://v1-9.docs.kubernetes.io/docs/reference/generated/kubernetes-api/v1.9/#clusterrolebinding-v1-rbac
[40]https://github.com/jenkinsci/kubernetes-plugin

Defining Continuous Deployment

 The work on defining Continuous Deployment (CDP) steps should not start in Jenkins or any other similar tool. Instead, we should focus on Shell commands and scripts and turn our attention to the CI/CD tools only once we are confident that we can execute the full process with only a few commands.

We should be able to execute most of the CDP steps from anywhere. Developers should be able to run them locally from a Shell. Others might want to integrate them into their favorite IDEs. The number of ways all or parts of the CDP steps can be executed might be quite huge. Running them as part of every commit is only one of those permutations. The way we execute CDP steps should be agnostic to the way we define them. If we add the need for very high (if not complete) automation, it is clear that the steps must be simple commands or Shell scripts. Adding anything else to the mix is likely to result in tight coupling which limits our ability to be independent of the tools we're using to run those steps.

Our goal in this chapter is to define the minimum number of steps a continuous deployment process might need. From there on, it would be up to you to extend those steps to serve a particular use-case you might be facing in your project.

Once we know what should be done, we'll proceed and define the commands that will get us there. We'll do our best to create the CDP steps in a way that they can be easily ported to other tools. We'll try to be tools agnostic. There will always be some steps that are very specific to the tools we'll use, but I hope that they will be limited to scaffolding, and not the CDP logic.

 This chapter assumes that you are already familiar with LimitRanges and ResourceQuotas, besides the requirements from the previous chapters. If you're not, please refer to The DevOps 2.3 Toolkit: Kubernetes[41] for more info.

Whether we'll manage to reach our goals entirely is yet to be seen. For now, we'll ignore the existence of Jenkins and all the other tools that could be used to orchestrate our continuous deployment processes. Instead, we'll focus purely on Shell and the commands we need to execute. We might write a script or two though.

To Continuously Deliver Or To Continuously Deploy?

Everyone wants to implement continuous delivery or deployment. After all, the benefits are too significant to be ignored. Increase the speed of delivery, increase the quality, decrease the costs, free

---
[41]https://amzn.to/2GvzDjy

people to dedicate time to what brings value, and so on and so forth. Those improvements are like music to any decision maker, especially if that person has a business background. If a tech geek can articulate the benefits continuous delivery brings to the table, when he asks a business representative for a budget, the response is almost always "Yes! Do it."

By now, you might be confused with the differences between continuous integration, delivery, and deployment, so I'll do my best to walk you through the primary objectives behind each.

You are doing continuous integration (CI) if you have a set of automated processes that are executed every time you commit a change to a code repository. What we're trying to accomplish with CI is a state when every commit is validated shortly after a commit. We want to know not only whether what we did works, but also whether it integrates with the work our colleagues did. That's why it is crucial that everyone merges code to the master branch or, at least, to some other common branch. It does not matter much how we name it. What does matter is that not much time passes since the moment we fork the code. That can be hours or maybe days. If we delay integration for more than that, we are risking spending too much time working on something that breaks work of others.

 Continuous integration assumes that only a part of the process is automated and that human intervention is needed after machines are finished with their work. That intervention often consists of manual tests or even manual deployments to one or more environments.

The problem with continuous integration is that the level of automation is not high enough. We do not trust the process enough. We feel that it provides benefits, but we also require a second opinion. We need humans to confirm the result of the process executed by machines.

Continuous delivery (CD) is a superset of continuous integration. It features a fully automated process executed on every commit. If none of the steps in the process fail, we declare the commit as ready for production.

 With continuous delivery, we do not deploy to production automatically because someone needs to make a business decision. The reason to postpone or skip deploying a release to production is anything but technical.

Finally, continuous deployment (CDP) is almost the same as continuous delivery. All the steps in the process are in both cases fully automated. The only difference is that the button that says "deploy to production" is gone.

 With continuous deployment (CDP), every commit that passed all the automated steps is deployed to production.

Even though CD and CDP are almost the same from the process perspective, the latter might require changes in the way we develop our applications. We might, for example, need to start using feature toggles that allow us to disable partially finished features. Most of the changes required for CDP are things that should be adopted anyways. However, with CDP that need is increased to an even higher level.

We won't go into all the cultural and development changes one would need to employ before attempting to reach the stage where CDP is desirable, or even possible. That would be a subject for a different book and would require much more space than what we have. I am not even going to try to convince you to embrace continuous deployment. There are many valid cases when CDP is not a good option and even more of those when it is not even possible without substantial cultural and technical changes which are outside Kubernetes domain. Statistically speaking, it is likely that you are not ready to embrace continuous deployment.

At this point, you might be wondering whether it makes sense for you to continue reading. Maybe you are indeed not ready for continuous deployment, and maybe thinking this is a waste of time. If that's the case, my message to you is that, it does not matter. The fact that you already have some experience with Kubernetes tells me that you are not a laggard. You chose to embrace a new way of working. You saw the benefits of distributed systems, and you are embracing what surely looked like madness when you made your first steps.

If you reached this far, you are ready to learn and practice the processes that follow. You might not be ready to do continuous deployment. That's OK. You can fall back to continuous delivery. If that is also too big of a scratch, you can start with continuous integration. The reason I'm saying that it does not matter lies in the fact that most of the steps are the same in all those cases. No matter whether you are planning to do CI, CD, or CDP, you have to build something, you have to run some tests, and you have to deploy your applications somewhere.

 The difference between continuous integration, delivery, and deployment is not in processes, but in the level of confidence we have in them.

From the technical perspective, it does not matter whether we deploy to a local cluster, to the one dedicated to testing, or to production. A deployment to a Kubernetes cluster is (more or less) the same no matter what its purpose is. You might choose to have a single cluster for everything. That's also OK. That's why we have Namespaces. You might not trust your tests. Still, that's not a problem from the start because the way we execute tests is the same no matter how much we trust them. I can continue for a while with statements like that. What truly matters is that the process is, more or less, the same, no matter how much you trust it. Trust is earned with time.

 If you do want to read very opinionated and politically incorrect thoughts on what you might be missing, please visit The Ten Commandments Of Continuous Delivery[42].

The goal of this book is to teach you how to employ continuous deployment into a Kubernetes cluster. It's up to you to decide when are your expertise, culture, and code ready for it. The pipeline we'll

---

[42]https://technologyconversations.com/2017/03/06/the-ten-commandments-of-continuous-delivery/

build should be the same no matter whether you're planning to use CI, CD, or CDP. Only a few arguments might change.

All in all, the first objective is to define the base set of steps for our continuous deployment processes. We'll worry about executing those steps later.

Defining Continuous Deployment Goals

The continuous deployment process is relatively easy to explain, even though implementation might get tricky. We'll split our requirements into two groups. We'll start with a discussion about the overall goals that should be applied to the whole process. To be more precise, we'll talk about what I consider non-negotiable requirements.

A Pipeline needs to be secure. Typically, that would not be a problem. In past before Kubernetes was born, we would run the pipeline steps on separate servers. We'd have one dedicated to building and another for testing. We might have one for integration and another for performance tests. Once we adopt container schedulers and move into clusters, we lose control of the servers. Even though it is possible to run something on a specific server, that is highly discouraged in Kubernetes. We should let Kubernetes schedule Pods with as few restraints as possible. That means that our builds and tests might run in the production cluster and that might prove not to be secure. If we are not careful, a malicious user might exploit shared space. Even more likely, our tests might contain an unwanted side-effect that could put production applications at risk.

We could create separate clusters. One can be dedicated to the production and the other to everything else. While that is indeed an option we should explore, Kubernetes already provides the tools we need to make a cluster secure. We have RBAC, ServiceAccounts, Namespaces, PodSecurityPolicies, NetworkPolicies, and a few other resources at our disposal. So we can share the same cluster and be reasonably secure at the same time.

Security is not the only requirement. Even when everything is secured, we still need to make sure that our pipelines do not affect negatively other applications running inside a cluster. If we are not careful, tests might, for example, request or use too many resources and, as a result, we might be left with insufficient memory for the other applications and processes running inside our cluster. Fortunately, Kubernetes has a solution for those problems as well. We can combine Namespaces with LimitRanges and ResourceQuotas. While they do not provide a complete guarantee that nothing will go wrong (nothing does), they do provide a set of tools that, when used correctly, do provide reasonable guarantees that the processes in a Namespace will not go "wild".

Our pipeline should be fast. If it takes too much time for it to execute, we might be compelled to start working on a new feature before the execution of the pipeline is finished. If it fails, we will have to decide whether to stop working on the new feature and incur context switching penalty or to ignore the problem until we are free to deal with it. While both scenarios are bad, the latter is worst and should be avoided at all costs. A failed pipeline must have the highest priority. Otherwise, what's the point of having automated and continuous processes if dealing with issues is eventual?

Continuous deployment pipeline must be secured, it should produce no side-effects to the rest of the applications in a cluster, and it should be fast.

The problem is that we often cannot accomplish those goals independently. We might be forced to make tradeoffs. Security often clashes with speed, and we might need to strike a balance between the two.

Finally, the primary goal, that one that is above all the others, is that our continuous deployment pipeline must be executed on every commit to the master branch. That will provide continuous feedback about the readiness of the system, and, in a way, it will force people to merge to the master often. When we create a branch, it is non-existent until it gets back to the master, or whatever is the name of the production-ready branch. The more time passes until the merge, the bigger the chance that our code does not integrate with the work of our colleagues.

Now that we have the high-level objectives straighten out, we should switch our focus to the particular steps a pipeline should contain.

Defining Continuous Deployment Steps

We'll try to define a minimum set of steps any continuous deployment pipeline should execute. Do not take them literally. Every company is different, and every project has something special. You will likely have to extend them to suit your particular needs. However, that should not be a problem. Once we get a grip on those that are mandatory, extending the process should be relatively straightforward, except if you need to interact with tools that do not have a well-defined API nor a good CLI. If that's the case, my recommendation is to drop those tools. They're not worthy of the suffering they often impose.

We can split the pipeline into several stages. We'll need to *build* the artifacts (after running static tests and analysis). We have to run *functional tests* because unit testing is not enough. We need to create a *release* and *deploy* it somewhere (hopefully to production). No matter how much we trust the earlier stages, we do have to run tests to validate that the deployment (to production) was successful. Finally, we need to do some cleanup at the end of the process and remove all the processes created for the Pipeline. It would be pointless to leave them running idle.

All in all, the stages are as follows.

- Build stage
- Functional testing stage
- Release stage
- Deploy stage
- Production testing stage
- Cleanup stage

Here's the plan. In the build stage, we'll build a Docker image and push it to a registry (in our case Docker Hub). However, since building untested artifacts should be stopped, we are going to run static tests before the actual build. Once our Docker image is pushed, we'll deploy the application and run tests against it. If everything works as expected, we'll make a new release and deploy it to production. To be on the safe side, we'll run another round of tests to validate that the deployment was indeed successful in production. Finally, we'll clean up the system by removing everything except the production release.

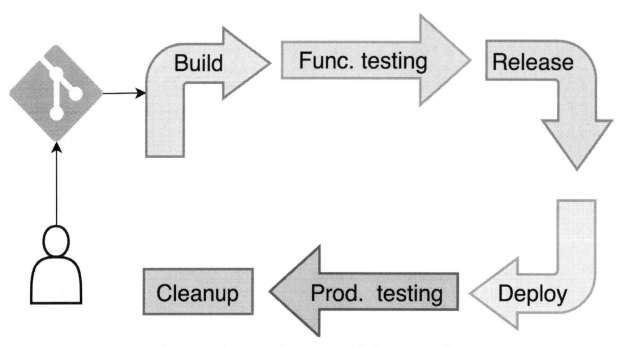

Figure 3-1: The stages of a continuous deployment pipeline

We'll discuss the steps of each of those stages later on. For now, we need a cluster we'll use for the hands-on exercises that'll help us get a better understanding of the pipeline we'll build later. If we are successful with the manually executed steps, writing pipeline script should be relatively simple.

 If you are not familiar with Docker Hub, please go to Docker Hub introduction[43] page and register. We'll need the hub ID later on.

Creating A Cluster

We'll start the hands-on part by going back to the local copy of the `vfarcic/k8s-specs` repository and pulling the latest version.

---

[43]https://docs.docker.com/docker-hub/

All the commands from this chapter are available in the 03-manual-cd.sh[44] Gist.

```
1   cd k8s-specs
2
3   git pull
```

Just as in the previous chapters, we'll need a cluster if we are to do the hands-on exercises. The rules are still the same. You can continue using the same cluster as before, or you can switch to a different Kubernetes flavor. You can continue using one of the Kubernetes distributions listed below, or be adventurous and try something different. If you go with the latter, please let me know how it went, and I'll test it myself and incorporate it into the list.

 Beware! The minimum requirements for the cluster are now slightly higher. We'll need at least 3 CPUs and 3 GB RAM if running a single-node cluster, and slightly more if those resources are spread across multiple nodes. If you're using Docker For Mac or Windows, minikube, or minishift, the specs are 1 CPU and 1 GB RAM higher. For GKE, we need at least 4 CPUs, so we changed the machine type to *n1-highcpu-2*. For everyone else, the requirements are still the same.

The Gists with the commands I used to create different variations of Kubernetes clusters are as follows.

- docker4mac-3cpu.sh[45]: **Docker for Mac** with 3 CPUs, 3 GB RAM, and with **nginx Ingress**.
- minikube-3cpu.sh[46]: **minikube** with 3 CPUs, 3 GB RAM, and with `ingress`, `storage-provisioner`, and `default-storageclass` addons enabled.
- kops.sh[47]: **kops in AWS** with 3 t2.small masters and 2 t2.medium nodes spread in three availability zones, and with **nginx Ingress** (assumes that the prerequisites are set through Appendix B).
- minishift-3cpu.sh[48]: **minishift** with 3 CPUs, 3 GB RAM, and version 1.16+.
- gke-2cpu.sh[49]: **Google Kubernetes Engine (GKE)** with 3 n1-highcpu-2 (2 CPUs, 1.8 GB RAM) nodes (one in each zone), and with **nginx Ingress** controller running on top of the "standard" one that comes with GKE. We'll use nginx Ingress for compatibility with other platforms. Feel free to modify the YAML files if you prefer NOT to install nginx Ingress.
- eks.sh[50]: **Elastic Kubernetes Service (EKS)** with 2 t2.medium nodes, with **nginx Ingress** controller, and with a **default StorageClass**.

---

[44]https://gist.github.com/bf33bf65299870b68b3de8dbe1b21c36
[45]https://gist.github.com/bf08bce43a26c7299b6bd365037eb074
[46]https://gist.github.com/871b5d7742ea6c10469812018c308798
[47]https://gist.github.com/2a3e4ee9cb86d4a5a65cd3e4397f48fd
[48]https://gist.github.com/2074633688a85ef3f887769b726066df
[49]https://gist.github.com/e3a2be59b0294438707b6b48adeb1a68
[50]https://gist.github.com/5496f79a3886be794cc317c6f8dd7083

Now that we have a cluster, we can move into a more exciting part of this chapter. We'll start defining and executing stages and steps of a continuous deployment pipeline.

Creating Namespaces Dedicated To Continuous Deployment Processes

If we are to accomplish a reasonable level of security of our pipelines, we need to run them in dedicated Namespaces. Our cluster already has RBAC enabled, so we'll need a ServiceAccount as well. Since security alone is not enough, we also need to make sure that our pipeline does not affect other applications. We'll accomplish that by creating a LimitRange and a ResourceQuota.

I believe that in most cases we should store everything an application needs in the same repository. That makes maintenance much simpler and enables the team in charge of that application to be in full control, even though that team might not have all the permissions to create the resources in a cluster.

We'll continue using go-demo-3 repository but, since we'll have to change a few things, it is better if you apply the changes to your fork and, maybe, push them back to GitHub.

```
1  open "https://github.com/vfarcic/go-demo-3"
```

If you're not familiar with GitHub, all you have to do is to log in and click the *Fork* button located in the top-right corner of the screen.

Next, we'll remove the go-demo-3 repository (if you happen to have it) and clone the fork.

Make sure that you replace [...] with your GitHub username.

```
1  cd ..
2
3  rm -rf go-demo-3
4
5  export GH_USER=[...]
6
7  git clone https://github.com/$GH_USER/go-demo-3.git
8
9  cd go-demo-3
```

The only thing left is to edit a few files. Please open *k8s/build.yml* and *k8s/prod.yml* files in your favorite editor and change all occurrences of vfarcic with your Docker Hub user.

The namespace dedicated for all building and testing activities of the go-demo-3 project is defined in the k8s/build-ns.yml file stored in the project repository.

```
1  git pull
2
3  cat k8s/build-ns.yml
```

The output is as follows.

```
1   apiVersion: v1
2   kind: Namespace
3   metadata:
4     name: go-demo-3-build
5
6   ---
7
8   apiVersion: v1
9   kind: ServiceAccount
10  metadata:
11    name: build
12    namespace: go-demo-3-build
13
14  ---
15
16  apiVersion: rbac.authorization.k8s.io/v1beta1
17  kind: RoleBinding
18  metadata:
19    name: build
20    namespace: go-demo-3-build
21  roleRef:
22    apiGroup: rbac.authorization.k8s.io
23    kind: ClusterRole
24    name: admin
25  subjects:
26  - kind: ServiceAccount
27    name: build
28
29  ---
30
31  apiVersion: v1
32  kind: LimitRange
33  metadata:
34    name: build
35    namespace: go-demo-3-build
36  spec:
37    limits:
```

```
38    - default:
39        memory: 200Mi
40        cpu: 0.2
41      defaultRequest:
42        memory: 100Mi
43        cpu: 0.1
44      max:
45        memory: 500Mi
46        cpu: 0.5
47      min:
48        memory: 10Mi
49        cpu: 0.05
50      type: Container
51
52  ---
53
54  apiVersion: v1
55  kind: ResourceQuota
56  metadata:
57    name: build
58    namespace: go-demo-3-build
59  spec:
60    hard:
61      requests.cpu: 2
62      requests.memory: 3Gi
63      limits.cpu: 3
64      limits.memory: 4Gi
65      pods: 15
```

If you are familiar with Namespaces, ServiceAccounts, LimitRanges, and ResourceQuotas, the definition should be fairly easy to understand.

We defined the go-demo-3-build Namespace which we'll use for all our CDP tasks. It'll contain the ServiceAccount build bound to the ClusterRole admin. As a result, containers running inside that Namespace will be able to do anything they want. It'll be their playground.

We also defined the LimitRange named build. It'll make sure to give sensible defaults to the Pods that running in the Namespace. That way we can create Pods from which we'll build and test without worrying whether we forgot to specify resources they need. After all, most of us do not know how much memory and CPU a build needs. The same LimitRange also contains some minimum and maximum limits that should prevent users from specifying too small or too big resource reservations and limits.

Finally, since the capacity of our cluster is probably not unlimited, we defined a ResourceQuota that specifies the total amount of memory and CPU for requests and limits in that Namespace. We also defined that the maximum number of Pods running in that Namespace cannot be higher than fifteen.

If we do have more Pods than what we can place in that Namespace, some will be pending until others finish their work and resources are liberated.

It is very likely that the team behind the project will not have sufficient permissions to create new Namespaces. If that's the case, the team would need to let cluster administrator know about the existence of that YAML. In turn, he (or she) would review the definition and create the resources, once he (or she) deduces that they are safe. For the sake of simplicity, you are that person, so please execute the command that follows.

```
1  kubectl apply \
2      -f k8s/build-ns.yml \
3      --record
```

As you can see from the output, the `go-demo-3-build` Namespace was created together with a few other resources.

Now that we have a Namespace dedicated to the lifecycle of our application, we'll create another one that to our production release.

```
1  cat k8s/prod-ns.yml
```

The `go-demo-3` Namespace is very similar to `go-demo-3-build`. The major difference is in the RoleBinding. Since we can assume that processes running in the `go-demo-3-build` Namespace will, at some moment, want to deploy a release to production, we created the RoleBinding `build` which binds to the ServiceAccount `build` in the Namespace `go-demo-3-build`.

We'll `apply` this definition while still keeping our cluster administrator's hat.

```
1  kubectl apply \
2      -f k8s/prod-ns.yml \
3      --record
```

Now we have two Namespaces dedicated to the `go-demo-3` application. We are yet to figure out which tools we'll need for our continuous deployment pipeline.

Defining A Pod With The Tools

Every application is different, and the tools we need for a continuous deployment pipeline vary from one case to another. For now, we'll focus on those we'll need for our *go-demo-3* application.

Since the application is written in Go, we'll need `golang` image to download the dependencies and run the tests. We'll have to build Docker images, so we should probably add a `docker` container as well. Finally, we'll have to execute quite a few `kubectl` commands. For those of you using OpenShift, we'll need `oc` as well. All in all, we need a Pod with `golang`, `docker`, `kubectl`, and (for some of you) `oc`.

The *go-demo-3* repository already contains a definition of a Pod with all those containers, so let's take a closer look at it.

```
1  cat k8s/cd.yml
```

The output is as follows.

```
1  apiVersion: v1
2  kind: Pod
3  metadata:
4    name: cd
5    namespace: go-demo-3-build
6  spec:
7    containers:
8    - name: docker
9      image: docker:18.03-git
10     command: ["sleep"]
11     args: ["100000"]
12     volumeMounts:
13     - name: workspace
14       mountPath: /workspace
15     - name: docker-socket
16       mountPath: /var/run/docker.sock
17     workingDir: /workspace
18   - name: kubectl
19     image: vfarcic/kubectl
20     command: ["sleep"]
21     args: ["100000"]
22     volumeMounts:
23     - name: workspace
24       mountPath: /workspace
25     workingDir: /workspace
26   - name: oc
27     image: vfarcic/openshift-client
28     command: ["sleep"]
29     args: ["100000"]
30     volumeMounts:
```

```
31      - name: workspace
32        mountPath: /workspace
33      workingDir: /workspace
34    - name: golang
35      image: golang:1.9
36      command: ["sleep"]
37      args: ["100000"]
38      volumeMounts:
39      - name: workspace
40        mountPath: /workspace
41      workingDir: /workspace
42    serviceAccount: build
43    volumes:
44    - name: docker-socket
45      hostPath:
46        path: /var/run/docker.sock
47        type: Socket
48    - name: workspace
49      emptyDir: {}
```

Most of the YAML defines the containers based on images that contain the tools we need. What makes it special is that all the containers have the same mount called workspace. It maps to /workspace directory inside containers, and it uses emptyDir volume type.

We'll accomplish two things with those volumes. On the one hand, all the containers will have a shared space so the artifacts generated through the actions we will perform in one will be available in the other. On the other hand, since emptyDir volume type exists only just as long as the Pod is running, it'll be deleted when we remove the Pod. As a result, we won't be leaving unnecessary garbage on our nodes or external drives.

To simplify the things and save us from typing cd /workspace, we set workingDir to all the containers.

Unlike most of the other Pods we usually run in our clusters, those dedicated to CDP processes are short lived. They are not supposed to exist for a long time nor should they leave any trace of their existence once they finish executing the steps we are about to define.

The ability to run multiple containers on the same node and with a shared file system and networking will be invaluable in our quest to define continuous deployment processes. If you were ever wondering what the purpose of having Pods as entities that envelop multiple containers is, the steps we are about to explore will hopefully provide a perfect use-case.

Let's create the Pod.

```
1   kubectl apply -f k8s/cd.yml --record
```

Pleases confirm that all the containers of the Pod are up and running by executing `kubectl -n go-demo-3-build get pods`. You should see that 4/4 are `ready`.

Now we can start working on our continuous deployment pipeline steps.

Executing Continuous Integration Inside Containers

The first stage in our continuous deployment pipeline will contain quite a few steps. We'll need to check out the code, to run unit tests and any other static analysis, to build a Docker image, and to push it to the registry. If we define continuous integration (CI) as a set of automated steps followed with manual operations and validations, we can say that the steps we are about to execute can be qualified as CI.

The only thing we truly need to make all those steps work is Docker client with the access to Docker server. One of the containers of the `cd` Pod already contains it. If you take another look at the definition, you'll see that we are mounting Docker socket so that the Docker client inside the container can issue commands to Docker server running on the host. Otherwise, we would be running Docker-in-Docker, and that is not a very good idea.

Now we can enter the `docker` container and check whether Docker client can indeed communicate with the server.

```
1   kubectl -n go-demo-3-build \
2       exec -it cd -c docker -- sh
3
4   docker container ls
```

Once inside the `docker` container, we executed `docker container ls` only as a proof that we are using a client inside the container which, in turn, uses Docker server running on the node. The output is the list of the containers running on top of one of our servers.

Let's get moving and execute the first step.

We cannot do much without the code of our application, so the first step is to clone the repository.

Make sure that you replace [. . .] with your GitHub username in the command that follows.

```
1  export GH_USER=[...]
2
3  git clone \
4      https://github.com/$GH_USER/go-demo-3.git \
5      .
```

 It is easy to overlook that there is a dot (.) in the git command. It specifies the current directory as the destination.

We cloned the repository into the workspace directory. That is the same folder we mounted as an emptyDir volume and is, therefore, available in all the containers of the cd Pod. Since that folder is set as workingDir of the container, we did not need to cd into it.

Please note that we cloned the whole repository and, as a result, we are having a local copy of the HEAD commit of the master branch. If this were a "real" pipeline, such a strategy would be unacceptable. Instead, we should have checked out a specific branch and a commit that initiated the process. However, we'll ignore those details for now, and assume that we'll solve them when we move the pipeline steps into Jenkins and other tools.

Next, we'll build an image and push it to Docker Hub. To do that, we'll need to login first.

Make sure that you replace [...] with your Docker Hub username in the command that follows.

```
1  export DH_USER=[...]
2
3  docker login -u $DH_USER
```

Once you enter your password, you should see the Login Succeeded message.

We are about to execute the most critical step of this stage. We'll build an image.

At this moment you might be freaking out. You might be thinking that I went insane. A Pastafarian and a firm believer that nothing should be built without running tests first just told you to build an image as the first step after cloning the code. Sacrilege!

However, this Dockerfile is special, so let's take a look at it.

```
1  cat Dockerfile
```

The output is as follows.

```
 1   FROM golang:1.9 AS build
 2   ADD . /src
 3   WORKDIR /src
 4   RUN go get -d -v -t
 5   RUN go test --cover -v ./... --run UnitTest
 6   RUN go build -v -o go-demo
 7
 8
 9   FROM alpine:3.4
10   MAINTAINER        Viktor Farcic <viktor@farcic.com>
11   RUN mkdir /lib64 && ln -s /lib/libc.musl-x86_64.so.1 /lib64/ld-linux-x86-64.so.2
12   EXPOSE 8080
13   ENV DB db
14   CMD ["go-demo"]
15   COPY --from=build /src/go-demo /usr/local/bin/go-demo
16   RUN chmod +x /usr/local/bin/go-demo
```

Normally, we'd run a container, in this case, based on the golang image, execute a few processes, store the binary into a directory that was mounted as a volume, exit the container, and build a new image using the binary created earlier. While that would work fairly well, multi-stage builds allow us to streamline the processes into a single docker image build command.

If you're not following Docker releases closely, you might be wondering what a multi-stage build is. It is a feature introduced in Docker 17.05 that allows us to specify multiple FROM statements in a Dockerfile. Each FROM instruction can use a different base, and each starts a new stage of the build process. Only the image created with the last FROM segment is kept. As a result, we can specify all the steps we need to execute before building the image without increasing its size.

In our example, we need to execute a few Go commands that will download all the dependencies, run unit tests, and compile a binary. Therefore, we specified golang as the base image followed with the RUN instruction that does all the heavy lifting. Please note that the first FROM statement is named build. We'll see why that matters soon.

Further down, we start over with a new FROM section that uses alpine. It is a very minimalist linux distribution (a few MB in size) that guarantees that our final image is minimal and is not cluttered with unnecessary tools that are typically used in "traditional" Linux distros like ubuntu, debian, and centos. Further down we are creating everything our application needs, like the DB environment variable used by the code to know where the database is, the command that should be executed when a container starts, and so on. The critical part is the COPY statement. It copies the binary we created in the build stage into the final image.

 Please consult Dockerfile reference[51] and Use multi-stage builds[52] for more information.

---

[51]https://docs.docker.com/engine/reference/builder/
[52]https://docs.docker.com/develop/develop-images/multistage-build/

Let's build the image.

```
1  docker image build \
2      -t $DH_USER/go-demo-3:1.0-beta \
3      .
```

 On some clusters you might receive `error parsing reference: "golang:1.9 AS build" is not a valid repository/tag: invalid reference format` error message. That probably means that Docker server is older than v17.05. You can check it with `docker version` command. If you are indeed unable to use multi-stage builds, you've stumbled into one of the problems with this approach. We'll solve this issue later (in one of the next chapters). For now, please execute the commands that follow as a workaround.

```
docker image pull vfarcic/go-demo-3:1.0-beta
```

```
docker image tag vfarcic/go-demo-3:1.0-beta $DH_USER/go-demo-3:1.0-beta
```

Those commands pulled my image and tagged it as yours. Remember that this is only a workaround until we find a better solution.

We can see from the output that the steps of our multi-stage build were executed. We downloaded the dependencies, run unit tests, and built the go-demo binary. All those things were temporary, and we do not need them in the final image. There's no need to have a Go compiler, nor to keep the code. Therefore, once the first stage was finished, we can see the message *Removing intermediate container*. Everything was discarded. We started over, and we built the production-ready image with the binary generated in the previous stage.

We have the whole continuous integration process reduced to a single command. Developers can run it on their laptops, and CI/CD tools can use it as part of their extended processes. Isn't that neat?

Let's take a quick look at the images on the node.

```
1  docker image ls
```

The output, limited to the relevant parts, is as follows.

```
1  REPOSITORY           TAG         IMAGE ID  CREATED          SIZE
2  vfarcic/go-demo-3 1.0-beta ...            54 seconds ago   25.8MB
3  <none>               <none>     ...        About a minute ago 779MB
4  ...
```

The first two images are the result of our build. The final image (vfarcic/go-demo-3) is only 25 MB. It's that small because Docker discarded all but the last stage. If you'd like to know how big your image would be if everything was built in a single stage, please combine the size of the vfarcic/go-demo-3 image with the size of the temporary image used in the first stage (it's just below vfarcic/go-demo-3 1.0-beta).

 If you had to tag my image as yours as a workaround for build problems, you won't see the second image (the one that is ~780 MB), on the other hand, if you succeded to build your own image, image name will be prefixed with your docker hub username.

The only thing missing is to push the image to the registry (e.g., Docker Hub).

```
1  docker image push \
2      $DH_USER/go-demo-3:1.0-beta
```

The image is in the registry and ready for further deployments and testing. Mission accomplished. We're doing continuous integration manually. If we'd place those few commands into a CI/CD tool, we would have the first part of the process up and running.

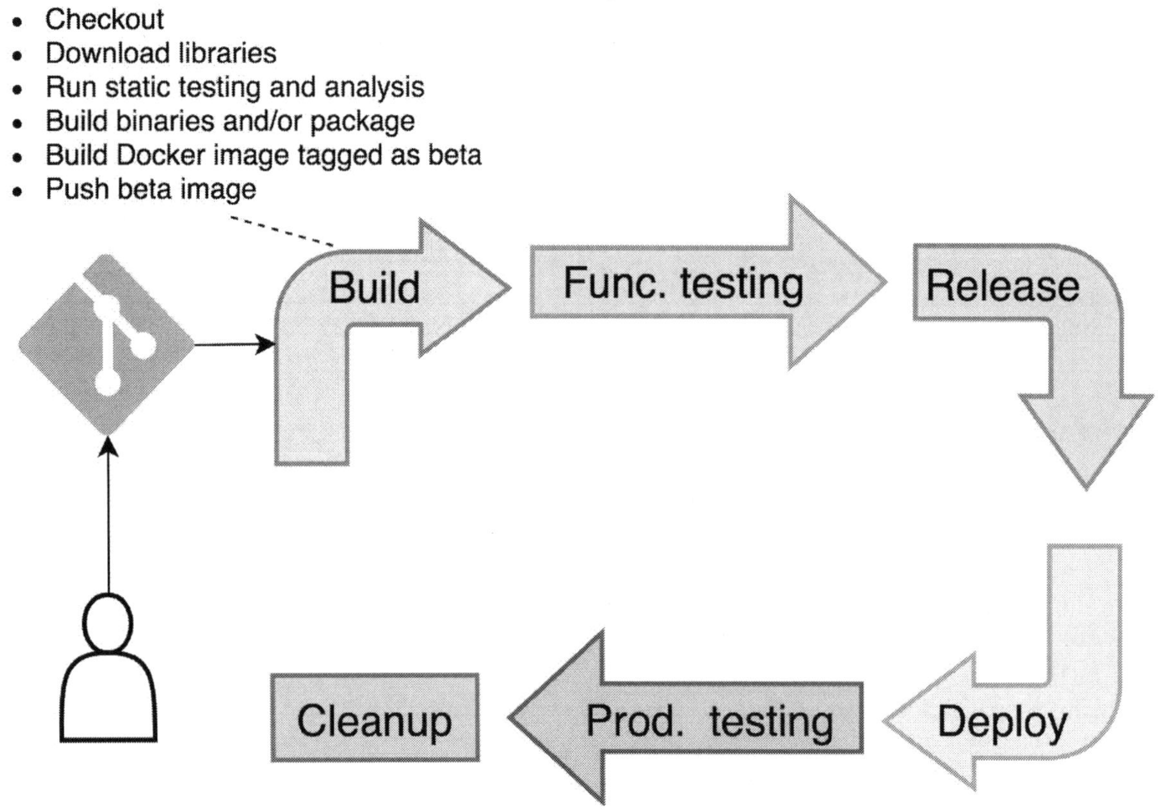

- Checkout
- Download libraries
- Run static testing and analysis
- Build binaries and/or package
- Build Docker image tagged as beta
- Push beta image

Figure 3-2: The build stage of a continuous deployment pipeline

We are still facing a few problems. Docker running in a Kubernetes cluster might be too old. It might not support all the features we need. As an example, most of the Kubernetes distributions before 1.10 supported Docker versions older than 17.05. If that's not enough, consider the possibility that you might not even use Docker in a Kubernetes cluster. It is very likely that ContainerD will be the preferable container engine in the future, and that is only one of many choices we can select. The point is that container engine in a Kubernetes cluster should be in charge of running container, and not much more. There should be no need for the nodes in a Kubernetes cluster to be able to build images.

Another issue is security. If we allow containers to mount Docker socket, we are effectively allowing them to control all the containers running on that node. That by itself makes security departments freak out, and for a very good reason. Also, don't forget that we logged into the registry. Anyone on that node could push images to the same registry without the need for credentials. Even if we do log out, there was still a period when everyone could exploit the fact that Docker server is authenticated and authorized to push images.

Truth be told, **we are not preventing anyone from mounting a Docker socket**. At the moment, our policy is based on trust. That should change with PodSecurityPolicy. However, security is not the focus of this book, so I'll assume that you'll set up the policies yourself, if you deem them worthy of your time.

 We should further restrict what a Pod can and cannot do through PodSecurityPolicy[53].

If that's not enough, there's also the issue of preventing Kubernetes to do its job. The moment we adopt container schedulers, we accept that they are in charge of scheduling all the processes running inside the cluster. If we start doing things behind their backs, we might end up messing with their scheduling capabilities. Everything we do without going through Kube API is unknown to Kubernetes.

We could use Docker inside Docker. That would allow us to build images inside containers without reaching out to Docker socket on the nodes. However, that requires privileged access which poses as much of a security risk as mounting a Docker socket. Actually, it is even riskier. So, we need to discard that option as well.

Another solution might be to use kaniko[54]. It allows us to build Docker images from inside Pods. The process is done without Docker so there is no dependency on Docker socket nor there is a need to run containers in privileged mode. However, at the time of this writing (May 2018) *kaniko* is still not ready. It is complicated to use, and it does not support everything Docker does (e.g., multi-stage builds), it's not easy to decipher its logs (especially errors), and so on. The project will likely have a bright future, but it is still not ready for prime time.

Taking all this into consideration, the only viable option we have, for now, is to build our Docker images outside our cluster. The steps we should execute are the same as those we already run. The only thing missing is to figure out how to create a build server and hook it up to our CI/CD tool. We'll revisit this subject later on.

[53]https://v1-9.docs.kubernetes.io/docs/reference/generated/kubernetes-api/v1.9/#podsecuritypolicy-v1beta1-extensions
[54]https://github.com/GoogleContainerTools/kaniko

For now, we'll exit the container.

```
1   exit
```

Let's move onto the next stage of our pipeline.

Running Functional Tests

Which steps do we need to execute in the functional testing phase? We need to deploy the new release of the application. Without it, there would be nothing to test. All the static tests were already executed when we built the image, so everything we do from now on will need a live application.

Deploying the application is not enough, we'll have to validate that at least it rolled out successfully. Otherwise, we'll have to abort the process.

We'll have to be cautious how we deploy the new release. Since we'll run it in the same cluster as production, we need to be careful that one does not affect the other. We already have a Namespace that provides some level of isolation. However, we'll have to be attentive not to use the same path or domain in Ingress as the one used for production. The two need to be accessible separately from each other until we are confident that the new release meets all the quality standards.

Finally, once the new release is running, we'll execute a set of tests that will validate it. Please note that we will run functional tests only. You should translate that into "in this stage, I run all kinds of tests that require a live application." You might want to add performance and integration tests as well. From the process point of view, it does not matter which tests you run. What matters is that in this stage you run all those that could not be executed statically when we built the image.

If any step in this stage fails, we need to be prepared to destroy everything we did and leave the cluster in the same state as before we started this stage. We'll postpone exploration of rollback steps until one of the next chapters. I'm sure you know how to do it anyway. If you don't, I'll leave you feeling ashamed until the next chapter.

As you probably guessed, we'll need to go into the `kubectl` container for at least some of the steps in this stage. It is already running as part of the `cd` Pod.

Remember, we are performing a manual simulation of a CDP pipeline. We must assume that everything will be executed from inside the cluster, not from your laptop.

```
1   kubectl -n go-demo-3-build \
2       exec -it cd -c kubectl -- sh
```

The project contains separate definitions for deploying test and production releases. For now, we are interested only in prior which is defined in `k8s/build.yml`.

```
1   cat k8s/build.yml
```

We won't comment on all the resources defined in that YAML since they are very similar to those we used before. Instead, we'll take a quick look at the differences between a test and a production release.

```
1   diff k8s/build.yml k8s/prod.yml
```

The two are almost the same. One is using `go-demo-3-build` Namespace while the other works with `go-demo-3`. The `path` of the Ingress resource also differs. Non-production releases will be accessible through `/beta/demo` and thus provide separation from the production release accessible through `/demo`. Everything else is the same.

It's a pity that we had to create two separate YAML files only because of a few differences (Namespace and Ingress). We'll discuss the challenges behind rapid deployments using standard YAML files later. For now, we'll roll with what we have.

Even though we separated production and non-production releases, we still need to modify the tag of the image on the fly. The alternative would be to change release numbers with each commit, but that would represent a burden to developers and a likely source of errors. So, we'll go back to exercising "magic" with `sed`.

```
1   cat k8s/build.yml | sed -e \
2       "s@:latest@:1.0-beta@g" | \
3       tee /tmp/build.yml
```

We output the contents of the `/k8s/build.yml` file, we modified it with `sed` so that the `1.0-beta` tag is used instead of the `latest`, and we stored the output in `/tmp/build.yml`.

Now we can deploy the new release.

```
1   kubectl apply \
2       -f /tmp/build.yml --record
3
4   kubectl rollout status deployment api
```

We applied the new definition and waited until it rolled out.

Even though we know that the rollout was successful by reading the output, we cannot rely on such methods when we switch to full automation of the pipeline. Fortunately, the `rollout status` command will exit with `0` if everything is OK, and with a different code if it's not.

Let's check the exit code of the last command.

```
1  echo $?
```

The output is 0 thus confirming that the rollout was successful. If it was anything else, we'd need to roll back or, even better, quickly fix the problem and roll forward.

A note to GKE users

GKE uses external load balancer as Ingress. To work properly, the type of the service related to Ingress needs to be NodePort. Since most of the other Kubernetes flavors do not need it, I kept it as ClusterIP (the default type). We'll have to patch the service. Please execute the command that follows.

```
kubectl -n go-demo-3-build patch svc api -p '{"spec":{"type": "NodePort"}}'
```

A note to minishift users

Since OpenShift does not support Ingress (at least not by default), we'll need to add a Route. Please execute the commands that follow.

```
exit

kubectl -n go-demo-3-build exec -it cd -c oc -- sh

oc apply -f k8s/build-oc.yml
```

We exited kubectl container, entered into oc, and deployed the route defined in k8s/build-oc.yml.

The only thing missing in this stage is to run the tests. However, before we do that, we need to find out the address through which the application can be accessed.

A note to GKE users

Please change hostname to ip in the command that follows. The jsonpath should be {.status.loadBalancer.ingress[0].ip}. GKE Ingress spins up an external load balancer, and it might take a while until the IP is generated. Therefore, you might need to repeat the modified command that follows until you get the IP.

A note to minikube users

Please open a separate terminal session and execute minikube ip. Remember the output. Change the command that follows to ADDR=[...]/beta where [...] is the IP you just retrieved.

A note to minishift users

Please change the command that follows to `ADDR=$(oc -n go-demo-3-build get routes -o jsonpath="{.items[0].spec.host}")`.

```
1  ADDR=$(kubectl -n go-demo-3-build \
2      get ing api \
3      -o jsonpath="{.status.loadBalancer.ingress[0].hostname}")/beta
4
5  echo $ADDR | tee /workspace/addr
6
7  exit
```

We retrieved the `hostname` from Ingress with the appended path (`/beta`) dedicated to beta releases. Further on, we stored the result in the `/workspace/addr` file. That way we'll be able to retrieve it from other containers running in the same Pod. Finally, we exited the container since the next steps will require a different one.

Ingress is painful, and its definition varies from one Kubernetes platform to another. If you choose to stick with one Kubernetes flavor forever and ever, that is not a big deal. On the other hand, if you want to be compatible and be able to deploy your applications to any Kubernetes cluster, you'll have to change the strategy. We'll try to address this issue in the next chapter.

Let's go inside the `golang` container. We'll need it to execute functional tests.

```
1  kubectl -n go-demo-3-build \
2      exec -it cd -c golang -- sh
```

Before we run the functional tests, we'll send a request to the application manually. That will give us confidence that everything we did so far works as expected.

```
1  curl "http://$(cat addr)/demo/hello"
```

In some cases (e.g., GKE), it might take a few minutes until the external load balancer is created. If you see 40x or 50x error message, please wait for a while and re-send the request.

We constructed the address using the information we stored in the `addr` file and sent a `curl` request. The output is `hello, world!`, thus confirming that the test release of application seems to be deployed correctly.

The tests require a few dependencies, so we'll download them using the go get command. Don't worry if you're new to Go. This exercise is not aimed at teaching you how to work with it, but only to show you the principles that apply to almost any language. In your head, you can replace the command that follows with maven this, gradle that, npm whatever.

```
1   go get -d -v -t
```

The tests expect the environment variable ADDRESS to tell them where to find the application under test, so our next step is to declare it.

```
1   export ADDRESS=api:8080
```

In this case, we chose to allow the tests to communicate with the application through the service called api.

Now we're ready to execute the tests.

```
1   go test ./... -v --run FunctionalTest
```

The output is as follows.

```
1   === RUN    TestFunctionalTestSuite
2   === RUN    TestFunctionalTestSuite/Test_Hello_ReturnsStatus200
3   2018/05/14 14:41:25 Sending a request to http://api:8080/demo/hello
4   === RUN    TestFunctionalTestSuite/Test_Person_ReturnsStatus200
5   2018/05/14 14:41:25 Sending a request to http://api:8080/demo/person
6   --- PASS: TestFunctionalTestSuite (0.03s)
7       --- PASS: TestFunctionalTestSuite/Test_Hello_ReturnsStatus200 (0.01s)
8       --- PASS: TestFunctionalTestSuite/Test_Person_ReturnsStatus200 (0.01s)
9   PASS
10  ok      _/go/go-demo-3  0.129s
```

We can see that the tests passed and we can conclude that the application is a step closer towards production. In a real-world situation, you'd run other types of tests or maybe bundle them all together. The logic is still the same. We deployed the application under test while leaving production intact, and we validated that it behaves as expected. We are ready to move on.

Testing an application through the service associated with it is a good idea,if for some reason we are not allowed to expose it to the outside world through Ingress. If there is no such restriction, executing the tests through a DNS which points to an external load balancer, which forwards to the Ingress service on one of the worker nodes, and from there load balances to one of the replicas, is much closer to how our users access the application. Using the "real" externally accessible address is a better option when that is possible, so we'll change our ADDRESS variable and execute the tests one more time.

```
1  export ADDRESS=$(cat addr)
2
3  go test ./... -v --run FunctionalTest
```

 ## A note to Docker For Mac/Windows users

Docker for Mac or Windows cluster is accessible through localhost. Since localhost has a different meaning depending on where it is invoked, the tests will fail by trying to access the application running inside the container from where we're running the tests. Please ignore the outcome and stick with using Service names (e.g., api) when running tests on Docker for Mac or Windows.

We're almost finished with this stage. The only thing left is to exit the golang container, go back to kubectl, and remove the application under test.

```
1  exit
2
3  kubectl -n go-demo-3-build \
4      exec -it cd -c kubectl -- sh
5
6  kubectl delete \
7      -f /workspace/k8s/build.yml
```

 ## A note to minishift users

The Route we created through build-oc.yml is still not deleted. For the sake of simplicity, we'll ignore it (for now) since it does not occupy almost any resources.

We exited the golang container and entered into kubectl to delete the test release.

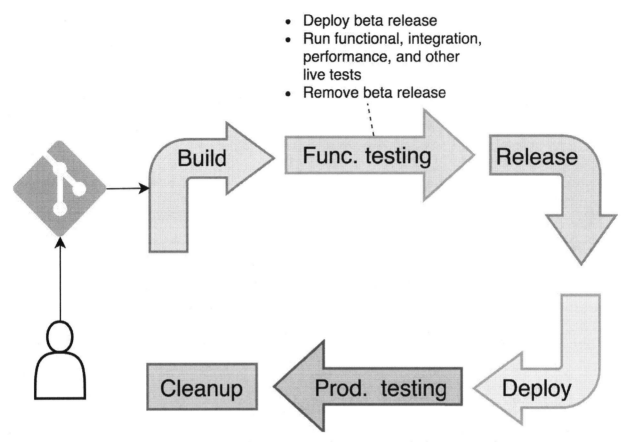

Figure 3-3: The functional testing stage of a continuous deployment pipeline

Let's take a look at what's left in the Namespace.

```
1   kubectl -n go-demo-3-build get all
```

The output is as follows.

```
1   NAME   READY STATUS   RESTARTS AGE
2   po/cd 4/4    Running 0        11m
```

Our `cd` Pod is still running. We will remove it later when we're confident that we don't need any of the tools it contains.

There's no need for us to stay inside the `kubectl` container anymore, so we'll exit.

```
1   exit
```

Creating Production Releases

We are ready to create our first production release. We trust our tests, and they proved that it is relatively safe to deploy to production. Since we cannot deploy to air, we need to create a production release first.

 We will not rebuild the image. The artifact we produced (our Docker image) and confirmed through our tests, is the one we care for. Rebuilding would not only be a waste, and it could potentially be a different artifact than the one we tested. That must never happen!

Please make sure to replace [...] with your Docker Hub user in one of the commands that follow.

```
1  kubectl -n go-demo-3-build \
2      exec -it cd -c docker -- sh
3
4  export DH_USER=[...]
5
6  docker image tag \
7      $DH_USER/go-demo-3:1.0-beta \
8      $DH_USER/go-demo-3:1.0
9
10 docker image push \
11     $DH_USER/go-demo-3:1.0
```

We went back to the `docker` container, we tagged the `1.0-beta` release as `1.0`, and we pushed it to the registry (in this case Docker Hub). Both commands should take no time to execute since we already have all the layers cashed in the registry.

We'll repeat the same process, but this time with the `latest` tag.

```
1  docker image tag \
2      $DH_USER/go-demo-3:1.0-beta \
3      $DH_USER/go-demo-3:latest
4
5  docker image push \
6      $DH_USER/go-demo-3:latest
7
8  exit
```

Now we have the same image tagged and pushed to the registry as `1.0-beta`, `1.0`, and `latest`.

You might be wondering why we have three tags. They are all pointing to the same image, but they serve different purposes.

The 1.0-beta is a clear indication that the image might not have been tested and might not be ready for prime. That's why we intentionally postponed tagging until this point. It would be simpler if we tagged and pushed everything at once when we built the image. However, that would send a wrong message to those using our images. If one of the steps failed during the pipeline, it would be an indication that the commit is not ready for production. As a result, if we pushed all tags at once, others might have decided to use 1.0 or latest without knowing that it is faulty.

We should always be explicit with versions we are deploying to production, so the 1.0 tag is what we'll use. That will help us control what we have and debug problems if they occur. However, others might not want to use explicit versions. A developer might want to deploy the last stable version of an application created by a different team. In those cases, developers might not care which version is in production. In such a case, deploying latest is probably a good idea, assuming that we take good care that it (almost) always works.

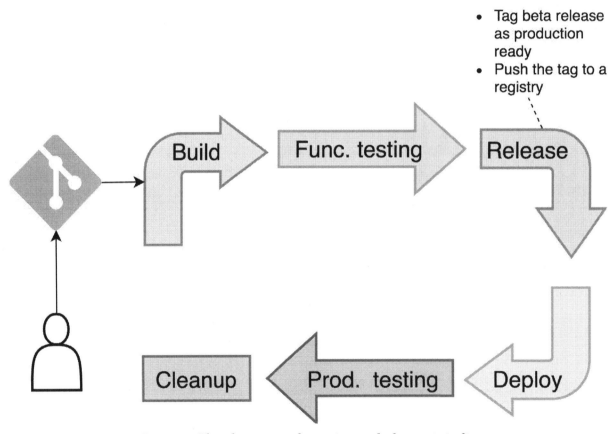

Figure 3-4: The release stage of a continuous deployment pipeline

We're making significant progress. Now that we have a new release, we can proceed and execute rolling updates against production.

Deploying To Production

We already saw that prod.yml is almost the same as build.yml we deployed earlier, so there's probably no need to go through it in details. The only substantial difference is that we'll create the resources in the go-demo-3 Namespace, and that we'll leave Ingress to its original path /demo.

```
1  kubectl -n go-demo-3-build \
2      exec -it cd -c kubectl -- sh
3
4  cat k8s/prod.yml \
5      | sed -e "s@:latest@:1.0@g" \
6      | tee /tmp/prod.yml
7
8  kubectl apply -f /tmp/prod.yml --record
```

We used sed to convert latest to the tag we built a short while ago, and we applied the definition. This was the first release, so all the resources were created. Subsequent releases will follow the rolling update process. Since that is something Kubernetes does out-of-the-box, the command will always be the same.

Next, we'll wait until the release rolls out before we check the exit code.

```
1  kubectl -n go-demo-3 \
2      rollout status deployment api
3
4  echo $?
```

The exit code is 0, so we can assume that the rollout was successful. There's no need even to look at the Pods. They are almost certainly running.

 ## A note to GKE users

GKE uses external load balancer as Ingress. To work properly, the type of the service related to Ingress needs to be NodePort. We'll have to patch the service to change its type. Please execute the command that follows.

```
kubectl -n go-demo-3 patch svc api -p '{"spec":{"type": "NodePort"}}'
```

A note to minishift users

Since OpenShift does not support Ingress (at least not by default), we'll need to add a Route. Please execute the commands that follow.

```
exit

kubectl -n go-demo-3-build exec -it cd -c oc -- sh

oc apply -f k8s/prod-oc.yml
```

We exited `kubectl` container, entered into `oc`, and deployed the route defined in `k8s/build-oc.yml`.

Now that the production release is up-and-running, we should find the address through which we can access it. Excluding the difference in the Namespace, the command for retrieving the hostname is the same.

 ## A note to GKE users

Please change `hostname` to `ip` in the command that follows. The `jsonpath` should be `{.status.loadBalancer.ingress[0].ip}`. Please note that GKE Ingress spins up an external load balancer and it might take a while until the IP is generated. Therefore, you might need to repeat the command that follows until you get the IP.

 ## A note to minikube users

Change the command that follows to `ADDR=[...]` where `[...]` is the minikube IP you retrieved earlier.

 ## A note to minishift users

Please change the command that follows to `ADDR=$(oc -n go-demo-3 get routes -o jsonpath="{.items[0].spec.host}")`.

```
1  ADDR=$(kubectl -n go-demo-3 \
2      get ing api \
3      -o jsonpath="{.status.loadBalancer.ingress[0].hostname}")
4
5  echo $ADDR | tee /workspace/prod-addr
```

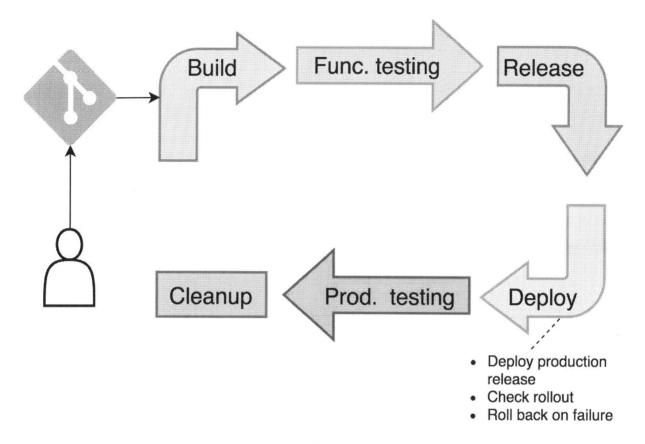

Figure 3-5: The deploy stage of a continuous deployment pipeline

To be on the safe side, we'll run another round of validation, which we'll call *production tests*. We don't need to be in the kubectl container for that, so let's exit.

```
1  exit
```

Running Production Tests

The process for running production tests is the same as functional testing we executed earlier. The difference is in the tests we execute, not how we do it.

The goal of production tests is not to validate all the units of our application. Unit tests did that. It is not going to validate anything on the functional level. Functional tests did that. Instead, they are very light tests with a simple goal of validating whether the newly deployed application is correctly integrated with the rest of the system. Can we connect to the database? Can we access the application from outside the cluster (as our users will)? Those are a few of the questions we're concerned with when running this last round of tests.

The tests are written in Go, and we still have the golang container running. All we have to do it to go through the similar steps as before.

```
1  kubectl -n go-demo-3-build \
2      exec -it cd -c golang -- sh
3
4  export ADDRESS=$(cat prod-addr)
```

Now that we have the address required for the tests, we can go ahead and execute them.

 ## A note to Docker For Mac/Windows users

DNS behind Docker for Mac or Windows is localhost. Since it has a different meaning depending on where it is invoked, the tests will fail, just as they did with the functional stage. Please change the address to api.go-demo-3:8080. This time we need to specify not only the name of the Service but also the Namespace since we are executing tests from go-demo-3-build and the application is running in the Namespace go-demo-3. Please execute the command export ADDRESS=api.go-demo-3:8080.

```
1  go test ./... -v --run ProductionTest
```

The output of the command is as follows.

```
1  === RUN    TestProductionTestSuite
2  === RUN    TestProductionTestSuite/Test_Hello_ReturnsStatus200
3  --- PASS: TestProductionTestSuite (0.10s)
4      --- PASS: TestProductionTestSuite/Test_Hello_ReturnsStatus200 (0.01s)
5  PASS
6  ok      _/go/go-demo-3   0.107s
```

 ## A note to GKE users

If your tests failed, the cause is probably due to a long time GKE needs to create a load balancer. Please wait for a few minutes and re-execute them.

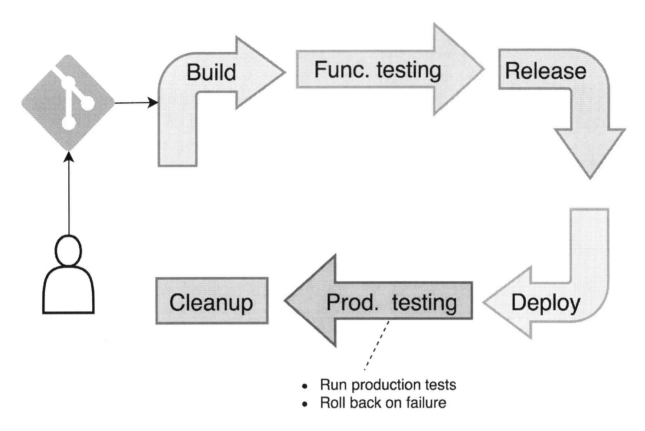

Figure 3-6: The production testing stage of a continuous deployment pipeline

Production tests were successful, and we can conclude that the deployment was successful as well. All that's left is to exit the container before we clean up.

```
1  exit
```

Cleaning Up Pipeline Leftovers

The last step in our manually-executed pipeline is to remove all the resources we created, except the production release. Since they are all Pods in the same Namespace, that should be reasonably easy. We can remove them all from `go-demo-3-build`.

```
1  kubectl -n go-demo-3-build \
2      delete pods --all
```

The output is as follows.

```
1  pod "cd" deleted
```

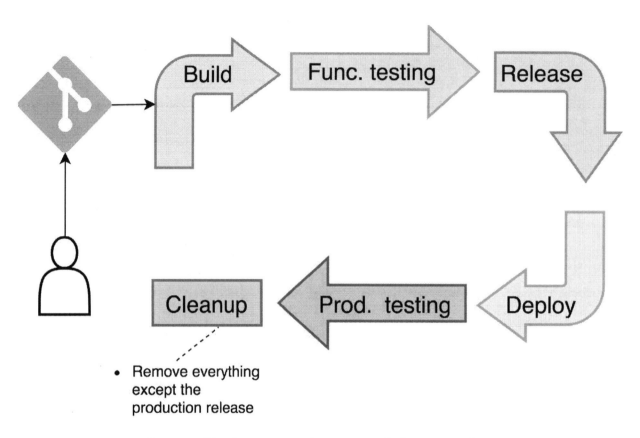

Figure 3-7: The cleanup stage of a continuous deployment pipeline

That's it. Our continuous pipeline is finished. Or, to be more precise, we defined all the steps of the pipeline. We are yet to automate everything.

Did We Do It?

We only partially succeeded in defining our continuous deployment stages. We did manage to execute all the necessary steps. We cloned the code, we run unit tests, and we built the binary and the Docker image. We deployed the application under test without affecting the production release, and we run functional tests. Once we confirmed that the application works as expected, we updated production with the new release. The new release was deployed through rolling updates but, since it was the first release, we did not see the effect of it. Finally, we run another round of tests to confirm that rolling updates were successful and that the new release is integrated with the rest of the system.

You might be wondering why I said that "we only partially succeeded." We executed the full pipeline. Didn't we?

One of the problems we're facing is that our process can run only a single pipeline for an application. If another commit is pushed while our pipeline is in progress, it would need to wait in a queue. We cannot have a separate Namespace for each build since we'd need to have cluster-wide permissions to create Namespaces and that would defy the purpose of having RBAC. So, the Namespaces need to be created in advance. We might create a few Namespaces for building and testing, but that would still be sub-optimal. We'll stick with a single Namespace with the pending task to figure out how to deploy multiple revisions of an application in the same Namespace given to us by the cluster administrator.

Another problem is the horrifying usage of `sed` commands to modify the content of a YAML file. There must be a better way to parametrize definition of an application. We'll try to solve that problem in the next chapter.

Once we start running multiple builds of the same application, we'll need to figure out how to remove the tools we create as part of our pipeline. Commands like `kubectl delete pods --all` will obviously not work if we plan to run multiple pipelines in parallel. We'll need to restrict the removal only to the Pods spin up by the build we finished, not all those in a Namespace. CI/CD tools we'll use later might be able to help with this problem.

We are missing quite a few steps in our pipeline. Those are the issues we will not try to fix in this book. Those that we explored so far are common to almost all pipelines. We always run different types of tests, some of which are static (e.g., unit tests), while others need a live application (e.g., functional tests). We always need to build a binary or package our application. We need to build an image and deploy it to one or more locations. The rest of the steps differs from one case to another. You might want to send test results to SonarQube, or you might choose to make a GitHub release. If your images can be deployed to different operating systems (e.g., Linux, Windows, ARM), you might want to create a manifest file. You'll probably run some security scanning as well. The list of the things you might do is almost unlimited, so I chose to stick with the steps that are very common and, in many cases, mandatory. Once you grasp the principles behind a well defined, fully automated, and container-based pipeline executed on top of a scheduler, I'm sure you won't have a problem extending our examples to fit your particular needs.

How about building Docker images? That is also one of the items on our TODO list. We shouldn't build them inside Kubernetes cluster because mounting Docker socket is a huge security risk and because we should not run anything without going through Kube API. Our best bet, for now, is to build them outside the cluster. We are yet to discover how to do that effectively. I suspect that will be a very easy challenge.

One message I tried to convey is that everything related to an application should be in the same repository. That applies not only to the source code and tests, but also to build scripts, Dockerfile, and Kubernetes definitions. Outside of that application-related repository should be only the code and configurations that transcends a single application (e.g., cluster setup). We'll continue using the same separation throughout the rest of the book. Everything required by go-demo-3 will be in the vfarcic/go-demo-3[55] repository. Cluster-wide code and configuration will continue living in

---

[55]https://github.com/vfarcic/go-demo-3

vfarcic/k8s-specs[56].

The logic behind everything-an-application-needs-is-in-a-single-repository mantra is vital if we want to empower the teams to be in charge of their applications. It's up to those teams to choose how to do something, and it's everyone else's job to teach them the skills they need. With some other tools, such approach would pose a big security risk and could put other teams in danger. However, Kubernetes provides quite a lot of tools that can help us to avoid those risks without sacrificing autonomy of the teams in charge of application development. We have RBAC and Namespaces. We have ResourceQuotas, LimitRanges, PodSecurityPolicies, NetworkPolicies, and quite a few other tools at our disposal.

 We can provide autonomy to the teams without sacrificing security and stability. We have the tools and the only thing missing is to change our culture and processes.

What Now?

We're done, for now. Please destroy the cluster if you're not planning to jump to the next chapter right away and if it is dedicated to the exercises in this book. Otherwise, execute the command that follows to remove everything we did.

```
1  kubectl delete ns \
2      go-demo-3 go-demo-3-build
```

---

[56]https://github.com/vfarcic/k8s-specs

Packaging Kubernetes Applications

 Using YAML files to install or upgrade applications in a Kubernetes cluster works well only for static definitions. The moment we need to change an aspect of an application we are bound to discover the need for templating and packaging mechanisms.

We faced quite a few challenges thus far. The good news is that we managed to solve most of them. The bad news is that, in some cases, our solutions felt sub-optimum (politically correct way to say *horrible*).

We spent a bit of time trying to define Jenkins resources while we were in the Deploying Stateful Applications At Scale chapter. That was a good exercise that can be characterized as a learning experience, but there's still some work in front of us to make it a truly useful definition. The primary issue with our Jenkins definition is that it is still not automated. We can spin up a master, but we still have to go through the setup wizard manually. Once we're done with the setup, we'd need to install some plugins, and we'd need to change its configuration. Before we go down that road, we might want to explore whether others already did that work for us. If we'd look for, let's say, a Java library that would help us solve a particular problem with our application, we'd probably look for a Maven repository. Maybe there is something similar for Kubernetes applications. Perhaps there is a community-maintained repository with installation solutions for commonly used tools. We'll make it our mission to find such a place.

Another problem we faced was customization of our YAML files. As a minimum, we'll need to specify different image tag every time we deploy a release. In the Defining Continuous Deployment chapter, we had to use `sed` to modify definitions before sending them through `kubectl` to Kube API. While that worked, I'm sure that you'll agree that commands like `sed -e "s@:latest@:1.7@g"` are not very intuitive. They look and feel awkward. To make things more complicated, image tags are rarely the only things that change from one deployment to another. We might need to change domains or paths of our Ingress controllers to accommodate the needs of having our applications deployed to different environments (e.g., staging and production). The same can be said for the number of replicas and many other things that define what we want to install. Using concatenated `sed` command can quickly become complicated, and it is not very user-friendly. Sure, we could modify YAML every time we, for example, make a new release. We could also create different definitions for each environment we're planning to use. But, we won't do that. That would only result in duplication and maintenance nightmare. We already have two YAML files for the `go-demo-3` application (one for testing and the other for production). If we continue down that route, we might end up with ten, twenty, or even more variations of the same definitions. We might also be forced to change it with every commit of our code so that the tag is always up to date. That road is not the one we'll take. It leads towards a cliff. What we need is a templating mechanism that will allow us to modify definitions before sending them to Kube API.

The last issue we'll try to solve in this chapter is the need to describe our applications and the possible changes others might apply to them before installing them inside a cluster. Truth be told, that is already possible. Anyone can read our YAML files to deduce what constitutes the application. Anyone could take one of our YAML files and modify it to suit their own needs. In some cases that might be challenging even for someone experienced with Kubernetes. However, our primary concern is related to those who are not Kubernetes ninjas. We cannot expect everyone in our organization to spend a year learning Kubernetes only so that they can deploy applications. On the other hand, we do want to provide that ability to everyone. We want to empower everyone. When faced with the need for everyone to use Kubernetes and the fact that not everyone will be a Kubernetes expert, it becomes apparent that we need a more descriptive, easier to customize, and more user-friendly way to discover and deploy applications.

We'll try to tackle those and a few other issues in this chapter. We'll try to find a place where community contributes with definitions of commonly used applications (e.g., Jenkins). We'll seek for a templating mechanism that will allow us to customize our applications before installing them. Finally, we'll try to find a way to better document our definitions. We'll try to make it so simple that even those who don't know Kubernetes can safely deploy applications to a cluster. What we need is a Kubernetes equivalent of package managers like *apt, yum, apk*, Homebrew[57], or Chocolatey[58], combined with the ability to document our packages in a way that anyone can use them.

I'll save you from searching for a solution and reveal it right away. We'll explore Helm[59] as the missing piece that will make our deployments customizable and user-friendly. If we are lucky, it might even turn out to be the solution that will save us from reinventing the wheel with commonly used applications.

Before we proceed, we'll need a cluster. It's time to get our hands dirty.

Creating A Cluster

It's hands-on time again. We'll need to go back to the local copy of the vfarcic/k8s-specs[60] repository and pull the latest version.

 All the commands from this chapter are available in the 04-helm.sh[61] Gist.

---

[57]https://brew.sh/
[58]https://chocolatey.org/
[59]https://helm.sh/
[60]https://github.com/vfarcic/k8s-specs
[61]https://gist.github.com/84adc5ad977f5c1a682bed524b781e0c

```
1  cd k8s-specs
2
3  git pull
```

Just as in the previous chapters, we'll need a cluster if we are to execute hands-on exercises. The rules are still the same. You can continue using the same cluster as before, or you can switch to a different Kubernetes flavor. You can keep using one of the Kubernetes distributions listed below, or be adventurous and try something different. If you go with the latter, please let me know how it went, and I'll test it myself and incorporate it into the list.

Cluster requirements in this chapter are the same as in the previous. We'll need at least 3 CPUs and 3 GB RAM if running a single-node cluster, and slightly more if those resources are spread across multiple nodes.

For your convenience, the Gists and the specs we used in the previous chapter are available here as well.

- docker4mac-3cpu.sh[62]: **Docker for Mac** with 3 CPUs, 3 GB RAM, and with nginx Ingress.
- minikube-3cpu.sh[63]: **minikube** with 3 CPUs, 3 GB RAM, and with `ingress`, `storage-provisioner`, and `default-storageclass` addons enabled.
- kops.sh[64]: **kops in AWS** with 3 t2.small masters and 2 t2.medium nodes spread in three availability zones, and with nginx Ingress (assumes that the prerequisites are set through Appendix B).
- minishift-3cpu.sh[65]: **minishift** with 3 CPUs, 3 GB RAM, and version 1.16+.
- gke-2cpu.sh[66]: **Google Kubernetes Engine (GKE)** with 3 n1-highcpu-2 (2 CPUs, 1.8 GB RAM) nodes (one in each zone), and with nginx Ingress controller running on top of the "standard" one that comes with GKE. We'll use nginx Ingress for compatibility with other platforms. Feel free to modify the YAML files if you prefer NOT to install nginx Ingress.
- eks.sh[67]: **Elastic Kubernetes Service (EKS)** with 2 t2.medium nodes, with **nginx Ingress** controller, and with a **default StorageClass**.

With a cluster up-and-running, we can proceed with an introduction to Helm.

What Is Helm?

I will not explain about Helm. I won't even give you the elevator pitch. I'll only say that it is a project with a big and healthy community, that it is a member of Cloud Native Computing Foundation

---

[62]https://gist.github.com/bf08bce43a26c7299b6bd365037eb074
[63]https://gist.github.com/871b5d7742ea6c10469812018c308798
[64]https://gist.github.com/2a3e4ee9cb86d4a5a65cd3e4397f48fd
[65]https://gist.github.com/2074633688a85ef3f887769b726066df
[66]https://gist.github.com/e3a2be59b0294438707b6b48adeb1a68
[67]https://gist.github.com/5496f79a3886be794cc317c6f8dd7083

(CNCF)[68], and that it has the backing of big guys like Google, Microsoft, and a few others. For everything else, you'll need to follow the exercises. They'll lead us towards an understanding of the project, and they will hopefully help us in our goal to refine our continuous deployment pipeline.

The first step is to install it.

Installing Helm

Helm is a client/server type of application. We'll start with a client. Once we have it running, we'll use it to install the server (Tiller) inside our newly created cluster.

The Helm client is a command line utility responsible for the local development of Charts, managing repositories, and interaction with the Tiller. Tiller server, on the other hand, runs inside a Kubernetes cluster and interacts with Kube API. It listens for incoming requests from the Helm client, combines Charts and configuration values to build a release, installs Charts and tracks subsequent releases, and is in charge of upgrading and uninstalling Charts through interaction with Kube API.

 Do not get too attached to Tiller. Helm v3 will remove the server component and operate fully from the client side. At the time of this writing (June 2018), it is still unknown when will v3 reach GA.

I'm sure that this brief explanation is more confusing than helpful. Worry not. Everything will be explained soon through examples. For now, we'll focus on installing Helm and Tiller.

If you are a **MacOS user**, please use Homebrew[69] to install Helm. The command is as follows.

```
1  brew install kubernetes-helm
```

If you are a **Windows user**, please use Chocolatey[70] to install Helm. The command is as follows.

```
1  choco install kubernetes-helm
```

Finally, if you are neither Windows nor MacOS user, you must be running **Linux**. Please go to the releases[71] page, download tar.gz file, unpack it, and move the binary to /usr/local/bin/.

If you already have Helm installed, please make sure that it is newer than 2.8.2. That version, and probably a few versions before, was failing on Docker For Mac/Windows.

Once you're done installing (or upgrading) Helm, please execute helm help to verify that it is working.

---

[68]https://www.cncf.io/
[69]https://brew.sh/
[70]https://chocolatey.org/
[71]https://github.com/kubernetes/helm/releases

We are about to install *Tiller*. It'll run inside our cluster. Just as `kubectl` is a client that communicates with Kube API, `helm` will propagate our wishes to `tiller` which, in turn, will issue requests to Kube API.

It should come as no surprise that Tiller will be yet another Pod in our cluster. As such, you should already know that we'll need a ServiceAccount that will allow it to establish communication with Kube API. Since we hope to use Helm for all our installation in Kubernetes, we should give that ServiceAccount very generous permissions across the whole cluster.

Let's take a look at the definition of a ServiceAccount we'll create for Tiller.

```
1  cat helm/tiller-rbac.yml
```

The output is as follows.

```
1   apiVersion: v1
2   kind: ServiceAccount
3   metadata:
4     name: tiller
5     namespace: kube-system
6
7   ---
8
9   apiVersion: rbac.authorization.k8s.io/v1beta1
10  kind: ClusterRoleBinding
11  metadata:
12    name: tiller
13  roleRef:
14    apiGroup: rbac.authorization.k8s.io
15    kind: ClusterRole
16    name: cluster-admin
17  subjects:
18    - kind: ServiceAccount
19      name: tiller
20      namespace: kube-system
```

Since by now you are an expert in ServiceAccounts, there should be no need for a detailed explanation of the definition. We're creating a ServiceAccount called `tiller` in the `kube-system` Namespace, and we are assigning it ClusterRole `cluster-admin`. In other words, the account will be able to execute any operation anywhere inside the cluster.

You might be thinking that having such broad permissions might seem dangerous, and you would be right. Only a handful of people should have the user permissions to operate inside `kube-system` Namespace. On the other hand, we can expect much wider circle of people being able to use Helm.

We'll solve that problem later in one of the next chapters. For now, we'll focus only on how Helm works, and get back to the permissions issue later.

Let's create the ServiceAccount.

```
1  kubectl create \
2      -f helm/tiller-rbac.yml \
3      --record --save-config
```

We can see from the output that both the ServiceAccount and the ClusterRoleBinding were created.

Now that we have the ServiceAccount that gives Helm full permissions to manage any Kubernetes resource, we can proceed and install Tiller.

```
1  helm init --service-account tiller
2
3  kubectl -n kube-system \
4      rollout status deploy tiller-deploy
```

We used `helm init` to create the server component called `tiller`. Since our cluster uses RBAC and all the processes require authentication and permissions to communicate with Kube API, we added `--service-account tiller` argument. It'll attach the ServiceAccount to the `tiller` Pod.

The latter command waits until the Deployment is rolled out.

We could have specified `--tiller-namespace` argument to deploy it to a specific Namespace. That ability will come in handy in one of the next chapters. For now, we omitted that argument, so Tiller was installed in the `kube-system` Namespace by default. To be on the safe side, we'll list the Pods to confirm that it is indeed running.

```
1  kubectl -n kube-system get pods
```

The output, limited to the relevant parts, is as follows.

```
1  NAME             READY STATUS   RESTARTS AGE
2  ...
3  tiller-deploy-... 1/1   Running 0        59s
```

Helm already has a single repository pre-configured. For those of you who just installed Helm for the first time, the repository is up-to-date. On the other hand, if you happen to have Helm from before, you might want to update the repository references by executing the command that follows.

```
1 helm repo update
```

The only thing left is to search for our favorite application hoping that it is available in the Helm repository.

```
1 helm search
```

The output, limited to the last few entries, is as follows.

```
1 ...
2 stable/weave-scope 0.9.2 1.6.5 A Helm chart for the Weave Scope cluster visual...
3 stable/wordpress   1.0.7 4.9.6 Web publishing platform for building blogs and ...
4 stable/zeppelin    1.0.1 0.7.2 Web-based notebook that enables data-driven, in...
5 stable/zetcd       0.1.9 0.0.3 CoreOS zetcd Helm chart for Kubernetes
```

We can see that the default repository already contains quite a few commonly used applications. It is the repository that contains the official Kubernetes Charts which are carefully curated and well maintained. Later on, in one of the next chapters, we'll add more repositories to our local Helm installation. For now, we just need Jenkins, which happens to be one of the official Charts.

I already mentioned Charts a few times. You'll find out what they are soon. For now, all you should know is that a Chart defines everything an application needs to run in a Kubernetes cluster.

Installing Helm Charts

The first thing we'll do is to confirm that Jenkins indeed exists in the official Helm repository. We could do that by executing `helm search` (again) and going through all the available Charts. However, the list is pretty big and growing by the day. We'll filter the search to narrow down the output.

```
1 helm search jenkins
```

The output is as follows.

```
1 NAME           CHART VERSION APP VERSION DESCRIPTION                              \
2
3 stable/jenkins 0.16.1        2.107       Open source continuous integration server. \
4 It s...
```

We can see that the repository contains `stable/jenkins` chart based on Jenkins version 2.107.

A note to minishift users

Helm will try to install Jenkins Chart with the process in a container running as user 0. By default, that is not allowed in OpenShift. We'll skip discussing the best approach to correct the permissions in OpenShift. I'll assume you already know how to set the permissions on the per-Pod basis. Instead, we'll do the simplest fix. Please execute the command that follows to allow the creation of restricted Pods to run as any user.

```
oc patch scc restricted -p '{"runAsUser":{"type": "RunAsAny"}}'
```

We'll install Jenkins with the default values first. If that works as expected, we'll try to adapt it to our needs later on.

Now that we know (through search) that the name of the Chart is stable/jenkins, all we need to do is execute helm install.

```
1  helm install stable/jenkins \
2      --name jenkins \
3      --namespace jenkins
```

We instructed Helm to install stable/jenkins with the name jenkins, and inside the Namespace also called jenkins.

The output is as follows.

```
1  NAME:    jenkins
2  LAST DEPLOYED: Sun May ...
3  NAMESPACE: jenkins
4  STATUS: DEPLOYED
5
6  RESOURCES:
7  ==> v1/Service
8  NAME           TYPE         CLUSTER-IP     EXTERNAL-IP PORT(S)       AGE
9  jenkins-agent ClusterIP    10.111.123.174 <none>      50000/TCP     1s
10 jenkins       LoadBalancer 10.110.48.57   localhost   8080:31294/TCP 0s
11
12 ==> v1beta1/Deployment
13 NAME    DESIRED CURRENT UP-TO-DATE AVAILABLE AGE
14 jenkins 1       1       1          0         0s
15
16 ==> v1/Pod(related)
17 NAME          READY STATUS    RESTARTS AGE
18 jenkins-... 0/1   Init:0/1 0        0s
19
20 ==> v1/Secret
```

```
21  NAME     TYPE    DATA AGE
22  jenkins Opaque 2     1s
23
24  ==> v1/ConfigMap
25  NAME           DATA AGE
26  jenkins         4    1s
27  jenkins-tests 1     1s
28
29  ==> v1/PersistentVolumeClaim
30  NAME      STATUS VOLUME   CAPACITY ACCESS MODES STORAGECLASS AGE
31  jenkins Bound  pvc-... 8Gi          RWO              gp2           1s
32
33
34  NOTES:
35  1. Get your 'admin' user password by running:
36    printf $(kubectl get secret --namespace jenkins jenkins -o jsonpath="{.data.jenkin\
37  s-admin-password}" | base64 --decode);echo
38  2. Get the Jenkins URL to visit by running these commands in the same shell:
39    NOTE: It may take a few minutes for the LoadBalancer IP to be available.
40         You can watch the status of by running 'kubectl get svc --namespace jenkins \
41  -w jenkins'
42    export SERVICE_IP=$(kubectl get svc --namespace jenkins jenkins --template "{{ ran\
43  ge (index .status.loadBalancer.ingress 0) }}{{ . }}{{ end }}")
44    echo http://$SERVICE_IP:8080/login
45
46  3. Login with the password from step 1 and the username: admin
47
48  For more information on running Jenkins on Kubernetes, visit:
49  https://cloud.google.com/solutions/jenkins-on-container-engine
```

At the top of the output, we can see some general information like the name we gave to the installed Chart (jenkins), when it was deployed, what the Namespace is, and the status.

Below the general information is the list of the installed resources. We can see that the Chart installed two services; one for the master and the other for the agents. Below is the Deployment and the Pod. It also created a Secret that holds the administrative username and password. We'll use it soon. Further on, we can see that it created two ConfigMaps. One (jenkins) holds all the configurations Jenkins might need. Later on, when we customize it, the data in this ConfigMap will reflect those changes. The second ConfigMap (jenkins-tests) is, at the moment, used only to provide a command used for executing liveness and readiness probes. Finally, we can see that a PersistentVolumeClass was created as well, thus making our Jenkins fault tolerant without losing its state.

Don't worry if you feel overwhelmed. We'll do a couple of iterations of the Jenkins installation process, and that will give us plenty of opportunities to explore this Chart in more details. If you are impatient, please `describe` any of those resources to get more insight into what's installed.

One thing worthwhile commenting right away is the type of the `jenkins` Service. It is, by default, set to `LoadBalancer`. We did not explore that type in The DevOps 2.3 Toolkit: Kubernetes[72], primarily because the book is, for the most part, based on minikube.

On cloud providers which support external load balancers, setting the type field to `LoadBalancer` will provision an external load balancer for the Service. The actual creation of the load balancer happens asynchronously, and information about the provisioned balancer is published in the Serviceâ€™s `status.loadBalancer` field.

When a Service is of the `LoadBalancer` type, it publishes a random port just as if it is the `NodePort` type. The additional feature is that it also communicates that change to the external load balancer (LB) which, in turn, should open a port as well. In most cases, the port opened in the external LB will be the same as the Service's `TargetPort`. For example, if the `TargetPort` of a Service is `8080` and the published port is `32456`, the external LB will be configured to accept traffic on the port `8080`, and it will forward traffic to one of the healthy nodes on the port `32456`. From there on, requests will be picked up by the Service and the standard process of forwarding it further towards the replicas will be initiated. From user's perspective, it seems as if the published port is the same as the `TargetPort`.

The problem is that not all load balancers and hosting vendors support the `LoadBalancer` type, so we'll have to change it to `NodePort` in some of the cases. Those changes will be outlined as notes specific to the Kubernetes flavor.

Going back to the Helm output...

At the bottom of the output, we can see the post-installation instructions provided by the authors of the Chart. In our case, those instructions tell us how to retrieve the administrative password from the Secret, how to open Jenkins in a browser, and how to log in.

 ## A note to minikube users

If you go back to the output, you'll notice that the type of the `jenkins` Service is `LoadBalancer`. Since we do not have a load balancer in front of our minikube cluster, that type will not work, and we should change it to `NodePort`. Please execute the command that follows.

```
helm upgrade jenkins stable/jenkins --set Master.ServiceType=NodePort
```

We haven't explained the `upgrade` process just yet. For now, just note that we changed the Service type to `NodePort`.

---

[72]https://amzn.to/2GvzDjy

A note to minishift users

OpenShift requires Routes to make services accessible outside the cluster. To make things more complicated, they are not part of "standard Kubernetes" so we'll need to create one using oc. Please execute the command that follows.

```
oc -n jenkins create route edge --service jenkins --insecure-policy Allow
```

That command created an edge Router tied to the jenkins Service. Since we do not have SSL certificates for HTTPS communication, we also specified that it is OK to use insecure policy which will allow us to access Jenkins through plain HTTP.

Next, we'll wait until jenkins Deployment is rolled out.

```
1  kubectl -n jenkins \
2      rollout status deploy jenkins
```

The rollout status command might exit with the error: watch closed before Until timeout message. Don't panic. Jenkins might need more time to initialize than that command's timeout. If that happens, wait until Jenkins Pod is running.

We are almost ready to open Jenkins in a browser. But, before we do that, we need to retrieve the hostname (or IP) through which we can access our first Helm install.

```
1  ADDR=$(kubectl -n jenkins \
2      get svc jenkins \
3      -o jsonpath="{.status.loadBalancer.ingress[0].hostname}"):8080
```

A note to minikube users

Unlike some other Kubernetes flavors (e.g., AWS with kops), minikube does not have a hostname automatically assigned to us through an external load balancer. We'll have to retrieve the IP of our minikube cluster and the port published when we changed the jenkins service to NodePort. Please execute the command that follows.

```
ADDR=$(minikube   ip):$(kubectl   -n   jenkins   get   svc   jenkins   -o
jsonpath="{.spec.ports[0].nodePort}")
```

A note to GKE users

Unlike some other Kubernetes flavors (e.g., AWS with kops), GKE does not have a hostname automatically assigned to us through an external load balancer. Instead, we got the IP of Google's LB. We'll have to get that IP. Please execute the command that follows.

```
ADDR=$(kubectl          -n      jenkins      get      svc      jenkins      -o
jsonpath="{.status.loadBalancer.ingress[0].ip}"):8080
```

A note to minishift users

Unlike all other Kubernetes flavors, OpenShift does not use Ingress. We'll have to retrieve the address from the `jenkins` Route we created previously. Please execute the command that follows.

```
ADDR=$(oc -n jenkins get route jenkins -o jsonpath="{.status.ingress[0].host}")
```

To be on the safe side, we'll `echo` the address we retrieved and confirm that it looks valid.

```
1  echo $ADDR
```

The format of the output will differ from one Kubernetes flavor to another. In case of AWS with kops, it should be similar to the one that follows.

```
1  ...us-east-2.elb.amazonaws.com
```

Now we can finally open Jenkins. We won't do much with it. Our goal, for now, is only to confirm that it is up-and-running.

```
1  open "http://$ADDR"
```

 Remember that if you are a **Windows user**, you'll have to replace `open` with `echo`, copy the output, and paste it into a new tab of your browser of choice.

You should be presented with the login screen. There is no setup wizard indicating that this Helm chart already configured Jenkins with some sensible default values. That means that, among other things, the Chart created a user with a password during the automatic setup. We need to discover it.

Fortunately, we already saw from the `helm install` output that we should retrieve the password by retrieving the `jenkins-admin-password` entry from the `jenkins` secret. If you need to refresh your memory, please scroll back to the output, or ignore it all together and execute the command that follows.

```
1  kubectl -n jenkins \
2      get secret jenkins \
3      -o jsonpath="{.data.jenkins-admin-password}" \
4      | base64 --decode; echo
```

The output should be a random set of characters similar to the one that follows.

```
1   shP7Fcsb9g
```

Please copy the output and return to Jenkins' login screen in your browser. Type *admin* into the *User* field, paste the copied output into the *Password* field and click the *log in* button.

Mission accomplished. Jenkins is up-and-running without us spending any time writing YAML file with all the resources. It was set up automatically with the administrative user and probably quite a few other goodies. We'll get to them later. For now, we'll "play" with a few other `helm` commands that might come in handy.

If you are ever unsure about the details behind one of the Helm Charts, you can execute `helm inspect`.

```
1   helm inspect stable/jenkins
```

The output of the `inspect` command is too big to be presented in a book. It contains all the information you might need before installing an application (in this case Jenkins).

If you prefer to go through the available Charts visually, you might want to visit Kubeapps[73] project hosted by bitnami[74]. Click on the *Explore Apps* button, and you'll be sent to the hub with the list of all the official Charts. If you search for Jenkins, you'll end up on the page with the Chart's details[75]. You'll notice that the info in that page is the same as the output of the `inspect` command.

We won't go back to Kubeapps[76] since I prefer command line over UIs. A firm grip on the command line helps a lot when it comes to automation, which happens to be the goal of this book.

With time, the number of the Charts running in your cluster will increase, and you might be in need to list them. You can do that with the `ls` command.

```
1   helm ls
```

The output is as follows.

```
1   NAME      REVISION UPDATED      STATUS    CHART          NAMESPACE
2   jenkins 1          Thu May ... DEPLOYED jenkins-0.16.1 jenkins
```

There is not much to look at right now since we have only one Chart. Just remember that the command exists. It'll come in handy later on.

If you need to see the details behind one of the installed Charts, please use the `status` command.

---

[73]https://kubeapps.com/
[74]https://bitnami.com/
[75]https://hub.kubeapps.com/charts/stable/jenkins
[76]https://kubeapps.com/

```
1  helm status jenkins
```

The output should be very similar to the one you saw when we installed the Chart. The only difference is that this time all the Pods are running.

Tiller obviously stores the information about the installed Charts somewhere. Unlike most other applications that tend to save their state on disk, or replicate data across multiple instances, tiller uses Kubernetes ConfgMaps to preserve its state.

Let's take a look at the ConfigMaps in the `kube-system` Namespace where tiller is running.

```
1  kubectl -n kube-system get cm
```

The output, limited to the relevant parts, is as follows.

```
1  NAME          DATA AGE
2  ...
3  jenkins.v1 1     25m
4  ...
```

We can see that there is a config named `jenkins.v1`. We did not explore revisions just yet. For now, only assume that each new installation of a Chart is version 1.

Let's take a look at the contents of the ConfigMap.

```
1  kubectl -n kube-system \
2      describe cm jenkins.v1
```

The output is as follows.

```
1  Name:        jenkins.v1
2  Namespace:   kube-system
3  Labels:      MODIFIED_AT=1527424681
4               NAME=jenkins
5               OWNER=TILLER
6               STATUS=DEPLOYED
7               VERSION=1
8  Annotations: <none>
9
10 Data
11 =====
12 release:
13 ----
14 [ENCRYPTED RELEASE INFO]
15 Events:  <none>
```

I replaced the content of the release Data with [ENCRYPTED RELEASE INFO] since it is too big to be presented in the book. The release contains all the info tiller used to create the first jenkins release. It is encrypted as a security precaution.

We're finished exploring our Jenkins installation, so our next step is to remove it.

```
1  helm delete jenkins
```

The output shows that the release "jenkins" was deleted.

Since this is the first time we deleted a Helm Chart, we might just as well confirm that all the resources were indeed removed.

```
1  kubectl -n jenkins get all
```

The output is as follows.

```
1  NAME            READY STATUS       RESTARTS AGE
2  po/jenkins-... 0/1   Terminating 0        5m
```

Everything is gone except the Pod that is still terminating. Soon it will disappear as well, and there will be no trace of Jenkins anywhere in the cluster. At least, that's what we're hoping for.

Let's check the status of the jenkins Chart.

```
1  helm status jenkins
```

The relevant parts of the output are as follows.

```
1  LAST DEPLOYED: Thu May 24 11:46:38 2018
2  NAMESPACE: jenkins
3  STATUS: DELETED
4
5  ...
```

If you expected an empty output or an error stating that jenkins does not exist, you were wrong. The Chart is still in the system, only this time its status is DELETED. You'll notice that all the resources are gone though.

When we execute helm delete [THE_NAME_OF_A_CHART], we are only removing the Kubernetes resources. The Chart is still in the system. We could, for example, revert the delete action and return to the previous state with Jenkins up-and-running again.

If you want to delete not only the Kubernetes resources created by the Chart but also the Chart itself, please add --purge argument.

```
1  helm delete jenkins --purge
```

The output is still the same as before. It states that the release "jenkins" was deleted. Let's check the status now after we purged the system.

```
1  helm status jenkins
```

The output is as follows.

```
1  Error: getting deployed release "jenkins": release: "jenkins" not found
```

This time, everything was removed, and helm cannot find the jenkins Chart anymore.

Customizing Helm Installations

We'll almost never install a Chart as we did. Even though the default values do often make a lot of sense, there is always something we need to tweak to make an application behave as we expect.

What if we do not want the Jenkins tag predefined in the Chart? What if for some reason we want to deploy Jenkins 2.112-alpine? There must be a sensible way to change the tag of the stable/jenkins Chart.

Helm allows us to modify installation through variables. All we need to do is to find out which variables are available.

Besides visiting project's documentation, we can retrieve the available values through the command that follows.

```
1  helm inspect values stable/jenkins
```

The output, limited to the relevant parts, is as follows.

```
1  ...
2  Master:
3    Name: jenkins-master
4    Image: "jenkins/jenkins"
5    ImageTag: "lts"
6    ...
```

We can see that within the Master section there is a variable ImageTag. The name of the variable should be, in this case, sufficiently self-explanatory. If we need more information, we can always inspect the Chart.

```
1  helm inspect stable/jenkins
```

I encourage you to read the whole output at some later moment. For now, we care only about the ImageTag.

The output, limited to the relevant parts, is as follows.

```
1  ...
2  | Parameter        | Description      | Default |
3  | ---------------- | ---------------- | ------- |
4  ...
5  | `Master.ImageTag` | Master image tag | `lts`   |
6  ...
```

That did not provide much more info. Still, we do not really need more than that. We can assume that Master.ImageTag will allow us to replace the default value lts with 2.112-alpine.

If we go through the documentation, we'll discover that one of the ways to overwrite the default values is through the --set argument. Let's give it a try.

```
1  helm install stable/jenkins \
2      --name jenkins \
3      --namespace jenkins \
4      --set Master.ImageTag=2.112-alpine
```

 ## A note to minikube users

We still need to change the jenkins Service type to NodePort. Since this is specific to minikube, I did not want to include it in the command we just executed. Instead, we'll run the same command as before. Please execute the command that follows.

```
helm upgrade jenkins stable/jenkins --set Master.ServiceType=NodePort --reuse-values
```

We still did not go through the upgrade process. For now, just note that we changed the Service type to NodePort.

Alternatively, you can delete the chart and install it again but, this time, the --set Master.ServiceType=NodePort argument needs to be added to helm install.

 ## A note to minishift users

The Route we created earlier still exists, so we do not need to create it again.

The output of the helm install command is almost the same as when we executed it the first time, so there's probably no need to go through it again. Instead, we'll wait until jenkins rolls out.

```
1  kubectl -n jenkins \
2      rollout status deployment jenkins
```

Now that the Deployment rolled out, we are almost ready to test whether the change of the variable had any effect. First, we need to get the Jenkins address. We'll retrieve it in the same way as before, so there's no need to lengthy explanation.

```
1  ADDR=$(kubectl -n jenkins \
2      get svc jenkins \
3      -o jsonpath="{.status.loadBalancer.ingress[0].hostname}"):8080
```

A note to minikube users

As a reminder, the command to retrieve the address from minikube is as follows.

```
ADDR=$(minikube    ip):$(kubectl    -n    jenkins    get    svc    jenkins    -o
jsonpath="{.spec.ports[0].nodePort}")
```

A note to GKE users

As a reminder, the command to retrieve the address from GKE is as follows.

```
ADDR=$(kubectl         -n         jenkins         get         svc         jenkins         -o
jsonpath="{.status.loadBalancer.ingress[0].ip}"):8080
```

A note to minishift users

As a reminder, the command to retrieve the address from the OpenShift route is as follows.

```
ADDR=$(oc -n jenkins get route jenkins -o jsonpath="{.status.ingress[0].host}")
```

As a precaution, please output the ADDR variable and check whether the address looks correct.

```
1  echo $ADDR
```

Now we can open Jenkins UI.

```
1  open "http://$ADDR"
```

This time there is no need even to log in. All we need to do is to check whether changing the tag worked. Please observe the version in the bottom-right corner of the screen. If should be *Jenkins ver. 2.112*.

Let's imagine that some time passed and we decided to upgrade our Jenkins from *2.112* to *2.116*. We go through the documentation and discover that there is the upgrade command we can leverage.

```
1  helm upgrade jenkins stable/jenkins \
2      --set Master.ImageTag=2.116-alpine \
3      --reuse-values
```

This time we did not specify the Namespace, but we did set the `--reuse-values` argument. With it, the upgrade will maintain all the values used the last time we installed or upgraded the Chart. The result is an upgrade of the Kubernetes resources so that they comply with our desire to change the tag, and leave everything else intact.

The output of the `upgrade` command, limited to the first few lines, is as follows.

```
1  Release "jenkins" has been upgraded. Happy Helming!
2  LAST DEPLOYED: Thu May 24 12:51:03 2018
3  NAMESPACE: jenkins
4  STATUS: DEPLOYED
5  ...
```

We can see that the release was upgraded.

To be on the safe side, we'll describe the `jenkins` Deployment and confirm that the image is indeed `2.116-alpine`.

```
1  kubectl -n jenkins \
2      describe deployment jenkins
```

The output, limited to the relevant parts, is as follows.

```
1  Name:           jenkins
2  Namespace:      jenkins
3  ...
4  Pod Template:
5    ...
6    Containers:
7     jenkins:
8      Image: jenkins/jenkins:2.116-alpine
9        ...
```

The image was indeed updated to the tag `2.116-alpine`.

To satisfy my paranoid nature, we'll also open Jenkins UI and confirm the version there. But, before we do that, we need to wait until the update rolls out.

```
1  kubectl -n jenkins \
2      rollout status deployment jenkins
```

Now we can open Jenkins UI.

```
1  open "http://$ADDR"
```

Please note the version in the bottom-right corner of the screen. It should say *Jenkins ver. 2.116.*

Rolling Back Helm Revisions

No matter how we deploy our applications and no matter how much we trust our validations, the truth is that sooner or later we'll have to roll back. That is especially true with third-party applications. While we could roll forward faulty applications we developed, the same is often not an option with those that are not in our control. If there is a problem and we cannot fix it fast, the only alternative is to roll back.

Fortunately, Helm provides a mechanism to roll back. Before we try it out, let's take a look at the list of the Charts we installed so far.

```
1  helm list
```

The output is as follows.

```
1  NAME      REVISION UPDATED      STATUS    CHART          NAMESPACE
2  jenkins 2          Thu May ... DEPLOYED jenkins-0.16.1 jenkins
```

As expected, we have only one Chart running in our cluster. The critical piece of information is that it is the second revision. First, we installed the Chart with Jenkins version 2.112, and then we upgraded it to 2.116.

 ### A note to minikube users

You'll see 3 revisions in your output. We executed `helm upgrade` after the initial install to change the type of the `jenkins` Service to `NodePort`.

We can roll back to the previous version (`2.112`) by executing `helm rollback jenkins 1`. That would roll back from the revision 2 to whatever was defined as the revision 1. However, in most cases that is unpractical. Most of our rollbacks are likely to be executed through our CD or CDP processes. In those cases, it might be too complicated for us to find out what was the previous release number.

Luckily, there is an undocumented feature that allows us to roll back to the previous version without explicitly setting up the revision number. By the time you read this, the feature might become documented. I was about to start working on it and submit a pull request. Luckily, while going through the code, I saw that it's already there.

Please execute the command that follows.

```
helm rollback jenkins 0
```

By specifying 0 as the revision number, Helm will roll back to the previous version. It's as easy as that.

We got the visual confirmation in the form of the "Rollback was a success! Happy Helming!" message.

Let's take a look at the current situation.

```
helm list
```

The output is as follows.

```
NAME            REVISION UPDATED      STATUS   CHART            NAMESPACE
jenkins         3        Thu May ... DEPLOYED jenkins-0.16.1 jenkins
```

We can see that even though we issued a rollback, Helm created a new revision 3. There's no need to panic. Every change is a new revision, even when a change means re-applying definition from one of the previous releases.

To be on the safe side, we'll go back to Jenkins UI and confirm that we are using version 2.112 again.

```
kubectl -n jenkins \
    rollout status deployment jenkins

open "http://$ADDR"
```

We waited until Jenkins rolled out, and opened it in our favorite browser. If we look at the version information located in the bottom-right corner of the screen, we are bound to discover that it is *Jenkins ver. 2.112* once again.

We are about to start over one more time, so our next step it to purge Jenkins.

```
helm delete jenkins --purge
```

Using YAML Values To Customize Helm Installations

We managed to customize Jenkins by setting `ImageTag`. What if we'd like to set CPU and memory. We should also add Ingress, and that would require a few annotations. If we add Ingress, we might want to change the Service type to ClusterIP and set HostName to our domain. We should also make sure that RBAC is used. Finally, the plugins that come with the Chart are probably not all the plugins we need.

Applying all those changes through `--set` arguments would end up as a very long command and would constitute an undocumented installation. We'll have to change the tactic and switch to `--values`. But before we do all that, we need to generate a domain we'll use with our cluster.

We'll use nip.io[77] to generate valid domains. The service provides a wildcard DNS for any IP address. It extracts IP from the nip.io subdomain and sends it back in the response. For example, if we generate 192.168.99.100.nip.io, it'll be resolved to 192.168.99.100. We can even add sub-sub domains like something.192.168.99.100.nip.io, and it would still be resolved to 192.168.99.100. It's a simple and awesome service that quickly became an indispensable part of my toolbox.

The service will be handy with Ingress since it will allow us to generate separate domains for each application, instead of resorting to paths which, as you will see, are unsupported by many Charts. If our cluster is accessible through *192.168.99.100*, we can have *jenkins.192.168.99.100.nip.io* and *go-demo-3.192.168.99.100.nip.io*.

We could use xip.ip[78] instead. For the end-users, there is no significant difference between the two. The main reason why we'll use nip.io instead of xip.io is integration with some of the tool. Minishift, for example, comes with Routes pre-configured to use nip.io.

 Do NOT use `nip.io`, `xip.io`, or similar services for production. They are not a substitute for "real" domains, but a convenient way to generate them for testing purposes when your corporate domains are not easily accessible.

First things first... We need to find out the IP of our cluster, or the external LB if it is available. The commands that follow will differ from one cluster type to another.

 Feel free to skip the sections that follow if you already know how to get the IP of your cluster's entry point.

If your cluster is running in **AWS** and was created with **kops**, we'll need to retrieve the hostname from the Ingress Service, and extract the IP from it. Please execute the commands that follow.

---

[77]http://nip.io
[78]http://xip.io

```
1 LB_HOST=$(kubectl -n kube-ingress \
2     get svc ingress-nginx \
3     -o jsonpath="{.status.loadBalancer.ingress[0].hostname}")
4
5 LB_IP="$(dig +short $LB_HOST \
6     | tail -n 1)"
```

If your cluster is running in **AWS** and was created as **EKS**, we'll need to retrieve the hostname from the Ingress Service, and extract the IP from it. Please execute the commands that follow.

```
1 LB_HOST=$(kubectl -n ingress-nginx \
2     get svc ingress-nginx \
3     -o jsonpath="{.status.loadBalancer.ingress[0].hostname}")
4
5 LB_IP="$(dig +short $LB_HOST \
6     | tail -n 1)"
```

If your cluster is running in **Docker For Mac/Windows**, the IP is 127.0.0.1 and all you have to do is assign it to the environment variable LB_IP. Please execute the command that follows.

```
1 LB_IP="127.0.0.1"
```

If your cluster is running in **minikube**, the IP can be retrieved using minikube ip command. Please execute the command that follows.

```
1 LB_IP="$(minikube ip)"
```

If your cluster is running in **GKE**, the IP can be retrieved from the Ingress Service. Please execute the command that follows.

```
1 LB_IP=$(kubectl -n ingress-nginx \
2     get svc ingress-nginx \
3     -o jsonpath="{.status.loadBalancer.ingress[0].ip}")
```

Next, we'll output the retrieved IP to confirm that the commands worked, and generate a sub-domain jenkins.

```
1   echo $LB_IP
2
3   HOST="jenkins.$LB_IP.nip.io"
4
5   echo $HOST
```

The output of the second `echo` command should be similar to the one that follows.

```
1   jenkins.192.168.99.100.nip.io
```

nip.io will resolve that address to `192.168.99.100`, and we'll have a unique domain for our Jenkins installation. That way we can stop using different paths to distinguish applications in Ingress config. Domains work much better. Many Helm charts do not even have the option to configure unique request paths and assume that Ingress will be configured with a unique domain.

 A note to minishift users

I did not forget about you. You already have a valid domain in the ADDR variable. All we have to do is assign it to the HOST variable. Please execute the command that follows.

```
HOST=$ADDR && echo $HOST
```

The output should be similar to `jenkins.192.168.99.100.nip.io`.

Now that we have a valid `jenkins.*` domain, we can try to figure out how to apply all the changes we discussed.

We already learned that we can inspect all the available values using `helm inspect` command. Let's take another look.

```
1   helm inspect values stable/jenkins
```

The output, limited to the relevant parts, is as follows.

```
1   Master:
2     Name: jenkins-master
3     Image: "jenkins/jenkins"
4     ImageTag: "lts"
5     ...
6     Cpu: "200m"
7     Memory: "256Mi"
8     ...
9     ServiceType: LoadBalancer
10    # Master Service annotations
```

```
11    ServiceAnnotations: {}
12    ...
13    # HostName: jenkins.cluster.local
14    ...
15    InstallPlugins:
16      - kubernetes:1.1
17      - workflow-aggregator:2.5
18      - workflow-job:2.15
19      - credentials-binding:1.13
20      - git:3.6.4
21    ...
22    Ingress:
23      ApiVersion: extensions/v1beta1
24      Annotations:
25        ...
26  ...
27  rbac:
28    install: false
29      ...
```

Everything we need to accomplish our new requirements is available through the values. Some of them are already filled with defaults, while others are commented. When we look at all those values, it becomes clear that it would be unpractical to try to re-define them all through --set arguments. We'll use --values instead. It will allow us to specify the values in a file.

I already prepared a YAML file with the values that will fulfill our requirements, so let's take a quick look at them.

```
1  cat helm/jenkins-values.yml
```

The output is as follows.

```
1  Master:
2    ImageTag: "2.116-alpine"
3    Cpu: "500m"
4    Memory: "500Mi"
5    ServiceType: ClusterIP
6    ServiceAnnotations:
7      service.beta.kubernetes.io/aws-load-balancer-backend-protocol: http
8    InstallPlugins:
9      - blueocean:1.5.0
10     - credentials:2.1.16
11     - ec2:1.39
```

```
12        - git:3.8.0
13        - git-client:2.7.1
14        - github:1.29.0
15        - kubernetes:1.5.2
16        - pipeline-utility-steps:2.0.2
17        - script-security:1.43
18        - slack:2.3
19        - thinBackup:1.9
20        - workflow-aggregator:2.5
21      Ingress:
22        Annotations:
23          nginx.ingress.kubernetes.io/ssl-redirect: "false"
24          nginx.ingress.kubernetes.io/proxy-body-size: 50m
25          nginx.ingress.kubernetes.io/proxy-request-buffering: "off"
26          ingress.kubernetes.io/ssl-redirect: "false"
27          ingress.kubernetes.io/proxy-body-size: 50m
28          ingress.kubernetes.io/proxy-request-buffering: "off"
29      HostName: jenkins.acme.com
30    rbac:
31      install: true
```

As you can see, the variables in that file follow the same format as those we output through the `helm inspect values` command. The only difference is in values, and the fact that `helm/jenkins-values.yml` contains only those that we are planning to change.

We defined that the `ImageTag` should be fixed to `2.116-alpine`.

We specified that our Jenkins master will need half a CPU and 500 MB RAM. The default values of 0.2 CPU and 256 MB RAM are probably not enough. What we set is also low, but since we're not going to run any serious load (at least not yet), what we re-defined should be enough.

The service was changed to `ClusterIP` to better accommodate Ingress resource we're defining further down.

If you are not using AWS, you can ignore `ServiceAnnotations`. They're telling ELB to use HTTP protocol.

Further down, we are defining the plugins we'll use throughout the book. Their usefulness will become evident in the next chapters.

The values in the `Ingress` section are defining the annotations that tell Ingress not to redirect HTTP requests to HTTPS (we don't have SSL certificates), as well as a few other less important options. We set both the old style (`ingress.kubernetes.io`) and the new style (`nginx.ingress.kubernetes.io`) of defining NGINX Ingress. That way it'll work no matter which Ingress version you're using. The `HostName` is set to a value that apparently does not exist. I could not know in advance what will be your hostname, so we'll overwrite it later on.

Finally, we set `rbac.install` to `true` so that the Chart knows that it should set the proper permissions.

Having all those variables defined at once might be a bit overwhelming. You might want to go through the Jenkins Chart documentation[79] for more info. In some cases, documentation alone is not enough, and I often end up going through the files that form the chart. You'll get a grip on them with time. For now, the important thing to observe is that we can re-define any number of variables through a YAML file.

Let's install the Chart with those variables.

```
1  helm install stable/jenkins \
2      --name jenkins \
3      --namespace jenkins \
4      --values helm/jenkins-values.yml \
5      --set Master.HostName=$HOST
```

We used the `--values` argument to pass the contents of the `helm/jenkins-values.yml`. Since we had to overwrite the `HostName`, we used `--set`. If the same value is defined through `--values` and `--set`, the latter always takes precedence.

 A note to minishift users

The values define Ingress which does not exist in your cluster. If we'd create a set of values specific to OpenShift, we would not define Ingress. However, since those values are supposed to work in any Kubernetes cluster, we left them intact. Given that Ingress controller does not exist, Ingress resources will have no effect, so it's safe to leave those values.

Next, we'll wait for `jenkins` Deployment to roll out and open its UI in a browser.

```
1  kubectl -n jenkins \
2      rollout status deployment jenkins
3
4  open "http://$HOST"
```

The fact that we opened Jenkins through a domain defined as Ingress (or Route in case of OpenShift) tells us that the values were indeed used. We can double check those currently defined for the installed Chart with the command that follows.

```
1  helm get values jenkins
```

The output is as follows.

---

[79]https://hub.kubeapps.com/charts/stable/jenkins

```
1   Master:
2     Cpu: 500m
3     HostName: jenkins.18.220.212.56.nip.io
4     ImageTag: 2.116-alpine
5     Ingress:
6       Annotations:
7         ingress.kubernetes.io/proxy-body-size: 50m
8         ingress.kubernetes.io/proxy-request-buffering: "off"
9         ingress.kubernetes.io/ssl-redirect: "false"
10        nginx.ingress.kubernetes.io/proxy-body-size: 50m
11        nginx.ingress.kubernetes.io/proxy-request-buffering: "off"
12        nginx.ingress.kubernetes.io/ssl-redirect: "false"
13    InstallPlugins:
14    - blueocean:1.5.0
15    - credentials:2.1.16
16    - ec2:1.39
17    - git:3.8.0
18    - git-client:2.7.1
19    - github:1.29.0
20    - kubernetes:1.5.2
21    - pipeline-utility-steps:2.0.2
22    - script-security:1.43
23    - slack:2.3
24    - thinBackup:1.9
25    - workflow-aggregator:2.5
26    Memory: 500Mi
27    ServiceAnnotations:
28      service.beta.kubernetes.io/aws-load-balancer-backend-protocol: http
29    ServiceType: ClusterIP
30  rbac:
31    install: true
```

Even though the order is slightly different, we can easily confirm that the values are the same as those we defined in `helm/jenkins-values.yml`. The exception is the `HostName` which was overwritten through the `--set` argument.

Now that we explored how to use Helm to deploy publicly available Charts, we'll turn our attention towards development. Can we leverage the power behind Charts for our applications?

Before we proceed, please delete the Chart we installed as well as the `jenkins` Namespace.

```
1  helm delete jenkins --purge
2
3  kubectl delete ns jenkins
```

Creating Helm Charts

Our next goal is to create a Chart for the *go-demo-3* application. We'll use the fork you created in the previous chapter.

First, we'll move into the fork's directory.

```
1  cd ../go-demo-3
```

To be on the safe side, we'll push the changes you might have made in the previous chapter and then we'll sync your fork with the upstream repository. That way we'll guarantee that you have all the changes I might have made.

You probably already know how to push your changes and how to sync with the upstream repository. In case you don't, the commands are as follows.

```
1  git add .
2
3  git commit -m \
4      "Defining Continuous Deployment chapter"
5
6  git push
7
8  git remote add upstream \
9      https://github.com/vfarcic/go-demo-3.git
10
11 git fetch upstream
12
13 git checkout master
14
15 git merge upstream/master
```

We pushed the changes we made in the previous chapter, we fetched the upstream repository *vfarcic/go-demo-3*, and we merged the latest code from it. Now we are ready to create our first Chart.

Even though we could create a Chart from scratch by creating a specific folder structure and the required files, we'll take a shortcut and create a sample Chart that can be modified later to suit our needs.

We won't start with a Chart for the *go-demo-3* application. Instead, we'll create a creatively named Chart *my-app* that we'll use to get a basic understanding of the commands we can use to create and manage our Charts. Once we're familiar with the process, we'll switch to *go-demo-3*.

Here we go.

```
1  helm create my-app
2
3  ls -1 my-app
```

The first command created a Chart named *my-app*, and the second listed the files and the directories that form the new Chart.

The output of the latter command is as follows.

```
1  Chart.yaml
2  charts
3  templates
4  values.yaml
```

We will not go into the details behind each of those files and directories just yet. For now, just note that a Chart consists of files and directories that follow certain naming conventions.

If our Chart has dependencies, we could download them with the dependency update command.

```
1  helm dependency update my-app
```

The output shows that no requirements were found in .../go-demo-3/my-app/charts. That makes sense because we did not yet declare any dependencies. For now, just remember that they can be downloaded or updated.

Once we're done with defining the Chart of an application, we can package it.

```
1  helm package my-app
```

We can see from the output that Helm successfully packaged chart and saved it to: .../go-demo-3/my-app-0.1.0.tgz. We do not yet have a repository for our Charts. We'll work on that in the next chapter.

If we are unsure whether we made a mistake in our Chart, we can validate it by executing lint command.

```
1  helm lint my-app
```

The output is as follows.

```
1  ==> Linting my-app
2  [INFO] Chart.yaml: icon is recommended
3
4  1 chart(s) linted, no failures
```

We can see that our Chart contains no failures, at least not those based on syntax. That should come as no surprise since we did not even modify the sample Chart Helm created for us.

Charts can be installed using a Chart repository (e.g., stable/jenkins), a local Chart archive (e.g., my-app-0.1.0.tgz), an unpacked Chart directory (e.g., my-app), or a full URL. So far we used Chart repository to install Jenkins. We'll switch to the local archive option to install my-app.

```
1  helm install ./my-app-0.1.0.tgz \
2      --name my-app
```

The output is as follows.

```
1  NAME:   my-app
2  LAST DEPLOYED: Thu May 24 13:43:17 2018
3  NAMESPACE: default
4  STATUS: DEPLOYED
5
6  RESOURCES:
7  ==> v1/Service
8  NAME    TYPE        CLUSTER-IP      EXTERNAL-IP PORT(S) AGE
9  my-app ClusterIP 100.65.227.236 <none>       80/TCP  1s
10
11 ==> v1beta2/Deployment
12 NAME    DESIRED CURRENT UP-TO-DATE AVAILABLE AGE
13 my-app 1       1       1          0         1s
14
15 ==> v1/Pod(related)
16 NAME                       READY STATUS          RESTARTS AGE
17 my-app-7f4d66bf86-dns28 0/1   ContainerCreating 0        1s
18
19
20 NOTES:
21 1. Get the application URL by running these commands:
22   export POD_NAME=$(kubectl get pods --namespace default -l "app=my-app,release=my-a\
23 pp" -o jsonpath="{.items[0].metadata.name}")
24   echo "Visit http://127.0.0.1:8080 to use your application"
25   kubectl port-forward $POD_NAME 8080:80
```

The sample application is a straightforward one with a Service and a Deployment. There's not much to say about it. We used it only to explore the basic commands for creating and managing Charts. We'll delete everything we did and start over with a more serious example.

```
1  helm delete my-app --purge
2
3  rm -rf my-app
4
5  rm -rf my-app-0.1.0.tgz
```

We deleted the Chart from the cluster, as well as the local directory and the archive we created earlier. The time has come to apply the knowledge we obtained and explore the format of the files that constitute a Chart. We'll switch to the *go-demo-3* application next.

Exploring Files That Constitute A Chart

I prepared a Chart that defines the *go-demo-3* application. We'll use it to get familiar with writing Charts. Even if we choose to use Helm only for third-party applications, familiarity with Chart files is a must since we might have to look at them to better understand the application we want to install.

The files are located in `helm/go-demo-3` directory inside the repository. Let's take a look at what we have.

```
1  ls -1 helm/go-demo-3
```

The output is as follows.

```
1  Chart.yaml
2  LICENSE
3  README.md
4  templates
5  values.yaml
```

A chart is organized as a collection of files inside a directory. The directory name is the name of the Chart (without versioning information). So, a Chart that describes *go-demo-3* is stored in the directory with the same name.

The first file we'll explore is *Chart.yml*. It is a mandatory file with a combination of compulsory and optional fields.

Let's take a closer look.

```
1  cat helm/go-demo-3/Chart.yaml
```

The output is as follows.

```
1  name: go-demo-3
2  version: 0.0.1
3  apiVersion: v1
4  description: A silly demo based on API written in Go and MongoDB
5  keywords:
6  - api
7  - backend
8  - go
9  - database
10 - mongodb
11 home: http://www.devopstoolkitseries.com/
12 sources:
13 - https://github.com/vfarcic/go-demo-3
14 maintainers:
15 - name: Viktor Farcic
16   email: viktor@farcic.com
```

The name, version, and apiVersion are mandatory fields. All the others are optional.

Even though most of the fields should be self-explanatory, we'll go through each of them just in case.

The name is the name of the Chart, and the version is the version. That's obvious, isn't it? The critical thing to note is that versions must follow SemVer 2[80] standard. The full identification of a Chart package in a repository is always a combination of a name and a version. If we package this Chart, its name would be *go-demo-3-0.0.1.tgz*. The apiVersion is the version of the Helm API and, at this moment, the only supported value is v1.

The rest of the fields are mostly informational. You should be able to understand their meaning so I won't bother you with lengthy explanations.

The next in line is the LICENSE file.

```
1  cat helm/go-demo-3/LICENSE
```

The first few lines of the output are as follows.

---

[80]http://semver.org/

```
1  The MIT License (MIT)
2
3  Copyright (c) 2018 Viktor Farcic
4
5  Permission is hereby granted, free ...
```

The *go-demo-3* application is licensed as MIT. It's up to you to decide which license you'll use, if any.

README.md is used to describe the application.

```
1  cat helm/go-demo-3/README.md
```

The output is as follows.

```
1  This is just a silly demo.
```

I was too lazy to write a proper description. You shouldn't be. As a rule of thumb, README.md should contain a description of the application, a list of the pre-requisites and the requirements, a description of the options available through values.yaml, and anything else you might deem important. As the extension suggests, it should be written in Markdown format.

Now we are getting to the critical part.

The values that can be used to customize the installation are defined in values.yaml.

```
1  cat helm/go-demo-3/values.yaml
```

The output is as follows.

```
1  replicaCount: 3
2  dbReplicaCount: 3
3  image:
4    tag: latest
5    dbTag: 3.3
6  ingress:
7    enabled: true
8    host: acme.com
9  service:
10   # Change to NodePort if ingress.enable=false
11   type: ClusterIP
12 rbac:
13   enabled: true
14 resources:
```

```
15    limits:
16      cpu: 0.2
17      memory: 20Mi
18    requests:
19      cpu: 0.1
20      memory: 10Mi
21  dbResources:
22    limits:
23      memory: "200Mi"
24      cpu: 0.2
25    requests:
26      memory: "100Mi"
27      cpu: 0.1
28  dbPersistence:
29    ## If defined, storageClassName: <storageClass>
30    ## If set to "-", storageClassName: "", which disables dynamic provisioning
31    ## If undefined (the default) or set to null, no storageClassName spec is
32    ##   set, choosing the default provisioner.  (gp2 on AWS, standard on
33    ##   GKE, AWS & OpenStack)
34    ##
35    # storageClass: "-"
36    accessMode: ReadWriteOnce
37    size: 2Gi
```

As you can see, all the things that may vary from one *go-demo-3* installation to another are defined here. We can set how many replicas should be deployed for both the API and the DB. Tags of both can be changed as well. We can disable Ingress and change the host. We can change the type of the Service or disable RBAC. The resources are split into two groups, so that the API and the DB can be controlled separately. Finally, we can change database persistence by specifying the storageClass, the accessMode, or the size.

I should have described those values in more detail in README.md, but, as I already admitted, I was too lazy to do that. The alternative explanation of the lack of proper README is that we'll go through the YAML files where those values are used, and everything will become much more apparent.

The important thing to note is that the values defined in that file are defaults that are used only if we do not overwrite them during the installation through --set or --values arguments.

The files that define all the resources are in the templates directory.

```
1  ls -1 helm/go-demo-3/templates/
```

The output is as follows.

```
1  NOTES.txt
2  _helpers.tpl
3  deployment.yaml
4  ing.yaml
5  rbac.yaml
6  sts.yaml
7  svc.yaml
```

The templates are written in Go template language[81] extended with add-on functions from Sprig library[82] and a few others specific to Helm. Don't worry if you are new to Go. You will not need to learn it. For most use-cases, a few templating rules are more than enough for most of the use-cases. With time, you might decide to "go crazy" and learn everything templating offers. That time is not today.

When Helm renders the Chart, it'll pass all the files in the templates directory through its templating engine.

Let's take a look at the NOTES.txt file.

```
1  cat helm/go-demo-3/templates/NOTES.txt
```

The output is as follows.

```
1  1. Wait until the applicaiton is rolled out:
2    kubectl -n {{ .Release.Namespace }} rollout status deployment {{ template "helm.fu\
3  llname" . }}
4
5  2. Test the application by running these commands:
6  {{- if .Values.ingress.enabled }}
7    curl http://{{ .Values.ingress.host }}/demo/hello
8  {{- else if contains "NodePort" .Values.service.type }}
9    export PORT=$(kubectl -n {{ .Release.Namespace }} get svc {{ template "helm.fullna\
10  me" . }} -o jsonpath="{.spec.ports[0].nodePort}")
11
12    # If you are running Docker for Mac/Windows
13    export ADDR=localhost
14
15    # If you are running minikube
16    export ADDR=$(minikube ip)
17
18    # If you are running anything else
19    export ADDR=$(kubectl -n {{ .Release.Namespace }} get nodes -o jsonpath="{.items[0\
```

---

[81]https://golang.org/pkg/text/template/
[82]https://github.com/Masterminds/sprig

```
20  ].status.addresses[0].address}")
21
22    curl http://$NODE_IP:$PORT/demo/hello
23  {{- else }}
24    If the application is running in OpenShift, please create a Route to enable access.
25
26    For everyone else, you set ingress.enabled=false and service.type is not set to No\
27  dePort. The application cannot be accessed from outside the cluster.
28  {{- end }}
```

The content of the NOTES.txt file will be printed after the installation or upgrade. You already saw a similar one in action when we installed Jenkins. The instructions we received how to open it and how to retrieve the password came from the NOTES.txt file stored in Jenkins Chart.

That file is our first direct contact with Helm templating. You'll notice that parts of it are inside if/else blocks. If we take a look at the second bullet, we can deduce that one set of instructions will be printed if ingress is enabled, another if the type of the Service is NodePort, and yet another if neither of the first two conditions is met.

Template snippets are always inside double curly braces (e.g., {{ and }}). Inside them can be (often simple) logic like an if statement, as well as predefined and custom made function. An example of a custom made function is {{ template "helm.fullname" . }}. It is defined in _helpers.tpl file which we'll explore soon.

Variables always start with a dot (.). Those coming from the values.yaml file are always prefixed with .Values. An example is .Values.ingress.host that defines the host that will be configured in our Ingress resource.

Helm also provides a set of pre-defined variables prefixed with .Release, .Chart, .Files, and .Capabilities. As an example, near the top of the NOTES.txt file is {{ .Release.Namespace }} snippet that will get converted to the Namespace into which we decided to install our Chart.

The full list of the pre-defined values is as follows (a copy of the official documentation).

- Release.Name: The name of the release (not the Chart)
- Release.Time: The time the chart release was last updated. This will match the Last Released time on a Release object.
- Release.Namespace: The Namespace the Chart was released to.
- Release.Service: The service that conducted the release. Usually this is Tiller.
- Release.IsUpgrade: This is set to true if the current operation is an upgrade or rollback.
- Release.IsInstall: This is set to true if the current operation is an install.
- Release.Revision: The revision number. It begins at 1, and increments with each helm upgrade.
- Chart: The contents of the Chart.yaml. Thus, the Chart version is obtainable as Chart.Version and the maintainers are in Chart.Maintainers.

- `Files`: A map-like object containing all non-special files in the Chart. This will not give you access to templates, but will give you access to additional files that are present (unless they are excluded using .helmignore). Files can be accessed using `{{index .Files "file.name"}}` or using the `{{.Files.Get name}}` or `{{.Files.GetString name}}` functions. You can also access the contents of the file as `[]byte` using `{{.Files.GetBytes}}`
- `Capabilities`: A map-like object that contains information about the versions of Kubernetes (`{{.Capabilities.KubeVersion}}`, Tiller (`{{.Capabilities.TillerVersion}}`), and the supported Kubernetes API versions (`{{.Capabilities.APIVersions.Has "batch/v1"}}`)

You'll also notice that our `if`, `else if`, `else`, and `end` statements start with a dash (-). That's the Go template way of specifying that we want all empty space before the statement (when - is on the left) or after the statement (when - is on the right) to be removed.

There's much more to Go templating that what we just explored. I'll comment on other use-cases as they come. For now, this should be enough to get you going. You are free to consult template package documentation[83] for more info. For now, the critical thing to note is that we have the NOTES.txt file that will provide useful post-installation information to those who will use our Chart.

I mentioned _helpers.tpl as the source of custom functions and variables. Let's take a look at it.

```
1  cat helm/go-demo-3/templates/_helpers.tpl
```

The output is as follows.

```
1   {{/* vim: set filetype=mustache: */}}
2   {{/*
3   Expand the name of the chart.
4   */}}
5   {{- define "helm.name" -}}
6   {{- default .Chart.Name .Values.nameOverride | trunc 63 | trimSuffix "-" -}}
7   {{- end -}}
8
9   {{/*
10  Create a default fully qualified app name.
11  We truncate at 63 chars because some Kubernetes name fields are limited to this (by \
12  the DNS naming spec).
13  If release name contains chart name it will be used as a full name.
14  */}}
15  {{- define "helm.fullname" -}}
16  {{- $name := default .Chart.Name .Values.nameOverride -}}
17  {{- if contains $name .Release.Name -}}
18  {{- .Release.Name | trunc 63 | trimSuffix "-" -}}
```

---

[83]https://golang.org/pkg/text/template/

```
19   {{- else -}}
20   {{- printf "%s-%s" .Release.Name $name | trunc 63 | trimSuffix "-" -}}
21   {{- end -}}
22   {{- end -}}
```

That file is the exact copy of the _helpers.tpl file that was created with the helm create command that generated a sample Chart. You can extend it with your own functions. I didn't. I kept it as-is. It consists of two functions with comments that describe them. The first (helm.name) returns the name of the chart trimmed to 63 characters which is the limitation for the size of some of the Kubernetes fields. The second function (helm.fullname) returns fully qualified name of the application. If you go back to the NOTES.txt file, you'll notice that we are using helm.fullname in a few occasions. Later on, you'll see that we'll use it in quite a few other places.

Now that NOTES.txt and _helpers.tpl are out of the way, we can take a look at the first template that defines one of the Kubernetes resources.

```
1   cat helm/go-demo-3/templates/deployment.yaml
```

The output is as follows.

```
1   apiVersion: apps/v1beta2
2   kind: Deployment
3   metadata:
4     name: {{ template "helm.fullname" . }}
5     labels:
6       app: {{ template "helm.name" . }}
7       chart: {{ .Chart.Name }}-{{ .Chart.Version | replace "+" "_" }}
8       release: {{ .Release.Name }}
9       heritage: {{ .Release.Service }}
10  spec:
11    replicas: {{ .Values.replicaCount }}
12    selector:
13      matchLabels:
14        app: {{ template "helm.name" . }}
15        release: {{ .Release.Name }}
16    template:
17      metadata:
18        labels:
19          app: {{ template "helm.name" . }}
20          release: {{ .Release.Name }}
21      spec:
22        containers:
23          - name: api
```

```
24          image: "vfarcic/go-demo-3:{{ .Values.image.tag }}"
25          env:
26          - name: DB
27            value: {{ template "helm.fullname" . }}-db
28          readinessProbe:
29            httpGet:
30              path: /demo/hello
31              port: 8080
32            periodSeconds: 1
33          livenessProbe:
34            httpGet:
35              path: /demo/hello
36              port: 8080
37          resources:
38 {{ toYaml .Values.resources | indent 10 }}
```

That file defines the Deployment of the *go-demo-3* API. The first thing I did was to copy the definition from the YAML file we used in the previous chapters. Afterwards, I replaced parts of it with functions and variables. The name, for example, is now {{ template "helm.fullname" . }}, which guarantees that this Deployment will have a unique name. The rest of the file follows the same logic. Some things are using pre-defined values like {{ .Chart.Name }} and {{ .Release.Name }}, while others are using those from the values.yaml. An example of the latter is {{ .Values.replicaCount }}.

The last line contains a syntax we haven't seen before. {{ toYaml .Values.resources | indent 10 }} will take all the entries from the resources field in the values.yaml, and convert them to YAML format. Since the final YAML needs to be correctly indented, we piped the output to indent 10. Since the resources: section of deployment.yaml is indented by eight spaces, indenting the entries from resources in values.yaml by ten will put them just two spaces inside it.

Let's take a look at one more template.

```
1 cat helm/go-demo-3/templates/ing.yaml
```

The output is as follows.

```
1   {{- if .Values.ingress.enabled -}}
2   {{- $serviceName := include "helm.fullname" . -}}
3   apiVersion: extensions/v1beta1
4   kind: Ingress
5   metadata:
6     name: {{ template "helm.fullname" . }}
7     labels:
8       app: {{ template "helm.name" . }}
9       chart: {{ .Chart.Name }}-{{ .Chart.Version | replace "+" "_" }}
10      release: {{ .Release.Name }}
11      heritage: {{ .Release.Service }}
12    annotations:
13      ingress.kubernetes.io/ssl-redirect: "false"
14      nginx.ingress.kubernetes.io/ssl-redirect: "false"
15  spec:
16    rules:
17    - http:
18        paths:
19        - backend:
20            serviceName: {{ $serviceName }}
21            servicePort: 8080
22      host: {{ .Values.ingress.host }}
23  {{- end -}}
```

That YAML defines the Ingress resource that makes the API Deployment accessible through its Service. Most of the values are the same as in the Deployment. There's only one difference worthwhile commenting.

The whole YAML is enveloped in the `{{- if .Values.ingress.enabled -}}` statement. The resource will be installed only if `ingress.enabled` value is set to `true`. Since that is already the default value in `values.yaml`, we'll have to explicitly disable it if we do not want Ingress.

Feel free to explore the rest of the templates. They are following the same logic as the two we just described.

There's one potentially significant file we did not define. We have not created `requirements.yaml` for *go-demo-3*. We did not need any. We will use it though in one of the next chapters, so I'll save the explanation for later.

Now that we went through the files that constitute the *go-demo-3* Chart, we should `lint` it to confirm that the format does not contain any apparent issues.

```
1   helm lint helm/go-demo-3
```

The output is as follows.

```
1  ==> Linting helm/go-demo-3
2  [INFO] Chart.yaml: icon is recommended
3
4  1 chart(s) linted, no failures
```

If we ignore the complaint that the icon is not defined, our Chart seems to be defined correctly, and we can create a package.

```
1  helm package helm/go-demo-3 -d helm
```

The output is as follows.

```
1  Successfully packaged chart and saved it to: helm/go-demo-3-0.0.1.tgz
```

The -d argument is new. It specified that we want to create a package in helm directory.

We will not use the package just yet. For now, I wanted to make sure that you remember that we can create it.

Upgrading Charts

We are about to install the *go-demo-3* Chart. You should already be familiar with the commands, so you can consider this as an exercise that aims to solidify what you already learned. There will be one difference when compared to the commands we executed earlier. It'll prove to be a simple, and yet an important one for our continuous deployment processes.

We'll start by inspecting the values.

```
1  helm inspect values helm/go-demo-3
```

The output is as follows.

```
1  replicaCount: 3
2  dbReplicaCount: 3
3  image:
4    tag: latest
5    dbTag: 3.3
6  ingress:
7    enabled: true
8    host: acme.com
9  route:
10   enabled: true
```

```
11  service:
12    # Change to NodePort if ingress.enable=false
13    type: ClusterIP
14  rbac:
15    enabled: true
16  resources:
17    limits:
18      cpu: 0.2
19      memory: 20Mi
20    requests:
21      cpu: 0.1
22      memory: 10Mi
23  dbResources:
24    limits:
25      memory: "200Mi"
26      cpu: 0.2
27    requests:
28      memory: "100Mi"
29      cpu: 0.1
30  dbPersistence:
31    ## If defined, storageClassName: <storageClass>
32    ## If set to "-", storageClassName: "", which disables dynamic provisioning
33    ## If undefined (the default) or set to null, no storageClassName spec is
34    ##   set, choosing the default provisioner.  (gp2 on AWS, standard on
35    ##   GKE, AWS & OpenStack)
36    ##
37    # storageClass: "-"
38    accessMode: ReadWriteOnce
39    size: 2Gi
```

We are almost ready to install the application. The only thing we're missing is the host we'll use for the application.

You'll find two commands below. Please execute only one of those depending on your Kubernetes flavor.

If you are **NOT** using **minishift**, please execute the command that follows.

```
1  HOST="go-demo-3.$LB_IP.nip.io"
```

If you are using minishift, you can retrieve the host with the command that follows.

```
1  HOST="go-demo-3-go-demo-3.$(minishift ip).nip.io"
```

No matter how you retrieved the host, we'll output it so that we can confirm that it looks OK.

```
1  echo $HOST
```

In my case, the output is as follows.

```
1  go-demo-3.192.168.99.100.nip.io
```

Now we are finally ready to install the Chart. However, we won't use `helm install` as before. We'll use `upgrade` instead.

```
1  helm upgrade -i \
2      go-demo-3 helm/go-demo-3 \
3      --namespace go-demo-3 \
4      --set image.tag=1.0 \
5      --set ingress.host=$HOST \
6      --reuse-values
```

The reason we are using `helm upgrade` this time lies in the fact that we are practicing the commands we hope to use inside our CDP processes. Given that we want to use the same process no matter whether it's the first release (install) or those that follow (upgrade). It would be silly to have `if/else` statements that would determine whether it is the first release and thus execute the install, or to go with an upgrade. We are going with a much simpler solution. We will always upgrade the Chart. The trick is in the `-i` argument that can be translated to "install unless a release by the same name doesn't already exist."

The next two arguments are the name of the Chart (`go-demo-3`) and the path to the Chart (`helm/go-demo-3`). By using the path to the directory with the Chart, we are experiencing yet another way to supply the Chart files. In the next chapter will switch to using `tgz` packages.

The rest of the arguments are making sure that the correct tag is used (`1.0`), that Ingress is using the desired host, and that the values that might have been used in the previous upgrades are still the same (`--reuse-values`).

If this command is used in the continuous deployment processes, we would need to set the tag explicitly through the `--set` argument to ensure that the correct image is used. The host, on the other hand, is static and unlikely to change often (if ever). We would be better of defining it in `values.yaml`. However, since I could not predict what will be your host, we had to define it as the `--set` argument.

Please note that minishift does not support Ingress (at least not by default). So, it was created, but it has no effect. I thought that it is a better option than to use different commands for OpenShift than for the rest of the flavors. If minishift is your choice, feel free to add `--set ingress.enable=false` to the previous command.

The output of the `upgrade` is the same as if we executed `install` (resources are removed for brevity).

```
1  NAME:   go-demo-3
2  LAST DEPLOYED: Fri May 25 14:40:31 2018
3  NAMESPACE: go-demo-3
4  STATUS: DEPLOYED
5
6  ...
7
8  NOTES:
9  1. Wait until the application is rolled out:
10    kubectl -n go-demo-3 rollout status deployment go-demo-3
11
12  2. Test the application by running these commands:
13    curl http://go-demo-3.18.222.53.124.nip.io/demo/hello
```

 ## A note to minishift users

We'll need to create a Route separately from the Helm Chart, just as we did with Jenkins. Please execute the command that follows.

```
oc -n go-demo-3 create route edge --service go-demo-3 --insecure-policy Allow
```

We'll wait until the Deployment rolls out before proceeding.

```
1  kubectl -n go-demo-3 \
2      rollout status deployment go-demo-3
```

The output is as follows.

```
1  Waiting for rollout to finish: 0 of 3 updated replicas are available...
2  Waiting for rollout to finish: 1 of 3 updated replicas are available...
3  Waiting for rollout to finish: 2 of 3 updated replicas are available...
4  deployment "go-demo-3" successfully rolled out
```

Now we can confirm that the application is indeed working by sending a curl request.

```
1  curl http://$HOST/demo/hello
```

The output should display the familiar hello, world! message, thus confirming that the application is indeed running and that it is accessible through the host we defined in Ingress (or Route in case of minishift).

Let's imagine that some time passed since we installed the first release, that someone pushed a change to the master branch, that we already run all our tests, that we built a new image, and that we pushed it to Docker Hub. In that hypothetical situation, our next step would be to execute another helm upgrade.

```
1 helm upgrade -i \
2     go-demo-3 helm/go-demo-3 \
3     --namespace go-demo-3 \
4     --set image.tag=2.0 \
5     --reuse-values
```

When compared with the previous command, the difference is in the tag. This time we set it to 2.0. We also removed --set ingress.host=$HOST argument. Since we have --reuse-values, all those used in the previous release will be maintained.

There's probably no need to further validations (e.g., wait for it to roll out and send a curl request). All that's left is to remove the Chart and delete the Namespace. We're done with the hands-on exercises.

```
1 helm delete go-demo-3 --purge
2
3 kubectl delete ns go-demo-3
```

Helm vs. OpenShift Templates

I could give you a lengthy comparison between Helm and OpenShift templates. I won't do that. The reason is simple. Helm is the de-facto standard for installing applications. It's the most widely used, and its adoption is going through the roof. Among the similar tools, it has the biggest community, it has the most applications available, and it is becoming adopted by more software vendors than any other solution. The exception is RedHat. They created OpenShift templates long before Helm came into being. Helm borrowed many of its concepts, improved them, and added a few additional features. When we add to that the fact that OpenShift templates work only on OpenShift, the decision which one to use is pretty straightforward. Helm wins, unless you chose OpenShift as your Kubernetes flavor. In that case, the choice is harder to make. On the one hand, Routes and a few other OpenShift-specific types of resources cannot be defined (easily) in Helm. On the other hand, it is likely that OpenShift will switch to Helm at some moment. So, you might just as well jump into Helm right away.

I must give a big thumbs up to RedHat for paving the way towards some of the Kubernetes resources that are in use today. They created Routes when Ingress did not exist. They developed OpenShift templates before Helm was created. Both Ingress and Helm were heavily influenced by their counterparts in OpenShift. There are quite a few other similar examples.

The problem is that RedHat does not want to let go of the things they pioneered. They stick with Routes, even though Ingress become standard. If Routes provide more features than, let's say, nginx Ingress controller, they could still maintain them as OpenShift Ingress (or whatever would be the name). Routes are not the only example. They continue forcing OpenShift templates, even though it's clear that Helm is the de-facto standard. By not switching to the standards that they pioneered, they are making their platform incompatible with others. In the previous chapters, we experienced the pain Routes cause when trying to define YAML files that should work on all other Kubernetes flavors. Now we experienced the same problem with Helm.

If you chose OpenShift, it's up to you to decide whether to use Helm or OpenShift templates. Both choices have pros and cons. Personally, one of the things that attract me the most with Kubernetes is the promise that our applications can run on any hosting solution and on any Kubernetes flavor. RedHat is breaking that promise. It's not that I don't expect different solutions to come up with new things that distinguish them from the competition. I do. OpenShift has quite a few of those. But, it also has features that have equally good or better equivalents that are part of Kubernetes core or widely accepted by the community. Helm is one of those that are better than their counterpart in OpenShift.

We'll continue using Helm throughout the rest of the book. If you do choose to stick with OpenShift templates, you'll have to do a few modifications to the examples. The good news is that those changes should be relatively easy to make. I believe that you won't have a problem adapting.

What Now?

We have a couple of problems left to solve. We did not yet figure out how to store the Helm charts in a way that they can be easily retrieved and used by others. We'll tackle that issue in the next chapter.

I suggest you take a rest. You deserve it. If you do feel that way, please destroy the cluster. Otherwise, jump to the next chapter right away. The choice is yours.

Distributing Kubernetes Applications

 Being able to package applications is of no use unless we can distribute them. A Kubernetes application is a combination of one or more container images and YAML files that describe them. If we are to distribute our applications, we need to store both container images and YAML definitions in repositories.

We are already storing our images in Docker Hub[84]. We could have chosen a different container registry but, since Docker Hub is so convenient, we'll continue using it throughout the book. Even though that might not be the best choice, if we move the discussion about repositories for container images out of the way, we can focus on YAML files or, to be more concrete, Helm Charts.

At this point, you might be thinking that being able to run Charts located on your laptop is an excellent way to go. All you have to do is check out the code of an application hoping that the Chart is there and execute a command like `helm upgrade -i go-demo-3 helm/go-demo-3`. You'd be correct that's the easiest way to install or upgrade an application that you are developing. However, your application is not the only one you'll be installing.

If you are a developer, you will almost certainly want to run many applications on your laptop. If you need to check whether your app integrates with those developed by your colleagues, you'll want to run theirs as well. You can continue down the same path of checking out their code and installing local Charts. But that already starts being tedious. You'll need to know which repositories they're using, and check out more code than you truly need. Wouldn't it be better to install your colleagues' applications in the same way as installing publicly available third-party applications? Wouldn't it be great if you could execute something like `helm search my-company-repo/`, get the list of all the apps created in your organization, and install those you need? We are already using the same approach with container images (e.g., `docker image pull`), with Linux packages (`apt install vim`), and many other packages and distributions. Why not do the same with Helm Charts? Why would we restrict the ability to pull a definition of an application only to those created by third-parties? We should be able to distribute our apps in the same way.

Helm Charts are still very young. The project just started, and there aren't many repositories to choose. Today (June 2018), ChartMuseum[85] is one of the few, if not the only one available. So, picking the right solution is very straightforward. When there aren't many choices, the selection process is easy.

In this chapter, we'll explore Helm repositories and how we can leverage them to distribute our Charts across an organization, or even publish them to a broader audience if we are in the business of providing software to the more general public.

---

[84]https://hub.docker.com/
[85]https://github.com/kubernetes-helm/chartmuseum

As always, we need to start from somewhere, and that is a Kubernetes cluster.

Creating A Cluster And Retrieving Its IP

You know the drill. Create a new cluster or reuse the one you dedicated to the exercises.

First, we'll go to the local copy of the *vfarcic/k8s-specs* repository and make sure that we have the latest revision. Who knows? I might have changed something since you read the last chapter.

 All the commands from this chapter are available in the 05-chart-museum.sh[86] Gist.

```
1  cd k8s-specs
2
3  git pull
```

The requirements for the cluster are now slightly different. We'll need **Helm server (tiller)**. On top of that, if you are a **minishift** user, you'll need a cluster with 4GB RAM.

For your convenience, the new Gists and the specs are available.

- docker4mac-helm.sh[87]: **Docker for Mac** with 3 CPUs, 3 GB RAM, with **nginx Ingress**, and with **tiller**.
- minikube-helm.sh[88]: **minikube** with 3 CPUs, 3 GB RAM, with `ingress`, `storage-provisioner`, and `default-storageclass` addons enabled, and with **tiller**.
- kops-helm.sh[89]: **kops in AWS** with 3 t2.small masters and 2 t2.medium nodes spread in three availability zones, with **nginx Ingress**, and with **tiller**. The Gist assumes that the prerequisites are set through Appendix B.
- minishift-helm.sh[90]: **minishift** with 3 CPUs, 3 GB RAM, with version 1.16+, and with **tiller**.
- gke-helm.sh[91]: **Google Kubernetes Engine (GKE)** with 3 n1-highcpu-2 (2 CPUs, 1.8 GB RAM) nodes (one in each zone), and with **nginx Ingress** controller running on top of the "standard" one that comes with GKE, and with **tiller**. We'll use nginx Ingress for compatibility with other platforms. Feel free to modify the YAML files and Helm Charts if you prefer NOT to install nginx Ingress.
- eks-helm.sh[92]: **Elastic Kubernetes Service (EKS)** with 2 t2.medium nodes, with **nginx Ingress** controller, with a **default StorageClass**, and with **tiller**.

---

[86]https://gist.github.com/e0657623045b43259fe258a146f05e1a
[87]https://gist.github.com/7e6b068c6d3d56fc53416ac2cd4086e3
[88]https://gist.github.com/728246d8be349ffb52770f72c39e9564
[89]https://gist.github.com/6c1ebd59305fba9eb0102a5a8cea863b
[90]https://gist.github.com/945ab1e68afa9e49f85cec3bc6df4959
[91]https://gist.github.com/1593ed36c4b768a462b1a32d5400649b
[92]https://gist.github.com/6de44c440c0d0facb20b743c079bd12f

Besides creating a cluster, we'll need an IP through which we can access it. The instructions that follow differ from one Kubernetes flavor to another. Please make sure you execute those matching your cluster.

If your cluster is running in **AWS** and if it was created with **kops**, we'll retrieve the IP by digging the hostname of the Elastic Load Balancer (ELB). Please execute the commands that follow.

```
1  LB_HOST=$(kubectl -n kube-ingress \
2      get svc ingress-nginx \
3      -o jsonpath="{.status.loadBalancer.ingress[0].hostname}")
4
5  LB_IP="$(dig +short $LB_HOST \
6      | tail -n 1)"
```

If your cluster is running in **AWS** and if it was created as **EKS**, we'll retrieve the IP by digging the hostname of the Elastic Load Balancer (ELB). Please execute the commands that follow.

```
1  LB_HOST=$(kubectl -n ingress-nginx \
2      get svc ingress-nginx \
3      -o jsonpath="{.status.loadBalancer.ingress[0].hostname}")
4
5  LB_IP="$(dig +short $LB_HOST \
6      | tail -n 1)"
```

If you're using **Docker For Mac or Windows**, the cluster is accessible through localhost. Since we need an IP, we'll use 127.0.0.1 instead. Please execute the command that follows.

```
1  LB_IP="127.0.0.1"
```

Minikube users can retrieve the IP through minikube ip. If you are one of them, please execute the command that follows.

```
1  LB_IP=$(minikube ip)
```

Retrieving IP from **minishift** is similar to minikube. If that's your Kubernetes flavor, please execute the command that follows.

```
1  LB_IP=$(minishift ip)
```

Finally, if you are using **GKE**, the IP we're looking for is available through the ingress-nginx service. Please execute the command that follows.

```
1  LB_IP=$(kubectl -n ingress-nginx \
2      get svc ingress-nginx \
3      -o jsonpath="{.status.loadBalancer.ingress[0].ip}")
```

No matter how you retrieved the IP of your cluster, we'll validate it by echoing the LB_IP variable.

```
1  echo $LB_IP
```

The output will differ from one case to another. In my case, it is 52.15.140.221.

There's only one more thing left before we jump into Chart repositories. We'll merge your fork of the *go-demo-3* code repository with the origin and thus ensure that you are up-to-date with changes I might have made in the meantime.

First, we'll move into the fork's directory.

```
1  cd ../go-demo-3
```

To be on the safe side, we'll push the changes you might have made in the previous chapter, and then we'll sync your fork with the upstream repository. That way, we'll guarantee that you have all the changes I might have made.

You probably already know how to push your changes and how to sync with the upstream repository. In case you don't, the commands are as follows.

```
1  git add .
2
3  git commit -m \
4      "Packaging Kubernetes Applications chapter"
5
6  git push
7
8  git remote add upstream \
9      https://github.com/vfarcic/go-demo-3.git
10
11 git fetch upstream
12
13 git checkout master
14
15 git merge upstream/master
```

We pushed the changes we made in the previous chapter, we fetched the upstream repository *vfarcic/go-demo-3*, and we merged the latest code from it. The only thing left is to go back to the k8s-specs directory.

```
1  cd ../k8s-specs
```

Now we are ready to explore Helm repositories with *ChartMuseum*.

Using ChartMuseum

Just as Docker Registry[93] is a place where we can publish our container images and make them accessible to others, we can use Chart repository to accomplish similar goals with our Charts.

A Chart repository is a location where packaged Charts can be stored and retrieved. We'll use ChartMuseum[94] for that. There aren't many other solutions to choose. We can say that we picked it because there were no alternatives. That will change soon. I'm sure that Helm Charts will become integrated into general purpose repositories. At the time of this writing (June 2018), Charts are already supported by JFrog's Artifactory[95]. You could easily build one yourself if you're adventurous. All you'd need is a way to store index.yaml file that contains all the Charts and an API that could be used to push and retrieve packages. Anything else would be a bonus, not a requirement.

That's it. That's all the explanation you need, except a note that we'll go with the easiest solution. We won't build a Charts repository ourselves, nor we are going to pay for Artifactory. We'll use ChartMuseum.

ChartMuseum is already available in the official Helm repository. We'll add it to your Helm installation just in case you removed it accidentally.

```
1  helm repo add stable \
2      https://kubernetes-charts.storage.googleapis.com
```

You should see the output claiming that "stable" has been added to your repositories.

Next, we'll take a quick look at the values available in chartmuseum.

```
1  helm inspect values stable/chartmuseum
```

The output, limited to the relevant parts, is as follows.

---

[93]https://docs.docker.com/registry/
[94]https://github.com/kubernetes-helm/chartmuseum
[95]https://www.jfrog.com/confluence/display/RTF/Helm+Chart+Repositories

```
1   ...
2   image:
3     repository: chartmuseum/chartmuseum
4     tag: v0.7.0
5     pullPolicy: IfNotPresent
6   env:
7     open:
8       ...
9       DISABLE_API: true
10      ...
11    secret:
12      # username for basic http authentication
13      BASIC_AUTH_USER:
14      # password for basic http authentication
15      BASIC_AUTH_PASS:
16      ...
17  resources: {}
18  #   limits:
19  #     cpu: 100m
20  #     memory: 128Mi
21  #   requests:
22  #     cpu: 80m
23  #     memory: 64Mi
24  ...
25  persistence:
26    enabled: false
27    ...
28  ## Ingress for load balancer
29  ingress:
30    enabled: false
31  ...
32  #   annotations:
33  #     kubernetes.io/ingress.class: nginx
34  #     kubernetes.io/tls-acme: "true"
35
36  ## Chartmuseum Ingress hostnames
37  ## Must be provided if Ingress is enabled
38  ##
39  #   hosts:
40  #     chartmuseum.domain.com:
41  #       - /charts
42  #       - /index.yaml
43  ...
```

We can, and we will change the image tag. We'll try to make that our practice with all installations. We'll always use a specific tag, and leave latest for developers and others who might not be concerned with stability of the system.

By default, access to the API is disabled through the DISABLE_API: true entry. We'll have to enable it if we are to interact with the API. We can see that there are, among others, BASIC_AUTH_USER and BASIC_AUTH_PASS secrets which we can use if we'd like to provide a basic HTTP authentication.

i> Please visit ChartMuseum API[96] documentation if you're interested in more details.

Further down are the commented resources. We'll have to define them ourselves.

We'll need to persist the state of the application and make it accessible through Ingress. Both can be accomplished by changing related enabled entries to true and, in case of Ingress, by adding a few annotations and a host.

Now that we went through the values we're interested in, we can proceed with the practical parts. We'll need to define the address (domain) we'll use for ChartMuseum.

We already have the IP of the cluster (hopefully the IP of the external LB), and we can use it to create a nip.io domain, just as we did in the previous chapter.

```
1  CM_ADDR="cm.$LB_IP.nip.io"
```

To be on the safe side, we'll echo the value stored in CM_ADDR, and check whether it looks OK.

```
1  echo $CM_ADDR
```

In my case, the output is cm.18.221.122.90.nip.io.

If you go back to the values output, you'll notice that the Chart requires host to be defined as a key/value pairs. The problem is that "special" characters cannot be used as part of keys. In the case of our address, we need to escape all the dots. We'll use a bit of sed magic for that.

```
1  CM_ADDR_ESC=$(echo $CM_ADDR \
2      | sed -e "s@\.@\\\.@g")
3
4  echo $CM_ADDR_ESC
```

We echoed the address, and we sent the output to the sed command that replaced every . character with \.. The output of the latter command should be similar to the one that follows.

```
1  cm\.18\.221\.122\.90\.nip\.io
```

I already prepared a file with all the values we'll want to customize. Let's take a quick look at it.

---

[96]https://github.com/helm/chartmuseum#api

```
1  cat helm/chartmuseum-values.yml
```

The output is as follows.

```
1  image:
2    tag: v0.7.0
3  env:
4    open:
5      DISABLE_API: false
6  resources:
7    limits:
8      cpu: 100m
9      memory: 128Mi
10   requests:
11     cpu: 80m
12     memory: 64Mi
13 persistence:
14   enabled: true
15 ingress:
16   enabled: true
17   annotations:
18     kubernetes.io/ingress.class: "nginx"
19     ingress.kubernetes.io/ssl-redirect: "false"
20     nginx.ingress.kubernetes.io/ssl-redirect: "false"
21   hosts:
22     cm.127.0.0.1.nip.io:
23     - /
```

This is becoming monotonous, and that's OK. It should be that way. Installations should be boring and follow the same pattern. We found that pattern in Helm.

The *chartmuseum-values.yml* file defines the values we discussed. It sets the tag we'll use, and it enables the API. It defines the resources, and you already know that the values we're using should be taken with a lot of skepticism. In the "real" production, the amount of memory and CPU your applications require will differ significantly from what we can observe in our examples. So we should always monitor our applications real usage patterns, and fine-tune the configuration instead of guessing.

We enabled persistence, and we'll use the default StorageClass, since we did not specify any explicitly.

Ingress section defines the same annotations as those we used with the other Helm installations. It also defines a single host that will handle requests from all paths (/). Think of it as a reminder only. We cannot rely on the host in the *chartmuseum-values.yml* file since it likely differs from the `nip.io` address you defined. I could not predict which one will be in your case. So, we'll overwrite that value with a `--set` argument.

Let's install the Chart.

```
1  helm install stable/chartmuseum \
2      --namespace charts \
3      --name cm \
4      --values helm/chartmuseum-values.yml \
5      --set ingress.hosts."$CM_ADDR_ESC"={"/"} \
6      --set env.secret.BASIC_AUTH_USER=admin \
7      --set env.secret.BASIC_AUTH_PASS=admin
```

The Chart is installed. Instead of waiting in silence for all the Pods to start running, we'll briefly discuss security.

We defined the username and the password through `--set` arguments. They shouldn't be stored in `helm/chartmuseum-values.yml` since that would defy the purpose of secrecy.

Personally, I believe that there's no reason to hide the Charts. They do not (should not) contain anything confidential. The applications are stored in a container registry. Even if someone decides to use our Charts, that person would not be able to deploy our images, if our registry is configured to require authentication.

If that is not enough, and we do want to protect our Charts besides protecting images, we should ask yourself who should not be allowed to access them. If we want to prevent only outsiders from accessing our Charts, the fix is easy. We can put our cluster inside a VPN and make the domain accessible only to internal users. On the other hand, if we want to prevent even internal users from accessing our Charts, we can add basic HTTP authentication. We already saw the `secret` section when we inspected the values. You could set `env.secret.BASIC_AUTH_USER` and `env.secret.BASIC_-AUTH_PASS` to enable basic authentication. That's what we did in our example.

If none of those methods is secure enough, we can implement the best security measure of all. We can disable access to all humans by removing Ingress and changing the Service type to `ClusterIP`. That would result in only processes running in Pods being able to access the Charts. A good example would be to allow Jenkins to push and pull the Charts, and no one else. Even though that approach is more secure, it does not provide access to the Charts to people who might need it. Humans are true users of ChartMuseum. For scripts, it is easy to know which repository contains the definitions they need and to clone the code, even if that is only for the purpose of retrieving Charts. Humans need a way to search for Charts, to inspect them, and to run them on their laptops or servers.

We opted to a middle solution. We set up basic authentication which is better than no authentication, but still less secure than allowing only those within a VPN to access Charts or disabling human access altogether.

A note to minishift users

OpenShift ignores Ingress resources so we'll have to create a Route to accomplish the same effect. Please execute the command that follows.

```
oc -n charts create route edge --service cm-chartmuseum --hostname $CM_ADDR
--insecure-policy Allow
```

By now, the resources we installed should be up-and-running. We'll confirm that just to be on the safe side.

```
1 kubectl -n charts \
2     rollout status deploy \
3     cm-chartmuseum
```

The output should show that the deployment "cm-chartmuseum" was successfully rolled out.

Next, we'll check whether the application is healthy.

```
1 curl "http://$CM_ADDR/health"
```

The output is as follows.

```
1 {"healthy":true}
```

Now we can open ChartMuseum in browser.

```
1 open "http://$CM_ADDR"
```

You will be asked for a username and a password. Please use *admin* for both and click the *Sign in* button.

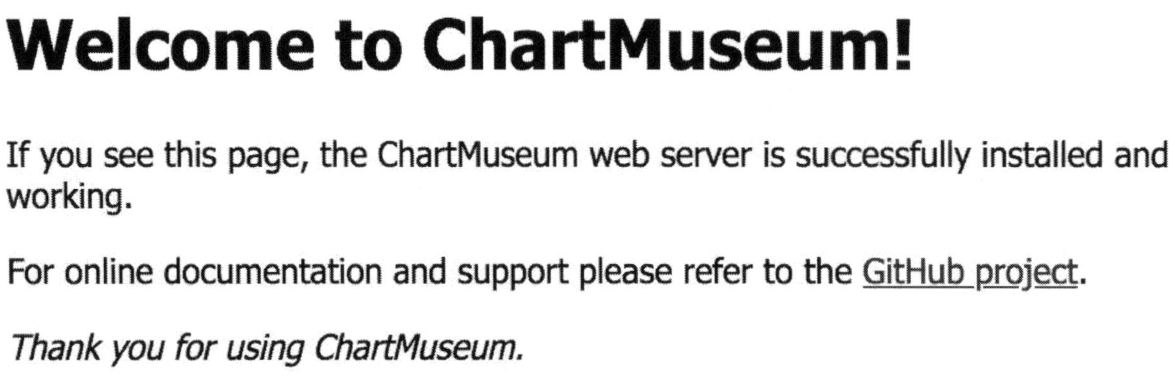

Welcome to ChartMuseum!

If you see this page, the ChartMuseum web server is successfully installed and working.

For online documentation and support please refer to the GitHub project.

Thank you for using ChartMuseum.

Figure 5-1: ChartMuseum's welcome screen

As you can see, there's not much of the UI to look. We are supposed to interact with ChartMuseum through its API. If we need to visualize our Charts, we'll need to look for a different solution.

Let's see the index.

```
1  curl "http://$CM_ADDR/index.yaml"
```

Since we did not specify the username and the password, we got {"error":"unauthorized"} as the output. We'll need to authenticate every time we want to interact with ChartMuseum API.

Let's try again but, this time, with the authentication info.

```
1  curl -u admin:admin \
2      "http://$CM_ADDR/index.yaml"
```

The output is as follows.

```
1  apiVersion: v1
2  entries: {}
3  generated: "2018-06-02T21:38:30Z"
```

It should come as no surprise that we have no entries to the museum. We did not yet push a Chart. Before we do any pushing, we should add a new repository to our Helm client.

```
1  helm repo add chartmuseum \
2      http://$CM_ADDR \
3      --username admin \
4      --password admin
```

The output states that "chartmuseum" has been added to your repositories. From now on, all the Charts we store in our ChartMuseum installation will be available through our Helm client.

The only thing left is to start pushing Charts to ChartMuseum. We could do that by sending curl requests. However, there is a better way, so we'll skip HTTP requests and install a Helm plugin instead.

```
1  helm plugin install \
2      https://github.com/chartmuseum/helm-push
```

This plugin added a new command helm push. Let's give it a spin.

```
1  helm push \
2      ../go-demo-3/helm/go-demo-3/ \
3      chartmuseum \
4      --username admin \
5      --password admin
```

The output is as follows.

```
1  Pushing go-demo-3-0.0.1.tgz to chartmuseum...
2  Done.
```

We pushed a Chart located in the ../go-demo-3/helm/go-demo-3/ directory into a repository chartmuseum. We can confirm that the push was indeed successful by retrieving index.yaml file from the repository.

```
1  curl "http://$CM_ADDR/index.yaml" \
2      -u admin:admin
```

The output is as follows.

```
1  apiVersion: v1
2  entries:
3    go-demo-3:
4    - apiVersion: v1
5      created: "2018-06-02T21:39:21Z"
6      description: A silly demo based on API written in Go and MongoDB
7      digest: d8443c78485e80644ff9bfddcf32cc9f270864fb50b75377dbe813b280708519
8      home: http://www.devopstoolkitseries.com/
9      keywords:
10     - api
11     - backend
12     - go
13     - database
14     - mongodb
15     maintainers:
16     - email: viktor@farcic.com
17       name: Viktor Farcic
18     name: go-demo-3
19     sources:
20     - https://github.com/vfarcic/go-demo-3
21     urls:
22     - charts/go-demo-3-0.0.1.tgz
23     version: 0.0.1
24 generated: "2018-06-02T21:39:28Z"
```

We can see that the `go-demo-3` Chart is now in the repository. Most of the information comes from the `Chart.yaml` file we explored in the previous chapter.

Finally, we should validate that our local Helm client indeed sees the new Chart.

```
1  helm search chartmuseum/
```

The output is probably disappointing. It states that `no results` were `found`. The problem is that even though the Chart is stored in the ChartMuseum repository, we did not update the repository information stored locally in the Helm client. So, let's update it first.

```
1  helm repo update
```

The output is as follows.

```
1  Hang tight while we grab the latest from your chart repositories...
2  ...Skip local chart repository
3  ...Successfully got an update from the "chartmuseum" chart repository
4  ...Successfully got an update from the "stable" chart repository
5  Update Complete. Happy Helming!
```

If you added more repositories to your Helm client, you might see a bigger output. Those additional repositories do not matter in this context. What does matter is that the `chartmuseum` was updated and that we can try to search it again.

```
1  helm search chartmuseum/
```

This time, the output is not empty.

```
1  NAME                       CHART VERSION    APP VERSION    DESCRIPTION
2
3  chartmuseum/go-demo-3      0.0.1                           A silly demo...
```

Our Chart is now available in ChartMuseum, and we can access it with our Helm client. Let's inspect the Chart.

```
1  helm inspect chartmuseum/go-demo-3
```

We won't go through the output since it is the same as the one we explored in the previous chapter. The only difference is that this time it is not retrieved from the Chart stored locally, but from ChartMuseum running inside our cluster. From now on, anyone with the access to that repository can deploy the *go-demo-3* application.

To be on the safe side, and fully confident in the solution, we'll deploy the Chart before announcing to everyone that they can use the new repository to install applications.

Just as with the other applications, we'll start by defining a domain we'll use for *go-demo-3*.

```
1  GD3_ADDR="go-demo-3.$LB_IP.nip.io"
```

Next, we'll output the address as a way to confirm that it looks OK.

```
1  echo $GD3_ADDR
```

The output should be similar to go-demo-3.18.221.122.90.nip.io.

Now we can finally install *go-demo-3* Chart stored in ChartMuseum running inside our cluster. We'll continue using upgrade with -i since that is more friendly to our yet-to-be-defined continuous deployment process.

```
1  helm upgrade -i go-demo-3 \
2      chartmuseum/go-demo-3 \
3      --namespace go-demo-3 \
4      --set image.tag=1.0 \
5      --set ingress.host=$GD3_ADDR \
6      --reuse-values
```

We can see from the first line of the output that the release "go-demo-3" does not exist, so Helm decided to install it, instead of doing the upgrade. The rest of the output is the same as the one you saw in the previous chapter. It contains the list of the resources created from the Chart as well as the post-installation instructions.

 A note to minishift users

OpenShift ignores Ingress resources so we'll have to create a Route to accomplish the same effect. Please execute the command that follows.

```
oc -n go-demo-3 create route edge --service go-demo-3 --hostname $GD3_ADDR
--insecure-policy Allow
```

Next, we'll wait until the application is rolled out and confirm that we can access it.

```
1  kubectl -n go-demo-3 \
2      rollout status deploy go-demo-3
3
4  curl "http://$GD3_ADDR/demo/hello"
```

The latter command output the familiar hello, world! message thus confirming that the application is up-and-running.

The only thing left to learn is how to remove Charts from ChartMuseum. But, before we do that, we'll delete *go-demo-3* from the cluster. We don't need it anymore.

```
1  helm delete go-demo-3 --purge
```

Unfortunately, there is no Helm plugin that will allow us to delete a Chart from a repository, so we'll accomplish our mission using `curl`.

```
1  curl -XDELETE \
2      "http://$CM_ADDR/api/charts/go-demo-3/0.0.1" \
3      -u admin:admin
```

The output is as follows.

```
1  {"deleted":true}
```

The chart is deleted from the repository.

Now you know everything there is to know about ChartMuseum. OK, maybe you don't know everything you should know, but you do know the basics that will allow you to explore it further.

Now that you know how to push and pull Charts to and from ChartMuseum, you might still be wondering if there is an UI that will allow us to visualize Charts. Read on.

Using Monocular

I don't think that UIs are useful. We tend to focus on the features they provide, and that distracts us from command line and code. We often get so immersed into filling fields and clicking buttons, that we often forget that the key to automation is to master CLIs and to write code that lives in a code repository. I think that UIs do more damage than good to software engineers.

That being said, I am fully aware that not everyone shares my views. Some like UIs and prefer pretty colors over black and white terminal screens. For those, I will guide you how to get a UI that will utilize Helm repositories and allow you to do some of the things we did through CLI by clicking buttons. We'll explore Monocular[97].

Monocular is web-based UI for managing Kubernetes applications packaged as Helm Charts. It allows us to search and discover available charts from multiple repositories, and install them in our clusters with one click.

Monocular can be installed with Helm. It is available through a Chart residing in its own repository[98]. So, our first step is to add the repository to our Helm client.

---

[97]https://github.com/kubernetes-helm/monocular
[98]https://kubernetes-helm.github.io/monocular

```
1  helm repo add monocular \
2      https://kubernetes-helm.github.io/monocular
```

Let's take a look at the available values.

```
1  helm inspect values monocular/monocular
```

The output, limited to the values we're interested in, is as follows.

```
1  api:
2    ...
3    image:
4      repository: bitnami/monocular-api
5      tag: v0.7.2
6      ...
7    resources:
8      limits:
9        cpu: 100m
10       memory: 128Mi
11     requests:
12       cpu: 100m
13       memory: 128Mi
14   ...
15 ui:
16   ...
17   image:
18     repository: bitnami/monocular-ui
19     tag: v0.7.2
20     ...
21 ingress:
22   enabled: true
23   hosts:
24   # Wildcard
25   -
26   # - monocular.local
27
28   ## Ingress annotations
29   ##
30   annotations:
31     ## Nginx ingress controller (default)
32     nginx.ingress.kubernetes.io/rewrite-target: /
33     kubernetes.io/ingress.class: nginx
34       ...
```

Just as with the other Charts, we'll use a fixed version of the images by customizing `image.tag` values in both the `api` and the `ui` sections.

We'll need to increase the resources since those specified by default are too low.

Ingress is already enabled, but we'll have to specify the host. Also, we'll add the "old" style annotations so that older versions of nginx Ingress are supported as well.

Those changes are already available in the `monocular-values.yml` file, so let's take a quick look at it.

```
1  cat helm/monocular-values.yml
```

The output is as follows.

```
1   api:
2     image:
3       tag: v0.7.0
4     resources:
5       limits:
6         cpu: 500m
7         memory: 1Gi
8       requests:
9         cpu: 200m
10        memory: 512Mi
11  ui:
12    image:
13      tag: v0.7.0
14  ingress:
15    annotations:
16      kubernetes.io/ingress.class: "nginx"
17      ingress.kubernetes.io/rewrite-target: /
18      nginx.ingress.kubernetes.io/rewrite-target: /
19      ingress.kubernetes.io/ssl-redirect: "false"
20      nginx.ingress.kubernetes.io/ssl-redirect: "false"
```

Before we proceed, we'll have to generate a valid hostname that we'll use with Monocular Ingress resource.

```
1  MONOCULAR_ADDR="monocular.$LB_IP.nip.io"
2
3  echo $MONOCULAR_ADDR
```

The output of the latter command should be similar to the one that follows.

```
1   monocular.18.221.122.90.nip.io
```

 A note to minishift users

Installing Monocular in OpenShift creates a few issues and requires quite a few changes to the commands that follow. Please use the instructions from Deploy Monocular on OpenShift[99] article instead of the command that follows.

Now we are ready to install Monocular Chart.

```
1   helm install monocular/monocular \
2       --namespace charts \
3       --name monocular \
4       --values helm/monocular-values.yml \
5       --set ingress.hosts={$MONOCULAR_ADDR}
```

The output follows the same pattern as the other charts. It shows the status at the top, followed with the resources it created. At the bottom are short instructions for the post-installation steps.

We should wait until the application rolls out before giving a spin to its UI.

```
1   kubectl -n charts \
2       rollout status \
3       deploy monocular-monocular-api
```

It will take a while until the API rolls out and the monocular-api Pods might fail a few times. Be patient.

Now we can open Monocular in a browser.

```
1   open "http://$MONOCULAR_ADDR"
```

---

[99]https://blog.openshift.com/deploy-monocular-openshift/

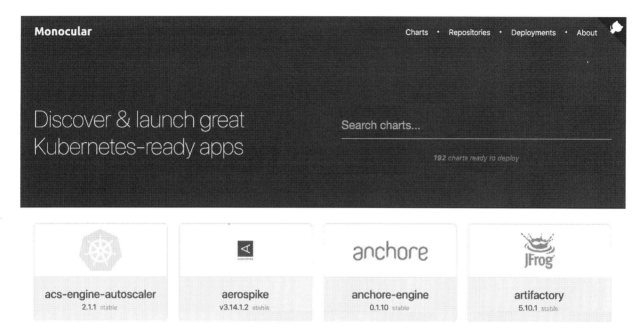

Figure 5-2: **Monocular's home screen**

If we click on the *Charts* link in top-right corner of the screen, we'll see all the charts available in the two default repositories (*stable* and *incubator*). We can use the link on the left-hand menu to filter them by a repository and to change the ordering. We can also use the *Search charts...* field to filter Charts.

The *Repositories* screen can be used to list those that are currently configured, as well as to add new ones.

The *Deployments* screen list all the Helm installations. At the moment, we have *cm* (ChartMuseum) and *monocular* running through Helm Charts. Additionally, there is the *New deployment* button that we can use to install a new Chart. Please click it and observe that you are taken back to the *Charts* screen. We are about to install Jenkins.

Type *jenkins* in the *Search charts...* field. The list of the Charts will be filtered, and we'll see only Jenkins. Click on the only Chart.

On the left-hand side of the screen is the same information we can see by executing `helm inspect stable/jenkins` command. On the right-hand side, there is the *Install* section which we can use for *one click installation* or to copy *Helm CLI* commands.

Please remain in the *One Click Installation* tab and click the *Install jenkins v...* button. You will be presented with a popup with a field to specify a Namespace where the Chart will be installed. Please type *jenkins* and click the *Deploy* button.

We were redirected to the screen with the same information we'd get if we executed `helm install stable/jenkins --namespace jenkins`.

Even though using Monocular might seem tempting at the begging, it has a few serious drawbacks. We'll discuss them soon. For now, please click the red *Delete deployment* button to remove Jenkins.

The major problem with Monocular is that it does not allow us to specify values during Charts installation. There will hardly ever be the case when we'll install Charts without any custom values. That inability alone should be enough to discard Monocular for any serious usage. On top of that, it does not provide the option to upgrade Charts.

Today (June 2018) Monocular project is still too young to be taken seriously. That will probably change as the project matures. For now, my recommendation is not to use it. That might provoke an adverse reaction. You might feel that I wasted your time by showing you a tool that is not useful. However, I thought that you should know that the UI exists and that it is the only free option we have today. I'll leave that decision to you. You know what it does and how to install it.

What Now?

We will continue using ChartMuseum throughout the rest of the book, and I will leave it to you to decide whether Monocular is useful or a waste of computing resources.

We could have set up a container registry, but we didn't. There are too many tools in the market ranging from free solutions like Docker Registry[100] all the way until enterprise products like Docker Trusted Registry[101] and JFrog' Artifactory[102]. The problem is that Docker Registry (free version) is very insecure. It provides only a very basic authentication. Still, the price is right (it's free). On the other hand, you might opt for one of the commercial solutions and leverage the additional features they provide. Never the less, I felt that for our use-case it is the best if we stick with Docker Hub[103]. Almost everyone has an account there, and it is an excellent choice for the examples we're having. Once you translate the knowledge from here to your "real" processes, you should have no problem switching to any other container registry if you choose to do so. By now, you should have all the skills required to run a registry in your cluster.

All in all, we'll continue using Docker Hub for storing container images, and we'll run ChartMuseum in our cluster and use it to distribute Helm Charts.

All that's left is for us to remove the Charts we installed. We'll delete them all at once. Alternatively, you can delete the whole cluster if you do plan to make a break. In any case, the next chapter will start from scratch.

```
1  helm delete $(helm ls -q) --purge
2
3  kubectl delete ns \
4      charts go-demo-3 jenkins
```

---

[100]https://docs.docker.com/registry/
[101]https://docs.docker.com/ee/dtr/
[102]https://www.jfrog.com/confluence/display/RTF/Docker+Registry
[103]https://hub.docker.com/

Installing and Setting Up Jenkins

 When used by engineers, UIs are evil. They sidetrack us from repeatability and automation.

UIs do have their purpose. They are supposed to provide enough colors and random graphs for CIO, CTO, and other C-level executives and mid-level managers. Management works in multi-color, while engineers should be limited to dual-color terminals, mixed with a slightly increased color pallet of IDEs and editors we use to code. We produce commits, while managers fake interest by looking at UIs.

The above phrase is a bit exaggerated. It's not true that UIs are useful only to managers nor that they fake interest. At least, that's not true for all of them. UIs do provide a lot of value but, unfortunately, they are often abused to the level of even postponing or even preventing automation. We'll try to make an additional effort to remove Jenkins UI for any setup related tasks. We'll try to automate everything.

We already improved a lot our ability to install Jenkins. A mere switch from custom-made YAML files to Helm Charts is a considerable step forward from the operational perspective. The addition of ServiceAccounts bound to Roles improved security. But, there's still one big thing left only partly explored. We did not yet reach the point where we can install and fully setup Jenkins from a command line. So far, there were always a few things we had to do manually from its UI. We'll try to get rid of those steps in the hope that the only command we'll need to execute is `helm install`.

As it often goes, we cannot hope to fully automate the setup without going through manual steps first. So, we'll start by exploring different use-cases. If we hit a road-block, we'll try to figure out how to overcome it. The chances are that another one will be waiting for us after the first, and another one after that. We're yet to see which obstacles we'll encounter and which steps are missing until we make Jenkins fully operational and, at the same time, reasonably secure. We'll try to automate the process only once we're confident in the way we set up Jenkins manually.

Creating A Cluster And Retrieving Its IP

You already know what the first steps are. Create a new cluster or reuse the one you dedicated to the exercises.

We'll start by going to the local copy of the *vfarcic/k8s-specs* repository and making sure that we have the latest revision.

All the commands from this chapter are available in the 06-jenkins-setup.sh[104] Gist.

```
1  cd k8s-specs
2
3  git pull
```

We'll need a few files from the *go-demo-3* repository you cloned in one of the previous chapters. To be on the safe side, please merge it the upstream. If you forgot the commands, they are available in the go-demo-3-merge.sh gist[105].

The requirements are the same as those from the previous chapters. The only difference is that I will assume that you'll store the IP of the cluster or the external load balancer as the environment variable LB_IP.

For your convenience, the Gists and the specs are available below. Please note that they are the same as those we used in the previous chapter with the addition of the export LB_IP command.

- docker4mac-ip.sh[106]: **Docker for Mac** with 3 CPUs, 3 GB RAM, with **nginx Ingress**, with **tiller**, and with LB_IP variable set to 127.0.0.1.
- minikube-ip.sh[107]: **minikube** with 3 CPUs, 3 GB RAM, with ingress, storage-provisioner, and default-storageclass addons enabled, with **tiller**, and with LB_IP variable set to the VM created by minikube.
- kops-ip.sh[108]: **kops in AWS** with 3 t2.small masters and 2 t2.medium nodes spread in three availability zones, with **nginx Ingress**, with **tiller**, and with LB_IP variable set to the IP retrieved by pinging ELB's hostname. The Gist assumes that the prerequisites are set through Appendix B.
- minishift-ip.sh[109]: **minishift** with 3 CPUs, 3 GB RAM, with version 1.16+, with **tiller**, and with LB_IP variable set to the VM created by minishift.
- gke-ip.sh[110]: **Google Kubernetes Engine (GKE)** with 3 n1-highcpu-2 (2 CPUs, 1.8 GB RAM) nodes (one in each zone), and with **nginx Ingress** controller running on top of the "standard" one that comes with GKE, with **tiller**, and with LB_IP variable set to the IP of the external load balancer created when installing nginx Ingress. We'll use nginx Ingress for compatibility with other platforms. Feel free to modify the YAML files and Helm Charts if you prefer NOT to install nginx Ingress.
- eks-ip.sh[111]: **Elastic Kubernetes Service (EKS)** with 2 t2.medium nodes, with **nginx Ingress** controller, with a **default StorageClass**, with **tiller**, and with LB_IP variable set tot he IP retrieved by pinging ELB's hostname.

[104]https://gist.github.com/4ea447d106c96cb088bc8d616719f6e8
[105]https://gist.github.com/171172b69bb75903016f0676a8fe9388
[106]https://gist.github.com/66842a54ef167219dc18b03991c26edb
[107]https://gist.github.com/df5518b24bc39a8b8cca95cc37617221
[108]https://gist.github.com/7ee11f4dd8a130b51407582505c817cb
[109]https://gist.github.com/fa902cc2e2f43dcbe88a60138dd20932
[110]https://gist.github.com/3e53def041591f3c0f61569d49ffd879
[111]https://gist.github.com/f7f3956cd39c3bc55638529cfeb2ff12

Now we're ready to install Jenkins.

Running Jenkins

We'll need a domain which we'll use to set Ingress' hostname and through which we'll be able to open Jenkins UI. We'll continue using *nip.io* service to generate domains. Just as before, remember that this is only a temporary solution and that you should use "real" domains with the IP of your external load balancer instead.

```
1  JENKINS_ADDR="jenkins.$LB_IP.nip.io"
2
3  echo $JENKINS_ADDR
```

The output of the latter command should provide a visual confirmation that the address we'll use for Jenkins looks OK. In my case, it is jenkins.52.15.140.221.nip.io.

 A note to minishift users

Helm will try to install Jenkins Chart with the process in a container running as user 0. By default, that is not allowed in OpenShift. We'll skip discussing the best approach to correct the issue, and I'll assume you already know how to set the permissions on the per-Pod basis. Instead, we'll do the most straightforward fix. Please execute the command that follows to allow the creation of restricted Pods to run as any user.

```
oc patch scc restricted -p '{"runAsUser":{"type": "RunAsAny"}}'
```

We'll start exploring the steps we'll need to run Jenkins in a Kubernetes cluster by executing the same helm install command we used in the previous chapters. It won't provide everything we need, but it will be a good start. We'll improve the process throughout the rest of the chapter with the objective of having a fully automated Jenkins installation process. We might not be able to accomplish our goal 100%. Or, we might conclude that full automation is not worth the trouble. Nevertheless, we'll use the installation from the Packaging Kubernetes Applications as the base and see how far we can go in our quest for full automation.

```
1  helm install stable/jenkins \
2      --name jenkins \
3      --namespace jenkins \
4      --values helm/jenkins-values.yml \
5      --set Master.HostName=$JENKINS_ADDR
```

Next, we'll confirm that Jenkins is rolled out.

```
1  kubectl -n jenkins \
2      rollout status deployment jenkins
```

The latter command will wait until jenkins Deployment rolls out. Its output is as follows.

```
1  Waiting for rollout to finish: 0 of 1 updated replicas are available...
2  deployment "jenkins" successfully rolled out
```

 ## A note to minishift users

OpenShift requires Routes to make services accessible outside the cluster. To make things more complicated, they are not part of "standard Kubernetes" so we'll need to create one using oc. Please execute the command that follows.

```
oc -n jenkins create route edge --service jenkins --insecure-policy Allow
--hostname $JENKINS_ADDR
```

That command created an edge Router tied to the jenkins Service. Since we do not have SSL certificates for HTTPS communication, we also specified that it is OK to use insecure policy which will allow us to access Jenkins through plain HTTP. Finally, the last argument defined the address through which we'd like to access Jenkins UI.

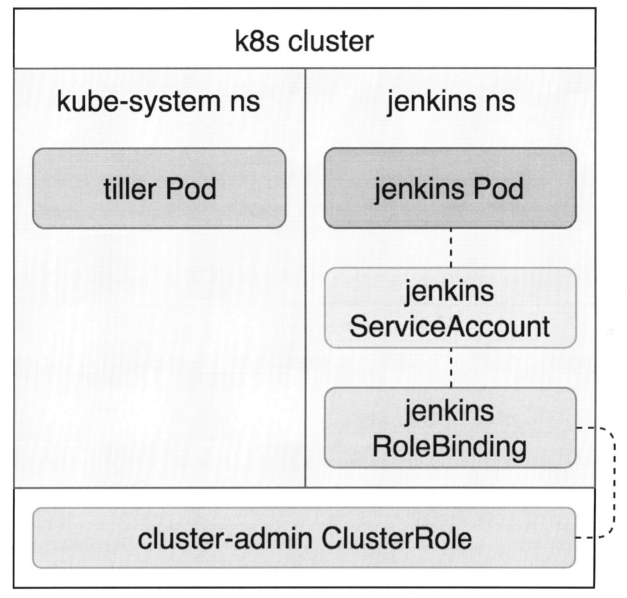

Figure 6-1: Jenkins setup operating in a single Namespace

Now that Jenkins is up-and-running, we can open it in your favorite browser.

```
1   open "http://$JENKINS_ADDR"
```

 ## A note to Windows users

Git Bash might not be able to use the open command. If that's the case, please replace the open command with echo. As a result, you'll get the full address that should be opened directly in your browser of choice.

Since this is the first time we're accessing this Jenkins instance, we'll need to login first. Just as before, the password is stored in the Secret `jenkins`, under `jenkins-admin-password`. So, we'll query the secret to find out the password.

```
1  JENKINS_PASS=$(kubectl -n jenkins \
2      get secret jenkins \
3      -o jsonpath="{.data.jenkins-admin-password}" \
4      | base64 --decode; echo)
5
6  echo $JENKINS_PASS
```

The output of the latter command should be a random string. As an example, I got `Ucg2tab4FK`. Please copy it, return to the Jenkins login screen opened in your browser, and use it to authenticate. We did not retrieve the username since it is hard-coded to *admin.*

We'll leave this admin user as-is since we won't explore authentication methods. When running Jenkins "for real", you should install a plugin that provides the desired authentication mechanism and configure Jenkins to use it instead. That could be LDAP, Google or GitHub authentication, and many other providers. For now, we'll continue using *admin* as the only god-like user.

Now that we got Jenkins up-and-running, we'll create a Pipeline which can be used to test our setup.

Using Pods to Run Tools

We won't explore how to write a continuous deployment pipeline in this chapter. That is reserved for the next one. Right now, we are only concerned whether our Jenkins setup is working as expected. We need to know if Jenkins can interact with Kubernetes, whether we can run the tools we need as Pods, and whether they can be spun across different Namespaces. On top of those, we still need to solve the issue of building container images. Since we already established that it is not a good idea to mount a Docker socket, nor to run containers in privileged mode, we need to find a valid alternative. In parallel to solving those and a few other challenges we'll encounter, we cannot lose focus from automation. Everything we do has to be converted into automatic setup unless we make a conscious decision that it is not worth the trouble.

I'm jumping ahead of myself by bombing you with too many things. We'll backtrack a bit and start with a simple requirement. Later on, we'll build on top of it. So, our first requirement is to run different tools packaged as containers inside a Pod.

Please go back to Jenkins UI and click the *New Item* link in the left-hand menu. Type *my-k8s-job* in the *item name* field, select *Pipeline* as the job type and click the *OK* button.

We created a new job which does not yet do anything. Our next step is to write a very simple Pipeline that will validate that we can indeed use Jenkins to spin up a Pod with the containers we need.

Please click the *Pipeline* tab and you'll be presented with the *Pipeline Script* field. Write the script that follows.

```
 1  podTemplate(
 2      label: "kubernetes",
 3      containers: [
 4          containerTemplate(name: "maven", image: "maven:alpine", ttyEnabled: true, co\
 5  mmand: "cat"),
 6          containerTemplate(name: "golang", image: "golang:alpine", ttyEnabled: true, \
 7  command: "cat")
 8      ]
 9  ) {
10      node("kubernetes") {
11          container("maven") {
12              stage("build") {
13                  sh "mvn --version"
14              }
15              stage("unit-test") {
16                  sh "java -version"
17              }
18          }
19          container("golang") {
20              stage("deploy") {
21                  sh "go version"
22              }
23          }
24      }
25  }
```

ℹ️ If you prefer to copy and paste, the job is available in the my-k8s-job.groovy Gist[112].

The script defines a Pod template with two containers. One is based on the maven image and the other on the golang image. Further down, we defined that Jenkins should use that template as the node. Inside it, we are using the maven container to execute two stages. One will return Maven version, and the other will output Java version. Further down, we switch to the golang container only to output Go version.

This job is straightforward, and it does not do anything related to our continuous deployment processes. Nevertheless, it should be enough to provide a necessary validation that we can use Jenkins to create a Pod, that we can switch from one container to another, and that we can execute commands inside them.

Don't forget to click the *Save* button before proceeding.

---

[112]https://gist.github.com/2cf872c3a9acac51409fbd5a2789cb02

If the job we created looks familiar, that's because it is the same as the one we used in the Enabling Process Communication With Kube API Through Service Accounts chapter. Since our goal is to confirm that our current Jenkins setup can create the Pods, that job is as good as any other to validate that claim.

Please click the *Open Blue Ocean* link from the left-hand menu. You'll see the *Run* button in the middle of the screen. Click it. As a result, a row will appear with a new build. Click it to see the details.

The build is running, and we should go back to the terminal window to confirm that the Pod is indeed created.

```
1  kubectl -n jenkins get pods
```

The output is as follows.

```
1  NAME                   READY STATUS          RESTARTS AGE
2  jenkins-...            1/1   Running         0        5m
3  jenkins-slave-... 0/3   ContainerCreating 0        16s
```

We can see that there are two Pods in the jenkins Namespace. One is hosting Jenkins itself, while the other was created when we run the Jenkins build. You'll notice that even though we defined two containers, we can see three. The additional container was added automatically to the Pod, and it's used to establish communication with Jenkins.

In your case, the status of the jenkins-slave Pod might be different. Besides ContainerCreating, it could be Running, Terminating, or you might not even see it. It all depends on how much time passed between initiating the build and retrieving the Pods in the jenkins Namespace.

What matters is the process. When we initiated a new build, Jenkins created the Pod in the same Namespace. Once all the containers are up-and-running, Jenkins will execute the steps we defined through the Pipeline script. When finished, the Pod will be removed, freeing resources for other processes.

Please go back to Jenkins UI and wait until the build is finished.

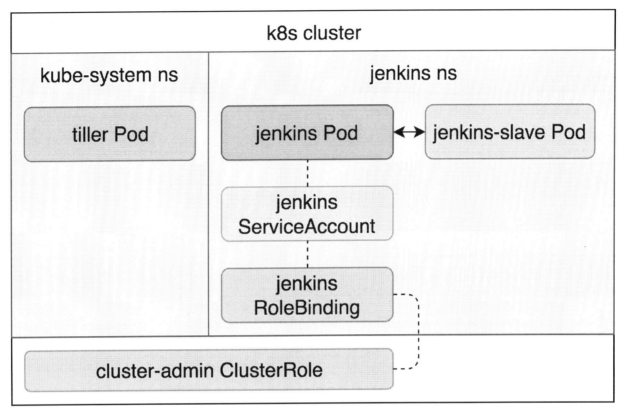

Figure 6-2: Jenkins spinning an agent (slave) Pod in the same Namespace

We proved that we could run a very simple job. We're yet to discover whether we can do more complicated operations.

On the first look, the script we wrote looks OK. However, I'm not happy with the way we defined podTemplate. Wouldn't it be better if we could use the same YAML format for defining the template as if we'd define a Pod in Kubernetes? Fortunately, jenkins-kubernetes-plugin[113] recently added that feature. So, we'll try to rewrite the script to better match Pod definitions.

We'll use the rewriting opportunity to replace maven with the tools we are more likely to use with a CD pipeline for the *go-demo-3* application. We still need golang. On top of it, we should be able to run kubectl, helm, and, openshift-client. The latter is required only if you're using OpenShift, and you are free to remove it if that's not your case.

Let's open my-k8s-job configuration screen and modify the job.

```
1  open "http://$JENKINS_ADDR/job/my-k8s-job/configure"
```

Please click the *Pipeline* tab and replace the script with the one that follows.

---

[113]https://github.com/jenkinsci/kubernetes-plugin

```
1   podTemplate(label: "kubernetes", yaml: """
2   apiVersion: v1
3   kind: Pod
4   spec:
5     containers:
6     - name: kubectl
7       image: vfarcic/kubectl
8       command: ["sleep"]
9       args: ["100000"]
10    - name: oc
11      image: vfarcic/openshift-client
12      command: ["sleep"]
13      args: ["100000"]
14    - name: golang
15      image: golang:1.9
16      command: ["sleep"]
17      args: ["100000"]
18    - name: helm
19      image: vfarcic/helm:2.8.2
20      command: ["sleep"]
21      args: ["100000"]
22  """
23  ) {
24      node("kubernetes") {
25          container("kubectl") {
26              stage("kubectl") {
27                  sh "kubectl version"
28              }
29          }
30          container("oc") {
31              stage("oc") {
32                  sh "oc version"
33              }
34          }
35          container("golang") {
36              stage("golang") {
37                  sh "go version"
38              }
39          }
40          container("helm") {
41              stage("helm") {
42                  sh "helm version"
43              }
```

```
44              }
45          }
46  }
```

 If you prefer to copy and paste, the job is available in the my-k8s-job-yaml.groovy Gist[114].

This time, the format of the script is different. Instead of the `containers` argument inside `podTemplate`, now we have `yaml`. Inside it is Kubernetes Pod definition just as if we'd define a standard Kubernetes resource.

The rest of the script follows the same logic as before. The only difference is that this time we are using the tools were are more likely to need in our yet-to-be-defined *go-demo-3* Pipeline. All we're doing is churning output of `kubectl`, `oc`, `go`, and `helm` versions.

Don't forget to click the *Save* button.

Next, we'll run a build of the job with the new script.

```
1  open "http://$JENKINS_ADDR/blue/organizations/jenkins/my-k8s-job/activity"
```

Please click the *Run* button, followed with a click on the row with the new build.

I have an assignment for you while the build is running. Try to find out what is wrong with our current setup without looking at the results of the build. You have approximately six minutes to complete the task. Proceed only if you know the answer or if you gave up.

Jenkins will create a Pod in the same Namespace. That Pod will have five containers, four of which will host the tools we specified in the `podTemplate`, and Jenkins will inject the fifth as a way to establish the communication between Jenkins and the Pod. We can confirm that by listing the Pods in the `jenkins` Namespace.

```
1  kubectl -n jenkins get pods
```

The output is as follows.

```
1  NAME               READY STATUS           RESTARTS AGE
2  jenkins-...        1/1   Running          0        16m
3  jenkins-slave-... 0/5   ContainerCreating 0        19s
```

So far, everything looks OK. Containers are being created. The `jenkins-slave-...` Pod will soon change its status to `Running`, and Jenkins will try to execute all the steps defined in the script.

Let's take a look at the build from Jenkins' UI.

After a while, the build will reach the `helm` stage. Click it, and you'll see the output similar to the one that follows.

---

[114]https://gist.github.com/a1b3b36c68323aea161d7364b1231de2

```
1   [my-k8s-job] Running shell script
2
3   + helm version
4
5   Client: &version.Version{SemVer:"v2.8.2", GitCommit:"...", GitTreeState:"clean"}
```

You'll notice that the build will hang at this point. After a few minutes, you might think that it will hang forever. It won't. Approximately five minutes later, the output of the step in the `helm` stage will change to the one that follows.

```
1   [my-k8s-job] Running shell script
2
3   + helm version
4
5   Client: &version.Version{SemVer:"v2.8.2", GitCommit:"...", GitTreeState:"clean"}
6
7   EXITCODE    0Error: cannot connect to Tiller
8
9   script returned exit code 1
```

 ## A note to Docker For Mac/Windows users

Even though Docker for Mac/Windows supports RBAC, it allows any internal process inside containers to communicate with Kube API. Unlike with other Kubernetes flavors, you will not see the same error. The build will complete successfully.

Our build could not connect to `Tiller`. Helm kept trying for five minutes. It reached its pre-defined timeout, and it gave up.

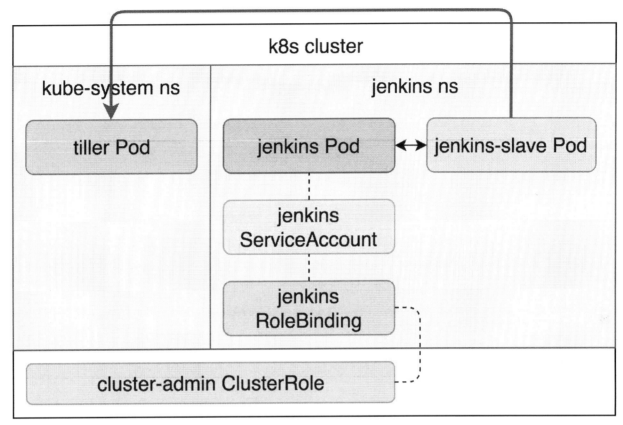

Figure 6-3: Jenkins agent (slave) Pod trying to connect to tiller in a different Namespace

If what we learned in the Enabling Process Communication With Kube API Through Service Accounts chapter is still fresh in your mind, that outcome should not be a surprise. We did not set ServiceAccount that would allow Helm running inside a container to communicate with Tiller. It is questionable whether we should even allow Helm running in a container to interact with Tiller running in kube-system. That would be a huge security risk that would allow anyone with access to Jenkins to gain access to any part of the cluster. It would defy one of the big reasons why we're using Namespaces. We'll explore this, and a few other problems next. For now, we'll confirm that Jenkins removed the Pod created by the failed build.

```
1  kubectl -n jenkins get pods
```

The output is as follows.

```
1  NAME          READY STATUS   RESTARTS AGE
2  jenkins-... 1/1    Running 0         42m
```

The jenkins-slave-... Pod is gone, and our system is restored to the state before the build started.

Running Builds In Different Namespaces

One of the significant disadvantages of the script we used inside my-k8s-job is that it runs in the same Namespace as Jenkins. We should separate builds from Jenkins and thus ensure that they do not affect its stability.

We can create a system where each application has two namespaces; one for testing and the other for production. We can define quotas, limitations, and other things we are used to defining on the Namespace level. As a result, we can guarantee that testing an application will not affect the production release. With Namespaces we can separate one set of applications from another. At the same time, we'll reduce the chance that one team will accidentally mess up with the applications of the other. Our end-goal is to be secure without limiting our teams. By giving them freedom in their own Namespace, we can be secure without impacting team's performance and its ability to move forward without depending on other teams.

Let's go back to the job configuration screen.

```
1  open "http://$JENKINS_ADDR/job/my-k8s-job/configure"
```

Please click the *Pipeline* tab and replace the script with the one that follows.

```
1  podTemplate(
2      label: "kubernetes",
3      namespace: "go-demo-3-build",
4      serviceAccount: "build",
5      yaml: """
6  apiVersion: v1
7  kind: Pod
8  spec:
9    containers:
10   - name: kubectl
11     image: vfarcic/kubectl
12     command: ["sleep"]
13     args: ["100000"]
14   - name: oc
15     image: vfarcic/openshift-client
16     command: ["sleep"]
17     args: ["100000"]
18   - name: golang
19     image: golang:1.9
20     command: ["sleep"]
21     args: ["100000"]
22   - name: helm
```

```
23        image: vfarcic/helm:2.8.2
24        command: ["sleep"]
25        args: ["100000"]
26    """
27  ) {
28      node("kubernetes") {
29          container("kubectl") {
30              stage("kubectl") {
31                  sh "kubectl version"
32              }
33          }
34          container("oc") {
35              stage("oc") {
36                  sh "oc version"
37              }
38          }
39          container("golang") {
40              stage("golang") {
41                  sh "go version"
42              }
43          }
44          container("helm") {
45              stage("helm") {
46                  sh "helm version --tiller-namespace go-demo-3-build"
47              }
48          }
49      }
50  }
```

> ℹ️ Getting spoiled with Gist and still do not want to type? The job is available in the my-k8s-job-ns.groovy Gist[115].

The only difference between that job and the one we used before is in podTemplate arguments namespace and serviceAccount. This time we specified that the Pod should be created in the go-demo-3-build Namespace and that it should use the ServiceAccount build. If everything works as expected, the instruction to run Pods in a different Namespace should provide the separation we crave, and the ServiceAccount will give the permissions the Pod might need when interacting with Kube API or other Pods.

Please click the *Save* button to persist the change of the Job definition.

---

[115]https://gist.github.com/ced1806af8e092d202942a79e81d5ba9

Next, we'll open Jenkins' BlueOcean screen and check whether we can run builds based on the modified Job.

```
1  open "http://$JENKINS_ADDR/blue/organizations/jenkins/my-k8s-job/activity"
```

Please click the *Run* button, and select the row with the new build. You'll see the same `Waiting for next available executor` message we've already seen in the past. Jenkins needs to wait until a Pod is created and is fully operational. However, this time the wait will be longer since Jenkins will not be able to create the Pod.

The fact that we defined that the Job should operate in a different Namespace will do us no good if such a Namespace does not exist. Even if we create the Namespace, we specified that it should use the ServiceAccount `build`. So, we need to create both. However, that's not where our troubles stop. There are a few other problems we'll need to solve but, for now, we'll concentrate on the missing Namespace.

Please click the *Stop* button in the top-right corner or the build. That will abort the futile attempt to create a Pod, and we can proceed and make the necessary changes that will allow us to run a build of that Job in the `go-demo-3-build` Namespace.

As a minimum, we'll have to make sure that the `go-demo-3-build` Namespace exists and that it has the ServiceAccount `build` which is bound to a Role with sufficient permissions. While we're defining the Namespace, we should probably define a LimitRange and a ResourceQuota. Fortunately, we already did all that in the previous chapters, and we already have a YAML file that does just that.

Let's take a quick look at the `build-ns.yml` file available in the *go-demo-3* repository.

```
1  cat ../go-demo-3/k8s/build-ns.yml
```

We won't go through the details behind that definition since we already explored it in the previous chapters. Instead, we'll imagine that we are cluster administrators and that the team in charge of *go-demo-3* asked us to `apply` that definition.

```
1  kubectl apply \
2      -f ../go-demo-3/k8s/build-ns.yml \
3      --record
```

The output shows that the resources defined in that YAML were created.

Even though we won't build a continuous deployment pipeline just yet, we should be prepared for running our application in production. Since it should be separated from the testing Pods and releases under test, we'll create another Namespace that will be used exclusively for *go-demo-3* production releases. Just as before, we'll `apply` the definition stored in the *go-demo-3* repository.

```
1  cat ../go-demo-3/k8s/prod-ns.yml
2
3  kubectl apply \
4      -f ../go-demo-3/k8s/prod-ns.yml \
5      --record
```

We're missing one more thing before the part of the setup related to Kubernetes resources is finished.

So far, we have a RoleBinding inside the jenkins Namespace that provides Jenkins with enough permissions to create Pods in the same Namespace. However, our latest Pipeline wants to create Pods in the go-demo-3-build Namespace. Given that we are not using ClusterRoleBinding that would provide cluster-wide permissions, we'll need to create a RoleBinding in go-demo-3-build as well. Since that is specific to the application, the definition is in its repository, and it should be executed by the administrator of the cluster, just as the previous two.

Let's take a quick look at the definition.

```
1  cat ../go-demo-3/k8s/jenkins.yml
```

The output is as follows.

```
1  apiVersion: rbac.authorization.k8s.io/v1
2  kind: RoleBinding
3  metadata:
4    name: jenkins-role-binding
5    namespace: go-demo-3-build
6    labels:
7      app: jenkins
8  roleRef:
9    apiGroup: rbac.authorization.k8s.io
10   kind: ClusterRole
11   name: cluster-admin
12 subjects:
13 - kind: ServiceAccount
14   name: jenkins
15   namespace: jenkins
```

The binding is relatively straightforward. It will bind the ServiceAccount in the jenkins Namespace with the ClusterRole cluster-admin. We will reduce those permissions in the next chapter. For now, remember that we're creating a RoleBinding in the go-demo-3-build Namespace and that it'll give ServiceAccount jenkins in the jenkins Namespace full permissions to do whatever it wants in the go-demo-3-build Namespace.

Let's apply this last Kubernetes definition before we proceed with changes in Jenkins itself.

```
1  kubectl apply \
2      -f ../go-demo-3/k8s/jenkins.yml \
3      --record
```

The next issue we'll have to solve is communication between Jenkins and the Pods spun during builds. Let's take a quick look at the configuration screen.

```
1  open "http://$JENKINS_ADDR/configure"
```

If you scroll down to the *Jenkins URL* field of the *Kubernetes* section, you'll notice that it is set to *http://jenkins:8080*. Similarly, *Jenkins tunnel* is *jenkins-agent:50000*. The two values correspond to the names of the Services through which agent Pods will establish communication with the master and vice versa. As you hopefully already know, using only the name of a Service allows communication between Pods in the same Namespace. If we'd like to extend that communication across different Namespaces, we need to use the *[SERVICE_NAME].[NAMESPACE]* format. That way, agent Pods will know where to find the Jenkins Pod, no matter where they're running. Communication will be established even if Jenkins is in the `jenkins` Namespace and the agent Pods are in `go-demo-3-build`, or anywhere else.

Let's change the config.

Please scroll to the *Kubernetes* section, and change the value of the *Jenkins URL* field to the address of the Service *http://jenkins.jenkins:8080*. Similarly, change the *Jenkins tunnel* field to *jenkins-agent.jenkins:50000*. Don't forget to click the *Save* button.

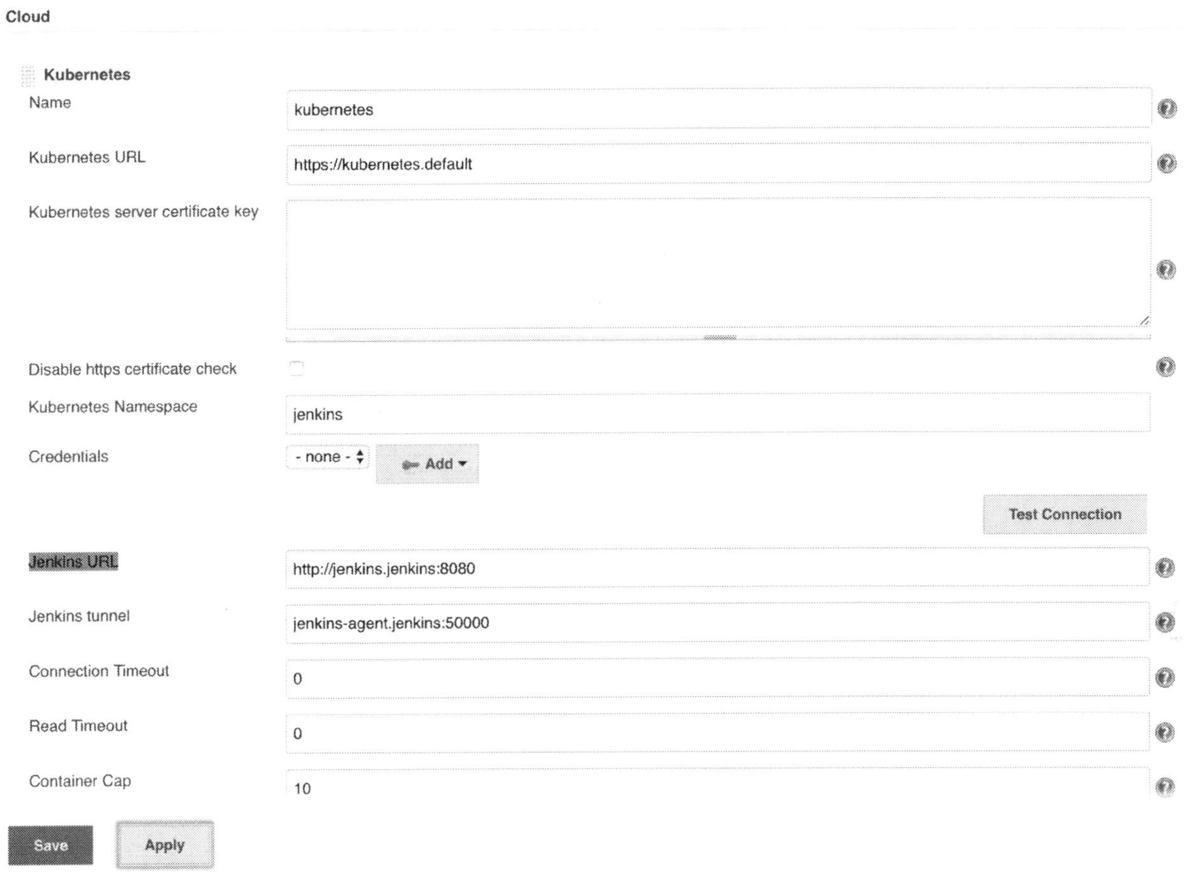

Figure 6-4: Jenkins configuration screen with Kubernetes plugin configured for cross-Namespace usage

Our troubles are not yet over. We need to rethink our Helm strategy.

We have Tiller running in the `kube-system` Namespace. However, our agent Pods running in `go-demo-3-build` do not have permissions to access it. We could extend the permissions, but that would allow the Pods in that Namespace to gain almost complete control over the whole cluster. Unless your organization is very small, that is often not acceptable. Instead, we'll deploy another Tiller instance in the `go-demo-3-build` Namespace and tie it to the ServiceAccount `build`. That will give the new tiller the same permissions in the `go-demo-3` and `go-demo-3-build` Namespaces. It'll be able to do anything in those, but nothing anywhere else.

That strategy has a downside. It is more expensive to run multiple Tillers than to run one. However, if we organize them per teams in our organization by giving each a separate Tiller instance, we can allow them full freedom within their Namespaces without affecting others. On top of that, remember that Tiller will be removed in Helm v3, so this is only a temporary fix.

```
1  helm init --service-account build \
2      --tiller-namespace go-demo-3-build
```

The output ends with the `Happy Helming!` message, letting us know that Tiller resources are installed. To be on the safe side, we'll wait until it rolls out.

```
1 kubectl -n go-demo-3-build \
2     rollout status \
3     deployment tiller-deploy
```

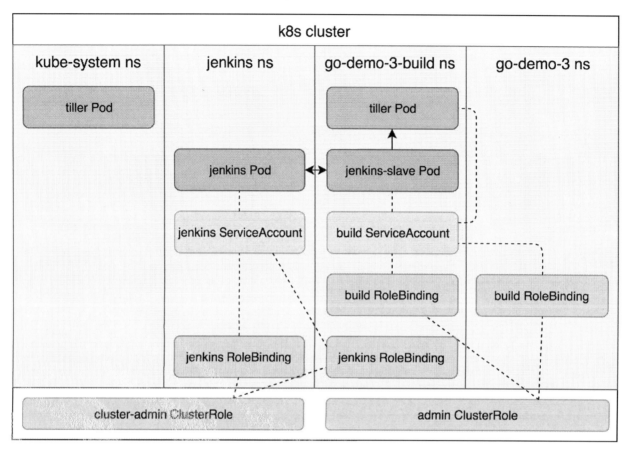

Figure 6-5: Jenkins with permissions to operate across multiple Namespaces

Now we are ready to re-run the job.

```
1 open "http://$JENKINS_ADDR/blue/organizations/jenkins/my-k8s-job/activity"
```

Please click the *Run* button followed with a click to the row of the new build.

While waiting for the build to start, we'll go back to the terminal and confirm that a new `jenkins-slave-...` Pod is created.

```
1 kubectl -n go-demo-3-build \
2     get pods
```

The output is as follows.

```
1  NAME                 READY STATUS   RESTARTS AGE
2  jenkins-slave-... 5/5   Running 0        36s
3  tiller-deploy-... 1/1   Running 0        3m
```

If you do not see the `jenkins-slave` Pod, you might need to wait for a few moments, and retrieve the Pods again.

Once the state of the `jenkins-slave` Pod is `Running`, we can go back to Jenkins UI and observe that it progresses until the end and that it turns to green.

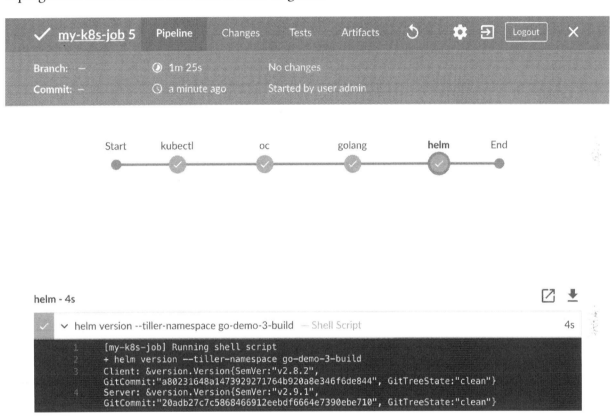

Figure 6-6: Jenkins job for testing tools

We managed to run the tools in the separate Namespace. However, we still need to solve the issue of building container images.

Creating Nodes For Building Container Images

We already discussed that mounting a Docker socket is a bad idea due to security risks. Running Docker in Docker would require privileged access, and that is almost as unsafe and Docker socket. On top of that, both options have other downsides. Using Docker socket would introduce processes unknown to Kubernetes and could interfere with it's scheduling capabilities. Running Docker in

Docker could mess up with networking. There are other reasons why both options are not good, so we need to look for an alternative.

Recently, new projects spun up attempting to help with building container images. Good examples are img[116], orca-build[117], umoci[118], buildah[119], FTL[120], and Bazel rules_docker[121]. They all have serious downsides. While they might help, none of them is a good solution which I'd recommend as a replacement for building container images with Docker.

kaniko[122] is a shiny star that has a potential to become a preferable way for building container images. It does not require Docker nor any other node dependency. It can run as a container, and it is likely to become a valid alternative one day. However, that day is not today (June 2018). It is still green, unstable, and unproven.

All in all, Docker is still our best option for building container images, but not inside a Kubernetes cluster. That means that we need to build our images in a VM outside Kubernetes.

How are we going to create a VM for building container images? Are we going to have a static VM that will be wasting our resources when at rest?

The answer to those questions depends on the hosting provider you're using. If it allows dynamic creation of VMs, we can create them when we need them, and destroy them when we don't. If that's not an option, we need to fall back to a dedicated machine for building images.

I could not describe all the methods for creating VMs, so I limited the scope to three combinations. We'll explore how to create a static VM in cases when dynamic provisioning is not an option. If you're using Docker For Mac or Windows, minikube, or minishift, that is your best bet. We'll use Vagrant, but the same principles can be applied to any other, often on-premise, virtualization technology.

On the other hand, if you're using a hosting provider that does support dynamic provisioning of VMs, you should leverage that to your benefit to create them when needed, and destroy them when not. I'll show you the examples of Amazon's Elastic Compute Cloud (EC2) and Google Cloud Engine (GCE). If you use something else (e.g., Azure, DigitalOcean), the principle will be the same, even though the implementation might vary significantly.

The primary question is whether Jenkins supports your provider. If it does, you can use a plugin that will take care of creating and destroying nodes. Otherwise, you might need to extend your Pipeline scripts to use provider's API to spin up new nodes. In that case, you might want to evaluate whether such an option is worth the trouble. Remember, if everything else fails, having a static VM dedicated to building container images will always work.

Even if you chose to build your container images differently, it is still a good idea to know how to connect external VMs to Jenkins. There's often a use-case that cannot (or shouldn't) be accomplished

---

[116]https://github.com/genuinetools/img
[117]https://github.com/cyphar/orca-build
[118]https://github.com/openSUSE/umoci
[119]https://github.com/projectatomic/buildah
[120]https://github.com/GoogleCloudPlatform/runtimes-common/tree/master/ftl
[121]https://github.com/bazelbuild/rules_docker
[122]https://github.com/GoogleContainerTools/kaniko

inside a Kubernetes cluster. You might need to execute some of the steps in Windows nodes. There might be processes that shouldn't run inside containers. Or, maybe you need to connect Android devices to your Pipelines. No matter the use-case, knowing how to connect external agents to Jenkins is essential. So, building container images is not necessarily the only reason for having external agents (nodes), and I strongly suggest exploring the sections that follow, even if you don't think it's useful at this moment.

Before we jump into different ways to create VMs for building and pushing container images, we need to create one thing common to all. We'll need to create a set of credentials that will allow us to login to Docker Hub.

```
1  open "http://$JENKINS_ADDR/credentials/store/system/domain/_/newCredentials"
```

Please type your Docker Hub *Username* and *Password*. Both the *ID* and the *Description* should be set to *docker* since that is the reference we'll use later. Don't forget to click the *OK* button.

Now we are ready to create some VMs. Please choose the section that best fits your use case. Or, even better, try all three of them.

Creating a VM with Vagrant and VirtualBox

 This section is appropriate for those using **Docker for Mac or Windows**, **minikube**, **minishift**, or anyone else planning to use static nodes as agents.

We'll use Vagrant[123] to create a local VM. Please install it if you do not have it already.

The *Vagrantfile* we'll use is already available inside the vfarcic/k8s-specs[124]. It's in the *cd/docker-build* directory, so let's go there and take a quick look at the definition.

```
1  cd cd/docker-build
2
3  cat Vagrantfile
```

The output of the latter command is as follows.

---

[123]https://www.vagrantup.com/
[124]https://github.com/vfarcic/k8s-specs

```
1  # vi: set ft=ruby :
2
3  Vagrant.configure("2") do |config|
4      config.vm.box = "ubuntu/xenial64"
5
6      config.vm.define "docker-build" do |node|
7        node.vm.hostname = "docker-build"
8        node.vm.network :private_network, ip: "10.100.198.200"
9        node.vm.provision :shell, inline: "apt remove -y docker docker-engine docker.i\
10 o"
11       node.vm.provision :shell, inline: "apt update"
12       node.vm.provision :shell, inline: "apt install apt-transport-https ca-certific\
13 ates curl software-properties-common"
14       node.vm.provision :shell, inline: "curl -fsSL https://download.docker.com/linu\
15 x/ubuntu/gpg | apt-key add -"
16       node.vm.provision :shell, inline: "add-apt-repository \"deb [arch=amd64] https\
17 ://download.docker.com/linux/ubuntu $(lsb_release -cs) stable\""
18       node.vm.provision :shell, inline: "apt update"
19       node.vm.provision :shell, inline: "apt install -y docker-ce"
20       node.vm.provision :shell, inline: "sudo apt install -y default-jre"
21     end
22 end
```

That Vagrantfile is very simple. Even if you never used Vagrant, you should have no trouble understanding what it does.

We're defining a VM called docker-build, and we're assigning it a static IP 10.100.198.200. The node.vm.provision will install Docker and JRE. The latter is required for establishing the connection between Jenkins and this soon-to-be VM.

Next, we'll create a VM based on that Vagrantfile definition.

```
1  vagrant up
```

Now that the VM is up and running, we can go back to Jenkins and add it as a new agent node.

```
1  open "http://$JENKINS_ADDR/computer/new"
```

Please type *docker-build* as the *Node name*, select *Permanent Agent*, and click the *OK* button.

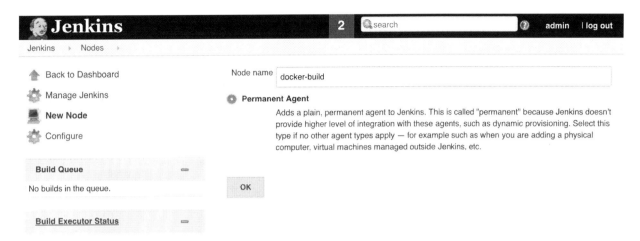

Figure 6-7: Jenkins screen for adding new nodes/agents

You are presented with a node configuration screen.

Please type *2* as the *# of executors*. That will allow us to run up to two processes inside this agent. To put it differently, up to two builds will be able to use it in parallel. If there are more than two, the new builds will wait in a queue until one of the executors is released. Depending on the size of your organization, you might want to increase the number of executors or add more nodes. As a rule of thumb, you should have one executor per CPU. In our case, we should be better of with one executor, but we'll roll with two mostly as a demonstration.

Next, we should set the *Remote root directory*. That's the place on the node's file system where Jenkins will store the state of the builds. Please set it to */tmp* or choose any other directory. Just remember that Jenkins will not create it, so the folder must already exist on the system.

We should set labels that define the machine we're going to use as a Jenkins agent. It is always a good idea to be descriptive, even if we're sure that we will use only one of the labels. Since that node is based on Ubuntu Linux distribution and it has Docker, our labels will be *docker ubuntu linux*. Please type the three into the *Labels* field.

There are a couple of methods we can use to establish the communication between Jenkins and the newly created node. Since it's Linux, the easiest, and probably the best method is SSH. Please select *Launch slave agents via SSH* as the *Launch Method*.

The last piece of information we'll define, before jumping into credentials, is the *Host*. Please type *10.100.198.200*.

We're almost finished. The only thing left is to create a set of credentials and assign them to this agent.

Please click the *Add* drop-down next to *Credentials* and select *Jenkins*.

Once in the credentials popup screen, select *SSH Username with private key* as the *Kind*, type *vagrant* as the *Username*, and select *Enter directly* as the *Private Key*.

We'll have to go back to the terminal to retrieve the private key created by Vagrant when it generated the VM.

```
1  cat .vagrant/machines/docker-build/virtualbox/private_key
```

Please copy the output, go back to Jenkins UI, and paste it into the *Key* field. Type *docker-build* as the *ID*, and click the *Add* button.

The credentials are generated, and we are back in the agent configuration screen. However, Jenkins did not pick the newly credentials automatically, so we'll need to select *vagrant* in the *Credentials* drop-down list. Finally, since we used the private key, we'll skip verification by selecting *Not verifying Verification Strategy* as the *Host Key Verification Strategy*.

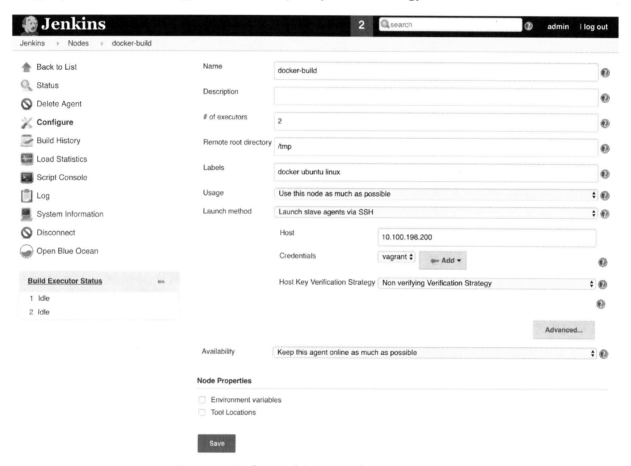

Figure 6-8: Jenkins node/agent configuration screen

Do not forget to click the *Save* button to persist the agent information.

You'll be redirected back to the Nodes screen. Please refresh the screen if the newly created agent is red.

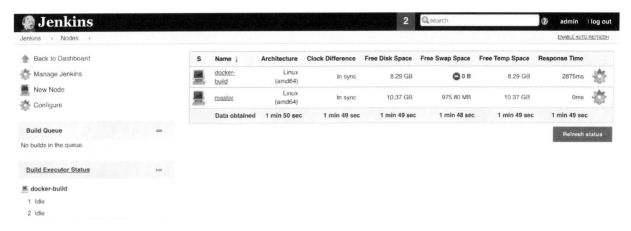

Figure 6-9: Jenkins nodes/agents screen

All that's left is to go back to the *k8s-specs* root directory.

```
1  cd ../../
2
3  export DOCKER_VM=true
```

We'll use the newly created agent soon. Feel free to skip the next two sections if this was the way you're planning to create agents for building container images.

Creating Amazon Machine Images (AMIs)

 This section is appropriate for those using **AWS**.

We'll use Jenkins EC2 plugin[125] to create agent nodes when needed and destroy them after a period of inactivity. The plugin is already installed. However, we'll need to configure it to use a specific Amazon Machine Image (AMI), so creating one is our first order of business.

Before we proceed, please make sure that the environment variables AWS_ACCESS_KEY_ID, AWS_-SECRET_ACCESS_KEY, and AWS_DEFAULT_REGION are set. If you followed the instructions for setting up the cluster with kops, the environment variables are already defined in source cluster/kops.

We'll build the image with Packer[126], so please make sure that it is installed in your laptop.

Packer definition we'll explore soon will require a security group. Please execute the command that follows to create one.

---

[125]https://plugins.jenkins.io/ec2
[126]https://www.packer.io/

```
1  export AWS_DEFAULT_REGION=us-east-2
2
3  aws ec2 create-security-group \
4      --description "For building Docker images" \
5      --group-name docker \
6      | tee cluster/sg.json
```

For convenience, we'll parse the output stored in cluster/sg.json to retrieve GroupId and assign it in an environment variable. Please install jq[127] if you don't have it already.

```
1  SG_ID=$(cat cluster/sg.json \
2      | jq -r ".GroupId")
3
4  echo $SG_ID
```

The output of the latter command should be similar to the one that follows.

```
1  sg-5fe96935
```

Next, we'll store the security group export in a file so that we can easily retrieve it in the next chapters.

```
1  echo "export SG_ID=$SG_ID" \
2      | tee -a cluster/docker-ec2
```

The security group we created is useless in its current form. We'll need to authorize it to allow communication on port 22 so that Packer can access it and execute provisioning.

```
1  aws ec2 \
2      authorize-security-group-ingress \
3      --group-name docker \
4      --protocol tcp \
5      --port 22 \
6      --cidr 0.0.0.0/0
```

We're done with the preparation steps and we can proceed to create the AMI.

Let's take a quick look at the Package definition we'll use.

---

[127]https://stedolan.github.io/jq/

```
1  cat jenkins/docker-ami.json
```

The output is as follows.

```
1  {
2    "builders": [{
3      "type": "amazon-ebs",
4      "region": "us-east-2",
5      "source_ami_filter": {
6        "filters": {
7          "virtualization-type": "hvm",
8          "name": "*ubuntu-xenial-16.04-amd64-server-*",
9          "root-device-type": "ebs"
10       },
11       "most_recent": true
12     },
13     "instance_type": "t2.micro",
14     "ssh_username": "ubuntu",
15     "ami_name": "docker",
16     "force_deregister": true
17   }],
18   "provisioners": [{
19     "type": "shell",
20     "inline": [
21       "sleep 15",
22       "sudo apt-get clean",
23       "sudo apt-get update",
24       "sudo apt-get install -y apt-transport-https ca-certificates nfs-common",
25       "curl -fsSL https://download.docker.com/linux/ubuntu/gpg | sudo apt-key add -",
26       "sudo add-apt-repository \"deb [arch=amd64] https://download.docker.com/linux/\
27  ubuntu $(lsb_release -cs) stable\"",
28       "sudo add-apt-repository -y ppa:openjdk-r/ppa",
29       "sudo apt-get update",
30       "sudo apt-get install -y docker-ce",
31       "sudo usermod -aG docker ubuntu",
32       "sudo apt-get install -y openjdk-8-jdk"
33     ]
34   }]
35  }
```

Most of the definition should be self-explanatory. We'll create an EBS image based on Ubuntu in the us-east-2 region and we'll use the `shell` `provisioner` to install Docker and JDK.

Let's create the AMI.

```
1  packer build -machine-readable \
2      jenkins/docker-ami.json \
3      | tee cluster/docker-ami.log
```

The last lines of the output are as follows.

```
1  ...
2  ...,amazon-ebs,artifact,0,id,us-east-2:ami-ea053b8f
3  ...,amazon-ebs,artifact,0,string,AMIs were created:\nus-east-2: ami-ea053b8f\n
4  ...,amazon-ebs,artifact,0,files-count,0
5  ...,amazon-ebs,artifact,0,end
6  ...,,ui,say,--> amazon-ebs: AMIs were created:\nus-east-2: ami-ea053b8f\n
```

The important line is the one that contains artifact,0,id. The last column in that row contains
the ID we'll need to tell Jenkins about the new AMI. We'll store it in an environment variable for
convenience.

```
1  AMI_ID=$(grep 'artifact,0,id' \
2      cluster/docker-ami.log \
3      | cut -d: -f2)
4
5  echo $AMI_ID
```

The output of the latter command should be similar to the one that follows.

```
1  ami-ea053b8f
```

Just as with the security group, we'll store the AMI_ID export in the docker-ec2 file so that we can
retrieve it easily in the next chapters.

```
1  echo "export AMI_ID=$AMI_ID" \
2      | tee -a cluster/docker-ec2
```

Now that we have the AMI, we need to move to Jenkins and configure the *Amazon EC2* plugin.

```
1  open "http://$JENKINS_ADDR/configure"
```

Please scroll to the *Cloud* section and click the *Add a new cloud* drop-down list. Choose *Amazon
EC2*. A new form will appear.

Type *docker-agents* as the *Name*, and expand the *Add* drop-down list next to *Amazon EC2
Credentials*. Choose *Jenkins*.

From the credentials screen, please choose *AWS Credentials* as the *Kind*, and type *aws* as both the
ID and the *Description*.

Next, we need to return to the terminal to retrieve the AWS access key ID.

```
1   echo $AWS_ACCESS_KEY_ID
```

Please copy the output, return to Jenkins UI, and paste it into the *Access Key ID* field.

We'll repeat the same process for the AWS secrets access key.

```
1   echo $AWS_SECRET_ACCESS_KEY
```

Copy the output, return to Jenkins UI, and paste it into the *Secret Access Key* field.

With the credentials information filled in, we need to press the *Add* button to store it and return to the EC2 configuration screen.

Please choose the newly created credentials and select *us-east-2* as the *Region*.

We need the private key next. It can be created through the aws ec2 command create-key-pair.

```
1   aws ec2 create-key-pair \
2       --key-name devops24 \
3       | jq -r '.KeyMaterial' \
4       >cluster/devops24.pem
```

We created a new key pair, filtered the output so that only the KeyMaterial is returned, and stored it in the devops24.pem file.

For security reasons, we should change the permissions of the devops24.pem file so that only the current user can read it.

```
1   chmod 400 cluster/devops24.pem
```

Finally, we'll output the content of the pem file.

```
1   cat cluster/devops24.pem
```

Please copy the output, return to Jenkins UI, and paste it into the *EC2 Key Pair's Private Key* field.

To be on the safe side, press the *Test Connection* button, and confirm that the output is *Success*.

We're finished with the general *Amazon EC2* configuration, and we can proceed to add the first and the only AMI.

Please click the *Add* button next to *AMIs*, and type *docker* as the *Description*.

We need to return to the terminal one more time to retrieve the AMI ID.

```
1  echo $AMI_ID
```

Please copy the output, return to Jenkins UI, and paste it into the *AMI ID* field.

To be on the safe side, please click the *Check AMI* button, and confirm that the output does not show any error.

We're almost done.

Select *T2Micro* as the *Instance Type*, type *docker* as the *Security group names*, and type *ubuntu* as the *Remote user*. The *Remote ssh port* should be set to *22*. Please write *docker ubuntu linux* as the labels, and change the *Idle termination time* to *10*.

Finally, click the *Save* button to preserve the changes.

We'll use the newly created EC2 template soon. Feel free to skip the next section if this was the way you're planning to create agents for building container images.

Creating Google Cloud Engine (GCE) Images

 This section is appropriate for those using **GKE**.

If you reached this far, it means that you prefer running your cluster in GKE, or that you are so curious that you prefer trying all three ways to create VMs that will be used to build container images. No matter the reason, we're about to create a GCE image and configure Jenkins to spin up VMs when needed and destroy them when they're not in use.

Before we do anything related to GCE, we need to authenticate.

```
1  gcloud auth login
```

Next, we need to create a service account that can be used by Packer to create GCE images.

```
1  gcloud iam service-accounts \
2      create jenkins
```

The output is as follows.

```
1  Created service account [jenkins].
```

We'll also need to know the project you're planning to use. We'll assume that it's the one that is currently active and we'll retrieve it with the `gcloud info` command.

```
1  export G_PROJECT=$(gcloud info \
2      --format='value(config.project)')
3
4  echo $G_PROJECT
```

Please note that the output might differ from what I've got. In my case, the output is as follows.

```
1  devops24-book
```

The last information we need is the email that was generated when we created the service account.

```
1  export SA_EMAIL=$(gcloud iam \
2      service-accounts list \
3      --filter="name:jenkins" \
4      --format='value(email)')
5
6  echo $SA_EMAIL
```

In my case, the output is as follows.

```
1  jenkins@devops24-book.iam.gserviceaccount.com
```

Now that we retrieved all the information we need, we can proceed and create a policy binding between the service account and the compute.admin role. That will give us more than sufficient privileges not only to create images but also to instantiate VMs based on them.

```
1  gcloud projects add-iam-policy-binding \
2      --member serviceAccount:$SA_EMAIL \
3      --role roles/compute.admin \
4      $G_PROJECT
```

The output shows all the information related to the binding we created. Instead of going into details, we'll create another one.

```
1  gcloud projects add-iam-policy-binding \
2      --member serviceAccount:$SA_EMAIL \
3      --role roles/iam.serviceAccountUser \
4      $G_PROJECT
```

Now that our service account is bound both to compute.admin and iam.serviceAccountUser roles, the only thing left before we create a GCE image is to create a set of keys.

```
1  gcloud iam service-accounts \
2      keys create \
3      --iam-account $SA_EMAIL \
4      cluster/gce-jenkins.json
```

The output is as follows.

```
1  created key [...] of type [json] as [cluster/gce-jenkins.json] for [jenkins@devops24\
2  -book.iam.gserviceaccount.com]
```

We're finally ready to create an image. We'll build it with Packer[128], so please make sure that it is installed in your laptop.

The definition of the image we'll create is stored in the docker-gce.json file. Let's take a quick look.

```
1  cat jenkins/docker-gce.json
```

The output is as follows.

```
1  {
2    "variables": {
3      "project_id": ""
4    },
5    "builders": [{
6      "type": "googlecompute",
7      "account_file": "cluster/gce-jenkins.json",
8      "project_id": "{{user `project_id`}}",
9      "source_image_project_id": "ubuntu-os-cloud",
10     "source_image_family": "ubuntu-1604-lts",
11     "ssh_username": "ubuntu",
12     "zone": "us-east1-b",
13     "image_name": "docker"
14   }],
15   "provisioners": [{
16     "type": "shell",
17     "inline": [
18       "sleep 15",
19       "sudo apt-get clean",
20       "sudo apt-get update",
21       "sudo apt-get install -y apt-transport-https ca-certificates nfs-common",
22       "curl -fsSL https://download.docker.com/linux/ubuntu/gpg | sudo apt-key add -",
```

---

[128]https://www.packer.io/

```
23        "sudo add-apt-repository \"deb [arch=amd64] https://download.docker.com/linux/\
24  ubuntu $(lsb_release -cs) stable\"",
25        "sudo add-apt-repository -y ppa:openjdk-r/ppa",
26        "sudo apt-get update",
27        "sudo apt-get install -y docker-ce",
28        "sudo usermod -aG docker ubuntu",
29        "sudo apt-get install -y openjdk-8-jdk"
30      ]
31    }]
32  }
```

That Packer definition should be self-explanatory. It containers the `builders` section that defines the parameters required to build an image in GCE, and the `provisioners` contain the `shell` commands that install Docker and JDK. The latter is required for Jenkins to establish the communication with the agent VMs we'll create from that image.

Feel free to change the zone if you're running your cluster somewhere other than `us-east1`.

Next, we'll execute `packer build` command that will create the image.

```
1  packer build -machine-readable \
2      --force \
3      -var "project_id=$G_PROJECT" \
4      jenkins/docker-gce.json \
5      | tee cluster/docker-gce.log
```

The output, limited to the last few lines, is as follows.

```
1  ...
2  ...,googlecompute,artifact,0,id,docker
3  ...,googlecompute,artifact,0,string,A disk image was created: docker
4  ...,googlecompute,artifact,0,files-count,0
5  ...,googlecompute,artifact,0,end
6  ...,,ui,say,--> googlecompute: A disk image was created: docker
```

Now that we have the image, we should turn our attention back to Jenkins and configure *Google Compute Engine Cloud*.

```
1  open "http://$JENKINS_ADDR/configure"
```

The chances are that your Jenkins session expired and that you'll need to log in again. If that's the case, please output the password we stored in the environment variable `JENKINS_PASS` and use it to authenticate.

```
1  echo $JENKINS_PASS
```

Once inside the Jenkins configuration screen, please expand the *Add a new cloud* drop-down list. It is located near the bottom of the screen. Select *Google Compute Engine*.

A new set of fields will appear. We'll need to fill them in so that Jenkins knows how to connect to GCE and what to do if we request a new node.

Type *docker* as the *Name*.

We'll need to go back to the terminal and retrieve the Project ID we stored in the environment variable G_PROJECT.

```
1  echo $G_PROJECT
```

Please copy the output, go back to Jenkins UI, and paste it into the *Project ID* field.

Next, we'll create the credentials.

Expand the *Add* drop-down list next to *Service Account Credentials* and select *Jenkins*.

You'll see a new popup with the form to create credentials.

Select *Google Service Account from private key* as the *Kind* and paste the name of the project to the *Project Name* field (the one you got from G_PROJECT variable).

Click *Choose File* button in the *JSON Key* field and select the *gce-jenkins.json* file we created earlier in the *cluster* directory.

Click the *Add* button, and the new credential will be persisted.

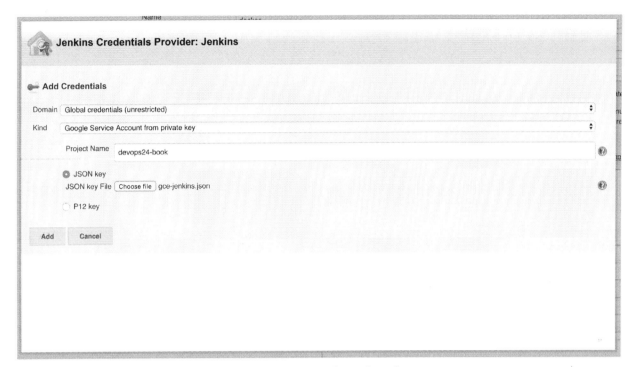

Figure 6-10: Jenkins Google credentials screen

We're back in the *Google Compute Engine* screen, and we need to select the newly created credential before we proceed.

Next, we'll add a definition of VMs we'd like to create through Jenkins.

Please click the *Add* button next to *Instance Configurations*, type *docker* as the *Name Prefix*, and type *Docker build instances* as the *Description*. Write *10* as the *Node Retention Time* and type *docker ubuntu linux* as the *Labels*. The retention time defines the period Jenkins will wait until destroying the VM. If in our case no other build needs that VM, it'll be destroyed after one minute. In "real" Jenkins, we'd need to think carefully what to use as retention. If the value is too low, we'll save on costs but builds execution will be longer since they'll need to wait until a new VM is created. On the other hand, if the value is too high, the same VM will be reused more often, but we'll be paying for compute time we don't use if there are no pending builds. For our experiments, one minute should do.

If you're running your cluster in *us-east-1*, please select it as the *Region*. Otherwise, switch to whichever region your cluster is running in and, more importantly, the region where the image was created. Similarly, select the appropriate zone. If you're following the exact steps, it should be *us-east1-b*. The important part is that the zone must be the same as the one where we built the image.

We're almost done with *Google Compute Engine* Jenkins' configuration.

Select *n1-standard-2* as the *Machine Type*, select *default* as both the *Network* and the *Subnetwork* and check both *External IP* and *Internal IP* check boxes.

In GCE, you will need to have either an external IP or a NAT gateway setup to download anything from the internet. As we do not want to bother you with the NAT gateway setup, we will configure an *External IP*. As we also want to have our connection traffic not unnecessarily going through the internet, we also select *Internal IP* to make sure Jenkins still uses the internal IP.

The *Image project* should be set to the same value as the one we stored in the environment variable `G_PROJECT`.

Finally, select *docker* as the *Image name* and click the *Save* button.

Testing Docker Builds Outside The Cluster

No matter whether you choose to use static VMs or you decided to create them dynamically in AWS or GCE, the steps to test them are the same. From Jenkins' perspective, all that matters is that there are agent nodes with the labels *docker*.

We'll modify our Pipeline to use the `node` labeled `docker`.

```
1  open "http://$JENKINS_ADDR/job/my-k8s-job/configure"
```

Please click the *Pipeline* tab and replace the script with the one that follows.

```
1  podTemplate(
2      label: "kubernetes",
3      namespace: "go-demo-3-build",
4      serviceAccount: "build",
5      yaml: """
6  apiVersion: v1
7  kind: Pod
8  spec:
9    containers:
10   - name: kubectl
11     image: vfarcic/kubectl
12     command: ["sleep"]
13     args: ["100000"]
14   - name: oc
15     image: vfarcic/openshift-client
16     command: ["sleep"]
17     args: ["100000"]
18   - name: golang
19     image: golang:1.9
```

```
20        command: ["sleep"]
21        args: ["100000"]
22      - name: helm
23        image: vfarcic/helm:2.8.2
24        command: ["sleep"]
25        args: ["100000"]
26    """
27    ) {
28        node("docker") {
29            stage("docker") {
30                sh "sudo docker version"
31            }
32        }
33        node("kubernetes") {
34            container("kubectl") {
35                stage("kubectl") {
36                    sh "kubectl version"
37                }
38            }
39            container("oc") {
40                stage("oc") {
41                    sh "oc version"
42                }
43            }
44            container("golang") {
45                stage("golang") {
46                    sh "go version"
47                }
48            }
49            container("helm") {
50                stage("helm") {
51                    sh "helm version --tiller-namespace go-demo-3-build"
52                }
53            }
54        }
55    }
```

If you prefer to copy and paste, the job is available in the my-k8s-job-docker.groovy Gist[129].

The only notable difference, when compared with the previous version of the job, is that we added

---
[129]https://gist.github.com/fbf9fc6611fe400c7950f43cfc89f406

the second node segment. Most of the steps will be executed inside the kubernetes node that hosts a few containers. The new node is called docker and will be in charge of the steps that require Docker server. Depending on the path you took, that node might be a static VM, a dynamically created (and destroyed) node in AWS or GCE, or something entirely different. From job's perspective, it does not matter how is that node created, but that it exists or that it will be created on demand. The job will request nodes docker and kubernetes, and it is up to Jenkins' internal configuration to figure out how to get them.

Please click the *Save* button to persist the updated job.

Next, we'll open the job in BlueOcean and run it as a way to confirm that everything works as expected.

```
1  open "http://$JENKINS_ADDR/blue/organizations/jenkins/my-k8s-job/activity"
```

Press the *Run* button, followed with a click on the row of the new build. Wait until all the stages are executed.

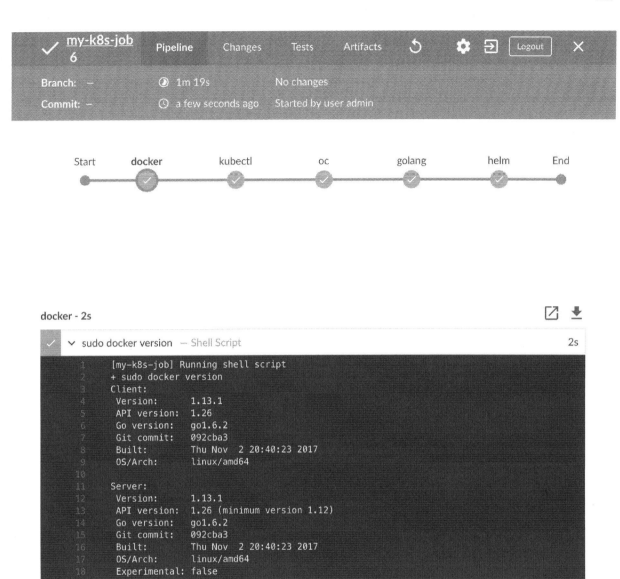

Figure 6-11: Jenkins job for testing tools

This time, everything worked, and the build is green. We managed to run the steps in a different Namespace without sacrificing security while keeping `docker` commands outside the Kubernetes cluster in a separate node.

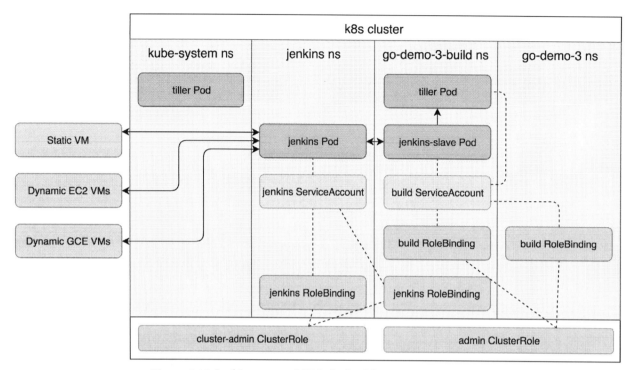

Figure 6-12: Jenkins external VMs for building container images

Now that we know what we want to accomplish, we'll switch our attention to full automation of Jenkins installation and setup.

Automating Jenkins Installation And Setup

One of the critical parts of Jenkins automation is the management of credentials. Jenkins uses `hudson.util.Secret` and `master.key` files to encrypt all the credentials. The two are stored in *secrets* directory inside Jenkins home directory. The credentials we uploaded or pasted are stored in `credentials.yml`. On top of those, each plugin (e.g., Google cloud) can add their files with credentials.

We need the credentials as well and the secrets if we are to automate Jenkins setup. One solution could be to generate the secrets, use them to encrypt credentials, and store them as Kubernetes secrets or config maps. However, that is a tedious process. Since we already have a fully configured Jenkins, we might just as well copy the files.

We'll persist the files we need to the local directories `cluster/jenkins` and `cluster/jenkins/secrets`. So, our first step is to create them.

```
1   mkdir -p cluster/jenkins/secrets
```

Next, we need to copy the files from the existing Jenkins instance. To do that, we need to find out the name of the Pod with Jenkins. We'll describe `jenkins` Deployment and check whether Jenkins Pods have labels that uniquely describe them.

```
1  kubectl -n jenkins \
2      describe deployment jenkins
```

The output, limited to the `Labels` section, is as follows.

```
1  ...
2  Labels: chart=jenkins-0.16.1
3          component=jenkins-jenkins-master
4          heritage=Tiller
5          release=jenkins
6  ...
```

The `component` label seems to be unique, and we can use it to retrieve the Jenkins Pod.

```
1  kubectl -n jenkins \
2      get pods \
3      -l component=jenkins-jenkins-master
```

The output is as follows.

```
1  NAME          READY STATUS  RESTARTS AGE
2  jenkins-... 1/1   Running 0          3h
```

We can combine that command with `jsonpath` output to retrieve only the name of the Pod and store it in an environment variable we'll use later to copy the files we need.

```
1  JENKINS_POD=$(kubectl -n jenkins \
2      get pods \
3      -l component=jenkins-jenkins-master \
4      -o jsonpath='{.items[0].metadata.name}')
5
6  echo $JENKINS_POD
```

The output of the latter command is as follows.

```
1  jenkins-c7f7c77b4-cgxx8
```

Now we can copy the files we need.

As a minimum, we'll need `credentials.xml`. That's where (most of) the credentials are stored. Since Jenkins uses the secrets to encrypt and decrypt credentials, we'll need them as well. Otherwise, Jenkins would generate new secrets when initializing and it could not decrypt the credentials.

```
1  kubectl -n jenkins cp \
2      $JENKINS_POD:var/jenkins_home/credentials.xml \
3      cluster/jenkins
4
5  kubectl -n jenkins cp \
6      $JENKINS_POD:var/jenkins_home/secrets/hudson.util.Secret \
7      cluster/jenkins/secrets
8
9  kubectl -n jenkins cp \
10     $JENKINS_POD:var/jenkins_home/secrets/master.key \
11     cluster/jenkins/secrets
```

A note to GKE users

Google cloud plugin stores authentication in a JSON file in the gauth directory. We'll need to copy the files from that folder as well.

```
kubectl    -n    jenkins    cp    $JENKINS_POD:var/jenkins_home/gauth/
cluster/jenkins/secrets

G_AUTH_FILE=$(ls cluster/jenkins/secrets/key*json | xargs -n 1 basename)

echo $G_AUTH_FILE
```

The first command copied all the files from the gauth directory inside Jenkins home, the second stored the name of the JSON file in the environment variable G_AUTH_FILE, and the last command output the name of the file so that we can confirm that it looks OK. In my case, the output of the latter command is key7754885476942296969.json.

Now that we stored the secrets and the credentials, we can remove Jenkins altogether and start over. This time, the goal is to have the installation and the setup fully automated or, if that's not possible, to reduce the number of manual steps to a minimum.

```
1  helm delete jenkins --purge
```

The output clearly states that the release "jenkins" was deleted.

We'll use a custom-made Helm chart this time. It is located in *helm/jenkins* directory inside the vfarcic/k8s-specs[130] repository that we already cloned.

Let's take a look at the files.

```
1  ls -1 helm/jenkins
```

The output is as follows.

[130]https://github.com/vfarcic/k8s-specs

```
1  Chart.yaml
2  requirements.yaml
3  templates
4  values.yaml
```

We can see that Chart follows a similar logic as the others. Chart.yaml defines metadata. You already used values.yaml so that should not come as a surprise, even though there is a twist which we'll experience a bit later. The templates directory contains the templates that form the Chart even though, as you will discover later, it has only one file. What makes this Chart unique, when compared with those we used so far, is the requirements.yaml file. We'll explore it first since it'll provide insights into the twists and weirdness we'll encounter in other files.

```
1  cat helm/jenkins/requirements.yaml
```

The output is as follows.

```
1  dependencies:
2    - name: jenkins
3      version: 0.16.1
4      repository:  https://kubernetes-charts.storage.googleapis.com
```

The requirements.yaml file lists all the dependencies of our Chart. Since all we need is Jenkins, it is the only requirement we specified.

Typically, we'd define our Chart and use requirements.yaml to add the dependencies our application needs. However, this use-case is a bit different. We do not have a Chart or, to be more precise, we did not define even a single YAML file in templates. All we want is to install Jenkins, customized to serve our needs.

At this point, you might be wondering why we do not install stable/jenkins directly with --values argument that will customize it. The reason behind using the requirements approach lies in our need to customize Jenkins config.xml file. README available in stable/jenkins Chart provides additional insight.

```
1  helm inspect readme stable/jenkins
```

The output, limited to the Custom ConfigMap section, is as follows.

```
 1  ...
 2  ## Custom ConfigMap
 3
 4  When creating a new parent chart with this chart as a dependency, the `CustomConfigM\
 5  ap` parameter can be used to override the default config.xml provided.
 6  It also allows for providing additional xml configuration files that will be copied \
 7  into `/var/jenkins_home`. In the parent chart's values.yaml,
 8  set the `jenkins.Master.CustomConfigMap` value to true...
 9  ...
10  and provide the file `templates/config.tpl` in your parent chart for your use case. \
11  You can start by copying the contents of `config.yaml` from this chart into your par\
12  ent charts `templates/config.tpl` as a basis for customization. Finally, you'll need\
13   to wrap the contents of `templates/config.tpl`...
14  ...
```

To comply with those instructions, I already created the values.yaml file, so let's take a quick look at it.

```
1  cat helm/jenkins/values.yaml
```

The output is as follows

```
 1  jenkins:
 2    Master:
 3      ImageTag: "2.121.1-alpine"
 4      Cpu: "500m"
 5      Memory: "500Mi"
 6      ServiceType: ClusterIP
 7      ServiceAnnotations:
 8        service.beta.kubernetes.io/aws-load-balancer-backend-protocol: http
 9      InstallPlugins:
10        - blueocean:1.5.0
11        - credentials:2.1.16
12        - ec2:1.39
13        - git:3.9.1
14        - git-client:2.7.2
15        - github:1.29.1
16        - kubernetes:1.7.1
17        - pipeline-utility-steps:2.1.0
18        - script-security:1.44
19        - slack:2.3
20        - thinBackup:1.9
```

```
21        - workflow-aggregator:2.5
22        - ssh-slaves:1.26
23        - ssh-agent:1.15
24        - jdk-tool:1.1
25        - command-launcher:1.2
26        - github-oauth:0.29
27        - google-compute-engine:1.0.4
28      Ingress:
29        Annotations:
30          kubernetes.io/ingress.class: "nginx"
31          nginx.ingress.kubernetes.io/ssl-redirect: "false"
32          nginx.ingress.kubernetes.io/proxy-body-size: 50m
33          nginx.ingress.kubernetes.io/proxy-request-buffering: "off"
34          ingress.kubernetes.io/ssl-redirect: "false"
35          ingress.kubernetes.io/proxy-body-size: 50m
36          ingress.kubernetes.io/proxy-request-buffering: "off"
37      HostName: jenkins.acme.com
38      CustomConfigMap: true
39      CredentialsXmlSecret: jenkins-credentials
40      SecretsFilesSecret: jenkins-secrets
41      # DockerAMI:
42      # GProject:
43      # GAuthFile:
44    rbac:
45      install: true
46      roleBindingKind: RoleBinding
```

If we compare that with `helm/jenkins-values.yml`, we'll notice that most entries are almost the same. There is one significant difference though. This time, all the entries are inside `jenkins`. That way, we're telling Helm that the values should be applied to the dependency named `jenkins` and defined in `requirements.yaml`.

If we ignore the fact that all the entries are now inside `jenkins`, there is another significant difference in that we set `jenkins.Master.CustomConfigMap` to `true`. According to the instructions we saw in the README, this flag will allow us to provide a custom ConfigMap that will replace Jenkins' `config.xml` file by parsing `templates/config.tmpl`. We'll take a closer look at it soon.

The other new parameter is `CredentialsXmlSecret`. It holds the name of the Kubernetes secret where we'll store Jenkins' `credentials.xml` file we copied earlier. That parameter is tightly coupled with `SecretsFilesSecret` which holds the name of yet another Kubernetes secret which, this time, will contain the secrets which we copied to the local directory `cluster/jenkins/secrets`.

Further on, we have four commented parameters which will enable specific behavior if they are set. We'll use `DockerAMI` to set AWS AMI in case we're hosting our cluster in AWS. The last pair of (new) parameters is `GProject` and `GAuthFile`. The former is the GCE project we'll use if we choose to use

Google as our hosting vendor, and the latter is the authentication file which, if you followed that part, we also copied from the prior Jenkins installation. The usage of those parameters will become clearer once we explore `config.tpl` file.

The `helm/jenkins/templates/config.tpl` file is the key to our goals, so let's take a closer look at it.

```
1  cat helm/jenkins/templates/config.tpl
```

The output is too big to be digested at once, so we'll break the explanation into various pieces.

How did I create that file? I started by following the instructions in Chart's README. I copied `config.yaml` and made the minor changes documented in the README. That was the easy part. Then I inspected the changes we made to `config.xml` inside our manually configured Jenkins (the one we deleted a few moments ago). They provided enough info about the entries that are missing, and I started modifying `config.tpl` file. The first change is in the snippet that follows.

```
1  {{- define "override_config_map" }}
2
3  apiVersion: v1
4  kind: ConfigMap
5  metadata:
6    name: {{ template "jenkins.fullname" . }}
7  data:
8    config.xml: |-
9      <?xml version='1.0' encoding='UTF-8'?>
10     <hudson>
11       ...
12     <clouds>
13       <org.csanchez.jenkins.plugins.kubernetes.KubernetesCloud plugin="kubernetes@\
14  {{ template "jenkins.kubernetes-version" . }}">
15         <name>kubernetes</name>
16         <templates>
17  {{- if .Values.Agent.Enabled }}
18         <org.csanchez.jenkins.plugins.kubernetes.PodTemplate>
19           ...
20         <containers>
21           <org.csanchez.jenkins.plugins.kubernetes.ContainerTemplate>
22             ...
23           <envVars>
24             <org.csanchez.jenkins.plugins.kubernetes.ContainerEnvVar>
25               <key>JENKINS_URL</key>
26               <value>http://{{ template "jenkins.fullname" . }}.{{ .Release.\
27  Namespace }}:{{.Values.Master.ServicePort}}{{ default "" .Values.Master.JenkinsUriPr\
28  efix }}</value>
```

```
29                    </org.csanchez.jenkins.plugins.kubernetes.ContainerEnvVar>
30                  </envVars>
31                </org.csanchez.jenkins.plugins.kubernetes.ContainerTemplate>
32              </containers>
33                ...
34            </org.csanchez.jenkins.plugins.kubernetes.PodTemplate>
35  {{- end -}}
36            ...
37            <jenkinsUrl>http://{{ template "jenkins.fullname" . }}.{{ .Release.Namespa\
38  ce }}:{{.Values.Master.ServicePort}}{{ default "" .Values.Master.JenkinsUriPrefix }}\
39  </jenkinsUrl>
40            <jenkinsTunnel>{{ template "jenkins.fullname" . }}-agent.{{ .Release.Names\
41  pace }}:50000</jenkinsTunnel>
42            ...
```

If you pay closer attention, you'll notice that those are the changes we did previously to the Kubernetes cloud section in Jenkins configuration. We added `.{{ .Release.Namespace }}` to Jenkins URL and the tunnel so that Pods spun up in a different Namespace can establish communication with the master.

The next difference is the section dedicated to the `ec2` plugin.

```
1   ...
2   {{- if .Values.Master.DockerAMI }}
3     <hudson.plugins.ec2.EC2Cloud plugin="ec2@1.39">
4       <name>ec2-docker-agents</name>
5       ...
6       <templates>
7         <hudson.plugins.ec2.SlaveTemplate>
8           <ami>{{.Values.Master.DockerAMI}}</ami>
9           ...
10  {{- end }}
11  ...
```

That section represents the addition that will be created if we use Jenkins' EC2 plugin. I'll be honest here and admit that I did not write that XML snippet. I don't think that anyone could. Instead, I copied it from the previous Jenkins setup, pasted it to `config.tpl`, wrapped it with `{{- if .Values.Master.DockerAMI }}` and `{{- end }}` instructions, and changed `<ami>` entry to use `{{.Values.Master.DockerAMI}}` as the value. That way, the section will be rendered only if we provide `jenkins.Master.DockerAMI` value and the `ami` entry will be set to whatever our AMI ID is.

Similarly to the section enabled through the existence of the `jenkins.Master.DockerAMI` value, we can enable Google cloud through the XML wrapped inside `{{- if .Values.Master.GProject }}` and `{{- end }}` block. The relevant snippet of the `config.tpl` file is as follows.

```
 1   ...
 2   {{- if .Values.Master.GProject }}
 3     <com.google.jenkins.plugins.computeengine.ComputeEngineCloud plugin="google-comput\
 4   e-engine@1.0.4">
 5       <name>gce-docker</name>
 6       <instanceCap>2147483647</instanceCap>
 7       <projectId>{{.Values.Master.GProject}}</projectId>
 8       <credentialsId>{{.Values.Master.GProject}}</credentialsId>
 9       ...
10   {{- end }}
11   ...
```

Just as with the EC2, that snippet was copied from the previous Jenkins instance. I enveloped it with the if/end block. All occurrences of the Google project were replaced with {{.Values.Master.GProject}}.

Unfortunately, changing the template that produces Jenkins' config.xml file is not enough, so I had to modify a few other entries in config.tpl.

If we continue walking through the differences, the next one is the docker-build entry of the ConfigMap. It contains the exact copy of the docker-build node we created when we configured a VM using Vagrant. Since all the credentials are external and the IP is fixed to 10.100.198.200, I did not have to modify it in any form or way. A simple copy & paste did the trick. However, we still need to figure out how to move the docker-build ConfigMap entry to nodes/docker-build/config.xml inside Jenkins home. The solution to that problem lies in apply_config.sh entry of the ConfigMap.

We're almost done with the exploration of the changes, the only thing missing is the mechanism with which we'll transfer the files generated through the ConfigMap into the adequate folders inside Jenkins home.

The last snippet from config.tpl comes from the apply_config.sh entry in the ConfigMap. The relevant parts are as follows.

```
 1   ...
 2     apply_config.sh: |-
 3       ...
 4       mkdir -p /var/jenkins_home/nodes/docker-build
 5       cp /var/jenkins_config/docker-build /var/jenkins_home/nodes/docker-build/config.\
 6   xml;
 7   {{- if .Values.Master.GAuthFile }}
 8       mkdir -p /var/jenkins_home/gauth
 9       cp -n /var/jenkins_secrets/{{.Values.Master.GAuthFile}} /var/jenkins_home/gauth;
10   {{- end }}
11   ...
12   {{- if .Values.Master.CredentialsXmlSecret }}
13       cp -n /var/jenkins_credentials/credentials.xml /var/jenkins_home;
```

```
14   {{- end }}
15   {{- if .Values.Master.SecretsFilesSecret }}
16      cp -n /var/jenkins_secrets/* /usr/share/jenkins/ref/secrets;
17   {{- end }}
18   ...
```

The `apply_config.sh` script will be executed during Jenkins initialization. The process is already defined in the official Jenkins Chart. I just had to extend it by adding `mkdir` and `cp` commands that will copy `docker-build` config into `/var/jenkins_home/nodes/docker-build/config.xml`. That should take care of the `docker-build` agent that uses the Vagrant VM we created earlier. If you choose to skip static VM in favor of AWS EC2 or Google cloud options, the agent will be created nevertheless, but it will be disconnected.

Further down, we can see a similar logic for the `gauth` directory that will be populated with the file provided as the Kubernetes secret with the name defined as the `jenkins.Master.GAuthFile` value.

Finally, it is worth mentioning the parts inside `{{- if .Values.Master.CredentialsXmlSecret }}` and `{{- if .Values.Master.SecretsFilesSecret }}` blocks. Those already existed in the original `config.yaml` file used as the base for `config.tpl`. They are responsible for copying the credentials and the secrets into the appropriate directories inside Jenkins home.

I must admit that all those steps are not easy to figure out. They require knowledge about internal Jenkins workings and are anything but intuitive. I should probably submit a few pull requests to the Jenkins Helm project to simplify the setup. Nevertheless, the current configuration should provide everything we need, even though it might not be easy to understand how we got here.

Now that we got a bit clearer understanding of the changes we did to the `config.tpl` file and the reasons behind creating a new Chart with `stable/jenkins` as the requirement, we can move forward and update the dependencies in the Chart located in the `helm/jenkins` directory.

```
1   helm dependency update helm/jenkins
```

The output is as follows.

```
1    Hang tight while we grab the latest from your chart repositories...
2    ...Unable to get an update from the "local" chart repository (http://127.0.0.1:8879/\
3    charts):
4          Get http://127.0.0.1:8879/charts/index.yaml: dial tcp 127.0.0.1:8879: connec\
5    t: connection refused
6    ...Unable to get an update from the "chartmuseum" chart repository (http://cm.127.0.\
7    0.1.nip.io):
8          Get http://cm.127.0.0.1.nip.io/index.yaml: dial tcp 127.0.0.1:80: connect: c\
9    onnection refused
10   ...Successfully got an update from the "stable" chart repository
11   Update Complete. Happy Helming!
```

```
12  Saving 1 charts
13  Downloading jenkins from repo https://kubernetes-charts.storage.googleapis.com
14  Deleting outdated charts
```

We can ignore the failures from the `local` and `chartmuseum` repositories. They are still configured in our local Helm even though they're not currently running.

The important parts of the output are the last entries showing that Helm downloaded `jenkins` from the official repository. We can confirm that further by listing the files in the `helm/jenkins/charts` directory.

```
1  ls -1 helm/jenkins/charts
```

The output is as follows.

```
1  jenkins-...tgz
```

We can see that the dependencies specified in the `requirements.yaml` file are downloaded to the `charts` directory. Since we specified `jenkins` as the only one, Helm downloaded a single `tgz` file.

We're only one step away from being able to install custom Jenkins Chart with (almost) fully automated setup. The only things missing are the `jenkins-credentials` and `jenkins-secrets` Secrets.

```
1  kubectl -n jenkins \
2      create secret generic \
3      jenkins-credentials \
4      --from-file cluster/jenkins/credentials.xml
5
6  kubectl -n jenkins \
7      create secret generic \
8      jenkins-secrets \
9      --from-file cluster/jenkins/secrets
```

The `jenkins-credentials` Secret contains the `credentials.xml` file we extracted from the previous Jenkins setup. Similarly, the `jenkins-secrets` Secret contains all the files we stored in `cluster/jenkins/secrets` directory.

This is it. The moment of truth is upon us. We are about to test whether our attempt to (almost) fully automate Jenkins setup indeed produces the desired effect.

```
1  helm install helm/jenkins \
2      --name jenkins \
3      --namespace jenkins \
4      --set jenkins.Master.HostName=$JENKINS_ADDR \
5      --set jenkins.Master.DockerVM=$DOCKER_VM \
6      --set jenkins.Master.DockerAMI=$AMI_ID \
7      --set jenkins.Master.GProject=$G_PROJECT \
8      --set jenkins.Master.GAuthFile=$G_AUTH_FILE
```

Please note that, depending on your choices, AMI_ID, G_PROJECT, and G_AUTH_FILE might not be set and, as a result, not all the changes we made to the Chart will be available.

Next, we'll wait until jenkins Deployment rolls out before we open Jenkins and confirm that all the changes we made are indeed applied correctly.

```
1  kubectl -n jenkins \
2      rollout status deployment jenkins
```

The output should show that deployment "jenkins" was successfully rolled out, and we can open Jenkins in our favorite browser.

```
1  open "http://$JENKINS_ADDR"
```

Just as before, you'll need the administrative password stored in the jenkins secret.

```
1  JENKINS_PASS=$(kubectl -n jenkins \
2      get secret jenkins \
3      -o jsonpath="{.data.jenkins-admin-password}" \
4      | base64 --decode; echo)
5
6  echo $JENKINS_PASS
```

Please copy the output of the latter command, go back to Jenkins' login screen, and use it as the password of the admin user.

The first thing we'll check is whether *Kubernetes* cloud section of the Jenkins' configuration screen is indeed populated with the correct values.

```
1  open "http://$JENKINS_ADDR/configure"
```

Please confirm that the *Kubernetes* section fields *Jenkins URL* and *Jenkins tunnel* are correctly populated. They should have *http://jenkins.jenkins:8080* and *jenkins-agent.jenkins:50000* set as values.

Now that we know that *Kubernetes* is configured correctly and will be able to communicate with Pods outside the `jenkins` Namespace, we'll proceed and confirm that other cloud sections are also configured correctly if we choose to use GKE.

 ## A note to AWS EC2 users

Unlike on-prem and GKE solutions, AWS requires a single manual step to complete the setup.

`cat cluster/devops24.pem`

Copy the output, scroll to the *EC2 Key Pair's Private Key* field, and paste it. Don't forget to click the *Apply* button to persist the change.

If you're using **GKE**, you should observe that the *Google Compute Section* section fields look OK and that there is the message *The credential successfully made an API request to Google Compute Engine* below the *Service Account Credentials* field.

Next, we'll confirm that the credentials were also created correctly and that Jenkins can decrypt them.

If you chose to use **Vagrant** to create a VM that will be used for building Docker images, please execute the command that follows to open the screen with the credentials.

```
1  open "http://$JENKINS_ADDR/credentials/store/system/domain/_/credential/docker-build\
2  /update"
```

If, on the other hand, you choose **AWS** to dynamically create nodes for building Docker images, the command that will open the screen with the credentials is as follows.

```
1  open "http://$JENKINS_ADDR/credentials/store/system/domain/_/credential/aws/update"
```

Finally, if Google makes you tick and you chose **GKE** to host your cluster, the command that follows will open the screen with GCE credentials.

```
1  open "http://$JENKINS_ADDR/credentials/store/system/domain/_/credential/$G_PROJECT/u\
2  pdate"
```

No matter which method you choose for hosting agents we'll use to build Docker images, you should confirm that the credentials look OK.

Next, we'll check whether the agents are indeed registered with Jenkins.

```
1  open "http://$JENKINS_ADDR/computer"
```

If you chose to create a VM with **Vagrant**, you should see that the *docker-build* agent is created and that it is available. Otherwise, the agent will still be created, but it will NOT be available. Don't panic if that's the case. Jenkins will use AWS or GCE to spin them up when needed.

If you chose to use AWS or GCE for spinning agent nodes, you'll notice the list saying *Provision via...* That allows us to spin up the VMs in GCE or AWS manually. However, we won't do that. We'll let Jenkins Pipeline use that option instead.

Everything seems to be configured correctly, and we can do the last verification. We'll create a new job and confirm that it works as expected.

```
1  open "http://$JENKINS_ADDR/newJob"
```

Please type *my-k8s-job* as the job name, select *Pipeline* as the job type, and click the *OK* button. Once inside the job configuration screen, click the *Pipeline* tab to jump to the *Script* field, and type the code that follows.

```
1  podTemplate(
2      label: "kubernetes",
3      namespace: "go-demo-3-build",
4      serviceAccount: "build",
5      yaml: """
6  apiVersion: v1
7  kind: Pod
8  spec:
9    containers:
10   - name: kubectl
11     image: vfarcic/kubectl
12     command: ["sleep"]
13     args: ["100000"]
14   - name: oc
15     image: vfarcic/openshift-client
16     command: ["sleep"]
17     args: ["100000"]
18   - name: golang
19     image: golang:1.9
20     command: ["sleep"]
21     args: ["100000"]
22   - name: helm
23     image: vfarcic/helm:2.8.2
24     command: ["sleep"]
25     args: ["100000"]
```

```
26   """
27   ) {
28       node("docker") {
29           stage("docker") {
30               sh "sudo docker version"
31           }
32       }
33       node("kubernetes") {
34           container("kubectl") {
35               stage("kubectl") {
36                   sh "kubectl version"
37               }
38           }
39           container("oc") {
40               stage("oc") {
41                   sh "oc version"
42               }
43           }
44           container("golang") {
45               stage("golang") {
46                   sh "go version"
47               }
48           }
49           container("helm") {
50               stage("helm") {
51                   sh "helm version --tiller-namespace go-demo-3-build"
52               }
53           }
54       }
55   }
```

ℹ️ If you prefer to copy and paste, the job is available in the my-k8s-job-docker.groovy Gist[131].

Please note that the job is the same as the one we used to validate the manual setup and, therefore, there's probably no need to comment on it again. You know what it does, so click the *Save* button to persist it.

Next, we'll open the job in BlueOcean and run a build.

---

[131]https://gist.github.com/fbf9fc6611fe400c7950f43cfc89f406

```
1  open "http://$JENKINS_ADDR/blue/organizations/jenkins/my-k8s-job/activity"
```

Press the *Run* button, followed with a click on the row with the new build. Wait until all the stages are finished, and the result is green. Open a bottle of Champagne to celebrate.

What Now?

If we exclude the case of entering AWS key, our Jenkins setup is fully automated. Kubernetes plugin is pre-configured to support Pods running in other Namespaces, Google and AWS clouds will be set up if we choose to use them, credentials are copied to the correct locations, and they are using the same encryption keys as those used to encrypt the credentials in the first place. All in all, we're finally ready to work on our continuous deployment pipeline. The next chapter will be the culmination of everything we did thus far.

Please note that the current setup is designed to support "one Jenkins master per team" strategy. Even though you could use the experience you gained so far to run a production-ready Jenkins master that will serve everyone in your company, it is often a better strategy to have one master per team. That approach provides quite a few benefits.

If each team gets a Jenkins master, each team will be able to work independently of others. A team can decide to upgrade their plugins without fear that they will affect others. We can choose to experiment with things that might cause trouble to others by creating a temporary master. Every team can have fine-tuned permissions on the Namespaces that matter to them, and no ability to do anything inside other Namespaces.

The productivity of a team is often directly proportional to the ability to do things without being limited with the actions of other teams and, at the same time freedom not to worry whether their work will negatively affect others. In Kubernetes, we get that freedom through Namespaces. In Jenkins, we get it by having masters dedicated to teams.

The Helm Chart we created is a step towards multi-master strategy. The Jenkins we installed can be considered dedicated to the team in charge of the *go-demo-3* application. Or it can be devoted to a bigger team. The exact division will differ from one organization to another. What matters is that no matter how many Jenkins masters we need, all we have to do is execute `helm install` for each. Given enough resources in the cluster, we can have a hundred fully operational Jenkins masters in only a few minutes time. And they will not be Jenkins masters waiting to be configured, but rather masters already loaded with everything a team needs. All they'd need to do is create Pipelines that will execute the steps necessary for their application to move from a commit into production. That's the subject of the next chapter.

One more chapter is finished and, like all the others, the next one will start from scratch. Please use the commands that follow to clean up the resources we created or, if you're using a temporary cluster, go ahead and destroy it.

```
1  helm delete $(helm ls -q) --purge
2
3  kubectl delete ns \
4      go-demo-3 go-demo-3-build jenkins
```

If you created a VM using **Vagrant**, I suggest you suspend it instead of destroying it. That way we'll preserve the same credentials and will be able to reuse those we stored in `cluster/jenkins/secrets/`.

```
1  cd cd/docker-build
2
3  vagrant suspend
4
5  cd ../../
```

Take some time to enjoy what we accomplished so far. The next chapter will be the culmination of our efforts.

Creating A Continuous Deployment Pipeline With Jenkins

 Having A Continuous Deployment pipeline capable of a fully automated application life-cycle is a real sign of maturity of an organization.

This is it. The time has come to put all the knowledge we obtained into good use. We are about to define a "real" continuous deployment pipeline in Jenkins. Our goal is to move every commit through a set of steps until the application is installed (upgraded) and tested in production. We will undoubtedly face some new challenges, but I am confident that we'll manage to overcome them. We already have all the base ingredients, and the main thing left is to put them all together into a continuous deployment pipeline.

Before we move into a practical section, we might want to spend a few moments discussing our goals.

Exploring The Continuous Deployment Process

Explaining continuous deployment (CDP) is easy. Implementing it is very hard, and the challenges are often hidden and unexpected. Depending on the maturity of your processes, architecture, and code, you might find out that the real problems do not lie in the code of a continuous deployment pipeline, but everywhere else. As a matter of fact, developing a pipeline is the easiest part. That being said, you might wonder whether you made a mistake by investing your time in reading this book since we are focused mostly on the pipeline that will be executed inside a Kubernetes cluster.

We did not discuss the changes in your other processes. We did not explore what a good architecture that will support CDP pipelines is. We did not dive into how to code your application to be pipeline-friendly. I assumed that you already know all that. I hope that you do understand the basic concepts behind Agile and DevOps movements and that you already started dismantling the silos in your company. I assume that you do know what it means for your software architecture to be cloud-native and that you do implement some if not all of the 12 factors[132]. I guessed that you are already practicing Test-Driven Development, Behavior-Driven Development, Acceptance-Driven Development, or any other technique that help you design your applications.

I might be wrong. To be more precise, I'm sure that I'm wrong. Most of you are not there yet. If you are one of those, please get informed. Read more books, do some courses, and convince your

---

[132]https://12factor.net/

managers to give you time, space, and resources you'll need to modernize your applications. It needs to be done. All those things and many others are what differentiates top performers (e.g., Google, Amazon, Netflix) and the rest of us. Still, none of them is the same. Every high-performing company is different, and yet, they all share some things in common. They all need to ship features fast. They all need to have a high level of quality. And they all acknowledge that highly-available, fault-tolerant, and distributed systems require a very different approach than what most of the rest of us are used to.

If you got depressed by thinking that you are not yet ready and that you are on the verge of quitting, my advice is to continue. Even though you might need to make a lot of changes before you are able to practice continuous deployment, knowing what the end result looks like will put you on the right path. We are about to design a fully operational continuous deployment pipeline. Once we're done, you'll know which other changes you'll need to make. You'll understand where the finish line is, and you will be able to go back to where you are and start moving in the right direction.

We already discussed what a continuous deployment pipeline looks like. In case you're forgetful (I know I am), here are a few of the rules that represent the short version.

Rule number one: Every commit to the master branch is deployed to production if it passes all the steps of a fully automated pipeline. If you need to involve humans after the commit, it's not continuous deployment, nor it is continuous delivery. At best, you're doing continuous integration.

Rule number two: You commit directly to the master branch, or you're using short-living feature branches. The master branch is the only one that matters. Production releases are made from it. If you do use branches, they are taken from the master branch, since that's the only one that truly matters. When you do create a feature branch, you are merging back to master soon afterward. You're not waiting for weeks to do so. If you are, you are not "continuously" validating whether your code integrates with the code of others. If that's the case, you're not even doing continuous integration. Unless, you have an elaborate branching strategy, in which case you are only making everyone's lives more complicated than they should be.

Rule number three: You trust your automation. When a test fails, there is a bug, and you fix it before anything else. I hope that you do not belong to a big group of companies that have flaky tests that sometimes work, and sometimes fail for random reasons. If you do, fix your tests first or remove those that are flaky. It's pointless to run tests you do not trust. The same can be said for builds, deployments, and just about any other step of the process. If you see yourself in the group of those that do not trust their code, you'll have to fix it first. Tests are code, just as builds, deployments, and everything else is. When code produces inconsistent results, we fix it, we do not restart it. Unfortunately, I do see a lot of companies that rather re-run a build that failed because of flaky tests than fix the cause of that flakiness. There's an alarming number of those that solve half of the production problems by restarting applications. Anyways, if you do not trust your automation, you cannot deploy to production automatically. You cannot even say that it is production ready.

Now that we established a set of straightforward ground rules, we can move on and describe the pipeline we should develop. We are going to build something. Since building without running unit and other types of static tests should be declared officially illegal and punishable with public shame, we'll include those in our **build stage**. Then we're going execute the steps of the **functional testing stage** that will run all sorts of tests that require a live application. Therefore, we'll need to deploy a test release during this stage. Once we're confident that our application behaves as expected, we're going to make a **production release**, followed with the **deploy stage** that will not only upgrade the production release but also run another round of tests to validate whether everything works as expected.

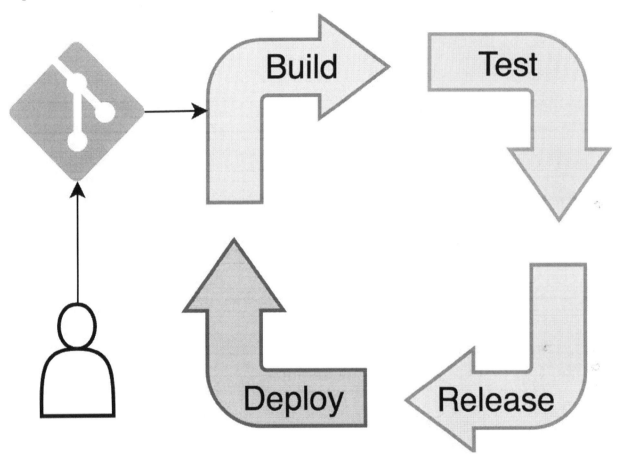

Figure 7-1: The stages of a continuous deployment pipeline

You might not agree with the names of the stages. That's OK. It does not matter much how you name things, nor how you group steps. What matters is that the pipeline has everything we need to feel confident that a release is safely deployed to production. Steps matter, stages are only labels.

We won't discuss the exact steps just yet. Instead, we'll break the stages apart and build one at the time. During the process, we'll discuss which steps are required.

It is almost certain that you'll need to add steps that I do not use. That's OK as well. It's all about principles and knowledge. Slight modifications should not be a problem.

Let's create a cluster.

Creating A Cluster

We'll start the practical section of the chapter by going to the *vfarcic/k8s-specs* repository and by making sure that we have the latest revision.

 All the commands from this chapter are available in the 07-jenkins-cdp.sh[133] Gist.

```
1  cd k8s-specs
2
3  git pull
```

Next, we'll merge your *go-demo-3* fork with the upstream. If you forgot the commands, they are available in the go-demo-3-merge.sh gist[134].

 It is imperative that you change all the references of vfarcic/go-demo-3 to the address of the image in your Docker Hub account. If, for example, your hub user is jdoe, you should change all vfarcic/go-demo-3 references to jdoe/go-demo-3. Even though I invite you to apply the modifications to all the files of the repository, the necessary changes are in files *helm/go-demo-3/Chart.yaml, helm/go-demo-3/templates/deployment.yaml*, and *k8s/build-config.yml*. Please make sure to **change all the branches**. Do not forget to **push** them to GitHub.

Now comes boring, but necessary part. We need to create a cluster unless you kept the one from the previous chapter running.

The additional requirements, when compared with the Gists from the previous chapter, are **ChartMuseum** and the environment variable CM_ADDR that contains the address through which we can access it.

If you're using a local cluster created through **Docker For Mac or Windows**, **minikube**, or **minishift**, we'll have to increase its size to **4GB RAM** and **4CPU**.

Docker For Mac or Windows users will also need to get the "real" IP of the cluster, instead of localhost we used so far. You should be able to get it by executing ifconfig and picking the address dedicated to Docker.

For your convenience, the Gists and the specs are available below.

- docker4mac-4gb.sh[135]: **Docker for Mac** with 3 CPUs, 4 GB RAM, with **nginx Ingress**, with **tiller**, with LB_IP variable set to the IP of the cluster, and with **ChartMuseum** and its address set as CM_ADDR variable.

---

[133]https://gist.github.com/d0cbca319360eb000098383a09fd65f7
[134]https://gist.github.com/171172b69bb75903016f0676a8fe9388
[135]https://gist.github.com/4b5487e707043c971989269883d20d28

- minikube-4gb.sh[136]: **minikube** with 3 CPUs, 4 GB RAM, with `ingress`, `storage-provisioner`, and `default-storageclass` addons enabled, with **tiller**, with `LB_IP` variable set to the VM created by minikube, and with **ChartMuseum** and its address set as `CM_ADDR` variable.
- kops-cm.sh[137]: **kops in AWS** with 3 t2.small masters and 2 t2.medium nodes spread in three availability zones, with **nginx Ingress**, with **tiller**, and with `LB_IP` variable set to the IP retrieved by pinging ELB's hostname, and with **ChartMuseum** and its address set as `CM_ADDR` variable. The Gist assumes that the prerequisites are set through Appendix B.
- minishift-4gb.sh[138]: **minishift** with 4 CPUs, 4 GB RAM, with version 1.16+, with **tiller**, and with `LB_IP` variable set to the VM created by minishift, and with **ChartMuseum** and its address set as `CM_ADDR` variable.
- gke-cm.sh[139]: **Google Kubernetes Engine (GKE)** with 3 n1-highcpu-2 (2 CPUs, 1.8 GB RAM) nodes (one in each zone), with **nginx Ingress** controller running on top of the "standard" one that comes with GKE, with **tiller**, with `LB_IP` variable set to the IP of the external load balancer created when installing nginx Ingress, and with **ChartMuseum** and its address set as `CM_ADDR` variable. We'll use nginx Ingress for compatibility with other platforms. Feel free to modify the YAML files and Helm Charts if you prefer NOT to install nginx Ingress.
- eks-cm.sh[140]: **Elastic Kubernetes Service (EKS)** with 2 t2.medium nodes, with **nginx Ingress** controller, with a **default StorageClass**, with **tiller**, with `LB_IP` variable set tot he IP retrieved by pinging ELB's hostname, and with **ChartMuseum** and its address set as `CM_ADDR` variable.

Now we are ready to install Jenkins.

Installing Jenkins

We already automated Jenkins installation so that it provides all the features we need out-of-the-box. Therefore, the exercises that follow should be very straightforward.

If you are a **Docker For Mac or Windows**, **minikube**, or **minishift** user, we'll need to bring back up the VM we suspended in the previous chapter. Feel free to skip the commands that follow if you are hosting your cluster in AWS or GCP.

---

[136]https://gist.github.com/0a29803842b62c5c033e4c75cd37f3d4
[137]https://gist.github.com/603e2dca21b4475985a078b0f78db88c
[138]https://gist.github.com/b3d9c8da6e6dfd3b49d3d707595f6f99
[139]https://gist.github.com/52b52500c469548e9d98c3f03529c609
[140]https://gist.github.com/fd9c0cdb3a104e7c745e1c91f7f75a2e

```
1  cd cd/docker-build
2
3  vagrant up
4
5  cd ../../
6
7  export DOCKER_VM=true
```

If you prefer running your cluster in **AWS with kops or EKS**, we'll need to retrieve the AMI ID we stored in docker-ami.log in the previous chapter.

```
1  AMI_ID=$(grep 'artifact,0,id' \
2      cluster/docker-ami.log \
3      | cut -d: -f2)
4
5  echo $AMI_ID
```

If **GKE** is your cluster of choice, we'll need to define variables G_PROJECT and G_AUTH_FILE which we'll pass to Helm Chart. We'll retrieve the project using gcloud CLI, and the authentication file is a reference to the one we stored in /cluster/jenkins/secrets directory in the previous chapter.

```
1  export G_PROJECT=$(gcloud info \
2      --format='value(config.project)')
3
4  echo $G_PROJECT
5
6  G_AUTH_FILE=$(\
7      ls cluster/jenkins/secrets/key*json \
8      | xargs -n 1 basename \
9      | tail -n 1)
10
11 echo $G_AUTH_FILE
```

Next, we'll need to create the Namespaces we'll need. Let's take a look at the definition we'll use.

```
1  cat ../go-demo-3/k8s/ns.yml
```

You'll notice that the definition is a combination of a few we used in the previous chapters. It contains three Namespaces.

The go-demo-3-build Namespace is where we'll run Pods from which we'll execute most of the steps of our pipeline. Those Pods will contain the tools like kubectl, helm, and Go compiler. We'll use the same Namespace to deploy our releases under test. All in all, the go-demo-3-build Namespace is for short-lived Pods. The tools will be removed when a build is finished, just as installations of releases under test will be deleted when tests are finished executing. This Namespace will be like a trash can that needs to be emptied whenever it gets filled or start smelling.

The second Namespace is go-demo-3. That is the Namespace dedicated to the applications developed by the go-demo-3 team. We'll work only on their primary product, named after the team, but we can imagine that they might be in charge of other application. Therefore, do not think of this Namespace as dedicated to a single application, but assigned to a team. They have full permissions to operate inside that Namespace, just as the others defined in ns.yml. They own them, and go-demo-3 is dedicated for production releases.

While we already used the two Namespaces, the third one is a bit new. The go-demo-3-jenkins is dedicated to Jenkins, and you might wonder why we do not use the jenkins Namespace as we did so far. The answer lies in my belief that it is a good idea to give each team their own Jenkins. That way, we do not need to create an elaborate system with user permissions, we do not need to think whether a plugin desired by one team will break a job owned by another, and we do not need to worry about performance issues when Jenkins is stressed by hundreds or thousands of parallel builds. So, we'll apply **"every team gets Jenkins"** type of logic. *"It's your Jenkins, do whatever you want to do with it,"* is the message we want to transmit to the teams in our company. Now, if your organization has only twenty developers, there's probably no need for splitting Jenkins into multiple instances. Fifty should be OK as well. But, when that number rises to hundreds, or even thousands, having various Jenkins masters has clear benefits. Traditionally, that would not be practical due to increased operational costs. But now that we are deep into Kubernetes, and that we already saw that a fully functional and configured Jenkins is only a few commands away, we can agree that monster instances do not make much sense. If you are small and that logic does not apply, the processes we'll explore are still the same, no matter whether you have one or a hundred Jenkins masters. Only the Namespace will be different (e.g., jenkins).

The rest of the definition is the same as what we used before. We have ServiceAccounts and RoleBindings that allow containers to interact with KubeAPI. We have LimitRanges and Resource-Quotas that protect the cluster from rogue Pods.

The LimitRange defined for the go-demo-3-build Namespace is especially important. We can assume that many of the Pods created through CDP pipeline will not have memory and CPU requests and limits. It's only human to forget to define those things in pipelines. Still, that can be disastrous since it might produce undesired effects in the cluster. If nothing else, that would limit Kubernetes' capacity to schedule Pods. So, defining LimitRange default and defaultRequest entries is a crucial step.

Please go through the whole ns.yml definition to refresh your memory of the things we explored in the previous chapters. We'll apply it once you're back.

```
1  kubectl apply \
2      -f ../go-demo-3/k8s/ns.yml \
3      --record
```

Now that we have the Namespaces, the ServiceAccounts, the RoleBindings, the LimitRanges, and the ResourceQuotas, we can proceed and create the secrets and the credentials required by Jenkins.

```
1  kubectl -n go-demo-3-jenkins \
2      create secret generic \
3      jenkins-credentials \
4      --from-file cluster/jenkins/credentials.xml
5
6  kubectl -n go-demo-3-jenkins \
7      create secret generic \
8      jenkins-secrets \
9      --from-file cluster/jenkins/secrets
```

Only one more thing is missing before we install Jenkins. We need to install Tiller in the go-demo-3-build Namespace.

```
1  helm init --service-account build \
2      --tiller-namespace go-demo-3-build
```

 A note to minishift users

Helm will try to install Jenkins Chart with the process in a container running as user 0. By default, that is not allowed in OpenShift. We'll skip discussing the best approach to correct the issue, and I'll assume you already know how to set the permissions on the per-Pod basis. Instead, we'll do the most straightforward fix by executing the command that follows that will allow the creation of restricted Pods to run as any user.

```
oc patch scc restricted -p '{"runAsUser":{"type": "RunAsAny"}}'
```

Now we are ready to install Jenkins.

```
1  JENKINS_ADDR="go-demo-3-jenkins.$LB_IP.nip.io"
2
3  helm install helm/jenkins \
4      --name go-demo-3-jenkins \
5      --namespace go-demo-3-jenkins \
6      --set jenkins.Master.HostName=$JENKINS_ADDR \
7      --set jenkins.Master.DockerVM=$DOCKER_VM \
8      --set jenkins.Master.DockerAMI=$AMI_ID \
9      --set jenkins.Master.GProject=$G_PROJECT \
10     --set jenkins.Master.GAuthFile=$G_AUTH_FILE
```

We generated a `nip.io` address and installed Jenkins in the `go-demo-3-jenkins` Namespace. Remember, this Jenkins is dedicated to the *go-demo-3* team, and we might have many other instances serving the needs of other teams.

A note to minishift users

OpenShift requires Routes to make services accessible outside the cluster. To make things more complicated, they are not part of "standard Kubernetes" so we'll need to create one using `oc`. Please execute the command that follows.

```
oc -n go-demo-3-jenkins create route edge --service go-demo-3-jenkins
--insecure-policy Allow --hostname $JENKINS_ADDR
```

That command created an `edge` Router tied to the `go-demo-3-jenkins` Service. Since we do not have SSL certificates for HTTPS communication, we also specified that it is OK to use insecure policy which will allow us to access Jenkins through plain HTTP. The last argument defined the address through which we'd like to access Jenkins UI.

So far, everything we did is almost the same as what we've done in the previous chapters. The only difference is that we changed the Namespace where we deployed Jenkins. Now, the only thing left before we jump into pipelines is to wait until Jenkins is rolled out and confirm a few things.

```
1  kubectl -n go-demo-3-jenkins \
2      rollout status deployment \
3      go-demo-3-jenkins
```

The only thing we'll validate, right now, is whether the node that we'll use to build and push Docker images is indeed connected to Jenkins.

A note to Windows users

Don't forget that `open` command might not work in Windows and that you might need to replace it with `echo`, copy the output, and paste it into a tab of your favorite browser.

```
1  open "http://$JENKINS_ADDR/computer"
```

Just as before, we'll need the auto-generated password.

```
1  JENKINS_PASS=$(kubectl -n go-demo-3-jenkins \
2      get secret go-demo-3-jenkins \
3      -o jsonpath="{.data.jenkins-admin-password}" \
4      | base64 --decode; echo)
5
6  echo $JENKINS_PASS
```

Please copy the output of the echo command, go back to the browser, and use it to log in as the admin user.

Once inside the nodes screen, you'll see different results depending on how you set up the node for building and pushing Docker images.

If you are a **Docker For Mac or Windows**, a **minikube** user, or a **minishift** user, you'll see a node called docker-build. That confirms that we successfully connected Jenkins with the VM we created with Vagrant.

If you created a cluster in **AWS** using **kops**, you should see a drop-down list called **docker-agents**.

GKE users should see a drop-down list called **docker**.

 A note to AWS EC2 users

Unlike on-prem and GKE solutions, AWS requires a single manual step to complete the Jenkins setup.

cat cluster/devops24.pem

Copy the output.

open "http://$JENKINS_ADDR/configure"

Scroll to the *EC2 Key Pair's Private Key* field, and paste the key. Don't forget to click the *Apply* button to persist the change.

Now that we confirmed that a node (static or dynamic) is available for building and pushing Docker images, we can start designing our first stage of the continuous deployment pipeline.

Defining The Build Stage

The primary function of the **build stage** of the continuous deployment pipeline is to build artifacts and a container image and push it to a registry from which it can be deployed and tested. Of course, we cannot build anything without code, so we'll have to check out the repository as well.

Since building things without running static analysis, unit tests, and other types of validation against static code should be illegal and punishable by public shame, we'll include those steps as well.

We won't deal with building artifacts, nor we are going to run static testing and analysis from inside the pipeline. Instead, we'll continue relying on Docker's multistage builds for all those things, just as we did in the previous chapters.

Finally, we couldn't push to a registry without authentication, so we'll have to log in to Docker Hub just before wc push a ncw image.

There are a few things that we are NOT going to do, even though you probably should when applying the lessons learned your "real" projects. We do NOT have static analysis. We are NOT generating code coverage, we are NOT creating reports, and we are not sending the result to analysis tools like SonarQube[141]. More importantly, we are NOT running any security scanning. There are many other things we could do in this chapter, but we are not. The reason is simple. There is an almost infinite number of tools we could uses and steps we could execute. They depend on programming languages, internal processes, and what so not. Our goal is to understand the logic and, later on, to adapt the examples to your own needs. With that in mind, we'll stick only to the bare minimum, not only in this stage but also in those that follow. It is up to you to extend them to fit your specific needs.

---

[141]https://www.sonarqube.org/

1. Check out the code
2. Run static analysis and testing
3. Build artifacts
4. Build images
5. Push image to the registry

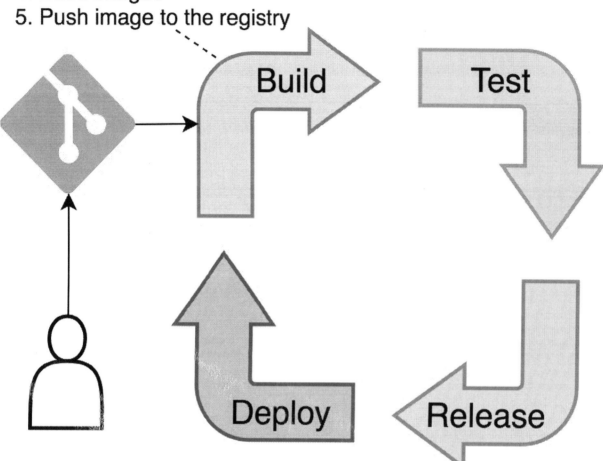

Figure 7-2: The essential steps of the build stage

Let's define the steps of the build stage as a Jenkins job.

```
1  open "http://$JENKINS_ADDR"
```

From the Jenkins home screen, please click the *New Item* link from the left-hand menu. The script for creating new jobs will appear.

Type *go-demo-3* as the *item name*, select *Pipeline* as the job type and click the *OK* button.

 As a rule of thumb, name your pipeline jobs after the repositories from which you're building the applications.

Once inside job's configuration screen, click the *Pipeline* tab in the top of the screen and type the script that follows inside the *Script* field.

```
1   import java.text.SimpleDateFormat
2
3   currentBuild.displayName = new SimpleDateFormat("yy.MM.dd").format(new Date()) + "-"\
4    + env.BUILD_NUMBER
5   env.REPO = "https://github.com/vfarcic/go-demo-3.git"
6   env.IMAGE = "vfarcic/go-demo-3"
7   env.TAG_BETA = "${currentBuild.displayName}-${env.BRANCH_NAME}"
8
9   node("docker") {
10    stage("build") {
11      git "${env.REPO}"
12      sh """sudo docker image build \
13        -t ${env.IMAGE}:${env.TAG_BETA} ."""
14      withCredentials([usernamePassword(
15        credentialsId: "docker",
16        usernameVariable: "USER",
17        passwordVariable: "PASS"
18      )]) {
19        sh """sudo docker login \
20          -u $USER -p $PASS"""
21      }
22      sh """sudo docker image push \
23        ${env.IMAGE}:${env.TAG_BETA}"""
24    }
25  }
```

ℹ️ If you prefer to copy and paste, the job is available in the cdp-jenkins-build.groovy Gist[142].

Since we already went through all those steps manually, the steps inside the Jenkins job should be self-explanatory. Still, we'll briefly explain what's going on since this might be your first contact with Jenkins pipeline.

First of all, the job is written using the **scripted pipeline** syntax. The alternative would be to use **declarative pipeline** which forces a specific structure and naming convention. Personally, I prefer the latter. A declarative pipeline is easier to write and read, and it provides the structure that makes implementation of some patterns much easier. However, it also comes with a few limitations. In our case, those limitations are enough to make the declarative pipeline a lousy choice. Namely, it does

---

not allow us to mix different types of agents, and it does not support all the options available in
`podTemplate` (e.g., `namespace`). Since scripted pipeline does not have such limitations, we opted for
that flavor, even though it makes the code often harder to maintain.

 Visit Pipeline documentation[143] if you're somewhat new to it and want to learn more.

What did we do so far?

We imported `SimpleDateFormat` library that allows us to retrieve dates. The reason for the `import`
becomes evident in the next line where we are changing the name of the build. By default, each build
is named sequentially. The first build is named `1`, the second `2`, and so on. We changed the naming
pattern so that it contains the date in `yy.MM.dd` format, followed with the sequential build number.

Next, we're defining a few environment variables that contain the information we'll need in the
pipeline steps. `REPO` holds the GitHub repository we're using, `IMAGE` is the name of the Docker image
we'll build, and `TAG_BETA` has the tag the image we'll use for testing. The latter is a combination of
the build and the branch name.

Before we proceed, please change the `REPO` and the `IMAGE` variables to match the address of the
repository you forked and the name of the image. In most cases, changing `vfarcic` to your GitHub
and Docker Hub user should be enough.

The `node` block is where the "real" action is happening.

By setting the `node` to `docker`, we're telling Jenkins to use the agent with the matching name or label
for all the steps within that block. The mechanism will differ from one case to another. It could match
the VM we created with Vagrant, or it could be a dynamically created node in AWS or GCP.

Inside the `node` is the `stage` block. It is used to group steps and has no practical purpose. It is purely
cosmetic, and it's used to visualize the pipeline.

Inside the `stage` are the steps. The full list of available steps depends on the available plugins. The
most commonly used ones are documented in the Pipeline Steps Reference[144]. As you'll see, most of
the pipeline we'll define will be based on the sh: Shell Script[145] step. Since we already determined
almost everything we need through commands executed in a terminal, using `sh` allows us to copy
and paste those same commands. That way, we'll have little dependency on Jenkins-specific way
of working, and we'll have parity between command line used by developers on their laptops and
Jenkins pipelines.

Inside the `build` stage, we're using `git` to retrieve the repository. Further on, we're using `sh` to
execute Docker commands to `build` an image, to `login` to Docker Hub, and to `push` the image.

The only "special" part of the pipeline is the `withCredentials` block. Since it would be very insecure
to hard-code into our jobs Docker Hub's username and password, we're retrieving the information

---

[143]https://jenkins.io/doc/book/pipeline/

[144]https://jenkins.io/doc/pipeline/steps/

[145]https://jenkins.io/doc/pipeline/steps/workflow-durable-task-step/#sh-shell-script

from Jenkins. The credentials with the ID `docker` will be converted into variables USER and PASS which are used with the `docker login` command. Besides the apparent do-not-hard-code-secrets reason, the primary motivation for using the `withCredentials` block lies in Jenkins' ability to obfuscate confidential information. As you'll see later on, the credentials will be removed from logs making them hidden to anyone poking around our builds.

 I split some of the instructions into multiple-lines to avoid potential problems with the width limitations in books. You won't have those limitations in your pipelines, and you might want to refactor examples into single-line steps thus making them easier to read and maintain.

Now that we had a brief exploration of our first draft of the pipeline, the time has come to try it out.

Please click the *Save* button to persist the job.

We'll use the new UI to run the builds and visualize them.

Click the *Open Blue Ocean* link from the left-hand menu, followed with the *Run* button.

Once the build starts, a new row will appear. Click it to enter into the details of the build and to observe the progress until it's finished and everything is green.

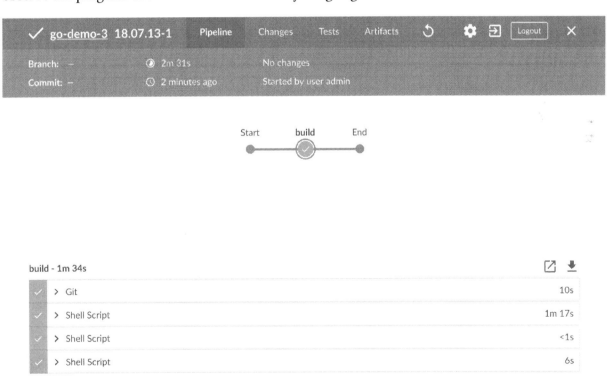

Figure 7-3: Jenkins build with a single stage

Let's check whether Jenkins executed the steps correctly. If it did, we should have a new image pushed to our Docker Hub account.

```
1  export DH_USER=[...]
2
3  open "https://hub.docker.com/r/$DH_USER/go-demo-3/tags/"
```

Please replace [. . .] with your Docker Hub username.

You should see a new image tagged as a combination of the date, build number (1), and the branch. The only problem so far is that the branch is set to null. That is the expected behavior since we did not tell Jenkins which branch to retrieve. As a result, the environment variable BRANCH_NAME is set to null and, with it, our image tag as well. We'll fix that problem later on. For now, we'll have to live with null.

Now that we finished defining and verifying the build stage, we can proceed to the *functional testing*.

Defining The Functional Testing Stage

For the *functional testing* stage, the first step is to install the application under test. To avoid the potential problems of installing the same release twice, we'll use helm upgrade instead of install.

As you already know, Helm only acknowledges that the resources are created, not that all the Pods are running. To mitigate that, we'll wait for rollout status before proceeding with tests.

Once the application is rolled out, we'll run the functional tests. Please note that, in this case, we will run only one set of tests. In the "real" world scenario, there would probably be others like, for example, performance tests or front-end tests for different browsers.

 When running multiple sets of different tests, consider using parallel construct. More information can be found in the Parallelism and Distributed Builds with Jenkins[146] article.

Finally, we'll have to delete the Chart we installed. After all, it's pointless to waste resources by running an application longer than we need it. In our scenario, as soon as the execution of the tests is finished, we'll remove the application under test. However, there is a twist. Jenkins, like most other CI/CD tools, will stop the execution of the first error. Since there is no guarantee that none of the steps in this stage will fail, we'll have to envelop all the inside a big try/catch/finally statement.

---

[146]https://www.cloudbees.com/blog/parallelism-and-distributed-builds-jenkins

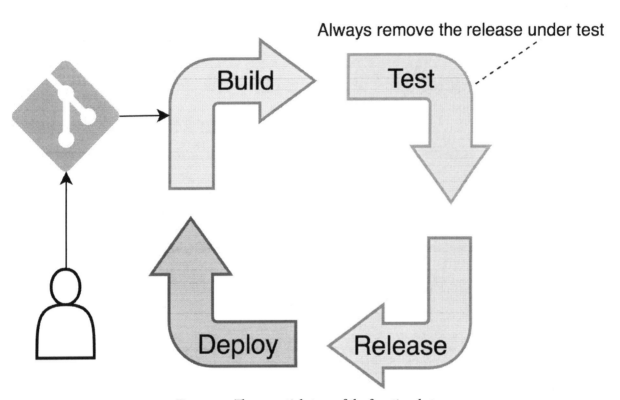

Figure 7-4: The essential steps of the functional stage

Before we move on and write a new version of the pipeline, we'll need an address that we'll use as Ingress host of our application under tests.

```
1  export ADDR=$LB_IP.nip.io
2
3  echo $ADDR
```

Please copy the output of the echo. We'll need it soon.

Next, we'll open the job's configuration screen.

```
1  open "http://$JENKINS_ADDR/job/go-demo-3/configure"
```

If you are **NOT using minishift**, please replace the existing code with the content of the cdp-jenkins-func.groovy Gist[147].

---

[147]https://gist.github.com/4edc53d5dd11814651485c9ff3672fb7

If you are **using minishift**, replace the existing code with the content of the cdp-jenkins-func-oc.groovy Gist[148].

We'll explore only the differences between the two revisions of the pipeline. They are as follows.

```
1   ...
2   env.ADDRESS = "go-demo-3-${env.BUILD_NUMBER}-${env.BRANCH_NAME}.acme.com"
3   env.CHART_NAME = "go-demo-3-${env.BUILD_NUMBER}-${env.BRANCH_NAME}"
4   def label = "jenkins-slave-${UUID.randomUUID().toString()}"
5
6   podTemplate(
7     label: label,
8     namespace: "go-demo-3-build",
9     serviceAccount: "build",
10    yaml: """
11  apiVersion: v1
12  kind: Pod
13  spec:
14    containers:
15    - name: helm
16      image: vfarcic/helm:2.9.1
17      command: ["cat"]
18      tty: true
19    - name: kubectl
20      image: vfarcic/kubectl
21      command: ["cat"]
22      tty: true
23    - name: golang
24      image: golang:1.9
25      command: ["cat"]
26      tty: true
27  """
28  ) {
29    node(label) {
30      node("docker") {
31        stage("build") {
32          ...
33        }
34      }
35      stage("func-test") {
36        try {
37          container("helm") {
```

---

[148]https://gist.github.com/1661c2527eda2bfe1e35c77f448f7c34

```
38              git "${env.REPO}"
39              sh """helm upgrade \
40                ${env.CHART_NAME} \
41                helm/go-demo-3 -i \
42                --tiller-namespace go-demo-3-build \
43                --set image.tag=${env.TAG_BETA} \
44                --set ingress.host=${env.ADDRESS} \
45                --set replicaCount=2 \
46                --set dbReplicaCount=1"""
47            }
48            container("kubectl") {
49              sh """kubectl -n go-demo-3-build \
50                rollout status deployment \
51                ${env.CHART_NAME}"""
52            }
53            container("golang") { // Uses env ADDRESS
54              sh "go get -d -v -t"
55              sh """go test ./... -v \
56                --run FunctionalTest"""
57            }
58          } catch(e) {
59              error "Failed functional tests"
60          } finally {
61            container("helm") {
62              sh """helm delete \
63                ${env.CHART_NAME} \
64                --tiller-namespace go-demo-3-build \
65                --purge"""
66            }
67          }
68        }
69      }
70  }
```

We added a few new environment variables that will simplify the steps that follow. The ADDRESS will be used to provide a unique host for the Ingress of the application under test. The uniqueness is accomplished by combining the name of the project (go-demo-3), the build number, and the name of the branch. We used a similar pattern to generate the name of the Chart that will be installed. All in all, both the address and the Chart are unique for each release of each application, no matter the branch.

We also defined label variable with a unique value by adding a suffix based on random UUID. Further down, when we define podTemplate, we'll use the label to ensure that each build uses its own Pod.

The `podTemplate` itself is very similar to those we used in quite a few occasions. It'll be created in the `go-demo-3-build` Namespace dedicated to building and testing applications owned by the `go-demo-3` team. The `yaml` contains the definitions of the Pod that includes containers with `helm`, `kubectl`, and `golang`. Those are the tools we'll need to execute the steps of the *functional testing* stage.

A note to minishift users

Your version of the pipeline contains a few things that other Kubernetes users do not need. You'll notice that there is an additional container named `oc` in the `podTemplate`. Further down, in the `func-test` stage, we're using that container to create an Edge Route that provides the same functionality as Ingress controller used by other Kubernetes flavors.

The curious part is the way nodes (agents) are organized in this iteration of the pipeline. Everything is inside one big block of `node(label)`. As a result, all the steps will be executed in one of the containers of the `podTemplate`. However, since we do not want the build steps to run inside the cluster, inside the node based on the `podTemplate` is the same `node("docker")` block we are using for building and pushing Docker images.

The reason for using nested `node` blocks lies in Jenkins' ability to delete unused Pods. The moment `podTemplate` node is closed, Jenkins will remove the associated Pod. To preserve the state we'll generate inside that Pod, we're making sure that it is alive through the whole build by enveloping all the steps (even those running somewhere else) inside one colossal `node(label)` block.

Inside the `func-test` stage is a `try` block that contains all the steps (except cleanup). Each of the steps is executed inside a different container. We enter `helm` to clone the code and execute `helm upgrade` that installs the release under test. Next, we jump into the `kubectl` container to wait for the `rollout status` that confirms that the application is rolled out completely. Finally, we switch into the `golang` container to run our tests.

Please note that we are installing only two replicas of the application under test and one replica of the DB. That's more than enough to validate whether it works as expected from the functional point of view. There's no need to have the same number of replicas as what we'll run in the production Namespace.

You might be wondering why we checked out the code for the second time. The reason is simple. In the first stage, we cloned the code inside the VM dedicated to (or dynamically created for) building Docker images. The Pod created through `podTemplate` does not have that code, so we had to clone it again. We did that inside the `helm` container since that's the first one we're using.

Why didn't we clone the code to all the containers of the Pod? After all, almost everything we do needs the code of the application. While that might not be true for the `kubectl` container (it only waits for the installation to roll out), it is undoubtedly true for `golang`. The answer lies in Jenkins `podTemplate` "hidden" features. Among other things, it creates a volume and mounts it to all the containers of the Pod as the directory `/workspace`. That directory happens to be the default directory in which it operates when inside those containers. So, the state created inside one of the containers, exists in all the others, as long as we do not switch to a different folder.

The try block is followed with catch that is executed only if one of the steps throws an error. The only purpose for having the catch block is to re-throw the error if there is any.

The sole purpose for using try/catch is in the finally block. In it, we are deleting the application we deployed. Since it executes no matter whether there was an error, we have a reasonable guarantee that we'll have a clean system no matter the outcome of the pipeline.

To summarize, try block ensures that errors are caught. Without it, the pipeline would stop executing on the first sign of failure, and the release under test would never be removed. The catch block re-throws the error, and the finally block deletes the release no matter what happens.

Before we test the new iteration of the pipeline, please replace the values of the environment variables to fit your situation. As a minimum, you'll need to change vfarcic to your GitHub and Docker Hub users, and you'll have to replace acme.com with the value stored in the environment variable ADDR in your terminal session.

Once finished with the changes, please click the *Save* button. Use the *Open Blue Ocean* link from the left-hand menu to switch to the new UI and click the *Run* button followed with a click on the row of the new build.

 If you configured Jenkins to spin up new Docker nodes in AWS or GCP, it will take around a minute until the VM is created and operational.

Please wait until the build reaches the func-test stage and finishes executing the second step that executes helm upgrade. Once the release under test is installed, switch to the terminal session to confirm that the new release is indeed installed.

```
1  helm ls \
2      --tiller-namespace go-demo-3-build
```

The output is as follows.

```
1  NAME             REVISION UPDATED         STATUS    CHART           NAMESPACE
2  go-demo-3-2-null 1          Tue Jul 17 ... DEPLOYED go-demo-3-0.0.1 go-demo-3-build
```

As we can see, Jenkins did initiate the process that resulted in the new Helm Chart being installed in the go-demo-3-build Namespace.

To be on the safe side, we'll confirm that the Pods are running as well.

```
1  kubectl -n go-demo-3-build \
2      get pods
```

The output is as follows

```
 1   NAME                        READY  STATUS     RESTARTS  AGE
 2   go-demo-3-2-null-...        1/1    Running 4            2m
 3   go-demo-3-2-null-...        1/1    Running 4            2m
 4   go-demo-3-2-null-db-0       2/2    Running 0            2m
 5   jenkins-slave-...           4/4    Running 0            6m
 6   tiller-deploy-...           1/1    Running 0            14m
```

As expected, the two Pods of the API and one of the DB are running together with `jenkins-slave` Pod created by Jenkins.

Please return to Jenkins UI and wait until the build is finished.

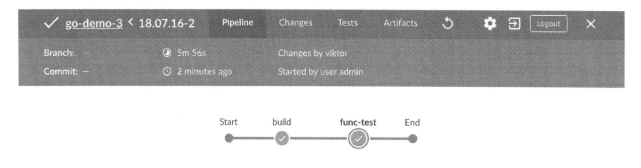

Figure 7-5: Jenkins build with the build and the functional testing stage

If everything works as we designed, the release under test was removed once the testing was finished. Let's confirm that.

```
 1   helm ls \
 2       --tiller-namespace go-demo-3-build
```

This time the output is empty, clearly indicating that the Chart was removed.

Let's check the Pods one more time.

```
1  kubectl -n go-demo-3-build \
2      get pods
```

The output is as follows

```
1  NAME                READY STATUS   RESTARTS AGE
2  tiller-deploy-... 1/1    Running 0          31m
```

Both the Pods of the release under tests as well as Jenkins agent are gone, leaving us only with Tiller. We defined the steps that remove the former, and the latter is done by Jenkins automatically.

Let's move onto the *release stage.*

Defining The Release Stage

In the *release stage*, we'll push Docker images to the registry as well as the project's Helm Chart. The images will be tags of the image under test, but this time they will be named using a convention that clearly indicates that they are production- ready.

In the *build stage*, we're tagging images by including the branch name. That way, we made it clear that an image is not yet thoroughly tested. Now that we executed all sorts of tests that validated that the release is indeed working as expected, we can re-tag the images so that they do not include branch names. That way, everyone in our organization can easily distinguish yet-to-be-tested from production-ready releases.

Since we cannot know (easily) whether the Chart included in the project's repository changed or not, during this stage, we'll push it to ChartMuseum. If the Chart's release number is unchanged, the push will merely overwrite the existing Chart. Otherwise, we'll have a new Chart release as well.

The significant difference between Docker images and Charts is in the way how we're generating releases. Each commit to the repository probably results in changes to the code, so building new images on each build makes perfect sense. Helm Charts, on the other hand, do not change that often.

One thing worth noting is that we will not use ChartMuseum for deploying applications through Jenkins' pipelines. We already have the Chart inside the repository that we're cloning. We'll store Charts in ChartMuseum only for those that want to deploy them manually without Jenkins. A typical user of those Charts are developers that want to spin up applications inside local clusters that are outside Jenkins' control.

Just as with the previous stages, we are focused only on the essential steps which you should extend to suit your specific needs. Examples that might serve as inspiration for the missing steps are those that would create a release in GitHub, GitLab, or Bitbucket. Also, it might be useful to build Docker images with manifest files in case you're planning on deploying them to different operating system families (e.g., ARM, Windows, etc.). Another thing that would be interesting to add is an automated way to create and publish release notes. Don't get your hopes too high because we'll skip those and quite a few other use-cases in an attempt to keep the pipeline simple, and yet fully functional.

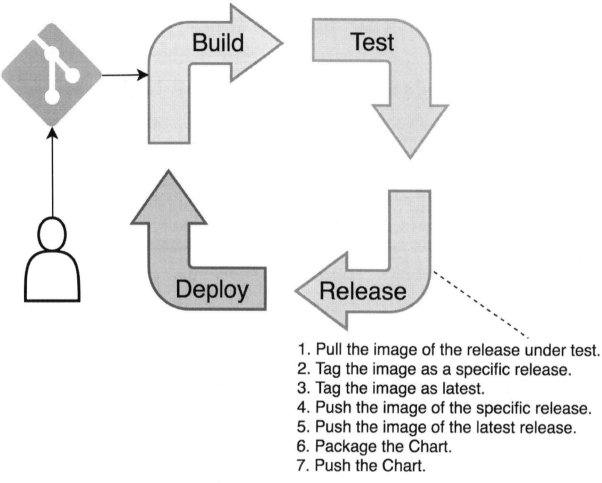

1. Pull the image of the release under test.
2. Tag the image as a specific release.
3. Tag the image as latest.
4. Push the image of the specific release.
5. Push the image of the latest release.
6. Package the Chart.
7. Push the Chart.

Figure 7-6: The essential steps of the release stage

Before we move on, we'll need to create a new set of credentials in Jenkins to store ChartMuseum's username and password.

```
1  open "http://$JENKINS_ADDR/credentials/store/system/domain/_/newCredentials"
```

Please type *admin* as both the *Username* and the *Password*. The *ID* and the *Description* should be set to *chartmuseum*. Once finished, please click the *OK* button to persist the credentials.

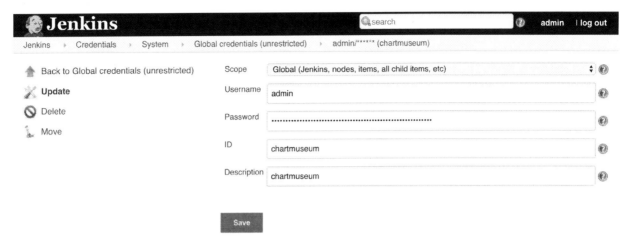

Figure 7-7: ChartMuseum Jenkins credentials

Next, we'll retrieve the updated `credentials.xml` file and store it in the `cluster/jenkins` directory. That way, if we want to create a new Jenkins instance, the new credentials will be available just as those that we created in the previous chapter.

```
1  JENKINS_POD=$(kubectl \
2      -n go-demo-3-jenkins \
3      get pods \
4      -l component=go-demo-3-jenkins-jenkins-master \
5      -o jsonpath='{.items[0].metadata.name}')
6
7  echo $JENKINS_POD
8
9  kubectl -n go-demo-3-jenkins cp \
10     $JENKINS_POD:var/jenkins_home/credentials.xml \
11     cluster/jenkins
```

We retrieved the name of the Pod hosting Jenkins, and we used it to copy the `credentials.xml` file.

Now we can update the job.

```
1  open "http://$JENKINS_ADDR/job/go-demo-3/configure"
```

If you are **NOT using minishift**, please replace the existing code with the content of the cdp-jenkins-release.groovy Gist[149].

If you are a **minishift user**, replace the existing code with the content of the cdp-jenkins-release-oc.groovy Gist[150].

Just as before, we'll explore only the differences between the two pipeline iterations.

---

[149]https://gist.github.com/2e89eec6ca991ab676d740733c409d35
[150]https://gist.github.com/33650e28417ceb1f2f349ec71b8a934d

```
1   ...
2   env.CM_ADDR = "cm.acme.com"
3   env.TAG = "${currentBuild.displayName}"
4   env.TAG_BETA = "${env.TAG}-${env.BRANCH_NAME}"
5   env.CHART_VER = "0.0.1"
6   ...
7       stage("release") {
8         node("docker") {
9           sh """sudo docker pull \
10            ${env.IMAGE}:${env.TAG_BETA}"""
11          sh """sudo docker image tag \
12            ${env.IMAGE}:${env.TAG_BETA} \
13            ${env.IMAGE}:${env.TAG}"""
14          sh """sudo docker image tag \
15            ${env.IMAGE}:${env.TAG_BETA} \
16            ${env.IMAGE}:latest"""
17          withCredentials([usernamePassword(
18            credentialsId: "docker",
19            usernameVariable: "USER",
20            passwordVariable: "PASS"
21          )]) {
22            sh """sudo docker login \
23              -u $USER -p $PASS"""
24          }
25          sh """sudo docker image push \
26            ${env.IMAGE}:${env.TAG}"""
27          sh """sudo docker image push \
28            ${env.IMAGE}:latest"""
29        }
30        container("helm") {
31          sh "helm package helm/go-demo-3"
32          withCredentials([usernamePassword(
33            credentialsId: "chartmuseum",
34            usernameVariable: "USER",
35            passwordVariable: "PASS"
36          )]) {
37            sh """curl -u $USER:$PASS \
38              --data-binary "@go-demo-3-${CHART_VER}.tgz" \
39              http://${env.CM_ADDR}/api/charts"""
40          }
41        }
42      }
43    }
```

```
44    }
```

Jut as before, we declared a few new environment variables. They should be self-explanatory.

We start the steps of the *release stage* inside the docker node. Since the nodes in AWS and GCP are dynamic, there is no guarantee that it'll be the same agent as the one used in the *build stage* since we set retention to ten minutes. Typically, that is more than enough time between the two requests for the node. However, some other build might have requested the node in between and, in that case, a new one would be created. Therefore, we cannot be sure that it's the same physical VM. To mitigate that, the first step is pulling the image we build previously. That way, we're ensuring that the cache is used in subsequent steps.

Next, we're creating two tags. One is based on the release (build display name), and the other on the latest. We'll use the more specific tag, while leaving the option to others to use the latest that that points to the last production-ready release.

Further on, we're logging to Docker Hub and pushing the new tags.

Finally, we are switching to the helm container of the podTemplate. Once inside, we are packaging the Chart and pushing it to ChartMuseum with curl. The essential element is the environment variable CHART_VER. It contains the version of the Chart that **must** correspond to the version in Chart.yaml file. We're using it to know which file to push. Truth be told, we could have parsed the output of the helm package command. However, since Charts do not change that often, it might be less work to update the version in two places than to add parsing to the code. It is true that having the same thing in two places increases the chances of an error by omission. I invite you to a challenge the current design by making a PR that will improve it.

Before we move on, you'll need to make the necessary changes to the values of the environment variables. Most likely, all you need to do is change vfarcic to your Docker Hub and GitHub users as well as acme.com to the value of the environment variable ADDR available in your terminal session.

Don't forget to click the *Save* button to persist the change. After that, follow the same process as before to run a new build by clicking the *Open Blue Ocean* link from the left-hand menu, followed with the *Run* button. Click on the row of the new build and wait until it's finished.

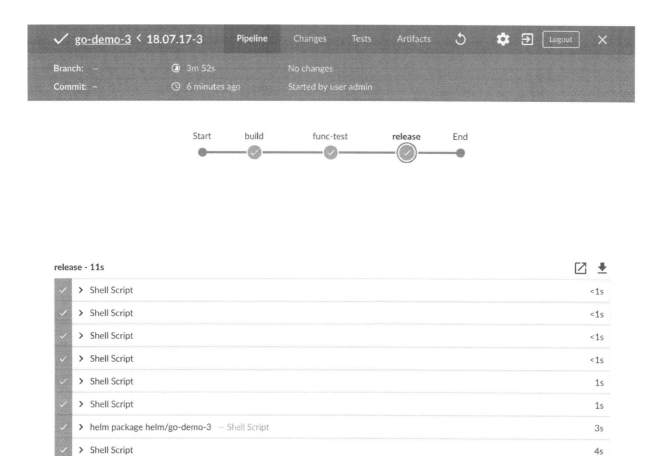

Figure 7-8: Jenkins build with the build, the functional testing, and the release stages

If everything went as expected, we should have a couple of new images pushed to Docker Hub. Let's confirm that.

```
1  open "https://hub.docker.com/r/$DH_USER/go-demo-3/tags/"
```

This time, besides the tags based on branches (for now with null), we got two new ones that represent the production-ready release.

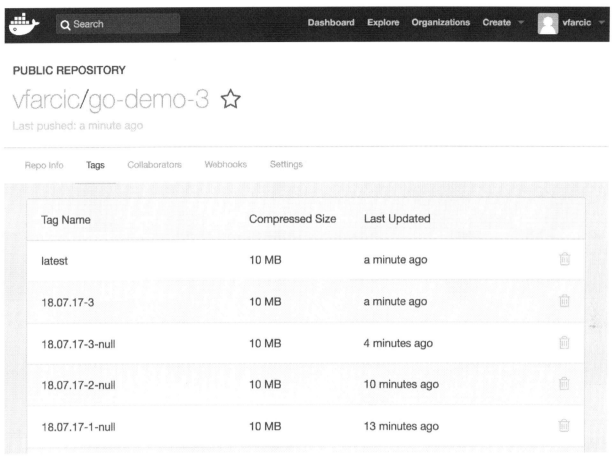

Figure 7-9: Images pushed to Docker Hub

Similarly, we should also have the Chart stored in ChartMuseum.

```
1  curl -u admin:admin \
2      "http://$CM_ADDR/index.yaml"
```

The output is as follows.

```
1  apiVersion: v1
2  entries:
3    go-demo-3:
4    - apiVersion: v1
5      created: "2018-07-17T21:53:30.760065856Z"
6      description: A silly demo based on API written in Go and MongoDB
7      digest: d73134fc9ff594e9923265476bac801b1bd38d40548799afd66328158f0617d8
8      home: http://www.devopstoolkitseries.com/
9      keywords:
10     - api
```

```
11        - backend
12        - go
13        - database
14        - mongodb
15      maintainers:
16      - email: viktor@farcic.com
17        name: Viktor Farcic
18      name: go-demo-3
19      sources:
20      - https://github.com/vfarcic/go-demo-3
21      urls:
22      - charts/go-demo-3-0.0.1.tgz
23      version: 0.0.1
24  generated: "2018-07-17T21:56:28Z"
```

Now that we confirmed that both the images and the Chart are being pushed to their registries, we can move onto the last stage of the pipeline.

Defining The Deploy Stage

We're almost finished with the pipeline, at least in its current form.

The purpose of the *deploy stage* is to install the new release to production and to do the last round of tests that only verify whether the new release integrates with the rest of the system. Those tests are often elementary since they do not validate the release on the functional level. We already know that the features work as expected and immutability of the containers guarantee that what was deployed as a test release is the same as what will be upgraded to production. What we're not yet sure is whether there is a problem related to the configuration of the production environment or, in our case, production Namespace.

If something goes wrong, we need to be able to act swiftly and roll back the release. I'll skip the discussion about the inability to roll back when changing database schemas and a few other cases. Instead, for the sake of simplicity, I'll assume that we'll roll back always if any of the steps in this stage fail.

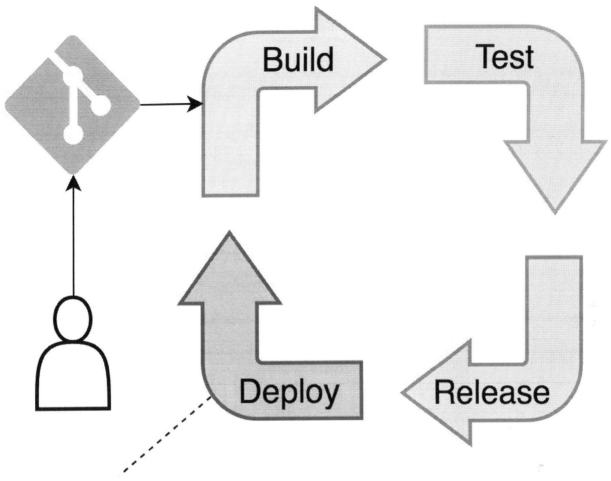

1. Upgrade the production release
2. Run production tests

Rollback in case of a failure

Figure 7-10: The essential steps of the deploy stage

Let's go back to *go-demo-3* configuration screen and update the pipeline.

```
1  open "http://$JENKINS_ADDR/job/go-demo-3/configure"
```

If you are **NOT using minishift**, please replace the existing code with the content of the cdp-jenkins-deploy.groovy Gist[151].

If you are **using minishift**, please replace the existing code with the content of the cdp-jenkins-deploy-oc.groovy Gist[152].

---

[151]https://gist.github.com/3657e7262b65749f29ddd618cf511d72
[152]https://gist.github.com/1a490bff0c90b021e3390a66dd75284e

The additions to the pipeline are as follows.

```
1    ...
2    env.PROD_ADDRESS = "go-demo-3.acme.com"
3    ...
4        stage("deploy") {
5          try {
6            container("helm") {
7              sh """helm upgrade \
8                go-demo-3 \
9                helm/go-demo-3 -i \
10                --tiller-namespace go-demo-3-build \
11                --namespace go-demo-3 \
12                --set image.tag=${env.TAG} \
13                --set ingress.host=${env.PROD_ADDRESS}
14                --reuse-values"""
15            }
16            container("kubectl") {
17              sh """kubectl -n go-demo-3 \
18                rollout status deployment \
19                go-demo-3"""
20            }
21            container("golang") {
22              sh "go get -d -v -t"
23              sh """DURATION=1 ADDRESS=${env.PROD_ADDRESS} \
24                go test ./... -v \
25                --run ProductionTest"""
26            }
27          } catch(e) {
28            container("helm") {
29              sh """helm rollback \
30                go-demo-3 0 \
31                --tiller-namespace go-demo-3-build"""
32              error "Failed production tests"
33            }
34          }
35        }
36      }
37    }
```

We added yet another environment variable (PROD_ADDRESS) that holds the address through which our production releases are accessible. We'll use it both for defining Ingress host as well as for the final round of testing.

Inside the stage, we're upgrading the production release with the `helm upgrade` command. The critical value is `image.tag` that specifies the image tag that should be used.

 ## A note to minishift users

Just as in the `func-test` stage, we had to add yet another Edge Route to the `deploy` stage so that we can gain the same functionality as what Ingress controller provides to other Kubernetes flavors.

Before we proceed with testing, we're waiting until the update rolls out. If there is something obviously wrong with the upgrade (e.g., the tag does not exist, or there are no available resources), the `rollout status` command will fail.

Finally, we're executing the last round of tests. In our case, the tests will run in a loop for one minute.

All the steps in this stage are inside a big `try` block, so a failure of any of the steps will be handled with the `catch` block. Inside it is a simple `helm rollback` command set to revision 0 which will result in a rollback to the previous release.

Just as in the other stages, we're jumping from one container to another depending on the tool we need at any given moment.

Before we move on, please make the necessary changes to the values of the environment variables. Just as before, you likely need to change `vfarcic` to your Docker Hub and GitHub users as well as `acme.com` to the value of the environment variable `ADDR` available in your terminal session.

Please click the *Save* button once you're finished with the changes that aim at making the pipeline work in your environment. The rest of the steps are the same as those we performed countless times before. Click the *Open Blue Ocean* link from the left-hand menu, press the *Run* button, and click on the row of the new build. Wait until the build is finished.

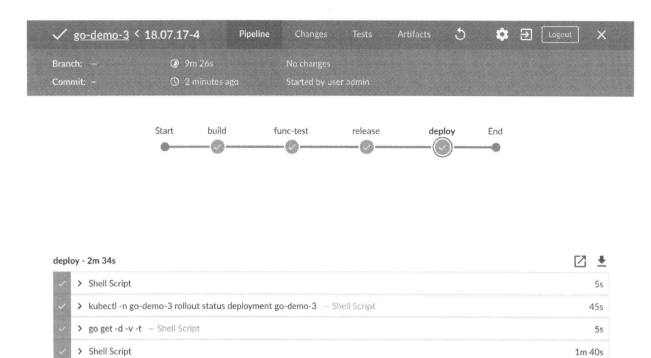

Figure 7-11: Jenkins build with all the continuous deployment stages

Since this is the first time we're running the *deploy stage*, we'll double-check that the production release was indeed deployed correctly.

```
1  helm ls \
2      --tiller-namespace go-demo-3-build
```

The output is as follows.

```
1  NAME        REVISION UPDATED        STATUS   CHART          NAMESPACE
2  go-demo-3 1          Wed Jul 18 ... DEPLOYED go-demo-3-0.0.1 go-demo-3
```

This is the first time we upgraded go-demo-3 production release, so the revision is 1.

How about Pods? Are they running as expected inside the go-demo-3 Namespace dedicated to production releases of that team?

```
1  kubectl -n go-demo-3 get pods
```

The output is as follows.

```
1  NAME               READY STATUS   RESTARTS AGE
2  go-demo-3-...       1/1   Running  2        6m
3  go-demo-3-...       1/1   Running  2        6m
4  go-demo-3-...       1/1   Running  2        6m
5  go-demo-3-db-0      2/2   Running  0        6m
6  go-demo-3-db-1      2/2   Running  0        6m
7  go-demo-3-db-2      2/2   Running  0        5m
```

All the Pods are indeed running. We have three replicas of the API and three replicas of the database.

Finally, we'll send a request to the newly deployed release and confirm that we are getting the correct response.

```
1  curl "http://go-demo-3.$ADDR/demo/hello"
```

The output should be the familiar `hello, world!` message.

What Are We Missing In Our Pipeline?

We already discussed some the steps that we might be missing. We might want to store test results in SonarQube. We might want to generate release notes and store them in GitHub. We might need to run performance tests. There are many things we could have done, but we didn't. Those additional steps will differ significantly from one organization to another. Even within a company, one team might have different steps than the other. Guessing which ones you might need would be an exercise in futility. I would have almost certainly guessed wrong.

One step that almost everyone needs is notification of failure. We need to be notified when something goes wrong and fix the issue. However, there are too many destinations where those notifications might need to be sent. Some prefer email, while others opt for chats. In the latter case, it could be Slack, HipChat, Skype, and many others. We might even choose to create a JIRA issue when one of the steps in the pipeline fails. Since even a simple notification can be performed in so many different ways, I'll skip adding them to the pipeline. I'm sure that you won't have a problem looking for a plugin you need (e.g., Slack Notification[153]) and injecting notifications into the stages. We already have a few `try` statements, and notifications can be inserted into `catch` blocks. You might need to add a few additional `try`/`catch` blocks or a big one that envelops the whole pipeline. I believe in you by being confident that you'll know how to do that. So, we'll move to the next subject.

Reusing Pipeline Snippets Through Global Pipeline Libraries

The pipeline we designed works as we expect. However, we'll have a problem on our hands if other teams start copying and pasting the same script for their pipelines. We'd end up with a lot

---

[153]https://plugins.jenkins.io/slack

of duplicated code that will be hard to maintain.

Most likely it will get worse than the simple practice of duplicating code since not all pipelines will be the same. There's a big chance each is going to be different, so copy and paste practice will only be the first action. People will find the pipeline that is closest to what they're trying to accomplish, replicate it, and then change it to suit their needs. Some steps are likely going to be the same for many (if not all) projects, while others will be specific to only one, or just a few pipelines.

The more pipelines we design, the more patterns will emerge. Everyone might want to build Docker images with the same command, but with different arguments. Others might use Helm to install their applications, but will not (yet) have any tests to run (be nice, do not judge them). Someone might choose to use Rust[154] for the new project, and the commands will be unique only to a single pipeline.

What we need to do is look for patterns. When we notice that a step, or a set of steps, are the same across multiple pipelines, we should be able to convert that snippet into a library, just as what we're likely doing when repetition happens in code of our applications. Those libraries need to be accessible to all those who need it, and they need to be flexible so that their behavior can be adjusted to slightly different needs. We should be able to provide arguments to those libraries.

What we truly need is the ability to create new pipeline steps that are tailored to our needs. Just as there is a general step `git`, we might want something like `k8sUpgrade` that will perform Helm's `upgrade` command. We can accomplish that, and quite a few other things through Jenkins' *Global Pipeline Libraries*.

We'll explore libraries through practical examples, so the firsts step is to configure them.

```
1   open "http://$JENKINS_ADDR/configure"
```

Please search for *Global Pipeline Libraries* section of the configuration, and click the *Add* button.

Type *my-library* as the *Name* (it can be anything else) and *master* as the *Default version*. In our context, the latter defines the branch from which we'll load the libraries.

Next, we'll click the *Load implicitly* checkbox. As a result, the libraries will be available automatically to all the pipeline jobs. Otherwise, our jobs would need to have `@Library('my-library')` instruction.

Select *Modern SCM* from the *Retrieval method* section and select *Git* from *Source Code Management*.

We're almost done. The only thing left is to specify the repository from which Jenkins will load the libraries. I already created a repo with all the libraries we'll use (and a few others we won't need). However, GitHub API has a limit to the number of requests that can be made per hour so if you (and everyone else) uses my repo, you might see some undesirable effects. My recommendation is to go to vfarcic/jenkins-shared-libraries.git[155] and fork it. Once the fork is created, copy the address from the *Clone and download* drop-down list, return to Jenkins UI, and paste it into the *Project Repository* field.

---

[154]https://www.rust-lang.org/
[155]https://github.com/vfarcic/jenkins-shared-libraries.git

We're finished with the configuration. Don't forget to click the *Save* button to persist the changes.

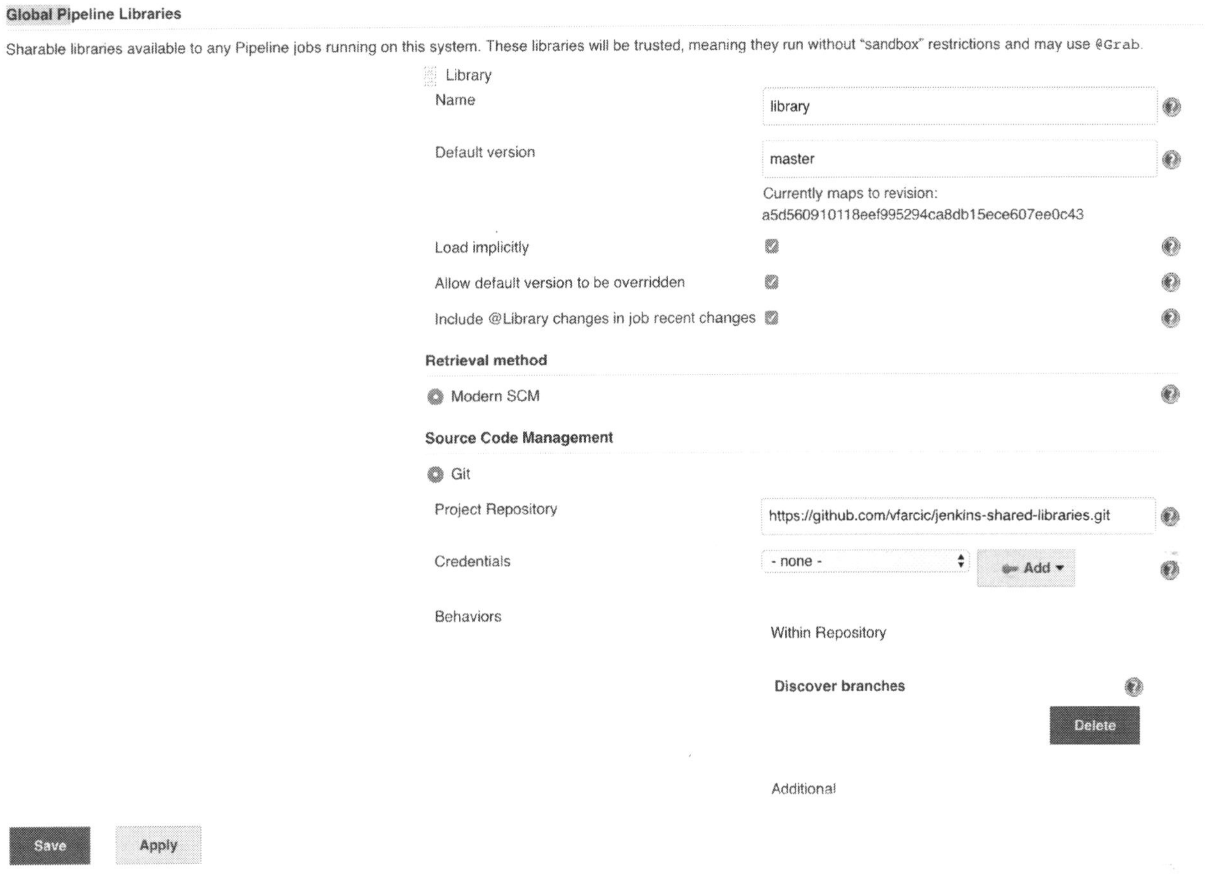

Figure 7-12: Jenkins Global Pipeline Libraries configuration screen

Let's take a closer look at the repository we'll use as the *global pipeline library*.

```
1  export GH_USER=[...]
2
3  open "https://github.com/$GH_USER/jenkins-shared-libraries.git"
```

Please replace [...] with your GitHub user before opening the forked repository in a browser.

You'll see that the repository has only .gitignore file and the vars dir in the root. Jenkins' *Global Pipeline Libraries* use a naming convention to discover the functions we'd like to use. They can be either in src or vars folder. The former is rarely used these days, so we're having only the latter.

If you enter into the vars directory, you'll see that there are quite a few *.groovy files mixed with a few *.txt files. We'll postpone exploration of the latter group of files and concentrate on the Groovy files instead. We'll use those with names that start with k8s and oc (in case you're using OpenShift).

Please find the *k8sBuildImageBeta.groovy* file and open it. You'll notice that the code inside it is almost the same as the one we used in the *build stage*. There are a few differences though, so let's go through the structure of the shared functions. It'll be a concise explanation.

The name of the file (e.g., *k8sBuildImageBeta.groovy*) becomes a pipeline step (e.g., k8sBuildImageBeta). If we use a step converted from a file, Jenkins will invoke the function call. So, every Groovy file needs to have such a function, even though additional internal functions can be defined as well. The call function can have any number of arguments. If we continue using the same example, you'll see that call inside *k8sBuildImageBeta.groovy* has a single argument image. It could have been defined with the explicit type like String image, but in most cases, there's no need for it. Groovy will figure out the type.

Inside the call function are almost the same steps as those we used inside the *build stage*. I copied and pasted them. The only modification to the steps was to replace Docker image references with the image argument. Since we already know that Groovy extrapolates arguments in a string when they are prefixed with the dollar sign ($) and optional curly braces ({ and }), our image argument became ${image}.

Using arguments in the functions is essential. They make them reusable across different pipelines. If *k8sBuildImageBeta.groovy* would have go-demo-3 image hard-coded, that would not be useful to anyone except those trying to build the *go-demo* application. The alternative would be to use environment variables and ditch arguments altogether. I've seen that pattern in many organizations, and I think it's horrible. It does not make it clear what is needed to use the function. There are a few exceptions though. My usage of environment variables is limited to those available to all builds. For example, ${env.BRANCH_NAME} is always available. One does not need to create it when writing a pipeline script. For everything else, please use arguments. That will be a clear indication to the users of those functions what is required.

I won't go through all the Groovy files that start with k8s (and oc) since they follow the same logic as *k8sBuildImageBeta.groovy*. They are copies of what we used in our pipeline, with the addition of a few arguments. So, instead of me going over all the functions, please take some time to explore them yourself. Return here once you're done, and we'll put those functions to good use and clarify a few other important aspects of Jenkins' shared libraries.

Before we continue, you might want to persist the changes we did to Jenkins configuration. All the information about the shared libraries is available in *org.jenkinsci.plugins.workflow.libs.GlobalLibraries.xml* file. We just need to copy it.

```
1  kubectl -n go-demo-3-jenkins cp \
2      $JENKINS_POD:var/jenkins_home/org.jenkinsci.plugins.workflow.libs.GlobalLibrarie\
3  s.xml \
4      cluster/jenkins/secrets
```

I already modified the template of the Jenkins Helm Chart to include the file we just copied. All you have to do the next time you install Jenkins with Helm is to add jenkins.Master.GlobalLibraries value. The full argument should be as follows.

```
1  --set jenkins.Master.GlobalLibraries=true
```

Now we can refactor our pipeline to use shared libraries and see whether that simplifies things.

```
1  open "http://$JENKINS_ADDR/job/go-demo-3/configure"
```

If you are **NOT using minishift**, please replace the existing code with the content of the cdp-jenkins-lib.groovy Gist[156].

If you are **using minishift**, please replace the existing code with the content of the cdp-jenkins-lib-oc.groovy Gist[157].

We'll explore only the differences from the previous iteration of the pipeline. They are as follows.

```
1   ...
2   env.PROJECT = "go-demo-3"
3   env.REPO = "https://github.com/vfarcic/go-demo-3.git"
4   env.IMAGE = "vfarcic/go-demo-3"
5   env.DOMAIN = "acme.com"
6   env.ADDRESS = "go-demo-3.acme.com"
7   env.CM_ADDR = "cm.acme.com"
8   env.CHART_VER = "0.0.1"
9   ...
10    node("kubernetes") {
11      node("docker") {
12        stage("build") {
13          git "${env.REPO}"
14          k8sBuildImageBeta(env.IMAGE)
15        }
16      }
17      stage("func-test") {
18        try {
19          container("helm") {
20            git "${env.REPO}"
21            k8sUpgradeBeta(env.PROJECT, env.DOMAIN, "--set replicaCount=2 --set dbRepl\
22  icaCount=1")
23          }
24          container("kubectl") {
25            k8sRolloutBeta(env.PROJECT)
26          }
27          container("golang") {
28            k8sFuncTestGolang(env.PROJECT, env.DOMAIN)
```

---

[156]https://gist.github.com/e9821d0430ca909d68eecc7ccbb1825d
[157]https://gist.github.com/ff6e0b04f165d2b26d326c116a7cc14f

```
29             }
30         } catch(e) {
31             error "Failed functional tests"
32         } finally {
33           container("helm") {
34             k8sDeleteBeta(env.PROJECT)
35           }
36         }
37       }
38     stage("release") {
39       node("docker") {
40         k8sPushImage(env.IMAGE)
41       }
42       container("helm") {
43         k8sPushHelm(env.PROJECT, env.CHART_VER, env.CM_ADDR)
44       }
45     }
46     stage("deploy") {
47       try {
48         container("helm") {
49           k8sUpgrade(env.PROJECT, env.ADDRESS)
50         }
51         container("kubectl") {
52           k8sRollout(env.PROJECT)
53         }
54         container("golang") {
55           k8sProdTestGolang(env.ADDRESS)
56         }
57       } catch(e) {
58         container("helm") {
59           k8sRollback(env.PROJECT)
60         }
61       }
62     }
63   }
64 }
```

We have fewer environment variables since part of the logic for constructing the values is moved into the functions. The podTemplate is still the same, and the real differences are noticeable inside stages.

All the stages now contain fewer steps. Everything is much simpler since the logic, steps, and the commands are moved to functions. All we're doing is treat those functions as simplified steps.

You might say that even though the pipeline is now much more straightforward, it is still not trivial. You'd be right. We could have replaced them with bigger and fewer functions. We could have had only four like build, test, release, and deploy. However, that would reduce flexibility. Every team in our organization would need to build, test, release, and deploy in the same way, or skip using the library and do the coding inside the pipeline. If the functions are too big, people must choose to adopt the whole process or not use them at all. By having a very focused function that does only one, or just a few things, we gain more flexibility when combining them.

Good examples are the functions used in the deploy stage. If there were only one (e.g., k8sDeploy), everyone would need to use Go to test. As it is now, a different team could choose to use k8sUpgrade and k8sRollout functions, but skip k8sProdTestGolang. Maybe their application is coded in Rust[158], and they will need a separate function. Or, there might be only one project that uses Rust, and there's no need for a function since there is no repetition. The point is that teams should be able to choose to re-use libraries that fit their process, and write themselves whatever they're missing.

 From my experience, functions from Jenkins' global pipeline libraries should be small and with a single purpose. That way, we can combine them as if they are pieces of a puzzle, instead of continually adding complexity by trying to fit all the scenarios into one or a few libraries.

Another thing worth mentioning is that node and container blocks are not inside libraries. There are two reasons for that. First, I think it is easier to understand the flow of the pipeline (without going into libraries) when those blocks are there. The second and the much more important reason is that they are not allowed in a declarative pipeline. We are using scripted flavor only because a few things are missing in declarative. However, the declarative pipeline is the future, and you should be prepared to switch once those issues are resolved. I will refactor the code into declarative once that becomes an option.

Before we move forward, please replace the values of the environment variables to fit your situation. As a reminder, you most likely need to change vfarcic with your GitHub and Docker Hub users, and acme.com with the value of the environment variable ADDR available in your terminal session.

Once you're finished adjusting the values, please click the *Save* button to persist the changes. Click the *Open Blue Ocean* link from the left-hand menu, followed with the *Run* button. Go to the new build and wait until it is finished.

We refactored the pipeline by making it more readable and easier to maintain. We did not introduce new functionalities, so the result of this build should be functionally the same as the previous that was done with the prior iteration of the code. Let's confirm that.

Did we push a new image to Docker Hub?

```
1   open "https://hub.docker.com/r/$DH_USER/go-demo-3/tags/"
```

[158]https://www.rust-lang.org/

The new image (with a few tags) was pushed.

How about Helm upgrades?

```
1  helm ls \
2      --tiller-namespace go-demo-3-build
```

The output is as follows.

```
1  NAME        REVISION UPDATED         STATUS   CHART          NAMESPACE
2  go-demo-3 2          Wed Jul 18 ... DEPLOYED go-demo-3-0.0.1 go-demo-3
```

We are now on the second revision, so that part seems to be working as expected. To be on the safe side, we'll check the history.

```
1  helm history go-demo-3 \
2      --tiller-namespace go-demo-3-build
```

The output is as follows.

```
1  REVISION UPDATED         STATUS     CHART          DESCRIPTION
2  1        Wed Jul 18 ... SUPERSEDED go-demo-3-0.0.1 Install complete
3  2        Wed Jul 18 ... DEPLOYED   go-demo-3-0.0.1 Upgrade complete
```

The first revision was superseded by the second.

Our mission has been accomplished, but our pipeline is still not as it's supposed to be.

Consulting Global Pipeline Libraries Documentation

We already saw that we can open a repository with global pipeline libraries and consult the functions to find out what they do. While the developer in me prefers that option, many might find it too complicated and might prefer something more "non-developer friendly". Fortunately, there is an alternative way to document and consult libraries.

Let's go back to the forked repository with the libraries.

```
1  open "https://github.com/$GH_USER/jenkins-shared-libraries/tree/master/vars"
```

If you pay closer attention, you'll notice that all Groovy files with names that start with k8s have an accompanying txt file. Let's take a closer look at one of them.

```
1  curl "https://raw.githubusercontent.com/$GH_USER/jenkins-shared-libraries/master/var\
2  s/k8sBuildImageBeta.txt"
```

The output is as follows.

```
1  ## Builds a Docker image with a beta release
2
3  The image is tagged with the **build display name** suffixed with the **branch name**
4
5  **Arguments:**
6
7  * **image**: the name of the Docker image (e.g. `vfarcic/go-demo-3`).
8
9  **Requirements:**
10
11 * A node with Docker
12 * Docker Hub credentials with the ID **docker**
```

Do not get confused with txt extension. Documentation can be written not only in plain text but also as HTML or Markdown. As you can see, I chose the latter. It is entirely up to you how you'll write corresponding documentation of a function. There is no prescribed formula. The only thing that matters is that the name of the txt file is the same as the name of the groovy function. The only difference is in the extension.

But, how do we visualize those helper files, besides visiting the repository where they reside? Before I answer that question, we'll make a slight change to Jenkins' security configuration.

```
1  open "http://$JENKINS_ADDR/configureSecurity/"
```

Please scroll down to the *Markup Formatter* section and change the value to *PegDown*. Click the *Apply* button to persist the change. From now on, Jenkins will format everything using the Markdown parser. Since our helper files are also written in Markdown, we should be able to visualize them correctly.

Let's find the documentation of the libraries.

```
1  open "http://$JENKINS_ADDR/job/go-demo-3/"
```

We are in the old view of the job we created short while ago. If you look at the left-hand menu, you'll see the link *Pipeline Syntax*. Click it.

The screen we're looking at contains quite a few useful links. There's *Snippet Generator* that we can use to generate code for each of the available steps. *Declarative Directive Generator* generates the code specific to Declarative Pipeline syntax that we're not (yet) using. I'll let you explore those and the other links at your own leisure. The one we're interested right now is the *Global Variables Reference* link. Please click it.

Inside the *Global Variable Reference* screen are all the variables and functions we can use. We're interested in those with names starting with *k8s*. Please scroll down until you find them. You'll see that *.txt* files are nicely formatted and available to anyone interested how to use our functions.

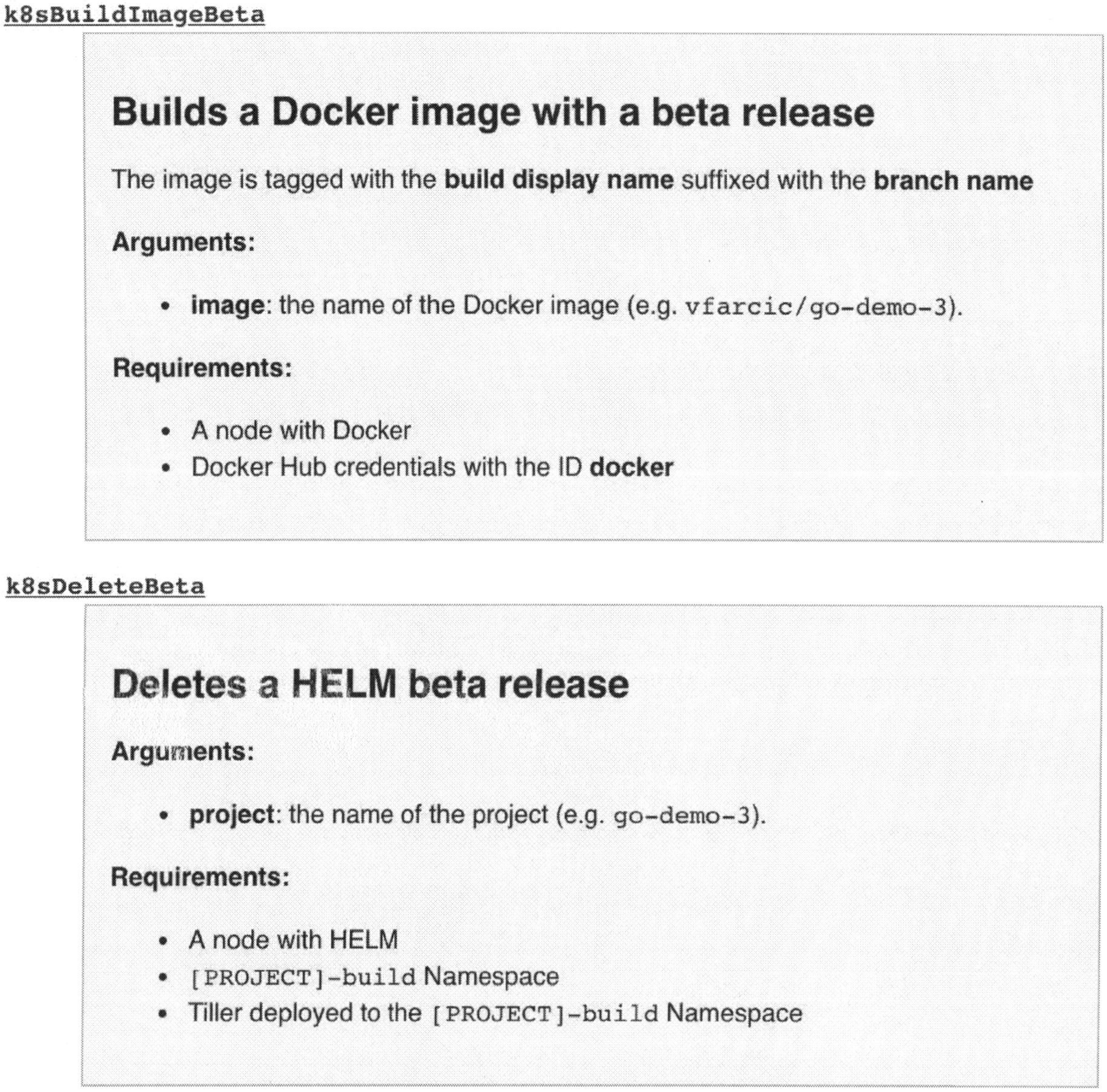

k8sBuildImageBeta

Builds a Docker image with a beta release

The image is tagged with the **build display name** suffixed with the **branch name**

Arguments:

- **image**: the name of the Docker image (e.g. `vfarcic/go-demo-3`).

Requirements:

- A node with Docker
- Docker Hub credentials with the ID **docker**

k8sDeleteBeta

Deletes a HELM beta release

Arguments:

- **project**: the name of the project (e.g. `go-demo-3`).

Requirements:

- A node with HELM
- `[PROJECT]-build` Namespace
- Tiller deployed to the `[PROJECT]-build` Namespace

Figure 7-13: Global Pipeline Libraries documentation

Using Jenkinsfile & Multistage Builds

The pipeline we designed has at least two significant shortcomings. It is not aware of branches, and it is not in source control.

Every time we instructed Jenkins to use the `git` step, it pulled the latest commit from the `master` branch. While that might be OK for demos, it is unacceptable in real-world situations. Our pipeline must pull the commit that initiated a build from the correct branch. In other words, no matter where we push a commit, that same commit must be used by the pipeline.

If we start processing all commits, no matter from which branch they're coming, we will soon realize that it does not make sense always to execute the same stages. As an example, the *release* and *deploy* stages should be executed only if a commit is made to the master branch. Otherwise, we'd create a new production release always, even if the branch is called *i-am-bored-so-i-decided-to-experiment*. As you can imagine, that is not what we'd like to happen.

Moving onto the second issue with the current pipeline...

I have a mantra that I already repeated quite a few times in this book. Everything we do, no matter whether its code, a configuration, or a properties file, **must** be in version control. I even go as far as to say that if someone finds something on some server that is not stored in version control, that person has full rights to remove that something. **If it's not in Git, it does not exist**. It's as simple as that. Everything else can be considered "hocus-pocus, ad-hoc, nobody knows what was done" type of things. CD pipeline is code and, as such, it must be stored in version control. There can be no exceptions.

Fortunately, we can solve those problems through a combination of Jenkinsfiles, Multistage Builds, and a bit of refactoring.

Let's take a look at *Jenkinsfile* located in the root of *go-demo-3* repository.

```
1  cat ../go-demo-3/Jenkinsfile
```

The output is as follows.

```
1  import java.text.SimpleDateFormat
2
3  def props
4  def label = "jenkins-slave-${UUID.randomUUID().toString()}"
5  currentBuild.displayName = new SimpleDateFormat("yy.MM.dd").format(new Date()) + "-"\
6    + env.BUILD_NUMBER
7
8  podTemplate(
9    label: label,
10   namespace: "go-demo-3-build",
```

```
11      serviceAccount: "build",
12      yaml: """
13  apiVersion: v1
14  kind: Pod
15  spec:
16    containers:
17    - name: helm
18      image: vfarcic/helm:2.9.1
19      command: ["cat"]
20      tty: true
21      volumeMounts:
22      - name: build-config
23        mountPath: /etc/config
24    - name: kubectl
25      image: vfarcic/kubectl
26      command: ["cat"]
27      tty: true
28    - name: golang
29      image: golang:1.9
30      command: ["cat"]
31      tty: true
32    volumes:
33    - name: build-config
34      configMap:
35        name: build-config
36  """
37  ) {
38    node(label) {
39      stage("build") {
40        container("helm") {
41          sh "cp /etc/config/build-config.properties ."
42          props = readProperties interpolate: true, file: "build-config.properties"
43        }
44        node("docker") {
45          checkout scm
46          k8sBuildImageBeta(props.image)
47        }
48      }
49      stage("func-test") {
50        try {
51          container("helm") {
52            checkout scm
53            k8sUpgradeBeta(props.project, props.domain, "--set replicaCount=2 --set db\
```

```
54  ReplicaCount=1")
55            }
56          container("kubectl") {
57            k8sRolloutBeta(props.project)
58            }
59          container("golang") {
60            k8sFuncTestGolang(props.project, props.domain)
61            }
62        } catch(e) {
63            error "Failed functional tests"
64        } finally {
65          container("helm") {
66            k8sDeleteBeta(props.project)
67            }
68          }
69        }
70      if ("${BRANCH_NAME}" == "master") {
71        stage("release") {
72          node("docker") {
73            k8sPushImage(props.image)
74            }
75          container("helm") {
76            k8sPushHelm(props.project, props.chartVer, props.cmAddr)
77            }
78        }
79        stage("deploy") {
80          try {
81            container("helm") {
82              k8sUpgrade(props.project, props.addr)
83            }
84            container("kubectl") {
85              k8sRollout(props.project)
86            }
87            container("golang") {
88              k8sProdTestGolang(props.addr)
89            }
90          } catch(e) {
91            container("helm") {
92              k8sRollback(props.project)
93            }
94          }
95        }
96      }
```

```
97    }
98  }
```

 ## A note to minishift users

Due to differences between OpenShift and other Kubernetes flavors, you'll have to explore the file called Jenkinsfile.oc. It contains a few OpenShift-specific differences we commented earlier.

As you can see, the content of Jenkinsfile is a pipeline similar to the one we previously created in Jenkins. Soon we'll discover how to tell Jenkins to use that file instead. For now, we'll explore the differences between the pipeline we defined in Jenkins and the one available in Jenkinsfile.

On the first inspection, you might say that both pipelines are the same. Take a closer look, and you'll notice that there are quite a few differences. They might be subtle, but they are important nevertheless.

The first difference is that there are no environment variables. Instead, there is a single variable props. We'll have to fast forward to the build stage to see its usage.

We added a set of new steps to the build stage. We are using readProperties to read the build-config.properties file and store interpolated values to the props variable. There is a bug in Jenkins that prevents us from using absolute paths so before we readProperies, we copy the file from /etc/config/ to the current directory.

If you go back to the podTemplate definition, you'll notice that the helm container has a mount to the directory /etc/config. Further down, the same volume is defined as configMap. In other words, we're injecting the build-config.properties file as Kubernetes ConfigMap and using its content to interpolate all the variables we need.

You don't have to use ConfigMap. It could be a Secret, or it could be a file located in the code repository. It does not matter how the file gets there, but that it contains the values we'll need for our pipeline. Those are the same ones we defined previously as environment variables. In my opinion, that's a much more elegant and easier way to define them. If you do not like the idea of a properties file, feel free to continue using environment variables as we did in previous iterations of the pipeline.

The next significant difference is that we changed git steps with checkout scm. Later on, we'll establish a connection between pipeline jobs and repositories and branches, and Jenkins will know which repository, which branch, and which commit to pull. Until now, we were always pulling HEAD of the master branch, and that is, obviously, apparently. We'll see how checkout scm works later on. For now, just remember that Jenkins will know what to pull with that instruction.

The step directly below checkout scm features the usage of readProperties step we declared earlier. Since we specified interpolate: true, Jenkins converted each property into a different variable or, to be more precise, a separate map entry. We're leveraging that with steps like k8sBuildImageBeta(props.image) where props.image is one of the interpolated property keys.

The rest of the pipeline is the same as what we had before, except that environment variables are replaced with props.SOMETHING variables.

There is one more important difference though. Two of the stages (release and deploy) are now enveloped in an if ("${BRANCH_NAME}" == "master") block. That allows us to control which parts of the pipeline are always executed, and which will run only if the branch is *master*. You might choose different conditions. For our use case, the logic is straightforward. If a commit (or a merge) is done to master, we want to execute the whole pipeline that, ultimately, upgrades the production release. All the other branches (typically feature branches), should only validate whether the commit works as expected. They should not make a (production) release, nor they should deploy to production.

 ## A note to minishift users

Please replace *Jenkinsfile* with *Jenkinsfile.oc*, commit the change, and push it to the forked repository. You'll have to repeat the same step for all the branches.

Now that we know that our pipeline needs a ConfigMap named go-demo-3-build, our next step will be to create it. We already have a YAML file in the application's repository.

```
1  cat ../go-demo-3/k8s/build-config.yml
```

The output is as follows.

```
1  kind: ConfigMap
2  apiVersion: v1
3  metadata:
4    creationTimestamp: 2016-02-18...
5    name: build-config
6    namespace: go-demo-3-build
7  data:
8    build-config.properties: |
9      project=go-demo-3
10     image=vfarcic/go-demo-3
11     domain=acme.com
12     addr=go-demo-3.acme.com
13     cmAddr=cm.acme.com
14     chartVer=0.0.1
```

If you focus on the build-config.properties data entry, you'll notice that it contains similar values as those we used before as environment variables. Obviously, we won't be able to create the ConfigMap as-is since we need to replace acme.com with the address and vfarcic with your Docker Hub user. We'll use a bit of sed magic to modify the YAML before passing it to kubectl.

```
1  cat ../go-demo-3/k8s/build-config.yml \
2      | sed -e "s@acme.com@$ADDR@g" \
3      | sed -e "s@vfarcic@$DH_USER@g" \
4      | kubectl apply -f - --record
```

We'll replace the Jenkins job we used so far with a different kind, so our next step is to delete it.

```
1  open "http://$JENKINS_ADDR/job/go-demo-3/"
```

Please click the *Delete Pipeline* link and confirm the action.

Now we are ready to create a job in the way we should have done it all along if we didn't need a playground that allows us to modify a pipeline easily.

```
1  open "http://$JENKINS_ADDR/blue/create-pipeline"
```

Please select *GitHub*, and you'll be asked for *Your GitHub access token*. If you do NOT have a token at hand, please click the *Create an access token here* link, and you will be redirected to the page in GitHub that is already pre-configured with all the permissions the token needs. All you have to do is type *Token description*. Anything should do. Feel free to type *jenkins* if today is not your creative day. Click the *Generate token* button at the bottom.

You'll see the newly generated token. Make sure to copy it and, optionally, save it somewhere. This is the first, and the last time you will see the value of the token.

Go back to Jenkins UI, paste the token into the *Your GitHub access token* field, and click the *Connect* button.

Next, we need to select the organization. You might have multiple entries if you are an active GitHub user. Choose the one where you forked *go-demo-3* repository.

Once you selected the organization, you'll see the list of all the repositories you own. Select *go-demo-3*. If there are too many, you can use the *Search...* field to filter the results.

The only thing left is to click the *Create Pipeline* button, and Jenkins will start creating new jobs. There will be one for each branch. You should, as a minimum, see three; *master*, *feature-3*, and *feature-4*. If we add a WebHook to our GitHub repository, Jenkins would be notified every time we create a new branch, and it would create a corresponding job. Similarly, when we delete a branch, the job would be removed as well.

Unfortunately, we might not be able to create a WebHook for our examples. At least, not for all of you. Those that are running a local cluster using Docker For Mac or Windows, minikube, or minishift, do not have an IP that is reachable from GitHub. Since I don't want to discriminate against those that run a cluster locally from those running it in one of the Cloud providers, I'll skip providing detailed instructions. Instead, when you translate lessons learned from this book into your production cluster, please follow the instructions from GitHub Webhook: Pipeline Multibranch[159] (jump to the *Validate*

---

[159]https://support.cloudbees.com/hc/en-us/articles/115003019232-GitHub-Webhook-Pipeline-Multibranch

GitHub WebHook section). Google is your friend if you prefer using GitLab, BitBucket, or some other Git solution.

Going back to Jenkins...

The first build of each job that corresponds to a different branch or a pull request is running. You can click on the *Branches* tab if you are interested only in jobs based on branches. Similarly, you can click on the *Pull Requests* tab to see the PRs. I did create a few pull requests in the *vfarcic/go-demo-3* repository, but they were not transferred to your fork. For now, you'll need to trust me when I say that new jobs will be created for each PR, as long as there is a GitHub WebHook that will notify Jenkins when you create them.

The communication between GitHub and Jenkins goes both ways. On the one hand, GitHub is notifying Jenkins whenever we created a new branch, commit something, or if we perform any other action configured through WebHooks. On the other hand, Jenkins will notify GitHub with a status of a build. A good example is a pull request. If we'd have one, would see that the state of the corresponding build would be available in PRs screen. We'd see both the activity while the build is running, as well as the outcome once it's finished.

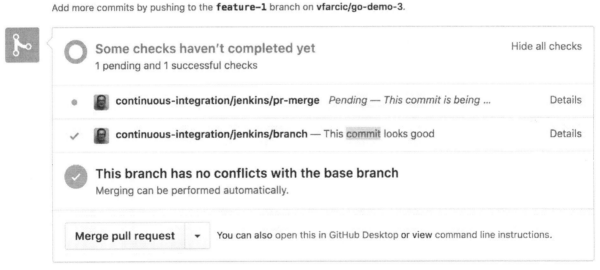

Figure 7-14: Jenkins integration with GitHub pull requests

Please note that each of the jobs based on different branches are now using `checkout scm` in their pipelines. Since now Jenkins keeps tracks of repositories, branches, and commits, there is no need for us to be explicit through steps like `git`. When a job is triggered by a commit, and Jenkins is notified via a webhook, it'll make sure it is that specific commit that is checked out. This by itself is a significant advantage of using Jenkins' multistage builds. Please note that when triggered manually, checkout scm will checkout the latest commit of the branch and the repository the job is pointing at.

The *Activity* tab shows all the builds, independently whether they come from a branch or a pull request.

We have a problem though. The `go-demo-3-build` Namespace does not have enough capacity to run more than one build at a time. I did my best to keep ResourceQuotas and overall cluster capacity to a minimum so that the cost for those running in Cloud is as small as possible. For those running a local cluster, we have limits of your laptops which we are probably already stretching to the limit.

Small capacity of our cluster and quotas is not really a big deal if we have enough patience. One of the builds is running while others are waiting in a queue. Once the first build is finished, the second one will start, and then the third, all the way until all the builds are completed. So, we'll have to be patient.

Please wait until a build of a feature branch is finished (e.g., *feature-3* or *feature-4*). Click on the row that represents that build and observe the stages. You'll notice that there are only two (`build` and `func-test`). The second half of the pipeline (`release` and `deploy`) was not executed since the `if` condition did not evaluate to `true`.

Similarly, once the build of the *master* branch is finished, enter inside it and observe that all the stages were executed thus upgrading our production release. Feel free to go to your cluster and confirm that a new Helm revision was created and that new Pods are running. Similarly, a new image should be available in Docker Hub.

STATUS	RUN	COMMIT	BRANCH	MESSAGE	DURATION	COMPLETED	
✓	18.07.21-	1cecfd0	PR-3	Branch indexing	26m 36s	4 minutes ago	↻
✓	18.07.21-	127f916	PR-4	Branch indexing	12m 55s	18 minutes ago	↻
✓	18.07.21-	eafe5bb	master	Branch indexing	7m 8s	23 minutes ago	↻
✓	18.07.21-	127f916	feature-4	Branch indexing	22m 7s	8 minutes ago	↻
✓	18.07.21-	1cecfd0	feature-3	Branch indexing	17m 17s	13 minutes ago	↻

Figure 7-15: The jobs from the go-demo-3 Multi-Branch Pipeline

What Now?

We are, finally, finished designing the first iteration of a fully functioning continuous deployment pipeline. All the subjects we explored in previous chapters and all the problems we solved led us to this point. Everything we learned before were prerequisites for the pipeline we just created.

We succeeded! We are victorious! And we deserve a break.

Before you run away, there are two things I'd like to comment.

Our builds were very slow. Realistically, they should be at least twice as fast. However, we are operating in a tiny cluster and, more importantly, go-demo-3-build Namespace has limited resources and very low defaults. Kubernetes throttled CPU usage of the containers involved in builds to maintain the default values we set on that Namespace. That was intentional. I wanted to keep the cluster and the Namespaces small so that the costs are at a minimum. If you're running a cluster in AWS or GCE, the total price should be very low. It should probably be less than a cup of coffee you had while reading the chapter. On the other hand, if you are running it locally, the chances are that you don't have a laptop in which you can spare much more CPU for the cluster (memory should be less of an issue). In either case, the critical thing to note is that you should be more generous when creating "real" production pipelines.

The second and the last note concerns the VM we're using to build and push Docker images. If you're using AWS or GCE, it was created dynamically with each build. If you recall the settings, the VMs are removed only after ten minutes of inactivity. Please make sure that period passed before you destroy your cluster. That way, we'll let Jenkins destroy the VM for us. If, on the other hand, you created a local VM with Vagrant, please execute the commands that follow to suspend it.

```
1  cd cd/docker-build
2
3  vagrant suspend
4
5  cd ../../
```

That's it. We reached the end of the chapter. Feel free to destroy the cluster if you're not planning to continue straight away.

Continuous Delivery With Jenkins And GitOps

 Continuous delivery is a step down from continuous deployment. Instead of deploying every commit from the master branch to production, we are choosing which build should be promoted. Continuous delivery has that single manual step that forces us (humans) to decide which release should be upgraded in production.

Given that we already explored continuous deployment, you might be wondering why are we even talking at this point about continuous delivery. There are a few reasons for that. First of all, I am conscious that many of you will not or can not implement continuous deployment. Your tests might not be as reliable as you'd need them to be. Your processes might not allow full automation. You might have to follow regulations that prevent you from reaching nirvana. There could be many other reasons. The point is that not everyone can apply continuous deployment. Even among those that can get there, there are indeed some that do not want that as the destination. So, we'll explore continuous delivery as an alternative to continuous deployment.

There are other reasons for writing this chapter. So far, I showed you one possible implementation of the continuous deployment pipeline. We could modify the existing pipeline by adding an `input` step before making the release and upgrading production. That would add *proceed* and *cancel* buttons that we could use to choose whether to upgrade the production release or not. This chapter would be the shortest chapter ever, and that would be boring. Where's the fun in doing a small variation of the same?

We'll use this chapter to explore a few alternative approaches to writing Jenkins pipeline. Just as the pipeline from the previous chapter could be easily converted from continuous deployment to continuous delivery process, what we're going to do next could also go both ways. So, even though our objective is to write a continuous delivery pipeline, the lessons from this chapter could be easily applied to continuous deployment as well.

We'll use this opportunity to explore declarative pipeline as an alternative to scripted. We'll switch from using a separate VM for building docker image to using the Docker socket to build it in one of the nodes of the cluster. We'll explore how we can define our whole productions environment differently. We'll even introduce GitOps.

The real goal is to give you valid alternatives to the approaches we used so far, thus allowing you to make better decisions when implementing lessons-learned in your organization. I hope that by the end of this chapter you will be able to cherry-pick things that suit you the best and assemble your own process.

That's it for the prep-talk. You know what continuous delivery is, and you know how to use Kubernetes. Let's define some pipelines.

Creating A Cluster

Just as before, we'll start the practical part by making sure that we have the latest version of the *k8s-specs* repository.

 All the commands from this chapter are available in the 08-jenkins-cd.sh[160] Gist.

```
1  cd k8s-specs
2
3  git pull
```

Unlike the previous chapters, you cannot use an existing cluster this time. The reason behind that lies in reduced requirements. This time, the cluster should **NOT have ChartMuseum**. Soon you'll see why. What we need are the same hardware specs (excluding GKE), with NGINX Ingress and Tiller running inside the cluster, and with the environment variable LB_IP that holds the address of the IP through which we can access the external load balancer, or with the IP of the VM in case of single VM local clusters like minikube, minishift, and Docker For Mac or Windows.

For **GKE** we'll need to increase memory slightly so we'll use **n1-highcpu-4** instance types instead of *n1-highcpu-2* we used so far.

- docker4mac-cd.sh[161]: **Docker for Mac** with 3 CPUs, 4 GB RAM, with **nginx Ingress**, with **tiller**, and with LB_IP variable set to the IP of the cluster.
- minikube-cd.sh[162]: **minikube** with 3 CPUs, 4 GB RAM, with ingress, storage-provisioner, and default-storageclass addons enabled, with **tiller**, and with LB_IP variable set to the VM created by minikube.
- kops-cd.sh[163]: **kops in AWS** with 3 t2.small masters and 2 t2.medium nodes spread in three availability zones, with **nginx Ingress**, with **tiller**, and with LB_IP variable set to the IP retrieved by pinging ELB's hostname. The Gist assumes that the prerequisites are set through Appendix B.
- minishift-cd.sh[164]: **minishift** with 4 CPUs, 4 GB RAM, with version 1.16+, with **tiller**, and with LB_IP variable set to the VM created by minishift.

---

[160]https://gist.github.com/cb0ececf6600745daeac8cc3ae400a86
[161]https://gist.github.com/d07bcbc7c88e8bd104fedde63aee8374
[162]https://gist.github.com/06bb38787932520906ede2d4c72c2bd8
[163]https://gist.github.com/d96c27204ff4b3ad3f4ae80ca3adb891
[164]https://gist.github.com/94cfcb3f9e6df965ec233bbb5bf54110

- gke-cd.sh[165]: **Google Kubernetes Engine (GKE)** with 3 n1-highcpu-4 (4 CPUs, 3.6 GB RAM) nodes (one in each zone), with **nginx Ingress** controller running on top of the "standard" one that comes with GKE, with **tiller**, and with LB_IP variable set to the IP of the external load balancer created when installing nginx Ingress. We'll use nginx Ingress for compatibility with other platforms. Feel free to modify the YAML files and Helm Charts if you prefer NOT to install nginx Ingress.
- eks-cd.sh[166]: **Elastic Kubernetes Service (EKS)** with 2 t2.medium nodes, with **nginx Ingress** controller, with a **default StorageClass**, with **tiller**, and with LB_IP variable set tot he IP retrieved by pinging ELB's hostname.

Here we go.

Defining The Whole Production Environment

All the chapters until this one followed the same pattern. We'd learn about a new tool and, from there on, we'd streamline its installation through Gists in all subsequent chapters. As an example, we introduced ChartMuseum a few chapters ago, we learned how to install it, and, from there on, there was no point reiterating the same set of steps in the chapters that followed. Instead, we had the installation steps in Gists. Knowing that, you might be wondering why we did not follow the same pattern now. Why was ChartMuseum excluded from the Gists we're using in this chapter? Why isn't Jenkins there as well? Are we going to install ChartMuseum and Jenkins with a different configuration? We're not. Both will have the same configuration, but they will be installed in a slightly different way.

We already saw the benefits provided by Helm. Among other things, it features a templating mechanism that allows us to customize our Kubernetes definitions. We used requirements.yaml file to create our own Jenkins distribution. Helm requirements are a nifty feature initially designed to provide means to define dependencies of our application. As an example, if we'd create an application that uses Redis DB, our application would be defined in templates and Redis would be a dependency defined in requirement.yaml. After all, if the community already has a Chart for Redis, why would we reinvent the wheel by creating our own definitions? Instead, we'd put it as an entry in requirements.yaml. Even though our motivation was slightly different, we did just that with Jenkins. As you might have guessed, dependencies in requirements.yaml are not limited to a single entry. We can define as many dependencies as we need.

We could, for example, create a Chart that would define Namespaces, RoleBindings, and all the other infrastructure-level things that our production environment needs. Such a Chart could treat all production releases as dependencies. If we could do something like that, we could store everything related to production in a single repository. That would simplify the initial installation as well as upgrades of the production applications. Such an approach does not need to be limited to production.

---

[165]https://gist.github.com/1b126df156abc91d51286c603b8f8718
[166]https://gist.github.com/2af71594d5da3ca550de9dca0f23a2c5

There could be another repository for other environments. Testing would be a good example if we still rely on manual tasks in that area.

Since we'd keep those Charts in Git repositories, changes to what constitutes production could be reviewed and, if necessary, approved before they're merged to the master branch. There are indeed other benefits to having a whole environment in a Git repository. I'll leave it to your imagination to figure them out.

The beauty of Helm requirements is that they still allow us to keep the definition of an application in the same repository as the code. If we take our *go-demo* application as an example, the Chart that defines the application can and should continue residing in its repository. However, a different repository could define all the applications running in the production environment as dependencies, including *go-demo*. That way, we'll accomplish two things. Everything related to an application, including its Chart would be in the same repository without breaking the everything-in-git rule. So far, our continuous deployment pipeline (the one we defined in the previous chapter) breaks that rule. Jenkins was upgrading production releases without storing that information in Git. We had undocumented deployments. While releases under test are temporary and live only for the duration of those automated tests, production releases last longer and should be documented, even if their life-span is also potentially short (until the next commit).

All in all, our next task is to have the whole production environment in a single repository, without duplicating the information already available in repositories where we keep the code and definitions of our applications.

I already created a repository vfarcic/k8s-prod[167] that defines a production environment. Since we'll have to make some changes to a few files, our first task is to fork it. Otherwise, I'd need to give you my GitHub credentials so that you could push those changes to my repo. As you can probably guess, that is not going to happen.

Please open vfarcic/k8s-prod[168] in a browser and fork the repository. I'm sure you already know how to do that. If you don't, all you have to do is to click on the *Fork* button located in the top-right corner and follow the wizard instructions.

Next, we'll clone the forked repository before we explore some of its files.

Please replace [...] with your GitHub username before running the commands that follow.

---

[167]https://github.com/vfarcic/k8s-prod
[168]https://github.com/vfarcic/k8s-prod

```
1  GH_USER=[...]
2
3  cd ..
4
5  git clone https://github.com/$GH_USER/k8s-prod.git
6
7  cd k8s-prod
```

We cloned the forked repository and entered into its root directory.

Let's see what we have.

```
1  cat helm/Chart.yaml
```

The output is as follows.

```
1  apiVersion: v1
2  name: prod-env
3  version: 0.0.1
4  description: Docker For Mac or Windows Production Environment
5  maintainers:
6  - name: Viktor Farcic
7    email: viktor@farcic.com
```

The Chart.yaml file is very uneventful, so we'll skip explaining it. The only thing that truly matters is the version.

 You might see a different version than the one from the output above. Don't panic! I probably bumped it in one of my tests.

Let's take a look at the requirements.yaml.

```
1  cp helm/requirements-orig.yaml \
2      helm/requirements.yaml
3
4  cat helm/requirements.yaml
```

We copied the original requirements as a precaution since I might have changed requirements.yaml during one of my experiments.

The output of the latter command is as follows.

```
1  dependencies:
2  - name: chartmuseum
3    repository: "@stable"
4    version: 1.6.0
5  - name: jenkins
6    repository: "@stable"
7    version: 0.16.6
```

We can see that the requirements for our production environments are chartmuseum and jenkins. Both are located in the stable repository (the official Helm repo).

Offcourse, just stating the requirements is not enough. Our applications almost always require customized versions of both public and private Charts.

We already know from the previous chapters that we can leverage values.yaml file to customize Charts. The repository already has one, so let's take a quick look.

```
1  cat helm/values-orig.yaml
```

The output is as follows.

```
1  chartmuseum:
2    env:
3      open:
4        DISABLE_API: false
5        AUTH_ANONYMOUS_GET: true
6      secret:
7        BASIC_AUTH_USER: admin # Change me!
8        BASIC_AUTH_PASS: admin # Change me!
9    resources:
10     limits:
11       cpu: 100m
12       memory: 128Mi
13     requests:
14       cpu: 80m
15       memory: 64Mi
16   persistence:
17     enabled: true
18   ingress:
19     enabled: true
20     annotations:
21       kubernetes.io/ingress.class: "nginx"
22       ingress.kubernetes.io/ssl-redirect: "false"
23       nginx.ingress.kubernetes.io/ssl-redirect: "false"
```

```
24      hosts:
25        cm.acme-escaped.com: # Change me!
26        - /
27
28    jenkins:
29      Master:
30        ImageTag: "2.129-alpine"
31        Cpu: "500m"
32        Memory: "500Mi"
33        ServiceType: ClusterIP
34        ServiceAnnotations:
35          service.beta.kubernetes.io/aws-load-balancer-backend-protocol: http
36        GlobalLibraries: true
37        InstallPlugins:
38        - durable-task:1.22
39        - blueocean:1.7.1
40        - credentials:2.1.18
41        - ec2:1.39
42        - git:3.9.1
43        - git-client:2.7.3
44        - github:1.29.2
45        - kubernetes:1.12.0
46        - pipeline-utility-steps:2.1.0
47        - pipeline-model-definition:1.3.1
48        - script-security:1.44
49        - slack:2.3
50        - thinBackup:1.9
51        - workflow-aggregator:2.5
52        - ssh-slaves:1.26
53        - ssh-agent:1.15
54        - jdk-tool:1.1
55        - command-launcher:1.2
56        - github-oauth:0.29
57        - google-compute-engine:1.0.4
58        - pegdown-formatter:1.3
59        Ingress:
60          Annotations:
61            kubernetes.io/ingress.class: "nginx"
62            nginx.ingress.kubernetes.io/ssl-redirect: "false"
63            nginx.ingress.kubernetes.io/proxy-body-size: 50m
64            nginx.ingress.kubernetes.io/proxy-request-buffering: "off"
65            ingress.kubernetes.io/ssl-redirect: "false"
66            ingress.kubernetes.io/proxy-body-size: 50m
```

```
67            ingress.kubernetes.io/proxy-request-buffering: "off"
68        HostName: jenkins.acme.com # Change me!
69        CustomConfigMap: true
70        CredentialsXmlSecret: jenkins-credentials
71        SecretsFilesSecret: jenkins-secrets
72        DockerVM: false
73    rbac:
74        install: true
```

We can see that the values are split into two groups; chartmuseum and jenkins. Other than that, they are almost the same as the values we used in the previous chapters. The only important difference is that both are now defined in the same file and that they will be used as values for the requirements.

 I hope that you noticed that the file is named values-orig.yaml instead of values.yaml. I could not predict in advance what will be the address through which you can access the cluster. We'll combine that file with a bit of sed magic to generate values.yaml that contains the correct address.

Next, we'll take a look at the templates of this Chart.

```
1  ls -1 helm/templates
```

The output is as follows.

```
1  config.tpl
2  ns.yaml
```

The config.tpl file is the same Jenkins configuration template we used before, so there should be no need explaining it. We'll skip it and jump straight into ns.yaml.

```
1  cat helm/templates/ns.yaml
```

The output is as follows.

```
1   apiVersion: v1
2   kind: ServiceAccount
3   metadata:
4     name: build
5
6   ---
7
8   apiVersion: rbac.authorization.k8s.io/v1beta1
9   kind: RoleBinding
10  metadata:
11    name: build
12  roleRef:
13    apiGroup: rbac.authorization.k8s.io
14    kind: ClusterRole
15    name: admin
16  subjects:
17  - kind: ServiceAccount
18    name: build
19
20  ---
21
22  apiVersion: rbac.authorization.k8s.io/v1beta1
23  kind: RoleBinding
24  metadata:
25    name: build
26    namespace: kube-system
27  roleRef:
28    apiGroup: rbac.authorization.k8s.io
29    kind: ClusterRole
30    name: admin
31  subjects:
32  - kind: ServiceAccount
33    name: build
34    namespace: {{ .Release.Namespace }}
```

That definition holds no mysteries. It is a very similar one to those we used before. The first two entries provide permissions Jenkins builds need for running in the same Namespace, while the third is meant to allow builds to interact with tiller running kube-system. You can see that through the namespace entry that is set to kube-system, and through the reference to the ServiceAccount in the Namespace where we'll install this Chart.

All in all, this chart is a combination of custom templates meant to provide permissions and a set of requirements that will install the applications our production environment needs. For now, those requirements are only two applications (ChartMuseum and Jenkins), and we are likely going to expand it later with additional ones.

I already mentioned that `values-orig.yaml` is too generic and that we should update it with the cluster address before we convert it into `values.yaml`. That's our next mission.

```
1  ADDR=$LB_IP.nip.io
2
3  echo $ADDR
4
5  ADDR_ESC=$(echo $ADDR \
6      | sed -e "s@\.@\\\.@g")
7
8  echo $ADDR_ESC
```

We defined the address of the cluster (`ADDR`) as well as the escaped variant required by ChartMuseum since it uses address as the key, not the value. As you already know from previous chapters, keys cannot contain "special" characters like dots (`.`).

Now that we have the address of your cluster, we can use `sed` to modify `values-orig.yaml` and output the result to `values.yaml`.

```
1  cat helm/values-orig.yaml \
2      | sed -e "s@acme-escaped.com@$ADDR_ESC@g" \
3      | sed -e "s@acme.com@$ADDR@g" \
4      | tee helm/values.yaml
```

Later on, we'll use Jenkins to install (or upgrade) the Chart, so we should push the changes to GitHub.

```
1  git add .
2
3  git commit -m "Address"
4
5  git push
```

All Helm dependencies need to be downloaded to the `charts` directory before they are installed. We'll do that through the `helm dependency update` command.

```
1  helm dependency update helm
```

The relevant part of the output is as follows.

```
1  ...
2  Saving 2 charts
3  Downloading chartmuseum from repo https://kubernetes-charts.storage.googleapis.com
4  Downloading jenkins from repo https://kubernetes-charts.storage.googleapis.com
5  Deleting outdated charts
```

Don't worry if some of the repositories are not reachable. You might see messages stating that Helm was unable to get an update from local or chartmuseum repositories. Local Helm configuration probably has those (and maybe other) references from previous exercises.

The last lines of the output are essential. We can see that Helm saved two Charts (chartmuseum and jenkins). Those are the Charts we specified as dependencies in requirements.yaml.

We can confirm that the dependencies were indeed downloaded by listing the files in the charts directory.

```
1  ls -1 helm/charts
```

The output is as follows.

```
1  chartmuseum-1.6.0.tgz
2  jenkins-0.16.6.tgz
```

Now that the dependencies are downloaded and saved to the charts directory, we can proceed and install our full production environment. It consists of only two applications. We'll increase that number soon, and I expect that you'll add other applications you need to your "real" environment if you choose to use this approach.

 A note to minishift users

Helm will try to install Jenkins dependency Chart with the process in a container running as user 0. By default, that is not allowed in OpenShift. We'll skip discussing the best approach to correct the issue, and I'll assume you already know how to set the permissions on the per-Pod basis. Instead, we'll do the most straightforward fix by executing the command that follows that will allow the creation of restricted Pods to run as any user.

```
oc patch scc restricted -p '{"runAsUser":{"type": "RunAsAny"}}'
```

```
1  helm install helm \
2      -n prod \
3      --namespace prod
```

The output, limited to the Pods, is as follows.

```
1  ...
2  ==> v1/Pod(related)
3  NAME                               READY  STATUS   RESTARTS  AGE
4  prod-chartmuseum-68bc575fb7-jgs98  0/1    Pending  0         1s
5  prod-jenkins-6dbc74554d-gbzp4      0/1    Pending  0         1s
6  ...
```

We can see that Helm sent requests to Kube API to create all the resources defined in our Chart. As a result, among other resources, we got the Pods which run containers with Jenkins and ChartMuseum.

However, Jenkins will fail to start without the secrets we were using in previous chapters, so we'll create them next.

```
1  kubectl -n prod \
2      create secret generic \
3      jenkins-credentials \
4      --from-file ../k8s-specs/cluster/jenkins/credentials.xml
5
6  kubectl -n prod \
7      create secret generic \
8      jenkins-secrets \
9      --from-file ../k8s-specs/cluster/jenkins/secrets
```

Let's list the Charts running inside the cluster and thus confirm that prod was indeed deployed.

```
1  helm ls
```

The output is as follows.

```
1  NAME REVISION UPDATED        STATUS    CHART          NAMESPACE
2  prod 1        Tue Aug  7 ... DEPLOYED prod-env-0.0.1 prod
```

Now that we saw that the Chart was installed, the only thing left is to confirm that the two applications are indeed running correctly. We won't do real testing of the two applications, but only superficial ones that will give us a piece of mind. We'll start with ChartMuseum.

First, we'll wait for ChartMuseum to roll out (if it didn't already).

```
1  kubectl -n prod \
2      rollout status \
3      deploy prod-chartmuseum
```

The output should state that the deployment `"prod-chartmuseum"` was `successfully rolled out`.

A note to minishift users

OpenShift ignores Ingress resources so we'll have to create a Route to accomplish the same effect. Please execute the command that follows.

```
oc -n prod create route edge --service prod-chartmuseum --hostname cm.$ADDR
--insecure-policy Allow
```

```
1   curl "http://cm.$ADDR/health"
```

The output is `{"healthy":true}`, so ChartMuseum seems to be working correctly.

Next, we'll turn our attention to Jenkins.

```
1   kubectl -n prod \
2       rollout status \
3       deploy prod-jenkins
```

Once the deployment `"prod-jenkins"` is `successfully rolled out`, we can open it in a browser as a very light validation.

A note to minishift users

OpenShift requires Routes to make services accessible outside the cluster. To make things more complicated, they are not part of "standard Kubernetes" so we'll need to create one using `oc`. Please execute the command that follows.

```
oc -n prod create route edge --service prod-jenkins --insecure-policy Allow
--hostname jenkins.$ADDR
```

That command created an `edge` Router tied to the `prod-jenkins` Service. Since we do not have SSL certificates for HTTPS communication, we also specified that it is OK to use insecure policy which will allow us to access Jenkins through plain HTTP. The last argument defined the address through which we'd like to access Jenkins UI.

```
1   JENKINS_ADDR="jenkins.$ADDR"
2
3   open "http://$JENKINS_ADDR"
```

We'll need the initial admin password to log in. Just as we did it countless times before, we'll fetch it from the `secret` generated through the Chart.

```
1  JENKINS_PASS=$(kubectl -n prod \
2      get secret prod-jenkins \
3      -o jsonpath="{.data.jenkins-admin-password}" \
4      | base64 --decode; echo)
5
6  echo $JENKINS_PASS
```

Please go back to Jenkins UI in your favorite browser and log in using *admin* as the username and the output of JENKINS_PASS as the password. If, later on, your Jenkins session expires and you need to log in again, all you have to do is output JENKINS_PASS variable to find the password.

Now that we have the base production environment, we can turn our attention towards defining a continuous delivery pipeline.

What Is The Continuous Delivery Pipeline?

Now that we have a cluster and the third-party applications running in the production environment, we can turn our attention towards defining a continuous delivery pipeline.

Before we proceed, we'll recap the definitions of continuous deployment and continuous delivery.

 Continuous deployment is a fully automated process that executes a set of steps with the goal of converting each commit to the master branch into a fully tested release deployed to production.

 Continuous delivery is almost a fully automated process that executes a set of steps with the goal of converting each commit to the master branch into a fully tested release that is ready to be deployed to production. We (humans) retain the ability to choose which of the production-ready releases will be deployed to production and when is that deployment going to happen.

When compared to continuous deployment, continuous delivery is split into two automated processes with a manual action in between. The first process ensures that a commit is built, tested, and converted into a release. The second is in charge of performing the actual deployment to production and executing a set of tests that validate that deployment.

In other words, the only significant difference between the two processes is that continuous delivery has a manual action that allows us to choose whether we want to proceed with the deployment to production. That choice is not based on technical knowledge since we already validated that a release is production ready. Instead, it is a business or a marketing decision what to deliver to our users and when should that happen.

Since this is not the first time we are discussing continuous deployment and continuous delivery, there's probably no need to dive deeper into the processes. Instead, we'll jump straight into one possible implementation of a continuous delivery pipeline.

If we compare the process that follows with the one from the previous chapter, some of the steps will be different. That is not to say that those described here are not well suited in a continuous deployment pipeline. Quite the contrary. The steps are interchangeable. My primary goal is not only to present a possible implementation of a continuous delivery pipeline but also to showcase a different approach that, with small adjustments, can be applied to any type of pipeline.

Exploring Application's Repository And Preparing The Environment

Before I wrote this chapter, I forked the vfarcic/go-demo-3[169] repository into vfarcic/go-demo-5[170]. Even though most the code of the application is still the same, I thought it would be easier to apply and demonstrate the changes in a new repository instead of creating a new branch or doing some other workaround that would allow us to have both processes in the same repository. All in all, *go-demo-5* is a copy of *go-demo-3* on top of which I made some changes which we'll comment soon.

Since we'll need to change a few configuration files and push them back to the repository, you should fork vfarcic/go-demo-5[171], just as you forked vfarcic/k8s-prod[172].

Next, we'll clone the repository before we explore the relevant files.

```
1  cd ..
2
3  git clone \
4      https://github.com/$GH_USER/go-demo-5.git
5
6  cd go-demo-5
```

The Chart located in `helm` directory is the same as the one we used in *go-demo-3* so we'll skip commenting it. Instead, we'll replace my GitHub user (`vfarcic`) with yours.

Before you execute the commands that follow, make sure you replace [...] with your Docker Hub user.

---

[169]https://github.com/vfarcic/go-demo-3
[170]https://github.com/vfarcic/go-demo-5
[171]https://github.com/vfarcic/go-demo-5
[172]https://github.com/vfarcic/k8s-prod

```
1  DH_USER=[...]
2
3  cat helm/go-demo-5/deployment-orig.yaml \
4      | sed -e "s@vfarcic@$DH_USER@g" \
5      | tee helm/go-demo-5/templates/deployment.yaml
```

In *go-demo-3*, the resources that define the Namespace, ServiceAccount, RoleBinding, LimitRange, and ResourceQuota were split between `ns.yml` and `build-config.yml` files. I got tired of having them separated, so I joined them into a single file `build.yml`. Other than that, the resources are the same as those we used before so we'll skip commenting on them as well. The only difference is that the Namespace is now *go-demo-5*.

```
1  kubectl apply -f k8s/build.yml --record
```

Finally, the only thing related to the setup of the environment we'll use for *go-demo-5* is to install Tiller, just as we did before.

```
1  helm init --service-account build \
2      --tiller-namespace go-demo-5-build
```

The two key elements of our pipeline will be *Dockerfile* and *Jenkinsfile* files. Let's explore the former first.

```
1  cat Dockerfile
```

The output is as follows.

```
1   FROM alpine:3.4
2   MAINTAINER              Viktor Farcic <viktor@farcic.com>
3
4   RUN mkdir /lib64 && ln -s /lib/libc.musl-x86_64.so.1 /lib64/ld-linux-x86-64.so.2
5
6   EXPOSE 8080
7   ENV DB db
8   CMD ["go-demo"]
9
10  COPY go-demo /usr/local/bin/go-demo
11  RUN chmod +x /usr/local/bin/go-demo
```

You'll notice that we are not using multi-stage builds. That makes me sad since I think that is one of the greatest additions to Docker's build process. The ability to run unit tests and build a binary served us well so far. The process was streamlined through a single `docker image build` command, it was documented in a single *Dockerfile* file, and we did not have to sacrifice the size of the final image. So, why did I choose not to use it now?

We'll switch from building Docker images in a separate VM outside the cluster to using Docker socket to build it in one of the Kubernetes worker nodes. That does reduce security (Docker on that node could be abducted), and it can cause potential problems with Kubernetes (we're using containers without its knowledge). Yet, using the socket is somewhat easier, cleaner, and faster. Even though we explored this option through Shell commands, we did not use it in our Jenkins pipelines. So, I thought that you should experience both ways of building images in a Jenkins pipeline and choose for yourself which method fits your use-case better. The goal is to find the balance and gain experience that will let you decide what works best for you. There will be quite a few other changes further on. They all aim at giving you better insight into different ways of accomplishing the same goals. You will have to make a choice on how to combine them into the solution that works the best in your organization.

Going back to the reason for NOT using Docker's multi-stage builds... Given that we're about to use Docker in one of the worker nodes of the cluster, we depend on Docker version running inside that cluster. At the time of this writing (August 2018), some Kubernetes clusters still use more than a year old Docker. If my memory serves me, multi-stage builds were added in Docker *17.05*, and some Kubernetes flavors (even when on the latest version), still use Docker *17.03* or even older. Kops is a good example, even though it is not the only one. Release *1.9.x* (the latest stable at the time of this writing), uses Docker *17.03*. Since I'm committed to making all the examples in this book working in many different Kubernetes flavors, I had to remove multi-stage builds.

Check Docker version in your cluster and, if it's *17.05* or newer, I'd greatly recommend you continue using multi-stage builds. They are too good of a feature to ignore it, if not necessary.

All in all, the *Dockerfile* assumes that we already executed our tests and that we built the binary. We'll see how to do that inside a Jenkins pipeline soon.

We'll explore the pipeline stored in Jenkinsfile in the repository we cloned. However, before we do that, we'll go through declarative pipeline syntax since that's the one we'll use in this chapter.

Switching From Scripted To Declarative Pipeline

A long time ago in a galaxy far, far away, a group of Jenkins contributors decided to reinvent the way Jenkins jobs are defined and how they operate. (A couple of years in software terms is a lot, and Jenkins contributors are indeed spread throughout the galaxy).

The new type of jobs became known as Jenkins pipeline. It was received well by the community, and the adoption started almost instantly. Everything was excellent, and the benefits of using Pipeline compared to FreeStyle jobs were evident from the start. However, it wasn't easy for everyone to adopt Pipeline. Those who were used to scripting, and especially those familiar with Groovy, had no difficulties to switch. But, many used Jenkins without being coders. They did not find Pipeline to be as easy as we thought it would be. While I do believe that there is no place in the software industry for those who do not know how to code, it was still evident that something needed to be done to simplify Pipeline syntax even more. So, a new flavor of Pipeline syntax was born. We renamed the existing Pipeline flavor to Scripted Pipeline and created a new one called Declarative Pipeline.

Declarative Pipeline forces more simplified and more opinionated syntax. Its goal is to provide an easier way to define pipelines, to make them more readable, and to lower the entry bar. You can think of the Scripted Pipeline being initially aimed at power users and Declarative Pipeline for everyone else. In the meantime, Declarative Pipeline started getting more and more attention, and today such a separation is not necessarily valid anymore. In some ways, Declarative Pipeline is more advanced, and it is recommended for all users except when one needs something that cannot be (easily) done without switching to Scripted.

 The recommendation is to always start with Declarative Pipeline and switch to Scripted only if you need to accomplish something that is not currently supported. Even then, you might be trying to do something you shouldn't.

Right now, you might be asking yourself something along the following lines. "Why did Viktor make us use Scripted Pipeline if Declarative is better?" The previous pipeline required two features that are not yet supported by Declarative. We wanted to use podTemplate for most of the process with an occasional jump into agents based on VMs for building Docker images. That is not yet supported with Declarative Pipeline. However, since we will now switch to using Docker socket to build images inside the nodes of the cluster, that is not an issue anymore. The second reason lies in the inability to define Namespace inside podTemplate. That also is not an issue anymore since we'll switch to the model of defining a separate Kubernetes cloud for each Namespace where builds should run. You'll see both changes in action soon when we start exploring the continuous delivery pipeline used for *go-demo-5*.

Before we jump into defining the pipeline for the *go-demo-5* application, we'll briefly explore the general structure of a Declarative pipeline.

The snippet that follows represents a skeleton of a Declarative pipeline.

```
 1  pipeline {
 2    agent {
 3      ...
 4    }
 5    environment {
 6      ...
 7    }
 8    options {
 9      ...
10    }
11    parameters {
12      ...
```

```
13      }
14      triggers {
15          ...
16      }
17      tools {
18          ...
19      }
20      stages {
21          ...
22      }
23      post {
24          ...
25      }
26  }
```

A Declarative Pipeline is always enclosed in a `pipeline` block. That allows Jenkins to distinguish the Declarative from the Scripted flavor. Inside it are different sections, each with a specific purpose.

The `agent` section specifies where the entire Pipeline, or a specific stage, will execute in the Jenkins environment depending on where the agent section is placed. The section must be defined at the top-level inside the pipeline block, but stage-level usage is optional. We can define different types of agents inside this block. In our case, we'll use `kubernetes` type which translates to `podTemplate` we used before. The `agent` section is mandatory.

The `post` section defines one or more additional steps that are run upon the completion of a Pipeline's or stage's run (depending on the location of the `post` section within the Pipeline). It supports any of the following post-condition blocks: `always`, `changed`, `fixed`, `regression`, `aborted`, `failure`, `success`, `unstable`, and `cleanup`. These condition blocks allow the execution of steps inside each condition depending on the completion status of the Pipeline or stage.

The `stages` block is where most of the action is happening. It contains a sequence of one or more `stage` directives inside of which are the `steps` which constitute the bulk of our pipeline. The `stages` section is mandatory.

The `environment` directive specifies a sequence of key-value pairs which will be defined as environment variables for the all steps, or stage-specific steps, depending on where the environment directive is located within the Pipeline. This directive supports a special helper method `credentials()` which can be used to access pre-defined Credentials by their identifier in the Jenkins environment.

The `options` directive allows configuring Pipeline-specific options from within the Pipeline itself. Pipeline provides a number of these options, such as `buildDiscarder`, but they may also be provided by plugins, such as `timestamps`.

The `parameters` directive provides a list of parameters which a user should provide when triggering the Pipeline. The values for these user-specified parameters are made available to Pipeline steps via the params object.

The `triggers` directive defines automated ways in which the Pipeline should be re-triggered. In most cases, we should trigger a build through a Webhook. In such situations, `triggers` block does not provide any value.

Finally, the last section is `tools`. It allows us to define tools to auto-install and put on the PATH. Since we're using containers, `tools` are pointless. The tools we need are already defined as container images and accessible through containers of the build Pod. Even if we'd use a VM for parts of our pipeline, like in the previous chapter, we should still bake the tools we need inside VM images instead of wasting our time installing them at runtime.

You can find much more info about the declarative pipeline in Pipeline Syntax[173] page. As a matter of fact, parts of the descriptions you just read are from that page.

You probably got bored to death with the previous explanations. If you didn't, the chances are that they were insufficient. We'll fix that by going through an example that will much better illustrate how Declarative Pipeline works. We'll use most of those blocks in the example that follows. The exceptions are `parameters` (we don't have a good use case for them), `triggers` (useless when we're using Webhooks), and `tools` (a silly feature in the era of containers and tools for building VM images). Once we're finished exploring the pipeline of the *go-demo-5* project, you'll have enough experience to get you started with your own Declarative Pipelines, if you choose to use them.

Demystifying Declarative Pipeline Through A Practical Example

Let's take a look at a *Jenkinsfile.orig* which we'll use as a base to generate *Jenkinsfile* that will contain the correct address of the cluster and the GitHub user.

```
1  cat Jenkinsfile.orig
```

The output is too big for us to explore it in one go, so we'll comment on each section separately. The first in line is the `options` block.

```
1  ...
2  options {
3    buildDiscarder logRotator(numToKeepStr: '5')
4    disableConcurrentBuilds()
5  }
6  ...
```

The first option will result in only the last five builds being preserved in history. Most of the time there is no reason for us to keep all the builds we ever made. The last successful build of a branch is

---

[173]https://jenkins.io/doc/book/pipeline/syntax/

often the only one that matters. We set them to five just to prove that I'm not cheap. By discarding the old builds, we're ensuring that Jenkins will perform faster. Please note that the last successful build is kept even if, in this case, more than five last builds failed.

The second option disables concurrent builds. Each branch will have a separate job (just as in the previous chapter). If commits to different branches happen close to each other, Jenkins will process them in parallel by running builds for corresponding jobs. However, there is often no need for us to run multiple builds of the same job (branch) at the same time. In some cases, that can even produce adverse effects. With `disableConcurrentBuilds`, if we ever make multiple commits rapidly, they will be queued and executed sequentially.

It's up to you to decide whether those options are useful. If they are, use them. If they aren't, discard them. My mission was to show you a few of the many `options` we can use.

The next block is `agent`.

```
1   ...
2   agent {
3     kubernetes {
4       cloud "go-demo-5-build"
5       label "go-demo-5-build"
6       serviceAccount "build"
7       yamlFile "KubernetesPod.yaml"
8     }
9   }
10  ...
```

In our case, the `agent` block contains a `kubernetes` block. That is an indication that the pipeline should create a Pod based on Kubernetes Cloud configuration. That is further refined with the `cloud` entry which specifies that it must be the cloud config named `go-demo-5-build`. We'll create that cloud later. For now, we'll have to assume that it'll exist.

The benefit of that approach is that we can define only part of the agent information outside Pipeline and help other teams worry less about the things they need to put into their Jenkinsfile. As an example, you will not see a mention of a Namespace where the build should create a Pod that acts as a Jenkins agent. That will be defined elsewhere, and every build that uses `go-demo-5-build` will be run in that same Namespace.

There is another, less apparent reason for using a `cloud` dedicated to the builds in `go-demo-5-build` Namespace. Declarative syntax does not allow us to specify Namespace. So, we'll have to have as many `cloud` configurations as there are Namespaces, or more.

The `label` defines the prefix that will be used to name the Pods that will be spin by the builds based on this pipeline.

Next, we're defining `serviceAccount` as `build`. We already created that ServiceAccount inside the *go-demo-5-build* Namespace when we applied the configuration from *build.yml*. Now we're telling Jenkins that it should use it when creating Pod.

Finally, we changed the way we define a Pod that will act as Jenkins agent. Instead of embedding Pod definition inside *Jenkinsfile*, we're using an external file defined as *yamlFile*. My opinion on that feature is still divided. Having a Pod definition in Jenkinsfile (as we did in the previous chapter) allows us to inspect everything related to the job from a single location. On the other hand, moving the Pod definition to yamlFile enable us to focus on the flow of the pipeline, and leave lengthy Pod definition outside. It's up to you to choose which approach you like more. We'll explore the content of the KubernetesPod.yaml a bit later.

The next section in Jenkinsfile.orig is environment.

```
1  ...
2  environment {
3    image = "vfarcic/go-demo-5"
4    project = "go-demo-5"
5    domain = "acme.com"
6    cmAddr = "cm.acme.com"
7  }
8  ...
```

The environment block defines a few variables that we'll use in our steps. They are similar to those we used before, and they should be self-explanatory. Later on, we'll have to change vfarcic to your Docker Hub user and acme.com to the address of your cluster.

You should note that Declarative Pipeline allows us to use the variables defined in environment block both as "normal" (e.g., ${VARIABLE_NAME}) and as environment variables ${env.VARIABLE_NAME}.

Now we reached the "meat" of the pipeline. The stages block contains three stage sub-blocks, with steps inside each.

```
1  ...
2  stages {
3    stage("build") {
4      steps {
5        ...
6      }
7    }
8    stage("func-test") {
9      steps {
10       ...
11     }
12   }
13   stage("release") {
14     steps {
15       ...
```

```
16        }
17      }
18    }
19  ...
```

Just as in the continuous deployment pipeline, we're having `build`, `func-test`, and `release` stages. However, the `deploy` stage is missing. This time, we are NOT going to deploy a new release to production automatically. We'll need a manual intervention to do that. One possible way to accomplish that would be to add the `deploy` block to the pipeline and an additional `input` step in front of it. It would pause the execution of the pipeline until we choose to click the button to proceed with deployment to production. However, we will not take that approach. Instead, we'll opt for GitOps principle which we'll discuss later. For now, just remember that our pipeline's goal is to make a release, not to deploy it to production.

Let us briefly go through each of the stages of the pipeline. The first one is the `build` stage.

```
1  ...
2  stage("build") {
3    steps {
4      container("golang") {
5        script {
6          currentBuild.displayName = new SimpleDateFormat("yy.MM.dd").format(new Date(\
7  )) + "-${env.BUILD_NUMBER}"
8        }
9        k8sBuildGolang("go-demo")
10     }
11     container("docker") {
12       k8sBuildImageBeta(image, false)
13     }
14   }
15 }
16 ...
```

The first set of steps of the `build` stage starts in the `golang` container. The first action is to customize the name of the build by changing the value of the `displayName`. However, that is not allowed in Declarative Pipeline. Luckily, there is a way to bypass that limitation by defining the `script` block. Inside it can be any set of pipeline instructions we'd typically define in a Scripted Pipeline. A `script` block is a nifty way to temporarily switch from Declarative to Scripted Pipeline which allows much more freedom and is not bound by Declarative's strict format rules.

There was no particular reason for using `golang` container to set the `displayName`. We could have done it in any of the other containers available in our agent defined through `yamlFile`. The only reason why we chose `golang` over any other lies in the next step.

Since, this time, our Dockerfile does not use multi-stage builds and, therefore, does not run unit tests nor it builds the binary needed for the final image, we have to run those steps separately. Given that the application is written in Go, we need its compiler available in the `golang` container. The actual steps are defined as k8sBuildGolang.groovy[174] inside the same repository we used in the previous chapter. Feel free to explore it, and you'll see that it contains the same commands we used before inside the first stage of our multi-stage build defined in *go-demo-3 Dockerfile*.

Once the unit tests are executed, and the binary is built, we're switching to the `docker` container to build the image. This one is based on the same shared libraries we used before, just as the most of the other steps in this pipeline. Since you're already familiar with them, I'll comment only if there is a substantial change in the way we utilize those libraries, or if we add a new one that we haven't used before. If you already forgot how those libraries work, please consult their code (`*.groovy`) or their corresponding helper files (`*.txt`) located in the *vars* dir of the *jenkins-shared-libraries* repository you already forked.

Let's move into the next stage.

```
 1  ...
 2  stage("func-test") {
 3    steps {
 4      container("helm") {
 5        k8sUpgradeBeta(project, domain, "--set replicaCount=2 --set dbReplicaCount=1")
 6      }
 7      container("kubectl") {
 8        k8sRolloutBeta(project)
 9      }
10      container("golang") {
11        k8sFuncTestGolang(project, domain)
12      }
13    }
14    post {
15      always {
16        container("helm") {
17          k8sDeleteBeta(project)
18        }
19      }
20    }
21  }
22  ...
```

The steps of the `func-test` stage are the same as those we used in the continuous deployment pipeline. The only difference is in the format of the blocks that surround them. We're jumping from one container to another and executing the same shared libraries as before.

---

[174]https://github.com/vfarcic/jenkins-shared-libraries/blob/master/vars/k8sBuildGolang.groovy

The real difference is in the post section of the stage. It contains an always block that guarantees that the steps inside it will execute no matter the outcome of the steps in this stage. In our case, the post section has only one step that invokes that k8sDeleteBeta library which deletes the installation of the release under test.

As you can see, the func-test stage we just explored is functionally the same as the one we used in the previous chapter when we defined the continuous deployment pipeline. However, I'd argue that the post section available in Declarative Pipeline is much more elegant and easier to understand than try/catch/finally blocks we used inside the Scripted Pipeline. That would be even more evident if we'd use a more complex type of post criteria, but we don't have a good use-case for them.

It's time to move into the next stage.

```
...
stage("release") {
  when {
      branch "master"
  }
  steps {
    container("docker") {
      k8sPushImage(image, false)
    }
    container("helm") {
      k8sPushHelm(project, "", cmAddr, true, true)
    }
  }
}
...
```

The release stage, just as its counterpart from the previous chapter, features the same step that tags and pushes the production release to Docker Hub (k8sPushImage) as well as the one that packages and pushes the Helm Chart to ChartMuseum (k8sPushHelm). The only difference is that the latter library invocation now uses two additional arguments. The third one, when set to true, replaces the image.tag value to the tag of the image built in the previous step. The fourth argument, also when set to true, fails the build if the version of the Chart is unchanged or, in other words, if it already exists in ChartMuseum. When combining those two, we are guaranteeing that the image.tag value in the Chart is the same as the image we built, and that the version of the Chart is unique. The latter forces us to update the version manually. If we'd work on continuous deployment, manual update (or any other manual action), would be unacceptable. But, continuous delivery does involve a human decision when and what to deploy to production. We're just ensuring that the human action of changing the version of the Chart was indeed performed. Please open the source code of k8sPushHelm.groovy[175] to check the code behind that library and compare it with the statements you just read.

---

[175]https://github.com/vfarcic/jenkins-shared-libraries/blob/master/vars/k8sPushHelm.groovy

You'll notice that there is a when statement above the steps. Generally speaking, it is used to limit the executions within a stage only to those cases that match the condition. In our case, that condition states that the stage should be executed only if the build is using a commit from the master branch. It is equivalent to the if ("${BRANCH_NAME}" == "master") block we used in the continuous deployment pipeline in the previous chapter. There are other conditions we could have used but, for our use-case, that one is enough.

 You might want to explore other types of when conditions by going through the when statement documentation[176].

You'll notice that we did not define git or checkout scm step anywhere in our pipeline script. There's no need for that with Declarative Pipeline. It is intelligent enough to know that we want to clone the code of the commit that initiated a build (through a Webhook, if we'd have it). When a build starts, cloning the code will be one of its first actions.

Now that we went through the content of the *Jenkinsfile.orig* file, we should go back to the referenced KubernetesPod.yaml file that defines the Pod that will be used as a Jenkins agent.

```
1  cat KubernetesPod.yaml
```

The output is as follows.

```
1  apiVersion: v1
2  kind: Pod
3  spec:
4    containers:
5    - name: docker
6      image: docker:18.06
7      command: ["cat"]
8      tty: true
9      volumeMounts:
10     - mountPath: /var/run/docker.sock
11       name: docker-socket
12   - name: helm
13     image: vfarcic/helm:2.9.1
14     command: ["cat"]
15     tty: true
16   - name: kubectl
17     image: vfarcic/kubectl
18     command: ["cat"]
19     tty: true
```

---

[176]https://jenkins.io/doc/book/pipeline/syntax/#when

```
20    - name: golang
21      image: golang:1.9
22      command: ["cat"]
23      tty: true
24    volumes:
25    - name: docker-socket
26      hostPath:
27        path: /var/run/docker.sock
28        type: Socket
```

That Pod definition is almost the same as the one we used inside *Jenkinsfile* in the *go-demo-3* repository. Apart from residing in a separate file, the only difference is in an additional container named docker. In this scenario, we are not using external VMs to build Docker images. Instead, we have an additional container through which we can execute Docker-related steps. Since we want to execute Docker commands on the node, and avoid running Docker-in-Docker, we mounted /var/run/docker.sock as a Volume.

 ## A note to minishift users

We need to relax security so that Pods are allowed to use hostPath volume plug-in. Please execute the command that follows.

```
oc adm policy add-scc-to-user hostmount-anyuid -z build -n go-demo-5-build
```

Creating And Running A Continuous Delivery Job

That's it. We explored (soon to be) *Jenkinsfile* that contains our continuous delivery pipeline and *KubernetesPod.yaml* that contains the Pod definition that will be used to create Jenkins agents. There are a few other things we need to do but, before we discuss them, we'll change the address and the Docker Hub user in *Jenkinsfile.orig*, store the output as *Jenkinsfile* and push the changes to the forked GitHub repository.

 ## A note to minishift users

We'll use a slightly modified version of Jenkins file. Just as in the previous chapter, we'll add the occCreateEdgeRouteBuild step that will accomplish the same results as if we'd have NGINX Ingress controller. Please use Jenkinsfile.oc instead of Jenkinsfile.orig in the command that follows.

```
 1  cat Jenkinsfile.orig \
 2      | sed -e "s@acme.com@$ADDR@g" \
 3      | sed -e "s@vfarcic@$DH_USER@g" \
 4      | tee Jenkinsfile
 5
 6  git add .
 7
 8  git commit -m "Jenkinsfile"
 9
10  git push
```

Since we are into running Git commands, we might just as well merge your *jenkins-shared-libraries* fork with the upstream/master. That will ensure that you have the latest version that includes potential changes I might have made since the time you forked the repository.

```
 1  cd ..
 2
 3  git clone https://github.com/$GH_USER/jenkins-shared-libraries.git
 4
 5  cd jenkins-shared-libraries
 6
 7  git remote add upstream \
 8      https://github.com/vfarcic/jenkins-shared-libraries.git
 9
10  git fetch upstream
11
12  git checkout master
13
14  git merge upstream/master
15
16  cd ../go-demo-5
```

We're almost ready to create a Jenkins pipeline for *go-demo-5*. The only thing missing is to create a new Kubernetes Cloud configuration.

For now, we have only one Kubernetes Cloud configured in Jenkins. Its name is *kubernetes*. However, the pipeline we just explored uses a cloud named go-demo-5-build. So, we should create a new one before we create jobs tied to the *go-demo-5* repository.

```
 1  open "http://$JENKINS_ADDR/configure"
```

Please scroll to the bottom of the page, expand the *Add a new cloud* list, and select *Kubernetes*. A new set of fields will appear.

Type *go-demo-5-build* as the name. It matches the `cloud` entry inside `kubernetes` block of our pipeline.

Next, type *go-demo-5-build* as the *Kubernetes Namespace*.

Just as with the other Kubernetes Cloud that was already defined in our Jenkins instance, the value of the *Jenkins URL* should be *http://prod-jenkins.prod:8080*, and the *Jenkins tunnel* should be set to *prod-jenkins-agent.prod:50000*.

Don't forget to click the *Save* button to persist the changes.

Right now, we have two Kubernetes Clouds configured in our Jenkins instance. One is called *kubernetes*, and it uses the *prod* Namespace, while the other (the new one) is called *go-demo-5-build* and it can be used for all the builds that should be performed in the *go-demo-5-build* Namespace.

Even though we have two Kubernetes Clouds, their configurations are almost the same. Besides having different names, the only substantial difference is in the Namespace they use. I wanted to keep it simple and demonstrate that multiple clouds are possible, and often useful. In the "real world" situations, you'll probably use more fields and differentiate them even further. As an example, we could have defined the default set of containers that will be used with those clouds.

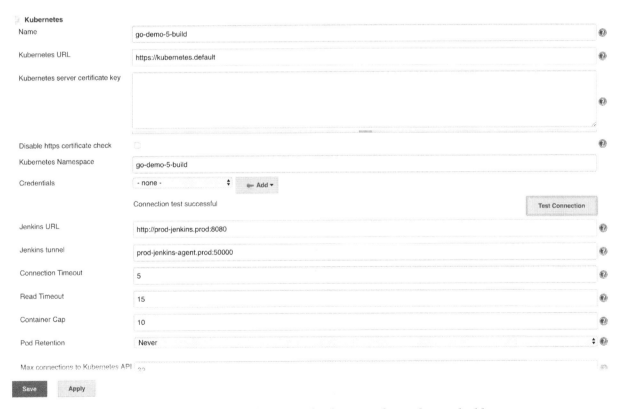

Figure 8-1: Jenkins Kubernetes Cloud settings for go-demo-5-build

Now we're ready to create a job that will be tied to the *go-demo-5* repository and validate whether the pipeline defined in the *Jenkinsfile* works as expected.

We'll create our job from the BlueOcean home screen.

```
1  open "http://$JENKINS_ADDR/blue/organizations/jenkins/"
```

Please click the *Create a New Pipeline* button and select *GitHub* as the repository type. Type *Your GitHub access token* and click the *Connect* button. A moment later, you'll see the list of organizations that token belongs to. Select the one where you forked the applications. The list of repositories will appear. Select *go-demo-5* and click the *Create Pipeline* button.

Jenkins will create jobs for each branch of the *go-demo-5* repository. There is only one (*master*), so there will be one job in total. We already explored in the previous chapter how Jenkins handles multiple repositories by creating a job for each, so I thought that there is no need to demonstrate the same feature again. Right now, *master* job/branch should be more than enough.

Please wait until the build is finished.

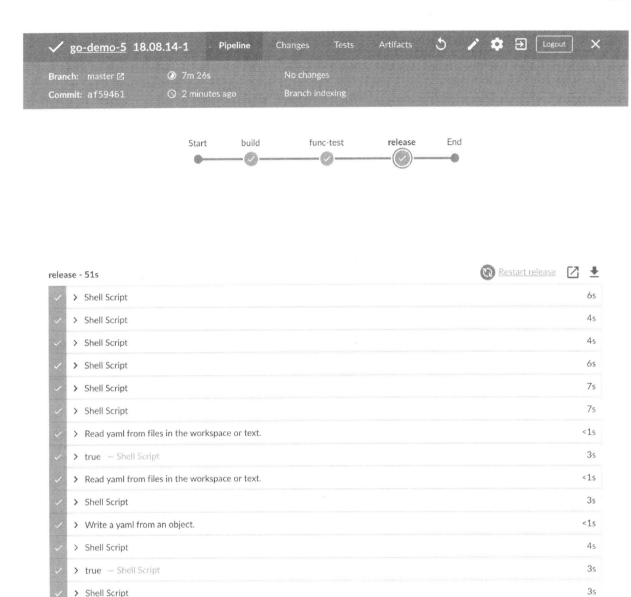

Figure 8-2: Continuous delivery Jenkins pipeline

Since the build was executed against the *master* branch, the `when` condition inside the `release` stage evaluated to `true` so the production-ready image was pushed to Docker Hub and the Helm Chart with the updated tag was pushed to ChartMuseum. We'll check the latter by retrieving the list of all the Charts.

```
1  curl "http://cm.$ADDR/index.yaml"
```

The output is as follows.

```
1  apiVersion: v1
2  entries:
3    go-demo-5:
4    - apiVersion: v1
5      created: "2018-08-08T20:47:34.322943263Z"
6      description: A silly demo based on API written in Go and MongoDB
7      digest: a30aa7921b890b1f919286113e4a8193a2d4d3137e8865b958acd1a2bfd97c7e
8      home: http://www.devopstoolkitseries.com/
9      keywords:
10     - api
11     - backend
12     - go
13     - database
14     - mongodb
15     maintainers:
16     - email: viktor@farcic.com
17       name: Viktor Farcic
18     name: go-demo-5
19     sources:
20     - https://github.com/vfarcic/go-demo-5
21     urls:
22     - charts/go-demo-5-0.0.1.tgz
23     version: 0.0.1
24 generated: "2018-08-08T21:03:01Z"
```

We can see that we have only one Chart (so far). It is the *go-demo-5* Chart. The important thing to note is the version of the Chart. In that output, it's `0.0.1`. However, I might have bumped it later since I wrote this text, so your version might be different. We'll need that version soon, so let's put it into an environment variable.

```
1  VERSION=[...]
```

Please make sure to change `[...]` with the version you obtained earlier from `index.yaml`.

Among other things, the build modified the Chart before pushing it to ChartMuseum. It changed the image tag to the new release. We'll add ChartMuseum as a repository in our local Helm client so that we can inspect the Chart and confirm that `image.tag` value is indeed correct.

```
1  helm repo add chartmuseum \
2      http://cm.$ADDR
3
4  helm repo list
```

The output of the latter command is as follows.

```
1  NAME            URL
2  stable          https://kubernetes-charts.storage.googleapis.com
3  local           http://127.0.0.1:8879/charts
4  chartmuseum     http://cm.18.219.191.38.nip.io
```

You might have additional repositories configured in your local Helm client. That's not of importance. What matters right now is that the output showed chartmuseum as one of the repositories.

Now that we added the new repository, we should update local cache.

```
1  helm repo update
```

Finally, we can inspect the Chart Jenkins pushed to ChartMuseum.

```
1  helm inspect chartmuseum/go-demo-5 \
2      --version $VERSION
```

The output, limited to relevant parts, is as follows.

```
1  ...
2  version: 0.0.1
3  ...
4  image:
5    tag: 18.08.08-3
6  ...
```

We can see that the build modified the image.tag before it packaged the Chart and pushed it to ChartMuseum.

The first build of our continuous delivery pipeline was successful. However, the whole process is still not finished. We are yet to design the process that will allow us to choose which release to deploy to production. Even though our goal is to let Jenkins handle deployments to production, we'll leave it aside for a while and first explore how we could do it manually from a terminal.

Did I mention that we'll introduce GitOps to the process?

What Is GitOps And Do We Want It?

Git is the only source of truth. If you understand that sentence, you know GitOps. Every time we want to apply a change, we need to push a commit to Git. Want to change the configuration of your servers? Commit a change to Git, and let an automated process propagate it to servers. Want to upgrade ChartMuseum? Change *requirements.yaml*, push the change to the *k8s-prod* repository, and let an automated process do the rest. Want to review a change before applying it? Make a pull request. Want to rollback a release? You probably get the point, and I can save you from listing hundreds of other "want to" questions.

Did we do GitOps in the previous chapter? Was our continuous deployment process following GitOps? The answer to both questions is *no*. We did keep the code, configurations, and Kubernetes definitions in Git. Most of it, at least. However, we were updating production releases with new image tags without committing those changes to Git. Our complete source of truth was the cluster, not Git. It contained most of the truth, but not all of it.

Does this mean that we should fully embrace GitOps? I don't think so. Some things would be impractical to do by committing them to Git.

Take installations of applications under test as an example. We need to install a test release inside a test environment (a Namespace), we need to run some automated tests, and we need to remove the applications once we're finished. If we'd fully embrace GitOps, we'd need to push a definition of the application under test to a Git repository and probably to initiate a different pipeline that would install it. After that, we'd run some tests and remove the information we just pushed to Git so that yet another process can remove it from the cluster. Using GitOps with temporary installations would only increase the complexity of the process and slow it down without any tangible benefit. Why would we store something in Git only to remove it a few minutes later?

There are other use cases where I think GitOps is not a right fit. Take auto-scaling as an example. We might want to use Horizontal Pod Autoscaler (HPA)[177]. Or, maybe we want Prometheus to fire alerts which will result in increasing and decreasing the number of replicas of our applications depending on, let's say, response times. If those changes are infrequent (e.g., once a month or even once a week), storing them in Git and firing Webhooks that will do the scaling makes sense. But, if scaling is more frequent, the information in Git would vary so much that it would only result in more confusion.

The same can be said to auto-scaling of infrastructure. Should we ignore the fact that GKE (and most other Kubernetes clusters) can automatically increase and decrease the number of nodes of the cluster depending on resource usage and how many pending Pods we have? We probably shouldn't.

Those examples should not discourage you from applying GitOps logic. Instead, they should demonstrate that we should not see the world as black-and-white. The fact that I think that we should not embrace GitOps hundred percent does not mean that we should not embrace it at all. We should always try to strike a balance between different practices and create a combination that best fits our scenarios.

---

[177]https://kubernetes.io/docs/tasks/run-application/horizontal-pod-autoscale/

In our case, we'll use GitOps to an extent, even though we might not follow the mantra to the fullest.

Now, let's try to upgrade our production environment by adding the *go-demo-5* release to it.

Upgrading The Production Environment Using GitOps Practices

Right now, our production environment contains Jenkins and ChartMuseum. On the other hand, we created a new production-ready release of *go-demo-5*. Now we should let our business, marketing, or some other department make a decision on whether they'd like to deploy the new release to production and when should that happen. We'll imagine that they gave us the green light to install the *go-demo-5* release and that it should be done now. Our users are ready for it.

We'll deploy the new release manually first. That way we'll confirm that our deployment process works as expected. Later on, we'll try to automate the process through Jenkins.

Our whole production environment is stored in the *k8s-prod* repository. The applications that constitute it are defined in *requirements.yaml* file. Let's take another look at it.

```
1  cd ../k8s-prod
2
3  cat helm/requirements.yaml
```

The output is as follows.

```
1  dependencies:
2  - name: chartmuseum
3    repository: "@stable"
4    version: 1.6.0
5  - name: jenkins
6    repository: "@stable"
7    version: 0.16.6
```

We already discussed those dependencies and used them to install Jenkins and ChartMuseum from the @stable repository. Since we do not want to bump versions of the two, we'll leave them intact, and we'll add *go-demo-5* to the mix.

```
1  echo "- name: go-demo-5
2    repository: \"@chartmuseum\"
3    version: $VERSION" \
4    | tee -a helm/requirements.yaml
5
6  cat helm/requirements.yaml
```

The output of the latter command is as follows.

```
1  dependencies:
2  - name: chartmuseum
3    repository: "@stable"
4    version: 1.6.0
5  - name: jenkins
6    repository: "@stable"
7    version: 0.16.6
8  - name: go-demo-5
9    repository: "@chartmuseum"
10   version: 0.0.1
```

Our dependencies increased from two to three dependencies.

Usually, that would be all, and we would upgrade the Chart. However, we still need to change the host value. In the "real world" situation, you'd have it pre-defined since hosts rarely change. But, in our case, I could not know your host in advance so we'll need to overwrite the ingress.host value of go-demo-5.

```
1  echo "go-demo-5:
2    ingress:
3      host: go-demo-5.$ADDR" \
4      | tee -a helm/values.yaml
5
6  cat helm/values.yaml
```

The latter command outputs the final version of the values. The section related to go-demo-5 should be similar to the one that follows.

```
1  ...
2  go-demo-5:
3    ingress:
4      host: go-demo-5.18.219.191.38.nip.io
```

We already discussed that we'll document production environment in Git and, therefore, adhere to GitOps principles.

Typically, we'd push the changes we made to a different branch or to a forked repo, and we'd make a pull request. Someone would review it and accept the changes or provide notes with potential improvements. I'm sure you already know how pull requests work, the value behind code reviews, and all the other good things we're doing with code in Git. So, we'll skip all that and push directly to the *master* branch. Just remember that we're not going to skip pull request and the rest because we should, but because I'm trying to skip the things you already know and jump straight to the point.

```
1  git add .
2
3  git commit -m "Added go-demo-5"
4
5  git push
```

As you already know, we need to update local Helm cache with the new dependencies.

```
1  helm dependency update helm
```

The last lines of the output are as follows.

```
1  ...
2  Saving 3 charts
3  Downloading chartmuseum from repo https://kubernetes-charts.storage.googleapis.com
4  Downloading jenkins from repo https://kubernetes-charts.storage.googleapis.com
5  Downloading go-demo-5 from repo http://cm.18.219.191.38.nip.io
6  Deleting outdated charts
```

We can see that this time Helm downloaded three Charts, including `go-demo-5` we just added as a dependency in `requirements.yaml`. We can confirm that by listing the files in the `helm/charts` directory.

```
1  ls -1 helm/charts
```

The output is as follows.

```
1  chartmuseum-1.6.0.tgz
2  go-demo-5-0.0.1.tgz
3  jenkins-0.16.6.tgz
```

The *go-demo-5* package is there, and we are ready to update our production environment.

```
1  helm upgrade prod helm \
2      --namespace prod
```

Let's take a look at the Pods running inside the prod Namespace.

```
1  kubectl -n prod get pods
```

The output is as follows.

```
1  NAME                                 READY   STATUS             RESTARTS   AGE
2  prod-chartmuseum-68bc575fb7-dn6h5    1/1     Running            0          4h
3  prod-go-demo-5-66c9d649bd-kq45m      1/1     Running            2          51s
4  prod-go-demo-5-66c9d649bd-lgjb7      1/1     Running            2          51s
5  prod-go-demo-5-66c9d649bd-pwnjg      1/1     Running            2          51s
6  prod-go-demo-5-db-0                  2/2     Running            0          51s
7  prod-go-demo-5-db-1                  0/2     ContainerCreating  0          15s
8  prod-jenkins-676cc64756-bj45v        1/1     Running            0          4h
```

Judging by the AGE, we can see that ChartMuseum and Jenkins were left intact. That makes sense since we did not change any of their properties. The new Pods are those related to *go-demo-5*. The output will differ depending on when we executed get pods. In my case, we can see that three replicas of the *go-demo-5* API are running and that we are in the process of deploying the second database Pod. Soon all three DB replicas will be running, and our mission will be accomplished.

 ## A note to minishift users

OpenShift ignores Ingress resources so we'll have to create a Route to accomplish the same effect. Please execute the command that follows.

```
oc -n prod create route edge --service prod-go-demo-5 --hostname go-demo-5.$ADDR
--insecure-policy Allow
```

To be on the safe side, we'll confirm that the newly deployed *go-demo-5* application is indeed accessible.

```
1  kubectl -n prod rollout status \
2      deployment prod-go-demo-5
3
4  curl -i "http://go-demo-5.$ADDR/demo/hello"
```

We waited until rollout status confirms that the application is deployed and we sent a request to it. The output of the latter command should show the status code 200 OK and the familiar message hello, world!.

As the last validation, we'll describe the application and confirm that the image is indeed correct (and not latest).

```
1  kubectl -n prod \
2      describe deploy prod-go-demo-5
```

The output, limited to the relevant parts, is as follows.

```
1  ...
2  Pod Template:
3    ...
4    Containers:
5     api:
6      Image: vfarcic/go-demo-5:18.08.08-3
7        ...
```

Now that we explored how to perform the upgrade manually, we'll try to replicate the same process from a Jenkins job.

Creating A Jenkins Job That Upgrades The Whole Production Environment

Before we upgrade the production environment, we'll create one more release of *go-demo-5* so that we have something new to deploy.

```
1  open "http://$JENKINS_ADDR/blue/organizations/jenkins/go-demo-5/branches"
```

We opened the *branches* screen of the *go-demo-5* job.

Please click the play button from the right side of the *master* row and wait until the new build is finished.

Lo and behold! Our build failed! If you explore the job in detail, you will know why it's broken. You'll see *"Did you forget to increment the Chart version?"* message.

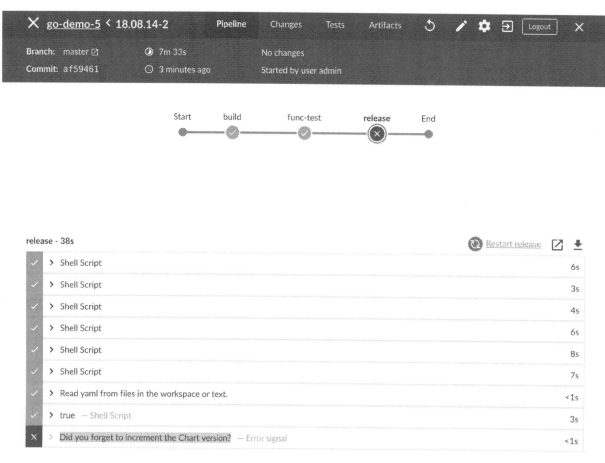

Figure 8-3: go-demo-5 failed build

Our job does not allow us to push a commit to the *master* branch without bumping the version of the *go-demo-5* Chart. That way, we guarantee that every production-ready release is versioned correctly. Let's fix that.

```
1  cd ../go-demo-5
```

Please open *helm/go-demo-5/Chart.yaml* in your favorite editor and increment the version. If, for example, the current version is `0.0.1`, change it to `0.02`, if it's `0.0.2`, change it to `0.0.3`, and so on. You get the point. Just increase it.

Next, we'll push the change to the *master* branch.

```
1  git add .
2
3  git commit -m "Version bump"
4
5  git push
```

Usually, you'd push the change to a branch, make a pull request, and let someone review it. Such a pull request would execute a Jenkins build that would give the reviewer the information about the quality of the changes. If the build was successful and the review did not reveal any deficiencies, we would merge the pull request.

We skipped all that, and we pushed the changes directly to the *master* branch only to speed things up.

Now let's go back to Jenkins and run another build.

```
1   open "http://$JENKINS_ADDR/blue/organizations/jenkins/go-demo-5/branches"
```

Please click the play button from the right side of the *master* row and wait until the new build is finished. This time, it should be successful, and we'll have a new *go-demo-5* release waiting to be deployed to the production environment.

Automating Upgrade Of The Production Environment

Now that we have a new release waiting, we would go through the same process as before. Someone would make a decision whether the release should be deployed to production or to let it rot until the new one comes along. If the decision is made that our users should benefit from the features available in that release, we'd need to update a few files in our *k8s-prod* repository.

```
1   cd ../k8s-prod
```

The first file we'll update is *helm/requirements.yaml*. Please open it in your favorite editor and change the *go-demo-5* version to match the version of the Chart we pushed a few moments ago.

We should also increase the version of the *prod-env* Chart as a whole. Open *helm/Chart.yaml* and bump the version.

Let's take a look at *Jenkinsfile.orig* from the repository.

```
1   cat Jenkinsfile.orig
```

The output is as follows.

```
1    import java.text.SimpleDateFormat
2
3    pipeline {
4      options {
5        buildDiscarder logRotator(numToKeepStr: '5')
6        disableConcurrentBuilds()
7      }
8      agent {
9        kubernetes {
10         cloud "kubernetes"
11         label "prod"
12         serviceAccount "build"
13         yamlFile "KubernetesPod.yaml"
14       }
15     }
16     environment {
17       cmAddr = "cm.acme.com"
18     }
19     stages {
20       stage("deploy") {
21         when {
22           branch "master"
23         }
24         steps {
25           container("helm") {
26             sh "helm repo add chartmuseum http://${cmAddr}"
27             sh "helm repo update"
28             sh "helm dependency update helm"
29             sh "helm upgrade -i prod helm --namespace prod --force"
30           }
31         }
32       }
33       stage("test") {
34         when {
35           branch "master"
36         }
37         steps {
38           echo "Testing..."
39         }
40         post {
41           failure {
42             container("helm") {
43               sh "helm rollback prod 0"
```

```
44                }
45              }
46            }
47          }
48        }
49      }
```

This time we're using the `kubernetes` Cloud configured to spin up Pods in the `prod` Namespace. The `build` ServiceAccount already has the permissions to access Tiller in `kube-system` thus allowing us to install applications anywhere inside the cluster. We won't need to go that far. Full permissions inside the `prod` Namespace are more than enough.

Just as with the *Jenkinsfile* inside the *go-demo-5* repository, the definition of the agent Pod is inside the `KubernetesPod.yaml` file. I'll let you explore it yourself.

The `environment` block contains `cmAddr` set to `cm.acme.com`. That's why we're exploring *Jenkinsfile.orig*. We'll need to create our own *Jenkinsfile* that will contain the correct address.

We have only two stages; `deploy` and `test`. Both of them have the `when` block that limits the execution of the steps only to builds initiated through a commit to the `branch "master"`.

The `deploy` stage runs in the `helm` container. The steps inside it are performing the same actions we did manually a while ago. They add `chartmuseum` to the list of repositories, they update the repos, the update the dependencies, and, finally, they `upgrade` the Chart. Since we already executed all those steps from a terminal, it should be pretty clear what they do.

The `test` stage has a simple `echo` step. I'll be honest with you. I did not write tests we'd need, and the `echo` is only a placeholder. You should know how to write your own tests for the applications you're developing, and there's probably no need for you to see yet another set of tests written in Go.

The critical part of the stage is the `post` section that'll rollback the `upgrade` if one of the tests fail. This is the part where we're ignoring GitOps principles. The chances that those tests will fail are meager. The new release was already tested, and containers guarantee that our applications will behave the same in any environment. The tests we're running in this pipeline are more like sanity checks, than some kind of in-depth validation.

If we'd adhere fully to GitOps, if tests do fail, we'd need to change the version of the Chart to the previous value, and we'd need to push it back to the repository. That would trigger yet another build that would perform another upgrade, only this time to the previous release. Instead, we're rolling back directly inside the pipeline assuming that someone will fix the issue soon after and initiate another upgrade that will contain the correction.

A note to minishift users

We already created a Route as a substitute for Ingress. Since, from now on, we're only updating the *go-demo-5* application while preserving the related Service, there's no need to add the `oc create route` command to the pipeline.

As you can see, we are applying GitOps principles only partially. In my opinion, they make sense in some cases and do not in others. It's up to you to decide whether you'll go towards full GitOps, or, like me, adopt it only partially.

Now, let's create *Jenkinsfile* with the correct address.

```
1  cat Jenkinsfile.orig \
2      | sed -e "s@acme.com@$ADDR@g" \
3      | tee Jenkinsfile
```

With all the files updated, we can proceed and push the changes to GitHub. Just as before, we're taking a shortcut by skipping the processes of making a pull request, reviewing it, approving it, and executing any other steps that we would normally do.

```
1  git add .
2
3  git commit -m "Jenkinsfile"
4
5  git push
```

The only thing left is to create a new Jenkins job and hope that everything works correctly.

```
1  open "http://$JENKINS_ADDR/blue/pipelines"
```

Please click the *New Pipeline* button, and select *GitHub* and the organization. Next, we'll choose *k8s-prod* repository and click the *Create Pipeline* button.

The new job was created, and all we have to do is wait for a few moments until it's finished.

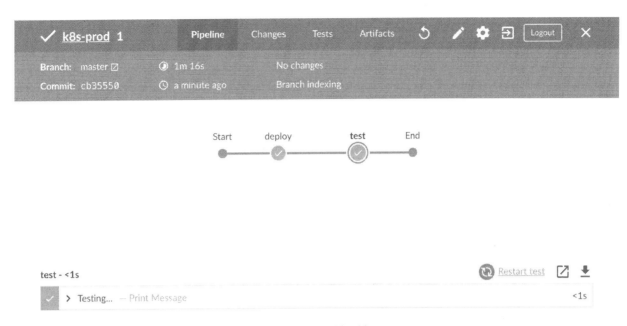

Figure 8-4: k8s-prod build screen

Let's see the `history` of the Chart.

```
1  helm history prod
```

The output is as follows.

```
1  REVISION  UPDATED        STATUS      CHART          DESCRIPTION
2  1         Wed Aug  ...   SUPERSEDED  prod-env-0.0.1 Install complete
3  2         Wed Aug  ...   SUPERSEDED  prod-env-0.0.1 Upgrade complete
4  3         Wed Aug  ...   DEPLOYED    prod-env-0.0.2 Upgrade complete
```

We can see from the CHART column that the currently deployed release is 0.0.2 (or whichever version you defined last).

Our system is working! We have a fully operational continuous delivery pipeline.

High-Level Overview Of The Continuous Delivery Pipeline

Let's step back and paint a high-level picture of the continuous delivery pipeline we created. To be more precise, we'll draw a diagram instead of painting anything. But, before we dive into a continuous delivery diagram, we'll refresh our memory with the one we used before for describing continuous deployment.

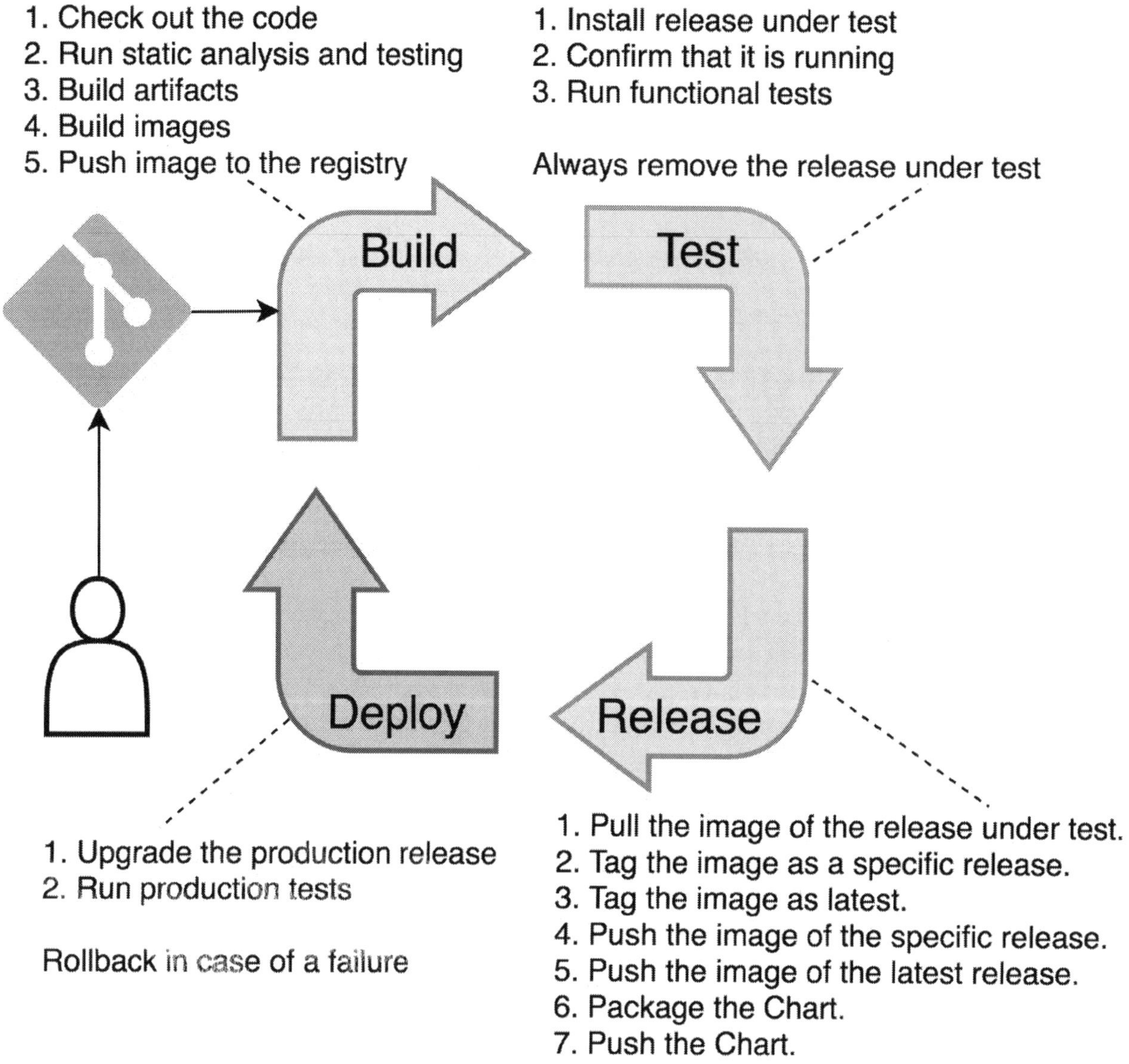

1. Check out the code
2. Run static analysis and testing
3. Build artifacts
4. Build images
5. Push image to the registry

1. Install release under test
2. Confirm that it is running
3. Run functional tests

Always remove the release under test

Build

Test

Deploy

Release

1. Upgrade the production release
2. Run production tests

Rollback in case of a failure

1. Pull the image of the release under test.
2. Tag the image as a specific release.
3. Tag the image as latest.
4. Push the image of the specific release.
5. Push the image of the latest release.
6. Package the Chart.
7. Push the Chart.

Figure 8-5: Continuous deployment process

The continuous deployment pipeline contains all the steps from pushing a commit to deploying and testing a release in production.

Continuous delivery removes one of the stages from the continuous deployment pipeline. We do NOT want to deploy a new release automatically. Instead, we want humans to decide whether a release should be upgraded in production. If it should, we need to decide when will that happen. Those (human) decisions are, in our case, happening as Git operations. We'll comment on them soon. For now, the important note is that the *deploy* stage is now removed from pipelines residing in application repositories.

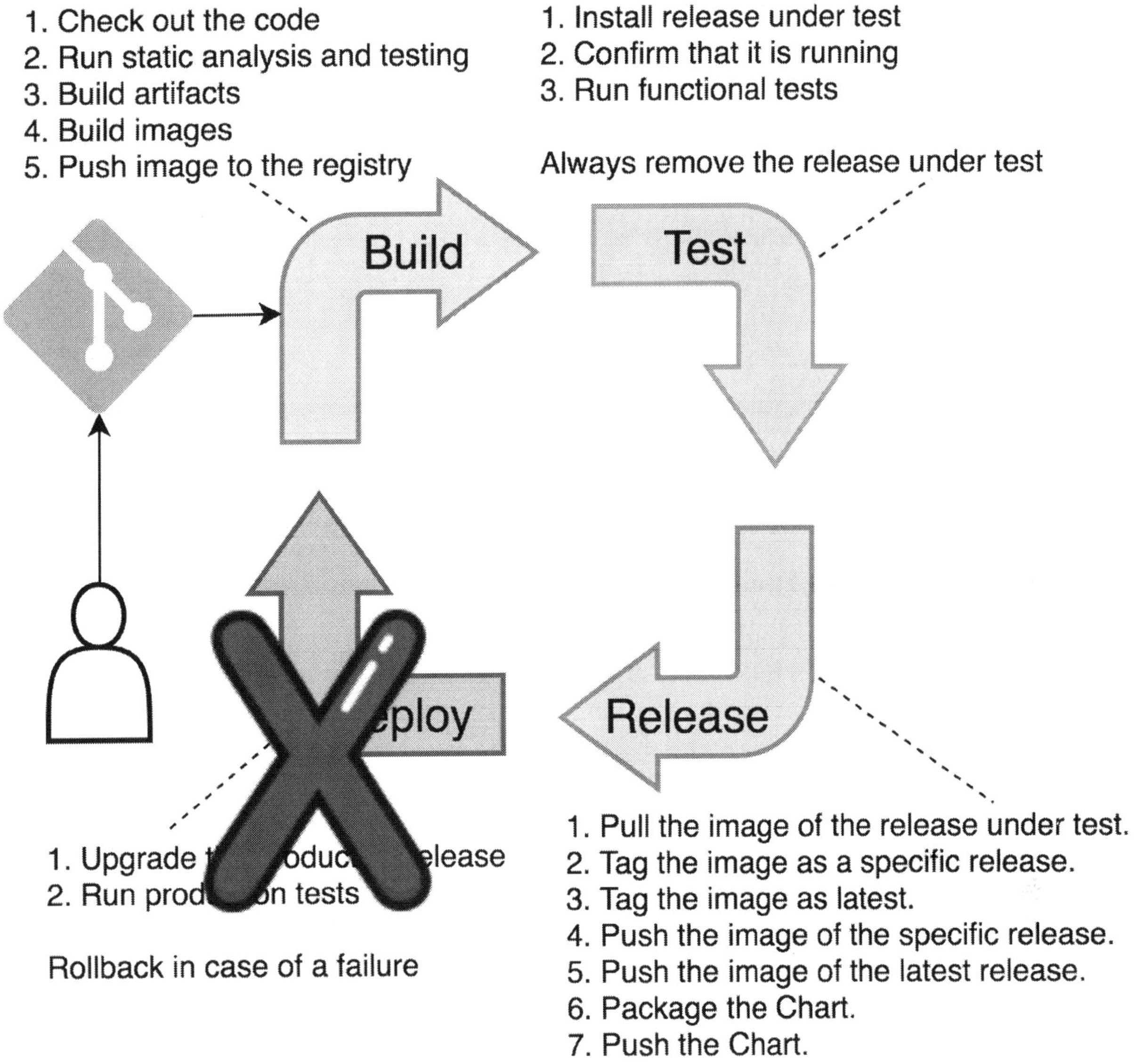

1. Check out the code
2. Run static analysis and testing
3. Build artifacts
4. Build images
5. Push image to the registry

1. Install release under test
2. Confirm that it is running
3. Run functional tests

Always remove the release under test

Build

Test

Deploy

Release

1. Upgrade the production release
2. Run production tests

Rollback in case of a failure

1. Pull the image of the release under test.
2. Tag the image as a specific release.
3. Tag the image as latest.
4. Push the image of the specific release.
5. Push the image of the latest release.
6. Package the Chart.
7. Push the Chart.

Figure 8-6: Continuous deployment process

The fact that our application pipeline (e.g., *go-demo-5*) does not perform deployment does not mean that it is not automated. The decisions which versions to use and when to initiate the upgrade process is manual, but everything else proceeding those actions is automated.

In our case, there is a separate repository (*k8s-prod*) that contains a full definition of what constitutes production environment. Whenever we make a decision to install a new application or to upgrade an existing one, we need to update files in *k8s-prod* and push them to the repository. Whether that push is performed directly to the *master* branch or to a separate branch, is of no importance to the process that relies solely on the *master* branch. If you choose to use separate branches (as you should), you can do pull requests, code reviews, and all the other things we usually do with code. But, as I already mentioned, those actions are irrelevant from the automation perspective. The *master* branch is the one that matters. Once a commit reaches it, it initiates a Webhook request that notifies Jenkins that there is a change and, from there on, we run a build that upgrades the production environment and executes light-weight tests with sanity checks. Except, that we did not set up GitHub Webhooks. I expect that you will have them once you create a "real" cluster with a "real" domain.

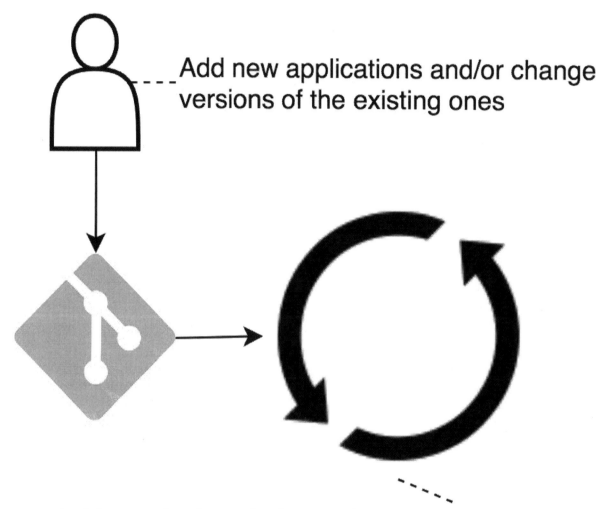

Add new applications and/or change versions of the existing ones

1. Upgrade the whole production environment
2. Run production tests

Rollback in case of a failure

Figure 8-7: Continuous deployment process

How does continuous delivery of applications combine with unified deployment to the production environment?

Let's imagine that we have four applications in total. We'll call them *app 1, app 2, app 3*, and *app 4*. Those applications are developed independently of each other. Whenever we push a commit to the *master* branch of one of those applications, corresponding continuous delivery pipeline is initiated and, if all the steps are successful, results in a new production-ready release. Pipelines are launched when code is pushed to other branches as well, but in those cases, production-ready releases are NOT created. So, we'll ignore them in this story.

We are accumulating production-ready releases in those applications and, at some point, someone makes a decision to upgrade the production environment. Those upgrades might involve an update of a single application, or it might entail update of a few. It all depends on the architecture of our applications (sometimes they are not independent), business decisions, and quite a few other criteria. No matter how we made the decision which applications to update and which releases to use, we need to make appropriate changes in the repository that serves as the source of truth of the production environment.

Let's say that we decided to upgrade app 1 to the release 2 and app 4 to release 4, to install the release 3 of app 2 for the first time, and to leave app 3 intact. In such a situation, we'd bump versions of app 1 and 4 in `requirements.yaml`. We'd add a new entry for app 2 since that's the first time we're installing that application. Finally, we'd leave app 3 in `requirements.yaml` as-is since we are not planning to upgrade it.

Once we're finished with modifications to `requirements.yaml`, all that's left is to bump the version in `Chart.yaml` and push the changes directly to master or to make a pull request and merge it after a review. No matter the route, once the change reaches the *master* branch, it fires a Webhook which, in turn, initiates a new build of the Jenkins job related to the repository. If all of the steps are successful, the Chart representing the production environment is upgraded and, with it, all the applications specified in `requirements.yaml` are upgraded as well. To be more precise, not all the dependencies are upgraded, but only those we modified. All in all, the production environment will converge to the desired stage after which we'll execute the last round of tests. If something fails, we roll back. Otherwise, another iteration of production deployments is finished, until we repeat the same process.

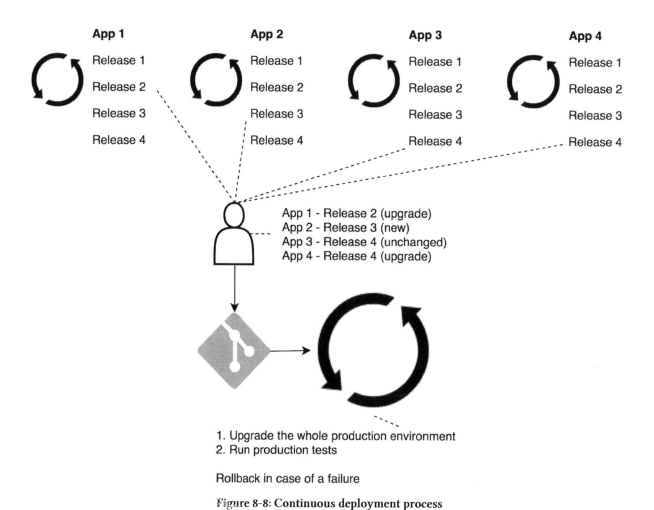

Figure 8-8: Continuous deployment process

To Continuously Deploy Or To Continuously Deliver?

Should we use the continuous deployment (CDP) or the continuous delivery (CD) process? That's a hard question to answer which mainly depends on your internal processes. There are a few questions that might guide us.

1. Are your applications truly independent and can be deployed without changing anything else in your cluster?
2. Do you have such a high level of trust in your automated tests that you are confident that there's no need for manual actions?
3. Are the teams working on applications authorized to make decisions on what to deploy to production and when?
4. Are those teams self-sufficient and do not depend on other teams?
5. Do you really want to upgrade production with every commit to the *master* branch?

If you answered with *no* to at least one of those questions, you cannot do continuous deployment. You should aim for continuous delivery, or not even that. Continuous delivery is almost as hard to practice as continuous deployment. The chances are that you cannot get there any time soon. If you can't, that's still not the end of the world. The lessons from this chapter can be easily modified to serve other processes.

If you answered with *no* to the second question (the one about tests), you cannot do either of those two processes. It's not that one requires less confidence in tests than the other. The level of trust is the same. We do not use continuous delivery because we trust our tests less, but because we choose not to deploy every commit to production. Our business might not be ready to deploy every production-ready release. Or, maybe, we need to wait for a marketing campaign to start (I'm ignoring the fact that we'd solve that with feature toggles). There might be many reasons to use continuous delivery instead of deployment, but none of them is technical. Both processes produce production-ready releases, and only one of them deploys it to production automatically.

Now, if you do NOT trust your tests, you need to fall back to continuous integration. Fortunately, the pipeline can be very similar. The major difference is that you should create one more repository (call it *k8s-test*) and have a similar Jenkinsfile inside it. When you think you're ready, you'll bump the versions in that repo and let Jenkins upgrade the test environment. From there on, you can let the army of manual testers do their work. They will surely find more problems than you're willing to fix but, once they stop finding those that impede you from upgrading the production, you can bump those versions in the repository that describes your production environment (*k8s-prod*). Apart from different Namespaces and, maybe, reduced number of replicas and Ingress hosts, the two repositories should contain the same Chart with similar dependencies, and changes to their *master* branch would result in very similar automated processes. You can even skip having the *k8s-test* repository and create a *test-env* branch in *k8s-prod*. That way, you can make changes to *test-env*, deploy them to the cluster, run manual testing, and, once you're confident that the release is production-ready, merge the branch to *master*.

What Now?

We are finished with the exploration of continuous delivery processes. Destroy the cluster if you created it only for the purpose of this chapter. Have a break. You deserve it.

Appendix A: Installing kubectl and Creating A Cluster With minikube

The text that follows provides the essential information you'll need to create a local Kubernetes cluster using minikube. This appendix contains a few sub-chapters from The DevOps 2.3 Toolkit: Kubernetes[178]. Please refer to it for a more detailed information.

Running Kubernetes Cluster Locally

Minikube creates a single-node cluster inside a VM on your laptop. While that is not ideal since we won't be able to demonstrate some of the features Kubernetes provides in a multi-node setup, it should be more than enough to explain most of the concepts behind Kubernetes. Later on, we'll move into a more production-like environment and explore the features that cannot be demonstrated in Minikube.

 A note to Windows users

Please run all the examples from *GitBash* (installed through *Git*). That way the commands you'll see throughout the book will be same as those that should be executed on *MacOS* or any *Linux* distribution. If you're using Hyper-V instead of VirtualBox, you may need to run the *GitBash* window as an Administrator.

Before we dive into Minikube installation, there are a few prerequisites we should set up. The first in line is kubectl.

Installing kubectl

Kubernetes' command-line tool, kubectl, is used to manage a cluster and applications running inside it. We'll use kubectl a lot throughout the book, so we won't go into details just yet. Instead, we'll discuss its commands through examples that will follow shortly. For now, think of it as your interlocutor with a Kubernetes cluster.

Let's install kubectl.

 All the commands from this chapter are available in the 02-minikube.sh[179] Gist.

---

[178]https://amzn.to/2GvzDjy
[179]https://gist.github.com/77ca05f4d16125b5a5a5dc30a1ade7fc

Feel free to skip the installation steps if you already have kubectl. Just make sure that it is version 1.8 or above.

If you are a **MacOS user**, please execute the commands that follow.

```
1  curl -LO https://storage.googleapis.com/kubernetes-release/release/`curl -s https://\
2  storage.googleapis.com/kubernetes-release/release/stable.txt`/bin/darwin/amd64/kubec\
3  tl
4
5  chmod +x ./kubectl
6
7  sudo mv ./kubectl /usr/local/bin/kubectl
```

If you already have Homebrew[180] package manager installed, you can "brew" it with the command that follows.

```
1  brew install kubectl
```

If, on the other hand, you're a **Linux user**, the commands that will install kubectl are as follows.

```
1  curl -LO https://storage.googleapis.com/kubernetes-release/release/$(curl -s https:/\
2  /storage.googleapis.com/kubernetes-release/release/stable.txt)/bin/linux/amd64/kubec\
3  tl
4
5  chmod +x ./kubectl
6
7  sudo mv ./kubectl /usr/local/bin/kubectl
```

Finally, **Windows users** should download the binary through the command that follows.

```
1  curl -LO https://storage.googleapis.com/kubernetes-release/release/$(curl -s https:/\
2  /storage.googleapis.com/kubernetes-release/release/stable.txt)/bin/windows/amd64/kub\
3  ectl.exe
```

Feel free to copy the binary to any directory. The important thing is to add it to your PATH.

Let's check kubectl version and, at the same time, validate that it is working correctly. No matter which OS you're using, the command is as follows.

---

[180]https://brew.sh/

```
1  kubectl version
```

The output is as follows.

```
1  Client Version: version.Info{Major:"1", Minor:"9", GitVersion:"v1.9.0", GitCommit:"9\
2  25c127ec6b946659ad0fd596fa959be43f0cc05", GitTreeState:"clean", BuildDate:"2017-12-1\
3  5T21:07:38Z", GoVersion:"go1.9.2", Compiler:"gc", Platform:"darwin/amd64"}
4  The connection to the server localhost:8080 was refused - did you specify the right \
5  host or port?
```

That is a very ugly and unreadable output. Fortunately, kubectl can use a few different formats for its output. For example, we can tell it to output the command in yaml format

```
1  kubectl version --output=yaml
```

The output is as follows.

```
1  clientVersion:
2    buildDate: 2017-12-15T21:07:38Z
3    compiler: gc
4    gitCommit: 925c127ec6b946659ad0fd596fa959be43f0cc05
5    gitTreeState: clean
6    gitVersion: v1.9.0
7    goVersion: go1.9.2
8    major: "1"
9    minor: "9"
10   platform: darwin/amd64
11
12 The connection to the server localhost:8080 was refused - did you specify the right \
13 host or port?
```

That was a much better (more readable) output.

We can see that the client version is 1.9. At the bottom is the error message stating that kubectl could not connect to the server. That is expected since we did not yet create a cluster. That's our next step.

 At the time of writing this book kubectl version was 1.9.0. Your version might be different when you install.

Installing Minikube

Minikube supports several virtualization technologies. We'll use VirtualBox throughout the book since it is the only virtualization supported in all operating systems. If you do not have it already, please head to the Download VirtualBox[181] page and get the version that matches your OS. Please keep in mind that for VirtualBox or HyperV to work, virtualization must be enabled in the BIOS. Most laptops should have it enabled by default.

Finally, we can install Minikube.

If you're using **MacOS**, please execute the command that follows.

```
1  brew cask install minikube
```

If, on the other hand, you prefer **Linux**, the command is as follows.

```
1  curl -Lo minikube https://storage.googleapis.com/minikube/releases/latest/minikube-l\
2  inux-amd64 && chmod +x minikube && sudo mv minikube /usr/local/bin/
```

Finally, you will not get a command if you are a Windows user. Instead, download the latest release from of the minikube-windows-amd64.exe[182] file, rename it to `minikube.exe`, and add it to your path.

We'll test whether Minikube works by checking its version.

```
1  minikube version
```

The output is as follows.

```
1  minikube version: v0.23.0
```

Now we're ready to give the cluster a spin.

Creating A Local Kubernetes Cluster With Minikube

The folks behind Minikube made creating a cluster as easy as it can get. All we need to do is to execute a single command. Minikube will start a virtual machine locally and deploy the necessary Kubernetes components into it. The VM will get configured with Docker and Kubernetes via a single binary called localkube.

---

[181]https://www.virtualbox.org/wiki/Downloads
[182]https://storage.googleapis.com/minikube/releases/latest/minikube-windows-amd64.exe

```
1  minikube start --vm-driver=virtualbox
```

 ## A note to Windows users

You might experience problems with `virtualbox`. If that's the case, you might want to use `hyperv` instead. Open a Powershell Admin Window and execute the `Get-NetAdapter` command, noting the name of your network connection. Create a `hyperv` virtual switch `New-VMSwitch -name NonDockerSwitch -NetAdapterName Ethernet -AllowManagementOS $true` replacing `Ethernet` with your network connection name. Then create the Minikube vm: `minikube start --vm-driver=hyperv --hyperv-virtual-switch "NonDockerSwitch" --memory=4096`. Other minikube commands such as `minikube start`, `minikube stop` and `minikube delete` all work the same whether you're using VirutalBox or Hyper-V.

A few moments later, a new Minikube VM will be created and set up, and a cluster will be ready for use.

When we executed the `minikube start` command, it created a new VM based on the Minikube image. That image contains a few binaries. It has both Docker[183] and rkt[184] container engines as well as *localkube* library. The library includes all the components necessary for running Kubernetes. We'll go into details of all those components later. For now, the important thing is that localkube provides everything we need to run a Kubernetes cluster locally.

Remember that this is a single-node cluster. While that is unfortunate, it is still the easiest way (as far as I know) to "play" with Kubernetes locally. It should do, for now. Later on, we'll explore ways to create a multi-node cluster that will be much closer to a production setup.

Let's take a look at the status of the cluster.

```
1  minikube status
```

The output is as follows.

```
1  minikube: Running
2  cluster: Running
3  kubectl: Correctly Configured: pointing to minikube-vm at 192.168.99.100
```

Minikube is running, and it initialized a Kubernetes cluster. It even configured `kubectl` so that it points to the newly created VM.

You won't see much UI in this book. I believe that a terminal is the best way to operate a cluster. More importantly, I am convinced that one should master a tool through its commands first. Later on, once we feel comfortable and understand how the tool works, we can choose to use a UI on top of it. We'll explore the Kubernetes UI in one of the later chapters. For now, I'll let you have a quick glimpse of it.

---

[183]https://www.docker.com/
[184]https://coreos.com/rkt/

```
1  minikube dashboard
```

Feel free to explore the UI but don't take too long. You'll only get confused with concepts that we did not yet study. Once we learn about pods, replica-sets, services, and a myriad of other Kubernetes components, the UI will start making much more sense.

Another useful Minikube command is docker-env.

```
1  minikube docker-env
```

The output is as follows.

```
1  export DOCKER_TLS_VERIFY="1"
2  export DOCKER_HOST="tcp://192.168.99.100:2376"
3  export DOCKER_CERT_PATH="/Users/vfarcic/.minikube/certs"
4  export DOCKER_API_VERSION="1.23"
5  # Run this command to configure your shell:
6  # eval $(minikube docker-env)
```

If you worked with Docker Machine, you'll notice that the output is the same. Both docker-machine env and minikube docker-env serve the same purpose. They output the environment variables required for a local Docker client to communicate with a remote Docker server. In this case, that Docker server is the one inside a VM created by Minikube. I assume that you already have Docker installed on your laptop. If that's not the case, please go to the Install Docker[185] page and follow the instructions for your operating system. Once Docker is installed, we can connect the client running on your laptop with the server in the Minikube VM.

```
1  eval $(minikube docker-env)
```

We evaluated (created) the environment variables provided through the minikube docker-env command. As a result, every command we send to our local Docker client will be executed on the Minikube VM. We can test that easily by, for example, listing all the running containers on that VM.

```
1  docker container ls
```

The containers listed in the output are those required by Kubernetes. We can, in a way, consider them system containers. We won't discuss each of them. As a matter of fact, we won't discuss any of them. At least, not right away. All you need to know, at this point, is that they make Kubernetes work.

Since almost everything in that VM is a container, pointing the local Docker client to the service inside it should be all you need (besides kubectl). Still, in some cases, you might want to SSH into the VM.

---

[185]https://docs.docker.com/engine/installation/

```
1  minikube ssh
2
3  docker container ls
4
5  exit
```

We entered into the Minikube VM, listed containers, and got out. There's no reason to do anything else beyond showing that SSH is possible, even though you probably won't use it.

What else is there to verify? We can, for example, confirm that kubectl is also pointing to the Minikube VM.

```
1  kubectl config current-context
```

The output should be a single word, minikube, indicating that kubectl is configured to talk to Kubernetes inside the newly created cluster.

As an additional verification, we can list all the nodes of the cluster.

```
1  kubectl get nodes
```

The output is as follows.

```
1  NAME      STATUS ROLES  AGE VERSION
2  minikube Ready   <none> 31m v1.8.0
```

It should come as no surprise that there is only one node, conveniently called minikube.

If you are experienced with Docker Machine or Vagrant, you probably noticed the similar pattern. Minikube commands are almost exactly the same as those from Docker Machine which, on the other hand, are similar to those from Vagrant.

We can do all the common things we would expect from a virtual machine. For example, we can stop it.

```
1  minikube stop
```

We can start it again.

```
1  minikube start
```

We can delete it.

```
1  minikube delete
```

One interesting feature is the ability to specify which Kubernetes version we'd like to use.

Since Kubernetes is still a young project, we can expect quite a lot of changes at a rapid pace. That will often mean that our production cluster might not be running the latest version. On the other hand, we should strive to have our local environment as close to production as possible (within reason).

We can list all the available versions with the command that follows.

```
1  minikube get-k8s-versions
```

The output, limited to the first few lines, is as follows.

```
1  The following Kubernetes versions are available:
2          - v1.9.0
3          - v1.8.0
4          - v1.7.5
5          - v1.7.4
6          - v1.7.3
7          - v1.7.2
8          - v1.7.0
9          ...
```

Now that we know which versions are available, we can create a new cluster based on, let's say, Kubernetes v1.7.0.

```
1  minikube start \
2      --vm-driver=virtualbox \
3      --kubernetes-version="v1.7.0"
4
5  kubectl version --output=yaml
```

We created a new cluster and output versions of the client and the server.

The output of the latter command is as follows.

```
1  clientVersion:
2    buildDate: 2017-10-24T19:48:57Z
3    compiler: gc
4    gitCommit: bdaeafa71f6c7c04636251031f93464384d54963
5    gitTreeState: clean
6    gitVersion: v1.8.2
7    goVersion: go1.8.3
8    major: "1"
9    minor: "8"
10   platform: darwin/amd64
11 serverVersion:
12   buildDate: 2017-10-04T09:25:40Z
13   compiler: gc
14   gitCommit: d3ada0119e776222f11ec7945e6d860061339aad
15   gitTreeState: dirty
16   gitVersion: v1.7.0
17   goVersion: go1.8.3
18   major: "1"
19   minor: "7"
20   platform: linux/amd64
```

If you focus on the `serverVersion` section, you'll notice that the `major` version is 1 and the `minor` is 7.

What Now?

We are finished with a short introduction to Minikube. Actually, this might be called a long introduction as well. We use it to create a single-node Kubernetes cluster, launch the UI, do common VM operations like stop, restart, and delete, and so on. There's not much more to it. If you are familiar with Vagrant or Docker Machine, the principle is the same, and the commands are very similar.

Before we leave, we'll destroy the cluster. The next chapter will start fresh. That way, you can execute commands from any chapter at any time.

```
1  minikube delete
```

That's it. The cluster is no more.

Appendix B: Using Kubernetes Operations (kops)

The text that follows provides the essential information you'll need to create a Kubernetes cluster in AWS using kops. This appendix contains a few sub-chapters from The DevOps 2.3 Toolkit: Kubernetes[186]. Please refer to it for a more detailed information.

Preparing For The Cluster Setup

We'll continue using the specifications from the `vfarcic/k8s-specs` repository, so the first thing we'll do is to go inside the directory where we cloned it, and pull the latest version.

 All the commands from this appendix are available in the 99-appendix-b.sh[187] Gist.

```
1   cd k8s-specs
2
3   git pull
```

I will assume that you already have an AWS account. If that's not the case, please head over to Amazon Web Services[188] and sign-up.

 If you are already proficient with AWS, you might want to skim through the text that follows and only execute the commands.

The first thing we should do is get the AWS credentials.

Please open Amazon EC2 Console[189], click on your name from the top-right menu and select *My Security Credentials*. You will see the screen with different types of credentials. Expand the *Access Keys (Access Key ID and Secret Access Key)* section and click the *Create New Access Key* button. Expand the *Show Access Key* section to see the keys.

---

[186]https://amzn.to/2GvzDjy
[187]https://gist.github.com/49bccadae317379bef6f81b4e5985f84
[188]https://aws.amazon.com/
[189]https://console.aws.amazon.com/ec2/

You will not be able to view the keys later on, so this is the only chance you'll have to *Download Key File.*

We'll put the keys as environment variables that will be used by the AWS Command Line Interface (AWS CLI)[190].

Please replace [. . .] with your keys before executing the commands that follow.

```
1  export AWS_ACCESS_KEY_ID=[...]
2
3  export AWS_SECRET_ACCESS_KEY=[...]
```

We'll need to install AWS Command Line Interface (CLI)[191] and gather info about your account.

If you haven't already, please open the Installing the AWS Command Line Interface[192] page, and follow the installation method best suited for your OS.

 A note to Windows users

I found the most convenient way to get AWS CLI installed on Windows is to use Chocolatey[193]. Download and install Chocolatey, then run `choco install awscli` from an Administrator Command Prompt. Later on in the chapter, Chocolatey will be used to install jq.

Once you're done, we'll confirm that the installation was successful by outputting the version.

 A note to Windows users

You might need to reopen your *GitBash* terminal for the changes to the environment variable PATH to take effect.

```
1  aws --version
```

The output (from my laptop) is as follows.

```
1  aws-cli/1.11.15 Python/2.7.10 Darwin/16.0.0 botocore/1.4.72
```

Amazon EC2 is hosted in multiple locations worldwide. These locations are composed of regions and availability zones. Each region is a separate geographic area composed of multiple isolated locations known as availability zones. Amazon EC2 provides you the ability to place resources, such as instances, and data in multiple locations.

Next, we'll define the environment variable AWS_DEFAULT_REGION that will tell AWS CLI which region we'd like to use by default.

---

[190]https://aws.amazon.com/cli/
[191]https://aws.amazon.com/cli/
[192]http://docs.aws.amazon.com/cli/latest/userguide/installing.html
[193]https://chocolatey.org/

```
1  export AWS_DEFAULT_REGION=us-east-2
```

For now, please note that you can change the value of the variable to any other region, as long as it has at least three availability zones. We'll discuss the reasons for using us-east-2 region and the need for multiple availability zones soon.

Next, we'll create a few Identity and Access Management (IAM) resources. Even though we could create a cluster with the user you used to register to AWS, it is a good practice to create a separate account that contains only the privileges we'll need for the exercises that follow.

First, we'll create an IAM group called kops.

```
1  aws iam create-group \
2      --group-name kops
```

The output is as follows.

```
1  {
2      "Group": {
3          "Path": "/",
4          "CreateDate": "2018-02-21T12:58:47.853Z",
5          "GroupId": "AGPAIF2Y6HJF7YFYQBQK2",
6          "Arn": "arn:aws:iam::036548781187:group/kops",
7          "GroupName": "kops"
8      }
9  }
```

We don't care much for any of the information from the output except that it does not contain an error message thus confirming that the group was created successfully.

Next, we'll assign a few policies to the group thus providing the future users of the group with sufficient permissions to create the objects we'll need.

Since our cluster will consist of EC2[194] instances, the group will need to have the permissions to create and manage them. We'll need a place to store the state of the cluster so we'll need access to S3[195]. Furthermore, we need to add VPCs[196] to the mix so that our cluster is isolated from prying eyes. Finally, we'll need to be able to create additional IAMs.

In AWS, user permissions are granted by creating policies. We'll need AmazonEC2FullAccess, AmazonS3FullAccess, AmazonVPCFullAccess, and IAMFullAccess.

The commands that attach the required policies to the kops group are as follows.

---

[194]https://aws.amazon.com/ec2
[195]https://aws.amazon.com/s3
[196]https://aws.amazon.com/vpc/

```
1  aws iam attach-group-policy \
2      --policy-arn arn:aws:iam::aws:policy/AmazonEC2FullAccess \
3      --group-name kops
4
5  aws iam attach-group-policy \
6      --policy-arn arn:aws:iam::aws:policy/AmazonS3FullAccess \
7      --group-name kops
8
9  aws iam attach-group-policy \
10     --policy-arn arn:aws:iam::aws:policy/AmazonVPCFullAccess \
11     --group-name kops
12
13 aws iam attach-group-policy \
14     --policy-arn arn:aws:iam::aws:policy/IAMFullAccess \
15     --group-name kops
```

Now that we have a group with the sufficient permissions, we should create a user as well.

```
1  aws iam create-user \
2      --user-name kops
```

The output is as follows.

```
1  {
2      "User": {
3          "UserName": "kops",
4          "Path": "/",
5          "CreateDate": "2018-02-21T12:59:28.836Z",
6          "UserId": "AIDAJ22UOS7JVYQIAVMWA",
7          "Arn": "arn:aws:iam::036548781187:user/kops"
8      }
9  }
```

Just as when we created the group, the contents of the output are not important, except as a confirmation that the command was executed successfully.

The user we created does not yet belong to the kops group. We'll fix that next.

```
1  aws iam add-user-to-group \
2      --user-name kops \
3      --group-name kops
```

Finally, we'll need access keys for the newly created user. Without them, we would not be able to act on its behalf.

```
1   aws iam create-access-key \
2       --user-name kops >kops-creds
```

We created access keys and stored the output in the kops-creds file. Let's take a quick look at its content.

```
1   cat kops-creds
```

The output is as follows.

```
1   {
2       "AccessKey": {
3           "UserName": "kops",
4           "Status": "Active",
5           "CreateDate": "2018-02-21T13:00:24.733Z",
6           "SecretAccessKey": "...",
7           "AccessKeyId": "..."
8       }
9   }
```

Please note that I removed the values of the keys. I do not yet trust you enough with the keys of my AWS account.

We need the SecretAccessKey and AccessKeyId entries. So, the next step is to parse the content of the kops-creds file and store those two values as the environment variables AWS_ACCESS_KEY_ID and AWS_SECRET_ACCESS_KEY.

In the spirit of full automation, we'll use jq[197] to parse the contents of the kops-creds file. Please download and install the distribution suited for your OS.

 ## A note to Windows users

Using Chocolatey, install jq from an Administrator Command Prompt via choco install jq.

---

[197]https://stedolan.github.io/jq/

```
1  export AWS_ACCESS_KEY_ID=$(\
2      cat kops-creds | jq -r \
3      '.AccessKey.AccessKeyId')
4
5  export AWS_SECRET_ACCESS_KEY=$(
6      cat kops-creds | jq -r \
7      '.AccessKey.SecretAccessKey')
```

We used `cat` to output contents of the file and combined it with `jq` to filter the input so that only the field we need is retrieved.

From now on, all the AWS CLI commands will not be executed by the administrative user you used to register to AWS, but as `kops`.

 It is imperative that the `kops-creds` file is secured and not accessible to anyone but people you trust. The best method to secure it depends from one organization to another. No matter what you do, do not write it on a post-it and stick it to your monitor. Storing it in one of your GitHub repositories is even worse.

Next, we should decide which availability zones we'll use. So, let's take a look at what's available in the `us-east-2` region.

```
1  aws ec2 describe-availability-zones \
2      --region $AWS_DEFAULT_REGION
```

The output is as follows.

```
1  {
2      "AvailabilityZones": [
3          {
4              "State": "available",
5              "RegionName": "us-east-2",
6              "Messages": [],
7              "ZoneName": "us-east-2a"
8          },
9          {
10             "State": "available",
11             "RegionName": "us-east-2",
12             "Messages": [],
13             "ZoneName": "us-east-2b"
14         },
15         {
```

```
16            "State": "available",
17            "RegionName": "us-east-2",
18            "Messages": [],
19            "ZoneName": "us-east-2c"
20        }
21    ]
22  }
```

As we can see, the region has three availability zones. We'll store them in an environment variable.

 ## A note to Windows users

Please use `tr '\r\n' ','` instead of `tr '\n' ','` in the command that follows.

```
1  export ZONES=$(aws ec2 \
2      describe-availability-zones \
3      --region $AWS_DEFAULT_REGION \
4      | jq -r \
5      '.AvailabilityZones[].ZoneName' \
6      | tr '\n' ',' | tr -d ' ')
7
8  ZONES=${ZONES%?}
9
10 echo $ZONES
```

Just as with the access keys, we used `jq` to limit the results only to the zone names, and we combined that with `tr` that replaced new lines with commas. The second command removes the trailing comma.

The output of the last command that echoed the values of the environment variable is as follows.

```
1  us-east-2a,us-east-2b,us-east-2c
```

We'll discuss the reasons behind the usage of three availability zones later on. For now, just remember that they are stored in the environment variable ZONES.

The last preparation step is to create SSH keys required for the setup. Since we might create some other artifacts during the process, we'll create a directory dedicated to the creation of the cluster.

```
1  mkdir -p cluster
2
3  cd cluster
```

SSH keys can be created through the `aws ec2` command `create-key-pair`.

```
1  aws ec2 create-key-pair \
2      --key-name devops23 \
3      | jq -r '.KeyMaterial' \
4      >devops23.pem
```

We created a new key pair, filtered the output so that only the `KeyMaterial` is returned, and stored it in the `devops.pem` file.

For security reasons, we should change the permissions of the `devops23.pem` file so that only the current user can read it.

```
1  chmod 400 devops23.pem
```

Finally, we'll need only the public segment of the newly generated SSH key, so we'll use `ssh-keygen` to extract it.

```
1  ssh-keygen -y -f devops23.pem \
2      >devops23.pub
```

All those steps might look a bit daunting if this is your first contact with AWS. Nevertheless, they are pretty standard. No matter what you do in AWS, you'd need to perform, more or less, the same actions. Not all of them are mandatory, but they are good practice. Having a dedicated (non-admin) user and a group with only required policies is always a good idea. Access keys are necessary for any `aws` command. Without SSH keys, no one can enter into a server.

The good news is that we're finished with the prerequisites, and we can turn our attention towards creating a Kubernetes cluster.

Creating A Kubernetes Cluster In AWS

We'll start by deciding the name of our soon to be created cluster. We'll choose to call it `devops23.k8s.local`. The latter part of the name (`.k8s.local`) is mandatory if we do not have a DNS at hand. It's a naming convention kops uses to decide whether to create a gossip-based cluster or to rely on a publicly available domain. If this would be a "real" production cluster, you would probably have a DNS for it. However, since I cannot be sure whether you do have one for the exercises in this book, we'll play it safe, and proceed with the gossip mode.

We'll store the name into an environment variable so that it is easily accessible.

```
1   export NAME=devops23.k8s.local
```

When we create the cluster, kops will store its state in a location we're about to configure. If you used Terraform, you'll notice that kops uses a very similar approach. It uses the state it generates when creating the cluster for all subsequent operations. If we want to change any aspect of a cluster, we'll have to change the desired state first, and then apply those changes to the cluster.

At the moment, when creating a cluster in AWS, the only option for storing the state are Amazon S3[198] buckets. We can expect availability of additional stores soon. For now, S3 is our only option.

The command that creates an S3 bucket in our region is as follows.

```
1   export BUCKET_NAME=devops23-$(date +%s)
2
3   aws s3api create-bucket \
4       --bucket $BUCKET_NAME \
5       --create-bucket-configuration \
6       LocationConstraint=$AWS_DEFAULT_REGION
```

We created a bucket with a unique name and the output is as follows.

```
1   {
2       "Location": "http://devops23-1519993212.s3.amazonaws.com/"
3   }
```

For simplicity, we'll define the environment variable KOPS_STATE_STORE. Kops will use it to know where we store the state. Otherwise, we'd need to use --store argument with every kops command.

```
1   export KOPS_STATE_STORE=s3://$BUCKET_NAME
```

There's only one thing missing before we create the cluster. We need to install kops.

If you are a **MacOS user**, the easiest way to install kops is through Homebrew[199].

```
1   brew update && brew install kops
```

As an alternative, we can download a release from GitHub.

---

[198]https://aws.amazon.com/s3
[199]https://brew.sh/

```
1  curl -Lo kops https://github.com/kubernetes/kops/releases/download/$(curl -s https:/\
2  /api.github.com/repos/kubernetes/kops/releases/latest | grep tag_name | cut -d '"' -\
3  f 4)/kops-darwin-amd64
4
5  chmod +x ./kops
6
7  sudo mv ./kops /usr/local/bin/
```

If, on the other hand, you're a **Linux user**, the commands that will install kops are as follows.

```
1  wget -O kops https://github.com/kubernetes/kops/releases/download/$(curl -s https://\
2  api.github.com/repos/kubernetes/kops/releases/latest | grep tag_name | cut -d '"' -f\
3   4)/kops-linux-amd64
4
5  chmod +x ./kops
6
7  sudo mv ./kops /usr/local/bin/
```

Finally, if you are a **Windows user**, you cannot install kops. At the time of this writing, its releases do not include Windows binaries. Don't worry. I am not giving up on you, dear *Windows user*. We'll manage to overcome the problem soon by exploiting Docker's ability to run any Linux application. The only requirement is that you have Docker For Windows[200] installed.

I already created a Docker image that contains kops and its dependencies. So, we'll create an alias kops that will create a container instead running a binary. The result will be the same.

The command that creates the kops alias is as follows. Execute it only if you are a **Windows user**.

```
1   mkdir config
2
3   alias kops="docker run -it --rm \
4       -v $PWD/devops23.pub:/devops23.pub \
5       -v $PWD/config:/config \
6       -e KUBECONFIG=/config/kubecfg.yaml \
7       -e NAME=$NAME -e ZONES=$ZONES \
8       -e AWS_ACCESS_KEY_ID=$AWS_ACCESS_KEY_ID \
9       -e AWS_SECRET_ACCESS_KEY=$AWS_SECRET_ACCESS_KEY \
10      -e KOPS_STATE_STORE=$KOPS_STATE_STORE \
11      vfarcic/kops"
```

We won't go into details of all the arguments the docker run command uses. Their usage will become clear when we start using kops. Just remember that we are passing all the environment variables

---

[200]https://www.docker.com/docker-windows

we might use as well as mounting the SSH key and the directory where kops will store kubectl configuration.

We are, finally, ready to create a cluster. But, before we do that, we'll spend a bit of time discussing the requirements we might have. After all, not all clusters are created equal, and the choices we are about to make might severely impact our ability to accomplish the goals we might have.

The first question we might ask ourselves is whether we want to have high-availability. It would be strange if anyone would answer no. Who doesn't want to have a cluster that is (almost) always available? Instead, we'll ask ourselves what the things that might bring our cluster down are.

When a node is destroyed, Kubernetes will reschedule all the applications that were running inside it into the healthy nodes. All we have to do is to make sure that, later on, a new server is created and joined the cluster, so that its capacity is back to the desired values. We'll discuss later how are new nodes created as a reaction to failures of a server. For now, we'll assume that will happen somehow.

Still, there is a catch. Given that new nodes need to join the cluster, if the failed server was the only master, there is no cluster to join. All is lost. The part is where master servers are. They host the critical components without which Kubernetes cannot operate.

So, we need more than one master node. How about two? If one fails, we still have the other one. Still, that would not work.

Every piece of information that enters one of the master nodes is propagated to the others, and only after the majority agrees, that information is committed. If we lose majority (50%+1), masters cannot establish a quorum and cease to operate. If one out of two masters is down, we can get only half of the votes, and we would lose the ability to establish the quorum. Therefore, we need three masters or more. Odd numbers greater than one are "magic" numbers. Given that we won't create a big cluster, three should do.

With three masters, we are safe from a failure of any single one of them. Given that failed servers will be replaced with new ones, as long as only one master fails at the time, we should be fault tolerant and have high availability.

 Always set an odd number greater than one for master nodes.

The whole idea of having multiple masters does not mean much if an entire data center goes down.

Attempts to prevent a data center from failing are commendable. Still, no matter how well a data center is designed, there is always a scenario that might cause its disruption. So, we need more than one data center. Following the logic behind master nodes, we need at least three. But, as with almost anything else, we cannot have any three (or more) data centers. If they are too far apart, the latency between them might be too high. Since every piece of information is propagated to all the masters in a cluster, slow communication between data centers would severely impact the cluster as a whole.

All in all, we need three data centers that are close enough to provide low latency, and yet physically separated, so that failure of one does not impact the others. Since we are about to create the cluster in AWS, we'll use availability zones (AZs) which are physically separated data centers with low latency.

Always spread your cluster between at least three data centers which are close enough to warrant low latency.

There's more to high-availability to running multiple masters and spreading a cluster across multiple availability zones. We'll get back to this subject later. For now, we'll continue exploring the other decisions we have to make.

Which networking shall we use? We can choose between *kubenet*, *CNI*, *classic*, and *external* networking.

The classic Kubernetes native networking is deprecated in favor of kubenet, so we can discard it right away.

The external networking is used in some custom implementations and for particular use cases, so we'll discard that one as well.

That leaves us with kubenet and CNI.

Container Network Interface (CNI) allows us to plug in a third-party networking driver. Kops supports Calico[201], flannel[202], Canal (Flannel + Calico)[203], kopeio-vxlan[204], kube-router[205], romana[206], weave[207], and amazon-vpc-routed-eni[208] networks. Each of those networks comes with pros and cons and differs in its implementation and primary objectives. Choosing between them would require a detailed analysis of each. We'll leave a comparison of all those for some other time and place. Instead, we'll focus on `kubenet`.

Kubenet is kops' default networking solution. It is Kubernetes native networking, and it is considered battle tested and very reliable. However, it comes with a limitation. On AWS, routes for each node are configured in AWS VPC routing tables. Since those tables cannot have more than fifty entries, kubenet can be used in clusters with up to fifty nodes. If you're planning to have a cluster bigger than that, you'll have to switch to one of the previously mentioned CNIs.

Use kubenet networking if your cluster is smaller than fifty nodes.

The good news is that using any of the networking solutions is easy. All we have to do is specify the `--networking` argument followed with the name of the network.

[201]http://docs.projectcalico.org/v2.0/getting-started/kubernetes/installation/hosted/

[202]https://github.com/coreos/flannel

[203]https://github.com/projectcalico/canal

[204]https://github.com/kopeio/networking

[205]https://github.com/kubernetes/kops/blob/master/docs/networking.md#kube-router-example-for-cni-ipvs-based-service-proxy-and-network-policy-enforcer

[206]https://github.com/romana/romana

[207]https://github.com/weaveworks/weave-kube

[208]https://github.com/kubernetes/kops/blob/master/docs/networking.md#amazon-vpc-backend

Given that we won't have the time and space to evaluate all the CNIs, we'll use kubenet as the networking solution for the cluster we're about to create. I encourage you to explore the other options on your own (or wait until I write a post or a new book).

Finally, we are left with only one more choice we need to make. What will be the size of our nodes? Since we won't run many applications, *t2.small* should be more than enough and will keep AWS costs to a minimum. *t2.micro* is too small, so we elected the second smallest among those AWS offers.

 You might have noticed that we did not mention persistent volumes. We'll explore them in the next chapter.

The command that creates a cluster using the specifications we discussed is as follows.

```
 1  kops create cluster \
 2      --name $NAME \
 3      --master-count 3 \
 4      --node-count 1 \
 5      --node-size t2.small \
 6      --master-size t2.small \
 7      --zones $ZONES \
 8      --master-zones $ZONES \
 9      --ssh-public-key devops23.pub \
10      --networking kubenet \
11      --authorization RBAC \
12      --yes
```

We specified that the cluster should have three masters and one worker node. Remember, we can always increase the number of workers, so there's no need to start with more than what we need at the moment.

The sizes of both worker nodes and masters are set to t2.small. Both types of nodes will be spread across the three availability zones we specified through the environment variable ZONES. Further on, we defined the public key and the type of networking.

We used --kubernetes-version to specify that we prefer to run version v1.8.4. Otherwise, we'd get a cluster with the latest version considered stable by kops. Even though running latest stable version is probably a good idea, we'll need to be a few versions behind to demonstrate some of the features kops has to offer.

By default, kops sets authorization to AlwaysAllow. Since this is a simulation of a production-ready cluster, we changed it to RBAC, which we already explored in one of the previous chapters.

The --yes argument specifies that the cluster should be created right away. Without it, kops would only update the state in the S3 bucket, and we'd need to execute kops apply to create the cluster.

Such two-step approach is preferable, but I got impatient and would like to see the cluster in all its glory as soon as possible.

The output of the command is as follows.

```
1   ...
2   kops has set your kubectl context to devops23.k8s.local
3
4   Cluster is starting.  It should be ready in a few minutes.
5
6   Suggestions:
7    * validate cluster: kops validate cluster
8    * list nodes: kubectl get nodes --show-labels
9    * ssh to the master: ssh -i ~/.ssh/id_rsa admin@api.devops23.k8s.local
10  The admin user is specific to Debian. If not using Debian please use the appropriate\
11   user based on your OS.
12   * read about installing addons: https://github.com/kubernetes/kops/blob/master/docs\
13  /addons.md
```

We can see that the kubectl context was changed to point to the new cluster which is starting, and will be ready soon. Further down are a few suggestions of the next actions. We'll skip them, for now.

A note to Windows users

Kops was executed inside a container. It changed the context inside the container that is now gone. As a result, your local kubectl context was left intact. We'll fix that by executing kops export kubecfg --name ${NAME} and export KUBECONFIG=$PWD/config/kubecfg.yaml. The first command exported the config to /config/kubecfg.yaml. That path was specified through the environment variable KUBECONFIG and is mounted as config/kubecfg.yaml on local hard disk. The latter command exports KUBECONFIG locally. Through that variable, kubectl is now instructed to use the configuration in config/kubecfg.yaml instead of the default one. Before you run those commands, please give AWS a few minutes to create all the EC2 instances and for them to join the cluster. After waiting and executing those commands, you'll be all set.

We'll use kops to retrieve the information about the newly created cluster.

```
1   kops get cluster
```

The output is as follows.

```
1  NAME               CLOUD ZONES
2  devops23.k8s.local aws   us-east-2a,us-east-2b,us-east-2c
```

This information does not tell us anything new. We already knew the name of the cluster and the zones it runs in.

How about kubectl cluster-info?

```
1  kubectl cluster-info
```

The output is as follows.

```
1  Kubernetes master is running at https://api-devops23-k8s-local-ivnbim-609446190.us-e\
2  ast-2.elb.amazonaws.com
3  KubeDNS is running at https://api-devops23-k8s-local-ivnbim-609446190.us-east-2.elb.\
4  amazonaws.com/api/v1/namespaces/kube-system/services/kube-dns:dns/proxy
5
6  To further debug and diagnose cluster problems, use 'kubectl cluster-info dump'.
```

We can see that the master is running as well as KubeDNS. The cluster is probably ready. If in your case KubeDNS did not appear in the output, you might need to wait for a few more minutes.

We can get more reliable information about the readiness of our new cluster through the kops validate command.

```
1  kops validate cluster
```

The output is as follows.

```
1  Using cluster from kubectl context: devops23.k8s.local
2
3  Validating cluster devops23.k8s.local
4
5  INSTANCE GROUPS
6  NAME               ROLE    MACHINETYPE MIN MAX SUBNETS
7  master-us-east-2a Master t2.small    1   1   us-east-2a
8  master-us-east-2b Master t2.small    1   1   us-east-2b
9  master-us-east-2c Master t2.small    1   1   us-east-2c
10 nodes             Node   t2.small    1   1   us-east-2a,us-east-2b,us-east-2c
11
12 NODE STATUS
13 NAME               ROLE   READY
14 ip-172-20-120-133... master True
```

```
15   ip-172-20-34-249...   master True
16   ip-172-20-65-28...    master True
17   ip-172-20-95-101...   node    True
18
19   Your cluster devops23.k8s.local is ready
```

That is useful. We can see that the cluster uses four instance groups or, to use AWS terms, four auto-scaling groups (ASGs). There's one for each master, and there's one for all the (worker) nodes.

The reason each master has a separate ASG lies in need to ensure that each is running in its own availability zone (AZ). That way we can guarantee that failure of the whole AZ will affect only one master. Nodes (workers), on the other hand, are not restricted to any specific AZ. AWS is free to schedule nodes in any AZ that is available.

We'll discuss ASGs in more detail later on.

Further down the output, we can see that there are four servers, three with masters, and one with worker node. All are ready.

Finally, we got the confirmation that our cluster devops23.k8s.local is ready.

Installing Ingress And Tiller (Server Side Helm)

To install Ingres, please execute the commands that follow.

```
1   kubectl create \
2       -f https://raw.githubusercontent.com/kubernetes/kops/master/addons/ingress-nginx\
3   /v1.6.0.yaml
4
5   kubectl -n kube-ingress \
6       rollout status \
7       deployment ingress-nginx
```

Destroying The Cluster

The appendix is almost finished, and we do not need the cluster anymore. We want to destroy it as soon as possible. There's no good reason to keep it running when we're not using it. But, before we proceed with the destructive actions, we'll create a file that will hold all the environment variables we used in this chapter. That will help us the next time we want to recreate the cluster.

```
1  echo "export AWS_ACCESS_KEY_ID=$AWS_ACCESS_KEY_ID
2  export AWS_SECRET_ACCESS_KEY=$AWS_SECRET_ACCESS_KEY
3  export AWS_DEFAULT_REGION=$AWS_DEFAULT_REGION
4  export ZONES=$ZONES
5  export NAME=$NAME" \
6      >kops
```

We echoed the variables with the values into the kops file, and now we can delete the cluster.

```
1  kops delete cluster \
2      --name $NAME \
3      --yes
```

The output is as follows.

```
1  ...
2  Deleted kubectl config for devops23.k8s.local
3
4  Deleted cluster: "devops23.k8s.local"
```

Kops removed references of the cluster from our kubectl configuration and proceeded to delete all the AWS resources it created. Our cluster is no more. We can proceed and delete the S3 bucket as well.

```
1  aws s3api delete-bucket \
2      --bucket $BUCKET_NAME
```

Now It's Your Turn

I showed you a very opinionated way of doing continuous delivery and continuous deployment using Jenkins in a Kubernetes cluster. I did not try to strike a balance and teach you everything you could do. I don't believe that balanced unopinionated writings are a good thing. I do not like to read an article or a book that compares different ways of doing something only to conclude with "they all have their pros and cons." To me, that's silly. I like to know how someone does something. I have no interest in wasting my time reading a comparison that tries to be "politically correct" so that no one gets offended. In my head, that's a sign that a writer is a spineless person that does not have a personal opinion nor real experience. Spending enough time with a technology or a process inevitably leads to opinions. "I tried this and that, I failed, I succeeded, and this is what, in my opinion, works best." Those are the types of writings I like to read, and those are the people I admire. I tried to follow the same logic. As a result, I gave you what I think works the best for me today (August 2018).

That being said, I'd love to get your point of view. I'd like to get my hands on your pipelines. They will inevitably be different than the ones I promoted in this book. Otherwise, I failed to convey the most important message. **Learn something new, combine it with your existing knowledge, and adapt it to your own needs. Never follow anything or anyone blindly.** Hopefully, you found at least parts of this book useful, you learned something new, and you adapted your existing processes. Please send me what you created. I want to see your processes and your pipelines. Even more, I'd love to work with you to publish them in a blog or as an appendix to this book. If you think you did something interesting, as I'm sure you did, please contact me on DevOps20[209] Slack and show me what you created. **You learned from others, now it's time for others to learn from you.**

I'm done explaining what I did, now it's your turn to share what you made.

---

[209]http://slack.devops20toolkit.com/

Contributions

Like the previous books, this one was also a collaboration effort. Many helped shape this book through discussions, notes, and bug reports. I was swarmed with comments through DevOps20[210] Slack (often private) messages and emails. The conversations I had with the readers of the early editions of the book influenced the end result significantly. I'm grateful to have such a great community behind me. **Thank you for helping me make this book great.**

A few rose above the crowd.

Joost van der Griendt is one of those people that embrace a challenge wholeheartedly. We worked together for the same customer and quickly established a great relationship. From there on, he started helping me with discussions and advice on the subjects I worked on. Later on, he began contributing to this book. At times he was so proactive and helpful that I could not keep up with his pull requests. Just when I would think that I'm done for the day, I'd see a new pull request with more questions, changes, additions, and corrections.

In his own words...

Joost started out a Java backend developer but found himself fascinated by developer productivity through tools like Jenkins and Maven. Inspired by Viktor's books and Workshops, he moved his attention to Docker, Cloud, and DevOps to the point where he joined CloudBees to help spread the knowledge.

Prageeth Warnak was continually sending pull requests with corrections and suggestions. He made this book much clearer than it would be if I had to rely on my, often incorrect, assumptions of what readers expect.

In his own words...

Prageeth is a seasoned IT professional currently working as the lead software architect for Australian telco giant Telstra. He enjoys working with new technologies, and he likes spending his leisure time reading books (especially those written by Viktor), watching Netflix and Fox news, yes he is an originalist and a conservative. He lives in Melbourne with his family. He is fascinated getting Microservices and DevOps done right.

Neeraj Kothari - Reviews, suggestions, windows testing, etc.

In his own words...

Neeraj is an architect who mostly works with American banks. New technologies excite him, and that makes him learn all the time. He likes to analyze and connect the dots in the fast-changing technology world. He is passionate about Microservices and DevOps. He likes to read, daydream and watch movies, His favorite author is Malcolm Gladwell.

---

[210]http://slack.devops20toolkit.com/

Tigran Mnatsakanyan, just like many others, contributed with corrections, advice, suggestions, and the like. We spent hours in discussions around Kubernetes, Jenkins, and CI/CD. He influenced the content of this books greatly. But, that's not his most significant contribution. He was brave enough to volunteer to write a whole chapter. It is still in progress so I won't give away spoilers, except to say that this edition will be updated as soon as Tigran's chapter is finished.

In his own words...

Tigran is a technologist who works as an independent contractor in London helping teams with technology and ways of working. He started as a Java developer then moved to functional programming using numerous architectural styles and patterns. At some point, he realized that in almost every team writing application code takes less time than everything else afterward, and he started to explore and learn more about the world of Microservices, DevOps, and Docker. And of course, he loves reading Viktor's books!

Made in the USA
Columbia, SC
24 October 2018